Women
and Men *in*
Management
Third Edition

To the memory of Edna Powell
for all the quarters and much more
and to
Vicky and Barry Graves
for all their love and guidance

Women and Men in Management
Third Edition

Gary N. Powell
University of Connecticut

Laura M. Graves
Clark University

SAGE Publications
International Educational and Professional Publisher
Thousand Oaks ▪ London ▪ New Delhi

For information:

Sage Publications, Inc.
2455 Teller Road
Thousand Oaks, California 91320
E-mail: order@sagepub.com

Sage Publications Ltd.
6 Bonhill Street
London EC2A 4PU
United Kingdom

Sage Publications India Pvt. Ltd.
B-42 Panchsheel Enclave
Post Box 4109
New Delhi 110 017 India

Printed in the United States of America

Library of Congress Cataloging-in-Publication Data
Powell, Gary N.
Women and men in management / by Gary N. Powell and Laura M. Graves.— 3rd ed.
   p. cm.
Rev. ed. of: Women & men in management. 2nd ed. c1993.
Includes bibliographical references and index.
ISBN 0–7619–2195–8
ISBN 0–7619–2196–6 (pbk.)
1. Women executives. 2. Executives. 3. Sex role in the work environment. I. Graves, Laura M. II. Powell, Gary N. Women & men in management. III. Title.
HD6054.3 .P69 2003
658.4′095—dc21

2002010312

This book is printed on acid-free paper.

02   03   04   05   10 9 8 7 6 5 4 3 2 1

Acquisitions Editor:	Al Bruckner
Editorial Assistant:	MaryAnn Vail
Copy Editor:	Robert Holm
Production Editor:	Denise Santoyo
Typesetter:	C&M Digitals (P) Ltd.
Indexer:	Kathy Papachontis
Cover Designer:	Michelle Lee

Contents

Foreword

Nancy J. Adler[1]

It's about time to realize, brethren, as best we can,

That a woman is not just a female man.

—Ogden Nash[2]

"Too often interlaced illusions trap professionals and society in a vicious circle of nonsense."[3] Such nonsense, unfortunately, still permeates most popular discussions focusing on the similarities and differences among women and men. Illusions continue to cloud supposedly professional perspectives on the effectiveness and relative success of female versus male managers. People still believe, for example, that few women have risen to their country's highest leadership position. Most women and men guess that fewer than 5 women have served as president or prime minister. The reality is that more than 50 women have led their country in the last half century—37 of whom served in just the last decade.[4] Similarly, people continue to believe that few, if any, male CEOs of major companies strongly support women's career advancement into senior management positions, and yet a growing number of powerful men have instituted major changes leading to increases at the highest levels.[5] Many women and men still believe that, even in today's global economy, women cannot succeed abroad. They can, they have, and they do.[6] Many people believe that the experience of male and female managers in the United States can be generalized to the rest of the world. It can't. Women outside the United States benefit from advantages and face disadvantages experienced by few of their American colleagues.[7] A veneer of politically correct vocabulary all too frequently substitutes for the type of thoughtful research and analysis that could produce deeper and more accurate understandings.

Which popular beliefs are illusions and which reflect fact? Are the overall trends optimistic or pessimistic? Why do women worldwide now comprise a greater proportion of both workers and managers than in any previous era? Why, at the same time, do many organizations continue to exclude women from their most senior management positions? Why do societies continue to segregate many women into low-paying occupations? Why do women in most countries continue to be paid less when performing similar work to men?

The third edition of Gary Powell and Laura Graves' *Women and Men in Management* addresses and answers these questions, not based on the authors' subjective experiences and personal opinions, but rather on their thorough review of over 900 studies and articles—a body of literature reflecting the explosion of research on gender and organizations in the last decade. Powell and Graves do not simply identify patterns and trends in the research. They go beyond mere synthesis (a difficult enough task in itself) to offer concrete rec-ommendations that individuals and organizations can implement concerning such seminal issues as employment decisions, work teams, leadership, sexual harassment, workplace romance, career development, the glass ceiling, work and family, and strategies for promoting an organizational culture of nondis-crimination, diversity, and inclusion.

Former U.S. First Lady Eleanor Roosevelt lived a life that proved the truth of her statement, "The future belongs to those who believe in the beauty of their dreams."[8] *Women and Men in Management* allows the future to belong to those who believe that human society is capable of equity based on nondiscrimina-tion, diversity, and inclusion, even if such a future resides today only in the dreams of those who choose to read Powell and Graves' excellent new book.

Notes

1. Nancy J. Adler is Professor of International Management at McGill University, Montreal, Canada.

2. Nash, O. (1950, July). It's about time. *Flair,* p. 56.

3. Palmer, P. J. (1990). *The active life: A spirituality of work, creativity, and caring.* New York: Harper & Row, p. 41.

4. Adler, N. J. (2001). Women joining men as global leaders in the new economy. In M. J. Gannon & K. L. Newman (Eds.), *The Blackwell handbook of cross-cultural management* (pp. 236–249). Oxford, U.K.: Blackwell; Adler, N. J. (1999). Global leaders: Women of influence. In G. N. Powell (Ed.), *Handbook of gender and work* (pp. 239–261). Thousand Oaks, CA: Sage; Adler, N. J. (1998). Did you hear? Global leadership in Charity's world. *Journal of Management Inquiry, 7,* 135–143.

5. Adler, N. J., Brody, L. W., & Osland, J. S. (2001). Going beyond twentieth century leadership: A CEO develops his company's global competitiveness. *Cross-Cultural Management: An International Journal, 8*(3–4), 11–34; Adler, N. J., Brody, L. W., & Osland, J. S. (2000). The Women's Global Leadership Forum: Enhancing one company's leadership capability. *Human Resource Management, 39*(2–3), 209–225.

6. Adler, N. J. (2000). Coaching global executives: Women succeeding in a world beyond here. In M. Goldsmith, L. Lyons, & A. Freas (Eds.), *Coaching for leadership* (pp. 359–368). San Francisco: Jossey-Bass; Adler, N. J. (1994). Competitive frontiers: Women managing across borders. In N. J. Adler & D. N. Izraeli (Eds.), *Competitive frontiers: Women managers in a Global economy* (pp. 22–40). Cambridge, MA: Blackwell.

7. Adler, N. J., & Izraeli, D. N. (Eds.). (1994). *Competitive frontiers: Women managers in a global economy.* Cambridge, MA: Blackwell; Adler, N. J. (1993). An international perspective on the barriers to the advancement of women managers. *Applied Psychology: An International Review, 42*(4), 289–300.

8. Roosevelt, E. (2002). *Quotes: Eleanor Roosevelt.* Retrieved June 23, 2002, from http://www.brainyquote.com.

Acknowledgments

Although we did all of the writing, there are many people who contributed to the preparation of this third edition of *Women and Men in Management*. We wish to express our deepest gratitude to

1. Our friend and copy editor, Julie Tamarkin, for expertly shaping our writing and, at times, providing comic relief in her commentary on our work

2. Tony Butterfield for his long-time friendship in the work and nonwork spheres of our lives

3. Our colleagues in the Gender and Diversity in Organizations Division of the Academy of Management, for providing both a forum for the sharing of research findings and a stimulus for creative thinking on this topic

4. Norm Powell, and to the memory of Zina Powell, for being as encouraging and supportive as parents could ever be

5. Vicky Graves, who became a professional woman long before it was acceptable to do so, and Barry Graves, for not imposing traditional gender roles on their children and for their ongoing interest in this project

6. Our friends for providing substantial support throughout the project, despite the fact that we sometimes ignored them while working on it

7. Tiger the Cat for sitting by (or on) our computers as we worked on this book and for providing unlimited love, affection, and play

1

Sex, Gender, and Work

ON THE PSYCHOLOGY OF SEX

> There is perhaps no field aspiring to be scientific where
> flagrant personal bias, logic martyred in the cause of support-
> ing a prejudice, unfounded assertions, and even sentimental
> rot and drivel, have run riot to such an extent as here.
>
> —Helen Thompson Woolley[1]

*W*omen and Men in Management, *Third Edition*, examines the evolving
roles and experiences of women and men in the global workplace.
Significant changes have occurred in recent years in the status of women and
men and in their interactions at work. Some believe that all of the needed
changes have taken place and that a person's sex no longer matters at work.
However, the evidence presents a more mixed picture.

The role of women in the workplace has been expanding steadily. In the
United States, the proportion of women in the labor force (i.e., the proportion
of all adults employed or seeking employment who are women), which was
42% in 1980, has risen to 47%.[2] A similar trend is exhibited in virtually every
country. As Table 1.1 indicates, the proportion of women in the labor force
increased between 1980 and 2000 by 1 to 16% in a diverse sample of countries
ranging from Argentina to Zimbabwe. Although the proportion of women in
the labor force in the countries listed in Table 1.1 varies widely (from 14% to
50%), the trend in all countries except one (Poland) is in the same direction,
toward the increased employment of women.

1

Table 1.1   Proportion of Women in the Labor Force

Country	1980	2000	Difference
Argentina	34%	40%	+6%
Australia	36	44	+8
Belgium	34	44	+10
Bermuda	43	50	+7
Botswana	23	39	+16
Brazil	31	40	+9
Canada	40	46	+6
Chile	29	33	+4
Denmark	45	46	+1
Egypt	7	19	+12
Finland	46	47	+1
France	39	45	+6
India	12	17	+5
Indonesia	33	38	+5
Ireland	32	40	+8
Israel	36	45	+9
Italy	32	37	+5
Japan	39	41	+2
Mauritius	26	37	+11
Mexico	31	34	+3
Netherlands	31	43	+12
New Zealand	41	45	+4
Norway	41	47	+6
Pakistan	10	14	+4
Panama	29	34	+5
Philippines	35	38	+3
Poland	49	45	−4
Singapore	35	39	+4
Spain	30	37	+7
Swaziland	25	29	+4
Sweden	45	48	+3
Switzerland	36	42	+6
United Kingdom	42	49	+7
United States	42	47	+5
Venezuela	28	35	+7
Zimbabwe	17	22	+5

SOURCE: International Labour Office. (2002). *LABORSTA-Internet database* (computed from Table 2A). Retrieved April 4, 2002, from http://laborsta.ilo.org

In addition, the representation of women in the managerial ranks is increasing. In the United States, the proportion of women managers, which was 26% in 1980, now is 45%. The proportion of women managers increased between 1980 and 2000 from 14% to 26% in Australia, 25% to 35% in Canada, and 16% to 29% in Sweden. Although the proportion of women in management in different countries varies widely due to differences in national culture and definitions of the term *manager*, the trend in almost all countries has been in the same direction, toward the increased representation of women in the managerial ranks.[3]

Despite these positive trends, the proportion of women decreases at progressively higher levels in managerial hierarchies within all countries. The higher the level of the organization, the fewer women are found. Although definitions of what constitutes "top management" vary among companies, the proportion of women in top management is only 13% in *Fortune* 500 corporations and less than 5% in most countries.[4]

The economic status of women in the workplace remains lower than that of men. The average female full-time worker continues to be paid less than the average male full-time worker. This gap is partly due to the lower average wages of workers in female-intensive occupations (i.e., occupations in which two thirds or more of the workforce is female) than that of workers in male-intensive occupations (i.e., occupations in which two thirds or more of the workforce is male). Also, women are paid less than men in the same occupation and often in the same job.[5]

The global labor force also remains sharply segregated on the basis of sex. In recent years, women have shown more interest in entering male-intensive occupations than men have shown in entering female-intensive occupations, which is not surprising because workers in male-intensive occupations are the higher paid. However, women continue to be crowded into a lower-paying set of occupations than are men.[6]

Thus, the influence of biological sex in the global workplace remains strong, even though there have been considerable changes. Is it only a matter of time until the proportions of women and men in all managerial levels and all occupations become essentially equal, until women and men are paid equal wages for equal work, and until individuals' work experiences are unaffected by their biological sex? As we shall see in this book, it will depend on actions that organizations and individuals take.

Sex Versus Gender

In this book, we make a distinction between two frequently used terms: sex and gender. *Sex* (biological sex) is the term suggested by the biological characteristics of individuals such as their physiological properties and reproductive apparatus. *Gender* is a term used in a social context. It refers to beliefs about what is appropriate for or typical of one sex more than the other, including feelings, attitudes, behavior, and interests. Thus, gender refers to the social role associated with being male or female.[7]

The study of sex differences examines how males and females actually differ. In contrast, the study of gender differences focuses on how people believe that males and females differ. For example, a sex difference in leadership style would exist if female leaders were more considerate of their subordinates than were male leaders. There would be a gender difference in leadership style if people believed that female leaders were more considerate of their subordinates than were male leaders. However, there could be a gender difference in leadership style without a corresponding sex difference, and vice versa. Furthermore, gender differences can *cause* sex differences. For example, if parents believe that the developmental needs of their sons differ from those of their daughters, they may raise their children in a way that reinforces that belief. The result is a *self-fulfilling prophecy*—when expectations cause behavior that makes the expectations come true. We identify many workplace situations in which self-fulfilling prophecies are likely to occur.[8]

As we consider the effects of sex differences on work-related behavior, we also need to consider the effects of gender differences. Sex differences influence how people are disposed to behave in work settings. Gender differences influence how people react to others' behavior in such settings. Gender differences are manifested in stereotypes, prejudice, and discrimination. A *stereotype* is a set of beliefs about the personal attributes of a group of people. Stereotyping is a cognitive activity, related to making, learning, and remembering distinctions between various groups of people. In contrast, people who display *prejudice*, or a negative attitude toward members of other groups, are engaging in an emotional activity. Finally, *discrimination*, a behavioral activity, is exhibited in how people treat members of other groups and in the decisions they make about others. We have reason to be concerned about all three of these phenomena. All of us may be targets of stereotyping, prejudice, and discrimination. In addition, we may engage in stereotyping, prejudice, and discrimination.[9]

Sex as a Primary Dimension of Diversity

Sex represents only one of many personal characteristics that may influence individuals' experiences in the workplace. People differ in many ways, some of which are changeable, others less amenable to change. *Primary dimensions of diversity* are essentially unchangeable personal characteristics that exert significant lifelong impacts. Sex is a primary dimension of diversity, along with race, ethnicity, age, sexual orientation, and physical abilities/disabilities. Together, primary dimensions of diversity shape our basic self-image and sense of identity. They affect our early learning experiences, and there is typically no escaping their impact throughout the course of our lives.[10]

Secondary dimensions of diversity, on the other hand, are changeable personal characteristics. These characteristics are acquired and may be modified or abandoned throughout life. Education, income, marital and parental status, religion, political affiliation, and work experience are some secondary dimensions of diversity of importance to many people. People also distinguish themselves in many other ways, such as in their choices of collegiate fraternities or sororities, hobbies, activities, voluntary associations, clothing and grooming style, and music preferences. Of course, a person does not completely determine his or her secondary characteristics. For instance, educational background, work experience, income, or marital status will be affected by other people's decisions. However, people generally have more control over the secondary dimensions of diversity in their lives than over the primary dimensions of diversity.

The primary dimensions of diversity may fall into different categories, including whether group membership is visible and whether it is regarded as changeable. For example, sexual orientation is not necessarily observable and opinions differ as to whether it is changeable. As a result, gays and lesbians face decisions about "coming out." They may decide to disclose their sexual orientation to family members and friends on a person-to-person basis based on the level of trust in the relationship and the anticipated reaction to the disclosure. However, they are unlikely to disclose their sexual orientation to coworkers if they perceive workplace discrimination on the basis of sexual orientation.[11]

In contrast, sex is highly visible and not easily changed. People have little choice about "coming out" as female or male. The psychologist Sandra Bem once asked audience members if they had ever known anyone personally without noticing that person's sex. Few could answer yes. Sex is an important characteristic to most people when forming their impression of someone, and in reacting to them. Even if sex is not important to a particular person's own sense of identity, other people may be influenced by *their* sense of that person's sex.

Thus, people categorize themselves and may be categorized by others along many different dimensions of diversity, both primary and secondary. The focus of this book is the influence of categorizations of people according to sex on what transpires in the workplace. However, sex is not isolated from other dimensions of diversity. The effect of sex on how people develop their senses of identity and on how they are treated in the workplace cannot be separated from the effects of race, ethnicity, age, sexual orientation, physical abilities/ disabilities, and various secondary dimensions of diversity.

Researchers often ignore the interdependence of sex and other dimensions of diversity. For example, many studies of sex or gender differences have not reported the racial or ethnic group of the individuals who were the focus of the study. By ignoring issues of race and ethnicity, such studies reflect an underlying assumption that sex and gender differences are similar across all racial and ethnic groups. That is, White women, Black women, Hispanic women, Asian women, and women of other racial and ethnic groups are assumed to have similar personal characteristics and experiences, as are White men, Black men, Hispanic men, Asian men, and so on. We need to guard against making such assumptions ourselves.[12]

Watching Out for Biases

People have strong beliefs about whether there are fundamental differences between the capabilities of females and males. In fact, speculation about such differences is a universal phenomenon. People seldom wonder whether children who differ in eye color or height also differ in personality, behavioral tendencies, or intellectual abilities. However, they do care if there are such differences between girls and boys.[13]

Views about the nature of sex differences certainly have evolved over time. For example, 19th-century scientists argued that brain size was a good indicator of basic intelligence, and that the tendency of women's brains to be smaller than men's meant that women were less intelligent. Such unfounded arguments were so prevalent in the early 1900s that Helen Thompson Woolley, the first psychologist to undertake an extensive and systematic experimental examination of the psychological characteristics of the sexes, offered the stinging indictment contained in the opening passage of this chapter.[14]

Some would say that Woolley's conclusion still applies a century later. Researchers may bring either of two types of bias to the study of sex differences, alpha bias or beta bias. *Alpha bias* consists of the tendency to exaggerate sex differences. *Beta bias* consists of the tendency to minimize or ignore sex differences. Either type of bias can lead to a distortion of how the researcher sees reality.[15]

Such biases may be the result of the personal prejudices of researchers. If the researcher's goal is to prove that traditional stereotypes of the sexes are inaccurate and that females and males are essentially equivalent in their personalities, behavioral tendencies, and intellectual abilities, he or she is likely to demonstrate beta bias by concluding that any sex differences that are found are trivial. On the other hand, if the researcher's goal is to prove that one sex is superior to the other in some way or to justify a status quo in which women and men are seen as naturally suited to different roles and thereby deserving of different treatment, he or she is likely to demonstrate alpha bias by concluding that sex differences in personal characteristics are large and fundamental to human functioning.[16]

Unfortunately, the mere presence of a two-category system leads people to view the two categories as opposites. For example, parents with two children tend to describe each in contrast to the other (e.g., "Tom is a leader and Joe is a follower"). However, parents with three or more children tend to focus on the unique aspects of each child (e.g., "Kristin enjoys being with people; Robby likes to play sports; Billy likes to work on science projects; Melissa loves to read; and Nathan enjoys playing the drums"). Similarly, anthropologists who have done fieldwork in only two cultures tend to emphasize the differences between these cultures, whereas anthropologists with wider field experience are more aware of the diversity of human experience. The same phenomenon may occur for sex. Because there are only two categories, no one has the opportunity to gain "wider field experience" with a third or fourth sex. As a result, people tend to focus on the differences between males and females, thereby reinforcing alpha bias. Also, every researcher of sex differences belongs to one of the two groups being examined. Researchers may be more likely to report sex differences that reflect favorably on members of their own sex. Moreover, the popular media exhibit alpha bias in their choice of which research results to publicize. Findings of sex differences are glamorized and magnified, whereas findings of sex similarities receive much less media attention.[17]

In conclusion, we need to pay close attention to the findings of research about sex similarities and differences in the workplace. However, we also need to be aware of the possibility of biases, both in researchers and in media accounts of research, that affect what research findings are reported and how they are reported.

Organization of the Book

The book begins its analysis of the transition in female/male work relationships by looking back in time. Chapter 2 considers the evolution of women's and men's work roles during the last century. It examines the effects of historical influences such as the occurrence of two major world wars, the passage of equal employment opportunity laws, and the development of the women's liberation movement. The current status of women and men in today's workforce is described in terms of sex differences in labor force participation, occupation, and pay.

Chapter 3 examines sex and gender differences that affect the behavior of women and men in the workplace. This chapter reviews some of the major findings of psychological research on sex differences. Key concepts such as gender stereotypes, gender roles, sexism, and gender identity that are critical to understanding male/female interactions are introduced. The ways in which parents, schools, and the mass media convey gender role expectations to children, as well as the limitations of strict adherence to gender roles in adults, are explored.

Chapter 4 considers how individuals and organizations make decisions about establishing employment relationships. For individuals, these decisions entail choosing which job opportunities to pursue and which job offers to accept; for organizations, they entail choosing which applicants to hire. The chapter describes how differences in men's and women's job search strategies and reactions to specific jobs and organizations lead them to seek and obtain very different employment opportunities. It also examines sex discrimination in organizations' hiring decisions, including how and when sex discrimination occurs and who discriminates against whom. Recommendations are offered for reducing sex and gender effects on the employment decisions of individuals and organizations.

Chapter 5 considers the effects of sex and gender on behavior in work teams. The chapter analyzes differences in how men and women behave and are evaluated in mixed-sex teams. It also examines how the sex composition of the team influences the experiences of male and female team members and the team's effectiveness. It suggests that mixed-sex teams are susceptible to a host of problems, the severity of which depends on a number of situational factors. The chapter concludes with recommendations for actions that team members and leaders may take to facilitate the functioning of mixed-sex teams.

Chapter 6 examines the effects of gender stereotypes and sexist attitudes on the work relationships between managers and their subordinates. It demonstrates that despite the increased proportion of women managers, managerial stereotypes continue to reflect the beliefs of "think manager—think male" and "think manager—think masculine" and that people still prefer to have a male boss. Sex differences in actual leader behavior and effectiveness are examined to determine whether there is any truth to these stereotypes. The chapter concludes that, contrary to managerial stereotypes, women may actually be better prepared to handle managerial roles in today's work environment. Organizations are urged to take actions to ensure that capable leaders of both sexes have equal chances to succeed.

Chapter 7 explores issues pertaining to the expression of sexuality in the workplace, which includes sexual harassment (unwelcome sexual attention directed toward others) and workplace romances (mutually desired relationships between two people at work). It examines the causes and consequences of both types of sexually oriented behavior. Actions are recommended for both organizations and individuals to deal with sexual harassment and to minimize the disruption caused by workplace romances.

Chapter 8 considers the career and life patterns typically followed by women and men. It examines sex differences in how people define career success and how their careers transpire, including employment gaps, developmental experiences, and promotions to top management. The intersection of employees' work and family lives is considered. It examines the impact of the organization's culture and work-family programs on how employees juggle their work and nonwork commitments. How family relationships influence an individual's ability to balance work and family roles is also explored. The chapter concludes with actions that organizations may take to facilitate the career success of their employees as well as actions that individuals may take to enhance their own success.

Chapters 1 through 8 identify numerous issues related to sex and gender that arise in today's workplace. Chapter 9 offers solutions to these problems. It details the relevant laws and regulations with which organizations must comply to avoid discrimination. The chapter presents the business case for going beyond legal compliance to promote diversity (i.e., representation of members of different groups in all jobs and levels) and inclusion (i.e., acceptance of members of all groups in the organizational culture). Actions are outlined for organizations to achieve nondiscriminatory, diverse, and inclusive cultures. This chapter concludes with a comprehensive summary of actions for organizations and individuals to improve women's and men's workplace interactions and experiences.

In summary, *Women and Men in Management* covers a wide range of topics. It describes female/male work roles in the past and the present. The effects of sex and gender on childhood development and adult behavior are considered. It examines how sex and gender influence individuals' experiences as job candidates, team members, and managers. Issues associated with the expression of sexuality in the workplace are explored. Finally, this book offers concrete recommendations for individuals and organizations to ensure that all people have fulfilling and productive careers, regardless of their biological sex.

Notes

1. Woolley, H. T. (1910). A review of the recent literature on the psychology of sex. *Psychological Bulletin, 7*(18), p. 335.

2. U.S. Department of Labor, Bureau of Labor Statistics. (2002). *Employment and earnings* (computed from data for March, 2002 from Table A-19). Retrieved April 24, 2002, from http://www.bls.gov/cps

3. International Labour Office. (2002). *LABORSTA-Internet database* (computed from Table 2C). Retrieved April 4, 2002, from http://laborsta.ilo.org; International Labour Office. (1993). Unequal race to the top. *World of Work: The Magazine of the International Labour Office* (U.S. ed.), no. 2, 6–7.

4. Powell, G. N. (1999). Reflections on the glass ceiling: Recent trends and future prospects. In G. N. Powell (Ed.), *Handbook of gender and work* (pp. 325–345). Thousand Oaks, CA: Sage; Wirth, L. (2001). *Breaking through the glass ceiling: Women in management.* Geneva: International Labour Office; Davidson, M. J., & Cooper, C. L. (1992). *Shattering the glass ceiling: The woman manager.* London: Chapman; Davidson, M. J., & Cooper, C. L. (Eds.). (1993). *European women in business and management.* London: Chapman; Catalyst. (2000). *Census of women corporate officers and top earners.* New York: Catalyst.

5. Roos, P. A., & Gatta, M. L. (1999). The gender gap in earnings: Trends, explanations, and prospects. In G. N. Powell (Ed.), *Handbook of gender and work* (pp. 95–123). Thousand Oaks, CA: Sage.

6. Jacobs, J. A. (1999). The sex segregation of occupations: Prospects for the 21st century. In G. N. Powell (Ed.), *Handbook of gender and work* (pp. 125–141). Thousand Oaks, CA: Sage.

7. Korabik, K. (1999). Sex and gender in the new millennium. In G. N. Powell (Ed.), *Handbook of gender and work* (pp. 3–16). Thousand Oaks, CA: Sage; Unger, R. K. (1979). Toward a redefinition of sex and gender. *American Psychologist, 34,* 1085–1094; Unger, R. K. (1998). *Resisting gender: Twenty-five years of feminist psychology.* London: Sage; Caplan, P. J., & Caplan, J. B. (1994). *Thinking critically about research on sex and gender.* New York: HarperCollins.

8. Geis, F. L. (1993). Self-fulfilling prophecies: A social psychological view of gender. In A. E. Beall & R. J. Sternberg (Eds.), *The psychology of gender* (pp. 9–54). New York: Guilford; Snyder, M. (1992). Motivational foundations of behavioral confirmation. In M. P. Zanna (Ed.), *Advances in experimental social psychology,* Vol. 25 (pp. 67–114). New York: Academic Press; Snyder, M. (1984). When belief creates reality. In L. Berkowitz (Ed.), *Advances in experimental social psychology,* Vol. 18 (pp. 247–305). New York: Academic Press; Jones, R. A. (1977). *Self-fulfilling prophecies: Social, psychological, and physiological effects of expectancies.* New York: Wiley.

9. Fiske, S. T. (1998). Stereotyping, prejudice, and discrimination. In D. T. Gilbert, S. T. Fiske, & G. Lindzey (Eds.), *The handbook of social psychology,* Vol. 2 (4th ed., pp. 357–411). Boston: McGraw-Hill; Stroebe, W. & Insko, C. A. (1989). Stereotype, prejudice and discrimination: Changing conceptions in theory and research. In D. Bar-Tal, C. F. Graumann, A. W. Kruglanski, & W. Stroebe (Eds.), *Stereotyping and prejudice: Changing conceptions* (pp. 3–34). London: Springer-Verlag; Oskamp, S. (Ed.). (2000). *Reducing prejudice and discrimination.* Mahwah, NJ: Erlbaum.

10. Loden, M., & Rosener, J. B. (1991). *Workforce America: Managing employee diversity as a vital resource.* Homewood, IL: Business One Irwin.

11. Ragins, B. R., & Cornwell, J. M. (2001). Pink triangles: Antecedents and consequences of perceived workplace discrimination against gay and lesbian employees. *Journal of Applied Psychology, 86,* 1244–1261; Croteau, J. M. (1996). Research on the work experiences of lesbian, gay, and bisexual people: An integrative review of methodology and findings. *Personnel Psychology, 48,* 195–209; Day, N. E., & Schoenrade, P. (1997). Staying in the closet versus coming out: Relationships between communication about sexual orientation and work attitudes. *Personnel Psychology, 50,* 147–163; Herek, G. M. (Ed.). (1998). *Stigma and sexual orientation: Understanding prejudice against lesbians, gay men, and bisexuals.* Thousand Oaks, CA: Sage; Bailey, J. M., & Pillard, R. C. (1997). The innateness of homosexuality. In M. R. Walsh (Ed.), *Women, men, and gender: Ongoing debates* (pp. 184–187). New Haven, CT: Yale University Press; Kitzinger, C., & Wilkinson, S. (1997). Transitions from heterosexuality to lesbianism: The discursive production of lesbian identities. In M. R. Walsh (Ed.), *Women, men, and gender: Ongoing debates* (pp. 188–203). New Haven, CT: Yale University Press.

12. Ferdman, B. M. (1999). The color and culture of gender in organizations: Attending to race and ethnicity. In G. N. Powell (Ed.), *Handbook of gender and work* (pp. 17–34). Thousand Oaks, CA: Sage; Reid, P. T. (1988). Racism and sexism: Comparisons and conflicts. In P. A. Katz

and D. A. Taylor (Eds.), *Eliminating racism: Profiles in controversy* (pp. 203–221). New York: Plenum.

13. Jacklin, C. N. (1989). Female and male: Issues of gender. *American Psychologist, 44,* 127–133.

14. Hyde, J. S. (1990). Meta-analysis and the psychology of gender differences. *Signs, 16,* 55–73; Milar, K. S. (2000). The first generation of women psychologists and the psychology of women. *American Psychologist, 55,* 616–619; Woolley.

15. Hare-Mustin, R. T., & Maracek, J. (1988). The meaning of difference: Gender theory, post-modernism, and psychology. *American Psychologist, 43,* 455–464.

16. Eagly, A. H. (1995). The science and politics of comparing women and men. *American Psychologist, 50,* 145–158; Hyde, J. S., & Plant, E. A. (1995). Magnitude of psychological gender differences: Another side to the story. *American Psychologist, 50,* 159–161; James, J. B. (1997). What are the social issues involved in focusing on *difference* in the study of gender? *Journal of Social Issues, 53,* 213–232; Epstein, C. F. (1999). Similarity and difference: The sociology of gender distinctions. In J. S. Chavetz (Ed.), *Handbook of the sociology of gender* (pp. 45–60). New York: Kluwer; Tavris, C. (1992). *The mismeasure of women: Why women are not the better sex, the inferior sex, or the opposite sex.* New York: Simon & Schuster.

17. Belle, D. (1985). Ironies in the contemporary study of gender. *Journal of Personality, 53,* 400–405; Eagly, A. H. (1987). *Sex differences in social behavior: A social-role interpretation.* Hillsdale, NJ: Erlbaum; Goodman, E. (2000, December 4). When men don't listen, their brains may not be the problem. *Hartford Courant,* p. A9.

2

Yesterday and Today

In Today's Workplace,
Women Feel Freer to Be, Well, Women

One young woman thinks of it as the Attractiveness Card. An older gentleman calls it the Cheerleader Promise. Either way, it's responsible for a fair amount of electricity—and confusion—in the office air these days.

A whole lot has changed in the workplace in a very short time. When an earlier generation marched to work 25 or 30 years ago, they found their best strategy lay in pretending their home lives didn't exist and in covering up their sexuality. Remember those awful suits and silly bow ties?

Their daughters are joining a very different work world. There are plenty of talented, able women around. Young people work around the clock and have little interest in erecting barriers between their social and work lives. Women are . . . less inhibited about using the personal tools at their disposal to get ahead professionally.

This, of course, is something that competent businessmen have always done. For example, attractive and athletic men have long drawn on their business skills, but also on their charm and golf game to help them get to the top. The difference now is that young women feel more comfortable doing the same thing. And that their style has a decidedly female bent to it.

Sometimes it is unabashed flirting. Other times it is teasing, bantering, a direct look in the eye. Just like the men, these women are confident about their business skills and not shy about showing it. Just as men feel no need to mask their masculinity, women are letting their femininity show.

—Ellen J. Pollock[1]

Yes, our daughters, sons, sisters, brothers, and friends are joining a very different work world. But *how different* are the current roles that women and men play in the workplace compared with those of the past? If traditional gender roles have been tossed aside, what has replaced them?

Traditional gender roles emphasize the differences rather than the similarities between women and men. They suggest that women should behave in a "feminine" manner, consistent with presumed feminine attributes, and that men should behave in a "masculine" manner, consistent with presumed masculine attributes. Traditionally, to deviate from these roles is to engage in abnormal behavior. Traditional gender roles have had a profound impact on relations between women and men in all spheres of our society—the family, the educational system, the legal system, and the workplace.

In this chapter, we first consider the evolution of the work roles of women and men over the last century. We trace the impact of diverse historical events, such as the advent of industrialization, two world wars, and the development of the women's liberation movement. Second, we look at the roles of men and women in the workforce today, considering differences between sexes and among various racial and ethnic groups. Finally, we consider the impact of the changes in traditional workplace gender roles on current economic realities and on the work relationships between men and women.

A Century of Changes

THE FIRST HALF

Although societies around the world have differed in their conceptions of gender roles, Western societies have shared similar notions. Throughout the recorded history of Western civilizations, a patriarchal social system, in which the male has authority over the female, has prevailed, or at least has been the norm.

Table 2.1   Labor Force Participation Rates

	Percentage in the U.S. Labor Force	
Year	Women	Men
1900	19	80
1910	23	81
1920	21	78
1930	22	76
1940	25	79
1950	31	80
1960	35	79
1970	43	80
1980	51	77
1990	58	76
2000	60	75

SOURCES: **1900–1960:** U.S. Department of Commerce, Bureau of the Census. (1975). *Historical statistics of the United States: Colonial times to 1970* (127–128, series D11–25). Washington, DC: Government Printing Office; **1970–2000:** U.S. Department of Labor, Bureau of Labor Statistics. (2002). *Employment and earnings,* Table 2. Retrieved April 22, 2002, from http://www.bls.gov/cps
NOTE: 1900–1930 data for persons 10 years old and over; 1940–1960 data for persons 14 years old and over; 1970–2000 data for persons 16 years old and over.

As the 20th century began, men were firmly established as the dominant sex in the workplace, both in numbers and in positions of authority. The stay-at-home wife who devoted herself exclusively to household and family responsibilities was a status symbol in U.S. society. This practice was the product of the existing patriarchal social system and the Industrial Revolution of the late 18th and early 19th centuries, which removed paid employment from the home. Although the role of stay-at-home wife was largely based on the experiences of White middle-class families that could afford to forgo the wife's wages, society embraced the notion that a woman's proper place was in the home.[2]

Thus, the U.S. labor force was clearly differentiated by sex at the beginning of the 20th century. Census statistics showed that 19% of women and 80% of men were in the labor force (Table 2.1). In other words, four of every five women *were not* engaged in paid employment, whereas four out of every five men *were.*

In the decades between 1900 and 1940, labor force participation rates for men and women remained essentially unchanged, despite the occurrence of several major events. World War I (1914 to 1918) created new jobs for women at higher wages than previous levels as large numbers of men went off to war. However, no sustained change in the employment of women resulted. In fact, the labor force participation rate of women in 1920 (21%) was slightly lower than it had been in 1910 (23%). Labor unions, government, and society in general were not ready for more than a temporary change in the economic role of women. Men received first priority in hiring when they returned from the war, and many women were driven from the labor force.

The passage of the Nineteenth Amendment to the U.S. Constitution in 1920, which gave women the right to vote, failed to influence economic roles. Backers of the amendment had hoped that ending sex discrimination in the right to vote would lead to the dismantling of sex discrimination in other areas and usher in a new era of equality between the sexes. However, women's suffrage brought about little change in women's economic status.[3]

The Great Depression, extending from the U.S. stock market crash in 1929 to the Japanese bombing of Pearl Harbor in 1941, threw millions of Americans out of work. The unemployment rate rose considerably, peaking at 25% during 1933. These conditions contributed to an identity crisis for unemployed men of all races. In the book *Puzzled America,* published in 1935, Sherwood Anderson concluded, "The breaking down of the moral fiber of the American man through being out of a job, losing that sense of being some part of the moving world of activity, so essential to an American man's sense of his manhood—the loss of this essential something in the jobless can never be measured in dollars."[4] The Depression caused great strains in family relations, as unemployed men suffered loss of status in their families. Those who relied upon holding an authoritative role in the family and society felt humbled and disgraced. In addition, the Depression triggered resentment toward working women, especially working wives. The attention being expended on the problems of men intensified the attitude that working women were depriving male breadwinners of employment. These gender dynamics were not reflected in the labor force participation rates of women and men shown in Table 2.1 because unemployed workers were still counted in the labor force.[5]

World War II, which closely followed the Depression, marked a turning point in the distribution of economic roles between women and men, although it did not necessarily cause the massive changes that were to follow. Similar to World War I, World War II created what was expected to be a temporary high demand for female labor. Women were attracted to war-related industries by an advertising campaign appealing to their patriotism, and they were given access to the more skilled, higher-paying jobs usually held by men. However, after the war was won in 1945, the labor force did not quickly "return to normal" as it did after World War I. Instead, a new sense of what is normal emerged.

THE SECOND HALF

Changes in the economic roles played by the sexes in the second half of the 20th century took several forms. The labor force participation rate of women rose steadily from 31% in 1950 to 60% by 2000, with the largest increase in labor force participation seen among non-Hispanic White women. In contrast, the labor force participation rate of men declined from 80% in 1950 to 75% in 2000. Although the gap between men and women remained at 15% in 2000, it had narrowed considerably over the 20th century.

This was the result of significant change in the composition of the female labor force. In 1900, 6% of married women and 44% of single (never married) women worked. In 1950, 24% of married women and 51% of single women worked. However, in 2000, 62% of married women and 65% of single women worked. Thus, the gap between the labor force participation rates of married and single women virtually disappeared over the century. In 2000, 53% of the female labor force was married, close to the 59% of male labor force that was married.[6]

Postwar changes in the female labor force demonstrated increasing disregard for the idea that the woman's proper place was in the home. In 1900, the women most accepted into the workplace were single, making up two thirds of the female labor force. Employment of single women required the least adjustment to public opinion; the notion that the *mother's* proper place was in the home could still be held as a standard when single women worked. The next group to enter the labor force in large numbers was older married women. Between 1940 and 1960, the proportion of 45- to 64-year-old women who worked went from 20% to 42%. These women were past their peak child-raising years. Their increasing presence in the workplace could be accepted begrudgingly by defenders of the status quo as long as *young* mothers stayed at home. The final group of women to increase its labor force participation consisted of younger married women with preschool or school-age children. By 2000, 81% of mothers with children between 14 and 17 years old, 78% of those with children between 6 and 13 years old, 74% of those with children between 3 and 5 years old, and 63% of those with children 2 years old or under were in the labor force. The increased employment of mothers of young children ended adherence to the belief that women belong at home.[7]

The educational attainment of women also changed considerably in the postwar years. In the United States, the proportion of college degrees earned by women increased between 1950 and 2000 from 24% to 57% at the bachelor's level and from 29% to 58% at the master's level. As Table 2.2 indicates, these increases were exhibited among members of the major racial and ethnic groups. Moreover, the proportion of college degrees in business earned by women increased between 1960 and 2000 from only 7% to 50% at the

Table 2.2   College Degrees Earned in the United States

	Percentage of Degrees Earned by Women					
	1950	1960	1970	1980	1990	2000
Bachelor's Level:						
Total, all disciplines:	24	35	43	50	53	57
Non-Hispanic White	—	—	—	50	53	57
Black	—	—	—	60	62	66
Hispanic	—	—	—	50	55	60
Asian	—	—	—	46	50	54
Total, business	—	7	9	34	47	50
Master's Level:						
Total, all disciplines:	29	32	40	50	53	58
Non-Hispanic White	—	—	—	52	55	60
Black	—	—	—	64	64	69
Hispanic	—	—	—	52	55	60
Asian	—	—	—	40	43	53
Total, business	—	4	4	22	34	40

SOURCE: U.S. Department of Education, National Center for Education Statistics. (2002). *Digest of education statistics 2001* (computed from Tables 247, 268, 271, and 284). Retrieved April 23, 2002, from http://nces.ed.gov

NOTE: — indicates data not available.

bachelor's level, and from only 4% to 40% at the master's level. These are striking increases.

The proportion of college degrees earned by women increased in many other countries as well. To cite a few examples, the proportion of bachelor's degrees earned by women increased between 1970 and 1997 from 42% to 59% in Australia, 38% to 58% in Canada, 31% to 52% in the United Kingdom, 20% to 34% in Japan, 26% to 64% in Norway, 40% to 62% in Sweden, and 29% to 59% in New Zealand. The proportion of master's degrees earned by women increased during the same period from 38% to 53% in Australia, 20% to 48% in Canada, 26% to 50% in the United Kingdom, 8% to 20% in Japan, 12% to 45% in Norway, 19% to 47% in Sweden, and 21% to 50% in New Zealand. These worldwide trends reflect a major societal shift toward the enhancement of women's academic credentials as well as an increased commitment of women to managerial and professional careers.[8]

These changes may in part be attributed to the power of "the pill," female oral contraceptives, regarded by *The Economist* as the most important advance in science and technology in the 20th century. The pill was approved for use by U.S. women in 1960 and was dispensed rapidly first to married women and,

Table 2.3   Participation in White-Collar Occupations

Year	Percentage of Labor Force		Percentage of Women Employed in Occupation	
	White-Collar	Managers	White-Collar	Managers
1900	18	6	19	4
1910	21	6	24	6
1920	25	7	32	7
1930	29	7	33	8
1940	31	7	35	11
1950	36	9	40	14
1960	43	11	42	16
1970	48	11	47	16
1980	52	11	53	26
1990	58	13	56	39
2000	59	15	57	45

SOURCES: **1900–1950:** U.S. Department of Commerce, Bureau of the Census. (1975). *Historical statistics of the United States: Colonial times to 1970* (139–140, series D182–232). Washington, DC: Government Printing Office; **1960–1980:** U.S. Department of Labor, Bureau of Labor Statistics. (1983). *Handbook of labor statistics* (44–48, Table 16). Washington, DC: Government Printing Office; **1990:** U.S. Department of Labor, Bureau of Labor Statistics. (1990). *Employment and earnings, 37*(2), 29, Table A-22; **2000:** U.S. Department of Labor, Bureau of Labor Statistics. (2002). *Employment and earnings* (computed from Table 9). Retrieved April 24, 2002, from http://www.bls.gov/cps

after several federal and state court actions, to single women. The pill greatly increased the reliability of contraception and reduced uncertainty about the consequences of sexual activity. Women could invest in a lengthy education without fearing that it would be interrupted by an unplanned pregnancy. Because the pill led to the postponing of marriage by most young women regardless of their educational aspirations, career women could delay marriage until completing their initial career preparation without being forced to choose from a reduced pool of eligible bachelors. Thus, the pill facilitated women's preparation for managerial and professional careers.[9]

The increased employment and educational attainment of women coincided with a rise in the proportion of white-collar jobs in the economy. White-collar jobs are those that do not require manual labor, including managerial jobs, professional jobs (e.g., engineers, teachers, lawyers, computer scientists), technical jobs (e.g., health and computer technicians), sales jobs (e.g., sales representatives and proprietors), and administrative support jobs (e.g., secretaries and clerical workers). In 1950, 36% of all jobs were white-collar, and women held 40% of these jobs (Table 2.3). By 1980, over half of all jobs were white-collar, and women held over half of these jobs.

Most important to the balance of power between the sexes were increases in the proportion of managers in the U.S. labor force and the proportion of managers who were women.[10] In 1900, as Table 2.3 indicates, the proportion of women managers was only 4%, or 1 in every 25. In 1940, it was 11%, or 1 in every 10. In 1970, it was 16%, or 1 in every 6. In 1980, it was 26%, or 1 in every 4. In 1990, it was 39%, or 2 in every 5. By 2000, it was 45%, or almost half, and ten times that of 1900. Thus, women dramatically gained representation in the growing managerial ranks over the 20th century. In countries throughout the world, changing societal and labor force patterns resulted in significant increases in the number and proportion of women managers.[11]

The women who entered the U.S. labor force after World War II came increasingly from the non-Hispanic White middle class. The growth in white-collar occupations created jobs that were compatible with middle-class status. Aspirations for a higher standard of living, consumerism, the desire to send children to college, and inflation made it necessary for some middle-class women to work to maintain a middle-class standard of living.

However, traditional attitudes concerning women's proper place in society persisted. During the 1950s, the mass media promoted an image of family togetherness that defined the mother's role as central to all domestic activity. According to Betty Friedan's *The Feminine Mystique,* women supposedly found true fulfillment as follows:

> Their only ambition was to be perfect wives and mothers; their highest ambition to have five children and a beautiful house, their only fight to get and keep their husbands. They had no thought for the unfeminine problems of the world outside the home; they wanted the men to make the major decisions. They gloried in their role as women, and wrote proudly on the census blank: "Occupation: housewife."[12]

Women were supposed to revel in this role and happily surrender control of and participation in economic and public life to men. According to opinion polls, both women and men accepted such gender roles. Yet the statistics that have been presented show that something else was actually happening in the workplace. As one observer put it, "A visitor from another planet who read the magazines and newspapers of the 1950s would never have guessed that the women portrayed as being engaged exclusively in homemaking activities were also joining the job market in unprecedented numbers."[13]

During this period, women workers were not perceived as crusading to achieve economic equality with men. Instead, their increased economic activity could be interpreted as consistent with their primary role as helpmates to their spouses. Most women who worked were citing "economic need" as the reason for their employment, even when the family income was solidly in the middle-class range. If women had not been portrayed, or portrayed themselves, as working temporarily to help meet immediate needs, male resistance to their entry into the labor force might have been greater.

Nonetheless, the contradiction between traditional attitudes and actual behavior could not last, especially when that contradiction became greater each year. What eventually changed was the public perception of traditional gender roles. In the late 1960s and early 1970s, a women's liberation movement emerged that had a major impact on the attitudes of women and, indirectly, men about their roles. This change was spurred both by the experiences of women in the civil rights movement of the 1960s and by the increasing resentment of middle-class business and professional women toward the barriers that held back their progress. This discontent found an early voice in Friedan's *The Feminine Mystique,* but mere recognition of the limits on women's achievements placed by society's attitudes was not enough. A full-fledged push for legislative and economic action ensued that would bring closer the goal of equality, or at least of equal opportunity, for men and women.[14]

The National Organization of Women (NOW), the first avowedly feminist organization since women gained the right to vote, held its inaugural meeting in 1966 with Betty Friedan the chief organizer. Its statement of purpose expressed concerns about discrimination in employment, education, and the legal system. It also called for a true partnership between the sexes to be brought about by equitable sharing of the responsibilities of home and children and their economic support. Women's groups such as NOW were successful in promoting change in many areas. Through lawsuits or the threat of legal action, large corporations were pressured into initiating "affirmative action" programs to increase their hiring and promotion of women. The federal government was pressured into investigating sex discrimination in federally funded contracts and federally sponsored programs and then devising programs to end it. Women's studies courses were added to the curriculum at many colleges and universities. Pressure from the women's liberation movement reduced the emphasis on gender stereotypes in children's books, stimulated the opening of day care centers, and contributed to the elimination of sexist language in professional journals and of separate advertising for "women's jobs" and "men's jobs" in the classified sections of newspapers. The women's movement had impact in many ways, large and small, and a whole generation of women became aware of the possibilities that could be open to them if they did not follow traditional norms.[15]

Starting in the 1960s, equal employment opportunity (EEO) laws were passed to restrict sex discrimination, as well as other types of discrimination. In the United States, Title VII of the Civil Rights Act of 1964 prohibited discrimination on the basis of sex, race, color, religion, or national origin in any employment condition, including hiring, firing, promotion, transfer, compensation, and access to training programs. Title VII was later extended to ban discrimination on the basis of pregnancy or childbirth and to ban sexual harassment. The Equal Pay Act of 1963 made it illegal to pay members of one sex less than the other if they are in equivalent jobs. All organizations with 50 or more employees and federal contracts exceeding $50,000 per year were required to file affirmative action programs with the federal government detailing the steps they were taking to eliminate discrimination. In addition, Title IX of the Education Amendments of 1972 banned sex discrimination in educational institutions receiving federal funds. Among other benefits, Title IX led to an enormous increase in opportunities for women to participate in college athletics.[16]

Ironically, the Title VII ban on sex discrimination in the United States was proposed as a last-minute amendment by a civil rights opponent as a strategy to prevent passage of the bill. Opponents felt the male-dominated Congress would be more reluctant to pass the legislation if sex was included. Indeed, one representative justified his opposition with the phrase, "Vive la différence!" However, women's rights advocates joined civil rights opponents to pass the amendment, and then joined civil rights advocates to pass the entire bill, amendment and all. Thus Title VII opened the door for significant gains for women in the workplace despite the intent of the representative who offered the amendment.[17]

EEO laws were passed in many other countries as well. In Canada, the Employment Equity Act in 1986 required organizations to commit to employment equity by analyzing their workforce, identifying employment barriers, implementing an Employment Equity Program, and reporting annually on their progress in achieving EEO goals; this law had an immediate impact on the hiring of women. In Japan, the Equal Employment Opportunity Law in 1985, which banned sex discrimination in employment, led to an increase in the employment of university-educated women. However, it was not until 1999 that Japan revised the law to end highly protective restrictions on women's overtime and work hours. Multinational associations such as the European Community (EC) and the United Nations also influenced social policy. For example, the EC's Social Protocol in 1992 encouraged member states to promote sex equality in labor market opportunities and treatment at work.[18]

The women's movement and EEO laws elicited mixed reactions from men. The men most threatened by these social and legal developments were those most committed to traditional roles in the family, the workplace, and public affairs. They were alarmed because their power in a patriarchal social system was being challenged. Other men were concerned about the impact on their job security and future advancement as more women entered the workplace. These men were inclined to dismiss newly mandated affirmative action programs as promoting "reverse discrimination."

A small number of men had the opposite reaction and promoted "men's liberation." Using consciousness-raising techniques borrowed from the women's movement, their goal was the liberation of men from the constraints imposed by the masculine sex role stereotype. "Men's studies" courses focusing on the male experience were offered on college campuses by the 1980s. Some saw men's studies as providing a necessary complement to women's studies. Many people with an interest in women's studies, however, believed that men's studies courses were not legitimate and marginally useful at best. The director of the National Women's Studies Association argued that *every* college course could be called a men's studies course.[19]

Most men, however, viewed the women's movement and EEO laws with ambivalence and anxiety. They took these developments seriously, but they did not know what to make of them or how to respond to them. As women entered the workplace in unprecedented numbers, men in turn faced confusion and discontent about their social, economic, and political roles. Many women, on the other hand, complained of a backlash against the women's liberation movement and were frustrated at the incomplete achievement of its goals. One woman characterized feminism as the Great Experiment That Failed, with its perpetuators as the casualties. Younger women, however, tended to see such complaints as tales from "the old days when, once upon a time, women had trouble getting into the schools or jobs they now hold."[20]

THE CENTURY DRAWS TO A CLOSE

In the last decade of the 20th century, tensions between women and men over public issues and events repeatedly emerged. Sexual harassment became a matter of considerable public discussion due to several widely publicized incidents. The National Football League fined players on the New England Patriots professional football team for locker-room sexual harassment of a female journalist, Lisa Olson. The response of the team's owner, Victor Kiam, to the charge of harassment was to call Olson a "classic bitch." Hounded by fans of the team when she returned to the Patriots' stadium to cover later games, Olson eventually left the country to pursue her profession in Australia.[21]

The secretary of the navy resigned and other naval officers were disciplined or dismissed after rampant sexual harassment and assault at the annual convention of the Tailhook Association, a group of retired and active naval aviators, came to public light. Female naval aviators were sexually assaulted by reportedly several hundred men as they were forced to walk a gauntlet of drunken officers lining the corridor outside hospitality suites at the convention hotel. The navy helicopter pilot who was the first to complain to navy officials about her treatment, Lt. Paula Coughlin, subsequently was the subject of a smear campaign by some of her fellow officers. In another case of sexual misconduct, Bob Packwood, a U.S. senator, was forced to resign under threat of expulsion for unwelcome advances toward numerous female office staff members.[22]

Feelings ran particularly high throughout the United States when Clarence Thomas, a nominee for the U.S. Supreme Court, was accused by Anita Hill, a law professor and former subordinate of Thomas, of sexual harassment. Hill's charges were dramatically aired and vehemently denied by Thomas in televised hearings. Battle lines were drawn over the merits of Hill's charges between men's organizations such as the National Organization for Men, feminist organizations such as NOW, and antifeminist organizations such as the Eagle Forum. To some, the hearings signified the extent of conflict between the sexes in society—women's strong feelings about sexual harassment and old-boy networks versus men's equally strong feelings of resentment about what they saw as unjust harassment complaints and loss of their traditional prerogatives.[23]

Workplace romance became a hotly contested public issue as well after it became known that President Bill Clinton had engaged in sexual activity with a White House intern, Monica Lewinsky. Clinton was impeached by the U.S. House of Representatives but was not convicted of the impeachment charges by the U.S. Senate, which would have forced him to leave office. Clinton claimed that the investigation of the affair infringed on his private life. However, the fact that the incidents occurred on White House premises and placed a burden on his office staff made it a very public affair. Observers were split over its implications for the workplace. Some claimed that corporate executives who behaved like Clinton would be terminated immediately, with one executive favoring "a good old-fashioned thrashing at high noon." Others said that no executive would ever receive the kind of severe punishment (conviction on impeachment charges, the equivalent of termination) that was seriously considered for Clinton.[24]

Even the merits of flirting by professional women, described approvingly in the *Wall Street Journal* article excerpted at the beginning of the chapter, were hotly debated in correspondence to the *Journal*. A female reader complained that giving the impression that young women were using their sexual appeal to compete in the workplace perpetuated the stereotype of women as sex objects and harmed women generally perceived as less attractive who were working hard to get ahead based on merit. A male reader complained that if he risked a sexual harassment complaint by flaunting his sexuality in the office, professional women should not be allowed to flaunt their feminine lures either. Gloria Steinem, a central figure in the women's liberation movement, was skeptical about whether flirting at work would truly benefit young women in the long run. The only people who seemed to be happy about the situation were the women who enjoyed and benefited from flirting and the men who welcomed their attention.[25] At the end of the 20th century, the intense feelings that these kinds of issues brought up for women and men were not fading.

A Snapshot of the Present

Let us now consider the current status of men and women in the workplace. Our review of key events and trends in the 20th century suggests that the economic roles played by the sexes became more similar over time. Sex differences in labor force participation, educational attainment, and employment in white-collar and managerial occupations decreased over the course of the century, and the marital status of the female labor force more closely reflected that of the male labor force. However, not all sex differences disappeared from the workplace in the 20th century. Significant differences in the status of men and women in the workforce remain.

Moreover, the employment status of men and women of various racial and ethnic groups differs. The three largest racial groups in the U.S. labor force according to government data are Whites (83%: 45% men and 38% women), Blacks (12%: 6% men and 6% women), and Asians (4%: 2% men and 2% women). Hispanics represent the largest ethnic group in the labor force tracked in government data (11%: 6% men and 5% women). Hispanics as an ethnic group are classified according to race; 95% of Hispanics in the labor force are classified as White and the remaining 5% are scattered across other racial groups. Thus, for purposes of comparison, we will examine the employment status of non-Hispanic White, Black, Asian, and Hispanic men and women.[26]

For example, the gap between the labor force participation rates of men and women varies across racial and ethnic groups. Table 2.4 reports the percentage of women and men in the labor force for each of the four groups examined. The sex difference in labor force participation rates ranges from 6% for Blacks to 20% for Hispanics. As we shall see, there are other significant differences in the employment status of members of different racial and ethnic groups within each sex.

THE SEX SEGREGATION OF OCCUPATIONS

If the workplace were completely integrated with regard to sex, the percentages of the male and female labor force in each occupation would be equal. For example, if 5% of all males were engineers, 5% of all females would be engineers, and the same would hold true for all occupations. As one sex increased in proportion in the labor force relative to the other, the percentages of

Table 2.4   Labor Force Participation Rates, by Racial/Ethnic Group

| | Percentage in the U.S. Labor Force | | |
Racial/Ethnic Group	Women	Men	Difference
Non-Hispanic White	59	72	13
Black	60	66	6
Asian	58	73	15
Hispanic	56	76	20
ALL RACES AND ETHNIC GROUPS	59	72	13

SOURCE: U.S. Department of Commerce, Bureau of the Census. (2002). *Current population survey* (computed from data for January, 2002). Retrieved April 24, 2002, from http://ferret.bls.census.gov

members of that sex in different occupations would remain equal to the equivalent percentages for the other sex.

Sex segregation exists when females and males are *not* similarly distributed across occupations. The level of sex segregation has dropped in most countries since the 1970s, primarily due to the increased employment of women in male-dominated occupations. However, the level of sex segregation remains very high. According to U.S. census data that divides the labor force into over 500 different types of work, just over half of the female or male labor force would have to change occupations for sex segregation to be eliminated completely. According to International Labor Office data, over half of the female or male labor force in countries such as Australia, Austria, Canada, Cyprus, Egypt, Finland, France, Germany, Ghana, Italy, Japan, Kuwait, Luxembourg, the Netherlands, New Zealand, Norway, Poland, Senegal, Spain, Sweden, Switzerland, and the United Kingdom would have to change occupations to eliminate sex segregation completely. Although there have been increases in the labor force participation of women worldwide (Table 1.1), the sex segregation of occupations is one of the most enduring features of the global economy.[27]

The nature of sex segregation in the U.S. workplace may be understood best by examining the employment of women and men in specific occupational categories. Women hold 47.0% of all jobs in the labor force (Table 2.5). Occupations are classified as male-intensive, female-intensive, or sex-neutral based on the proportion of women in the occupation. *Male-intensive* occupations are defined as those in which one third (33.3%) or less of the work force is female. *Female-intensive* occupations are defined as those in which two thirds (66.7%) or more of the work force is female. The remaining occupations, in which women hold more than one third but fewer than two thirds of the jobs (33.4% to 66.6%), are defined as *sex-neutral.* Overall, only 8.8% of

Table 2.5   Employment of Women and Men in Occupations

Occupation	Percentage of Male Labor Force	Percentage of Female Labor Force	Percentage of Female Workers in Occupation	Occupation Type
1. Executive, administrative, & managerial:				
Officials & administrators, public administration	.6	.7	51.8	
Other executive, administrative, & managerial	12.2	9.5	40.9	
Management-related occupations	3.1	4.5	56.4	
2. Professional specialty:				
Engineers	2.6	.4	11.1	M
Mathematical & computer scientists	1.9	1.1	34.5	
Natural scientists	.4	.3	36.1	
Health diagnosing occupations	1.1	.5	27.4	M
Health assessment & treating occupations	.6	4.4	86.5	F
Teachers, college & university	.9	.7	43.4	
Teachers, except college & university	2.1	6.8	74.2	F
Lawyers & judges	.9	.4	26.7	M
Other professional specialties	3.3	4.3	53.8	
3. Technicians & related support:				
Health technologists & technicians	.7	2.4	81.5	F
Engineering & science technicians	1.2	.5	26.2	M
Other technicians	1.0	1.0	45.5	
4. Sales occupations:				
Supervisors & proprietors	4.0	3.0	40.1	
Sales representatives, finance & business services	2.3	2.1	44.7	
Sales representatives, commodities, except retail	1.7	.6	26.2	M
Sales workers, retail & personal services	3.5	6.5	62.4	
Sales-related occupations	.0	.1	69.4	F

Occupation	Percentage of Male Labor Force	Percentage of Female Labor Force	Percentage of Female Workers in Occupation	Occupation Type
5. Administrative support, including clerical:				
Supervisors	.4	.7	59.0	
Computer equipment operators	.2	.3	52.7	
Secretaries, stenographers, & typists	.1	4.6	97.1	F
Financial records processing	.2	3.2	91.9	F
Mail & message distributing	.8	.5	37.4	
Other administrative support, including clerical	3.6	13.5	76.8	F
6. Service occupations:				
Private household	.0	1.0	96.2	F
Protective service	2.9	.9	21.0	M
Food service	4.0	5.7	56.0	
Health service	.4	4.1	89.3	F
Cleaning & building service	2.3	2.2	46.0	
Personal service	.8	4.2	82.6	F
7. Precision production, craft, & repair:				
Mechanics & repairers	6.3	.4	4.7	M
Construction trades	8.2	.2	2.6	M
Other precision production, craft, & repair	3.9	1.3	23.5	M
8. Operators, fabricators, & laborers:				
Machine operators, assemblers, & inspectors	5.9	3.8	36.2	
Transportation & material moving	7.2	.9	10.3	M
Handlers, equipment cleaners, helpers, & laborers	5.5	1.6	20.8	M
9. Farming, forestry, & fishing:				
Farm operators & managers	1.2	.5	27.6	M
Other farming, forestry, & fishing	2.0	.6	21.1	M
TOTAL-ALL OCCUPATIONS	100.0	100.0	47.0	

SOURCE: U.S. Department of Labor, Bureau of Labor Statistics. (2002). *Employment and earnings* (computed from data for March, 2002, from Table A-19). Retrieved April 24, 2002, from http://www.bls.gov/cps

NOTE: Occupation Type equals M for a male-intensive occupation and F for a female-intensive occupation. No symbol indicates a sex-neutral occupation. The table includes both full-time and part-time employees.

women work in male-intensive occupations, with other women equally divided between female-intensive (44.3%) and sex-neutral (46.9%) occupations. Similarly, only 8.5% of men work in female-intensive occupations, with other men equally divided between male-intensive (44.7%) and sex-neutral (46.8%) occupations.

As Table 2.5 demonstrates, executive, managerial, and administrative positions are sex-neutral. Professional, technical, and sales occupations are male-intensive, female-intensive, or sex-neutral according to the particular occupation being considered. The engineering and legal professions are male-intensive, whereas the teaching profession, except at the college and university level, is female-intensive. Health diagnosing (e.g., medicine) is male-intensive, whereas health assessment and treating (e.g., nursing) is female-intensive. Technical occupations in the health area are female-intensive, whereas those in engineering and science are male-intensive. The sale of commodities is male-intensive. Administrative support occupations, including clerical work, are predominantly female-intensive. The delivery of household, health, and personal services is female-intensive, whereas the delivery of protective services (e.g., security) is male-intensive. The remaining occupations, including precision production, craft, and repair; operators, fabricators, and laborers; and farming, forestry, and fishing are predominantly male-intensive.

The percentages of women and men employed in various occupations may be examined for members of different racial and ethnic groups. Table 2.6 displays these percentages for the nine major types of occupations. The table reveals large racial and ethnic differences in employment for both sexes. For example, the percentage employed in managerial and professional occupations is highest for non-Hispanic Whites and Asians of both sexes. However, the percentage employed in service occupations is highest for Hispanic and Black women. Also, the percentage employed as operators, fabricators, and laborers is highest for Black and Hispanic men. Overall, there is considerable racial/ethnic disparity in employment.[28]

The gap between the proportions of women in the labor force (47.0%) and in management overall (45.1% for all executive, administrative, and managerial workers) has virtually disappeared. Management as an occupation, once male-intensive, is now sex-neutral in composition. However, the large gap between the proportions of women in management overall and in *top* management remains. In all countries, the proportion of women decreases at progressively higher levels in the managerial ranks.[29]

For example, the proportion of female corporate officers in *Fortune* 500 corporations is currently 13%. The proportion of women in "clout" officer positions that wield the most power and influence (chief executive officer, chairman, vice chairman, president, chief operating officer, senior executive vice president, and

Table 2.6 Employment of Women and Men in Occupations, by Racial/Ethnic Group

Occupation	Percentage of Male Labor Force				Percentage of Female Labor Force			
	Non-Hispanic White	Black	Asian	Hispanic	Non-Hispanic White	Black	Asian	Hispanic
1. Executive, administrative, & managerial	17.0	8.9	16.1	6.3	16.2	9.9	13.8	8.7
2. Professional specialty	14.6	9.3	25.1	5.0	20.0	14.3	20.9	9.0
3. Technicians & related support	2.8	1.9	5.6	2.0	3.8	3.1	5.2	2.3
4. Sales occupations	12.7	8.6	10.3	7.4	12.8	11.8	11.6	13.7
5. Administrative support, including clerical	5.0	8.9	6.7	5.4	23.5	24.0	17.0	21.0
6. Service occupations	8.6	18.1	12.6	16.0	15.6	25.3	19.1	27.3
7. Precision production, craft, & repair	18.7	13.9	10.4	24.3	1.8	1.7	4.0	2.9
8. Operators, fabricators, & laborers	17.2	28.2	11.9	26.7	5.2	9.7	7.9	12.7
9. Farming, forestry, & fishing	3.4	2.2	1.3	6.9	1.1	.2	.5	2.4
TOTAL-ALL OCCUPATIONS	100.0	100.0	100.0	100.0	100.0	100.0	100.0	100.0

SOURCE: U.S. Department of Commerce, Bureau of the Census. (2002). *Current population survey* (computed from data for January, 2002). Retrieved April 24, 2002, from http://ferret.bls.census.gov

executive vice president) in *Fortune* 500 corporations is only 6%. Although the proportion of women in top management, however top management is defined, has increased over time, this proportion remains less than 5% in most countries. Thus, although the lower managerial ranks have become sex-neutral, the top managerial levels remain male-intensive. Further, the top managerial ranks in the United States are non-Hispanic White–intensive. Over 95% of both male and female top managers in the U.S. labor force are non-Hispanic Whites.[30]

THE SEX GAP IN EARNINGS

Not only do women and men tend to work in different occupations, they also differ in earnings. The ratio of female-to-male earnings (F/M ratio) for full-time U.S. workers across all occupations is 76%. Although this ratio has risen since the 1970s, when it was about 60%, the gap between male and female earnings remains considerable.[31]

The sex difference in earnings exists across occupations. The wages earned in female-intensive occupations are typically lower than those earned in male-intensive occupations. In fact, the reduction in the earnings gap since the 1970s has been primarily due to the increased employment of women in occupations that were previously male-intensive (e.g., management) or are still male-intensive (e.g., engineering and law).

The sex difference in earnings also exists within occupations. To cite a few examples, the F/M ratio for full-time workers is 68% for physicians, 88% for registered nurses (who earn 66% of what physicians earn), 75% for college and university teachers, 95% for elementary school teachers (who earn 73% of what college and university teachers earn), 93% for social workers, 69% for lawyers, 89% for cashiers, 77% for computer operators, 85% for male carriers, 87% for food servers in restaurants (i.e., waiters and waitresses), 82% for janitors and cleaners, 72% for machine operators, assemblers, and inspectors, 85% for bus drivers, and 89% for farm workers. Looking at the managerial ranks, female managers earn 67% as much as male managers. However, in rare examples of occupations in which women earn more than men, the F/M ratio is 103% for special education teachers and 102% for electrical and electronic engineers.[32]

The gap between the earnings of males and females does not diminish with educational attainment. Although education has a strong positive effect on earnings for both women and men, it yields greater economic benefits for men. The earnings gap exists at every educational level—for workers with less than a high school education, a high school diploma, a bachelor's degree, and even an advanced graduate degree. Earnings data suggest that the higher the educational level, the lower the F/M ratio, a depressing thought for females.[33]

The earnings gap exists across racial and ethnic groups. For example, the F/M ratio is 73% for non-Hispanic White workers, 87% for Black workers, and

88% for Hispanic workers. There is also an earnings gap between racial and ethnic groups; Black workers earn 76% and Hispanic workers earn 64% of what non-Hispanic White workers earn. As a result, non-Hispanic White men are the most highly paid in the U.S. labor force. Black men earn 70% of what non-Hispanic White men earn, Black women 61%, Hispanic men 59%, and Hispanic women only 52%.[34]

Finally, the earnings gap exists across national cultures. Although men invariably earn more than women overall, the size of the F/M ratio varies considerably across countries. Australia has one of the highest F/M ratios, about 90% for nonagricultural jobs; the Scandinavian countries of Norway, Denmark, and Sweden also have high F/M ratios. Japan has had one of the lowest F/M ratios, about 50% for nonagricultural jobs. Countries such as the United Kingdom, Germany, and Switzerland, as well as the United States, have intermediate F/M ratios. Interestingly, although U.S. women have higher work qualifications with respect to educational and professional attainment than do women in most other countries, the United States does not have one of the highest earnings ratios.[35]

Thus, there is a "cost of being female" that prevails within occupations as well as across occupations, educational levels, racial and ethnic groups, and cultures. The gap between male and female earnings is a long-standing attribute of the global economy, and it is not likely that this gap will disappear anytime soon.

In conclusion, women and men tend to play different economic roles in the workplace today. Current employment and compensation patterns send a powerful message to young people planning to enter and adults planning to reenter the labor force. The message is that although all occupations are theoretically open to all individuals, (a) some occupations are more appropriate for members of one sex than the other sex, (b) the lower-paying occupations are more appropriate for females, (c) the higher-paying occupations are more appropriate for males, (d) work in male-intensive occupations is worth more than work in female-intensive occupations, and (e) work performed by men is worth more than equivalent work performed by women.

Looking Forward

Traditional gender roles have less to do with present-day economic realities than at any previous time. The changes experienced by women in the labor force over the last century have been striking. Women entering male-intensive organizations have gone from being the only woman holding a particular job, to being a member of a small group of women amid a larger group of men in the job, sometimes to being a member of the majority group, and increasingly more often to being in charge. The changes experienced by men have been less dramatic. However, men have been required to adapt to the presence of more women as their peers, superiors, and subordinates. Both sexes have had to adjust.

Some important differences between the economic roles played by women and men remain. Men, especially non-Hispanic Whites, continue to hold most top management positions in organizations. Even when organizations consist predominantly of female employees, the leaders are typically male. The gap between male and female wages also persists. Among full-time workers, women consistently earn lower wages than men. Even with the same job in the same occupation, women's average earnings are typically lower than those of men. The highest paid occupations are those with predominantly male workers. Pay is an important indicator of the value attached to work, and the work of women, Blacks, and Hispanics continues to be valued less than the work of non-Hispanic White men.

Thus we find ourselves in a period of flux. Even though work and its rewards are not distributed equally between the sexes, enough change has occurred to make traditional gender roles no longer an appropriate guideline for workplace behavior. However, new standards of behavior have not replaced the old standards. Whether consciously or unconsciously, people often are influenced by their own sex and others' sex in their work behavior.

What *does* it mean to be a woman or a man in today's workplace? How *should* women and men take into account their own sex and others' sex in their workplace interactions, if at all? Widely accepted answers to these questions, promoting either a unisex standard of behavior or separate standards of behavior for men and women, have not emerged.

Due to the increase in the proportion of working women, more workplace interactions between people of the opposite sex are occurring than ever before. One of the few advantages of adhering to traditional gender roles was that men and women knew how they were expected to treat each other. That advantage is gone. In replacement, women and men need to understand each other better in their work roles. The remainder of the book explores men's and women's work roles, including their experiences as job seekers, recruiters, employees, team members, and leaders.

Notes

1. Pollock, E. J. (2000, February 7). In today's workplace, women feel freer to be, well, women. *Wall Street Journal*, p. A1. WALL STREET JOURNAL CLASSROOM EDITION (STAFF PRODUCED COPY ONLY) by E. J. POLLOCK. Copyright 2000 by DOW JONES & CO INC. Reproduced with permission of DOW JONES & CO INC. in the format Textbook via Copyright Clearance Center.

2. Chafe, W. H. (1976). Looking backward in order to look forward: Women, work, and social values in America. In J. M. Kreps (Ed.), *Women and the American economy: A look to the 1980s* (pp. 6–30). Englewood Cliffs, NJ: Prentice Hall; Tilly, L. A., & Scott, J. W. (1978). *Women, work, and family.* New York: Holt, Rinehart & Winston; Smith, B. G. (2000). Industrial revolution. In A. M. Howard & F. M. Kavenik (Eds.), *Handbook of American women's history* (pp. 269–270). Thousand Oaks, CA: Sage.

3. Buenker, J. D. (2000). Nineteenth Amendment to the Constitution—1920. In A. M. Howard & F. M. Kavenik (Eds.), *Handbook of American women's history* (p. 402). Thousand Oaks, CA: Sage; Chafe.

4. Anderson, S. (1935). *Puzzled America.* Mamaroneck, NY: Appel, p. 46., quoted in Dubbert, J. L. (1979). *A man's place: Masculinity in transition.* Englewood Cliffs, NJ: Prentice-Hall, p. 210.

5. Fox, M. F., & Hesse-Biber, S. (1984). *Women at work.* Palo Alto, CA: Mayfield; Dubbert; Howard, A. M. (2000). Depression era. In A. M. Howard & F. M. Kavenik (Eds.), *Handbook of American women's history* (p. 146). Thousand Oaks, CA: Sage.

6. U.S. Department of Commerce, Bureau of the Census. (1975). *Historical statistics of the United States: Colonial times to 1970* (p. 133, series D49–62). Washington, DC: Government Printing Office; U.S. Department of Labor, Bureau of Labor Statistics. (1989). *Handbook of labor statistics* (pp. 235–239, table 55). Washington, DC: Government Printing Office; U.S. Department of Commerce, Bureau of the Census. (2000). *Current population survey* (computed from data for October, 2000). Retrieved December 6, 2000, from http://ferret.bls.census.gov

7. Weiner, L. Y. (1985). *From working girl to working mother: The female labor force in the United States, 1820–1980.* Chapel Hill: University of North Carolina Press; U.S. Department of Commerce. (1975), pp. 131–132, series D29–41, and p. 133, series D49–62; U.S. Department of Commerce. (2000). (computed from data for October, 2000).

8. United Nations Educational, Scientific and Cultural Organization, Institute for Statistics. (2002). *Database: Education and literary statistics* (computed from data on graduates by ISCED level). Retrieved April 25, 2002, from http://www.uis.unesco.org

9. *The Economist* (1999, December 31). Oral contraceptives: The liberator, p.102; Goldin, C. (2000). *The power of the pill: Oral contraceptives and women's career and marriage decisions.* Cambridge, MA: Harvard University. (NBER Working Paper 7527).

10. We refer to individuals classified as executives, administrators, and managers in nonfarm occupations in U.S. government reports of labor statistics as simply "managers" throughout the book.

11. Adler, N. J., & Izraeli, D. N. (Eds.). (1994). *Competitive frontiers: Women managers in a global economy.* Cambridge, MA: Blackwell.

12. Friedan, B. (1974). *The feminine mystique* (10th anniversary ed.). New York: Norton, p. 18.

13. Chafe, p. 20.

14. Yelton-Stanley, S. K., & Howard, A. M. (2000). Women's liberation movement. In A. M. Howard & F. M. Kavenik (Eds.), *Handbook of American women's history* (pp. 640–641). Thousand Oaks, CA: Sage.

15. Yelton-Stanley, S. K. (2000). National Organization for Women (NOW). In A. M. Howard & F. M. Kavenik (Eds.), *Handbook of American women's history* (p. 382). Thousand Oaks, CA: Sage; *Ms.* (1979, December). *Special issue: The decade of women.*

16. Sedmak, N. J., & Vidas, C. (1994). *Primer on equal employment opportunity* (6th ed.). Washington, DC: Bureau of National Affairs.

17. Ledvinka, J., & Scarpello, V. G. (1991). *Federal regulation of personnel and human resource management* (2nd ed.). Boston: PWS-Kent, pp. 63–65.

18. Leck, J. D., & Saunders, D. M. (1992). Hiring women: The effects of Canada's Employment Equity Act. *Canadian Public Policy–Analyse de Politiques, 18* (2), 203–220; Cannings, K., & Lazonick, W. (1994). Equal employment opportunity and the "managerial woman" in Japan. *Industrial Relations, 33,* 44–69; Thornton, E. (1999, April 19). Make way for women with welding guns. *Business Week,* 54; Konrad, A. M., & Linnehan, F. (1999). Affirmative action: History, effects, and attitudes. In G. N. Powell (Ed.), *Handbook of gender and work* (pp. 429–452). Thousand Oaks,

CA: Sage; Davidson, M. J., & Cooper, C. L. (Eds.). (1993). *European women in business and management.* London: Chapman.

19. Pleck, J. H., & Sawyer, J. (Eds.). (1974). *Men and masculinity.* Englewood Cliffs, NJ: Prentice-Hall; Shiffman, M. (1987). The men's movement: An exploratory empirical investigation. In M. S. Kimmel (Ed.), *Changing men: New directions in research on men and masculinity* (pp. 295–314). Newbury Park, CA: Sage; Brod, H. (1987). A case for men's studies. In M. S. Kimmel (Ed.), *Changing men: New directions in research on men and masculinity* (pp. 263–277). Newbury Park, CA: Sage; Petzke, D. (1986, February 11). "Men's studies" catches on at colleges, setting off controversy and infighting. *Wall Street Journal,* p. 35.

20. Tiger, L. (1999). *The decline of males.* New York: Golden; Faludi, S. (1999). *Stiffed: The betrayal of the American man.* New York: Morrow; Faludi, S. (1991). *Backlash: The undeclared war against American women.* New York: Crown; Ebeling, K. (1990, November 19). The failure of feminism. *Newsweek,* 9; Goodman, E. (1985, March 8). Feminists' mid-life shock. *Hartford Courant,* p. B9.

21. Disch, L., & Kane, M. J. (1996). When a looker is really a bitch: Lisa Olson, sport, and the heterosexual matrix. *Signs, 21,* 278–308; Roessner, B. T. (1990, October 3). Episode makes sport a whole new ballgame. *Hartford Courant,* p. B1.

22. Salholz, E. (1992, August 10). Deepening shame. *Newsweek,* 30–36; U.S. Department of Defense, Inspector General. (1993). *Tailhook 91, part 2: Events at the 35th Annual Tailhook Symposium.* Washington, DC: Government Printing Office; Smolowe, J. (1995, September 18). Betrayed by his kisses: Packwood's final hours. *Time.* Retrieved June 4, 2001, from http://www.time.com

23. Blonston, G., & Scanlan, C. (1991, October 12). Hill, Thomas hold their ground: A conflict between the sexes. *Hartford Courant,* pp. A1, A9; Schafly, P. (1991, October 15). A feminist mob tries to smear a conservative judge. *Hartford Courant,* p. B13.

24. Isikoff, M., & Thomas, E. (1998, February 2). Clinton and the intern. *Newsweek,* 31–46; Powell, G. N. (1998, September 30). How "the affair" would be handled in the private sector. *Hartford Courant,* p. A13; Kronholz, J., & Bodipo-Memba, A. (1998, September 11). What if it were a corporate executive and an intern? *Wall Street Journal,* p. B1.

25. Letters to the editor: So now we're sex kittens again? (2000, February 18). *Wall Street Journal,* p. A15; Pollock, pp. A1, A20.

26. U.S. Department of Commerce, Bureau of the Census. (2002). *Current population survey* (computed from data for January, 2002). Retrieved April 26, 2002, from http://ferret.bls.census.gov. The terms "White," "Black," "Asian," and "Hispanic" are used in this book because these are the terms most frequently used in U.S. government reports on employment. The terms "Caucasian," "African American," "Pacific Islander," and "Latino" or "Chicano/Chicana" may just as well be used. Further, each of these groups may be divided into multiple subgroups. "American Indians" (i.e., "Native Americans") are also tracked as a racial group in government reports. However, since this group represents only 1% of the U.S. labor force, employment statistics are often incomplete and are not reported in this chapter. For more on the status of the many racial and ethnic groups in U.S. society, see Shinagawa, L. H., & Jang, M. (1998). *Atlas of American diversity.* Walnut Creek, CA: AltaMira; Amott, T., & Matthaei, J. (1996). *Race, gender, and work: A multicultural economic history of women in the United States* (Rev. ed.). Boston: South End Press; Higginbotham, E., & Romero, M. (Eds.). (1997). *Women and work: Exploring race, ethnicity, and class.* Thousand Oaks, CA: Sage; Vaz, K. M. (Ed.). (1995). *Black women in America.* Thousand Oaks, CA: Sage; Takaki, R. (1989). *Strangers from a different shore: A history of Asian Americans.* New York: Penguin; Knouse, S. B., Rosenfeld, P., & Culbertson, A. L. (Eds.). (1992). *Hispanics in the workplace.* Newbury Park, CA: Sage.

27. Jacobs, J. A. (1999). The sex segregation of occupations: Prospects for the 21st century. In G. N. Powell (Ed.), *Handbook of gender and work* (pp. 125–141). Thousand Oaks, CA: Sage; Anker, R. (1998). *Gender and jobs: Sex segregation of occupations in the world.* Geneva: International Labour Office, 176–177, Table 9.1.

28. For more on job segregation by sex, race, and ethnicity, see Reskin, B. F., & Padavic, I. (1999). Sex, race, and ethnic inequality in United States workplaces. In J. S. Chafetz (Ed.), *Handbook of the sociology of gender* (pp. 343–374). New York: Kluwer Academic/Plenum.

29. Powell, G. N. (1999). Reflections on the glass ceiling: Recent trends and future prospects. In G. N. Powell (Ed.), *Handbook of gender and work* (pp. 325–345). Thousand Oaks, CA: Sage.

30. Catalyst. (2000). *Census of women corporate officers and top earners.* New York: Catalyst; Wirth, L. (2001). *Breaking through the glass ceiling: Women in management.* Geneva: International Labour Office; Adler & Izraeli; Davidson, M. J., & Cooper, C. L. (1992). *Shattering the glass ceiling: The woman manager.* London: Chapman; Davidson, M. J., & Cooper, C. L. (Eds.). (1993). *European women in business and management.* London: Chapman; Federal Glass Ceiling Commission. (1995). *Good for business: Making full use of the nation's human capital: An environmental scan.* Washington, DC: U.S. Department of Labor, Glass Ceiling Commission.

31. U.S. Department of Labor, Bureau of Labor Statistics. (2002). *Employment and earnings* (computed from Table 39). Retrieved April 29, 2002, from http://www.bls.gov/cps; Roos, P. A., & Gatta, M. L. (1999). The gender gap in earnings: Trends, explanations, and prospects. In G. N. Powell (Ed.), *Handbook of gender and work* (pp. 95–123). Thousand Oaks, CA: Sage.

32. U.S. Department of Labor. (2002). (computed from Table 39).

33. Roos & Gatta.

34. U.S. Department of Labor. (2002). (computed from Table 37).

35. Roos & Gatta; Dunn, D., & Skaggs, S. (1999). Gender and paid work in industrial nations. In J. S. Chafetz (Ed.), *Handbook of the sociology of gender* (pp. 321–342). New York: Kluwer Academic/Plenum; Joshi, H., & Paci, P. (1998). *Unequal pay for women and men: Evidence from the British Birth Cohort Studies.* Cambridge, MA: MIT Press.

3

Becoming Women and Men

EMPHATICALLY FEMININE BARBIE

Adorable; billowy, breathtaking; charming, chic; dazzling, delicate, dramatic; elegant and exquisite; fanciful, fashionable, and fetching; glamorous and glittering; graceful; lovely; radiant, regal, romantic; shimmering, sparkling, stunning. These adjectives pervade Mattel's advertisements for Barbie. They also show up in [media] stories about Barbie. Young people and adults favor these same words when describing Barbie. Needless to say, these are the adjectives of modern middle-class femininity. They also describe youthful femininity, heterosexual femininity, and white femininity. . . . Above all, it seems, Barbie is an icon of the femininity associated with the middle reaches of contemporary Western societies. . . .

Despite her pervasive presence Barbie cannot readily become a part of ordinary lives in any full-blown sense because her femininity is fantastic. It goes way beyond what sociologist R. W. Connell calls "emphasized femininity," that style of looking and acting feminine that is most widely expected and enforced in a given society. Barbie's style might be called emphatic femininity. It takes feminine appearances and demeanor to unattainable extremes. Nothing about Barbie ever looks masculine, even when she is on the police force. Police Officer Barbie comes with a night stick and walkie-talkie but no gun and no handcuffs. She also comes with a "glittery evening dress" to wear to the awards dance when she will get the "Best Police Officer Award for her courageous acts in the community," yet Police Officer Barbie is pictured on the box "lov[ing] to teach safety tips to children." Barbie thus feminizes, even maternalizes, law enforcement. More generally, nothing about her appearance ever looks andro-gynous or gender-neutral even when she is being athletic, as with Baseball Barbie or Golf Date Barbie. Barbie's pink pack-aging, soft and billowing fabrics, form-fitting fashions, and shapely figure shout "Feminine!"

—Mary F. Rogers[1]

A re there sex differences beyond the obvious ones? What do people believe sex differences to be? How are beliefs about sex differences conveyed? What causes sex differences, and what effects do they have on individuals' well-being?

Sex differences influence how people are disposed to behave in work settings. Females and males are similar in some ways and different in others. Despite thousands of studies, however, researchers do not agree about the scope, magnitude, or cause of sex differences. As we noted in Chapter 1, this may be due to researchers' inclinations to engage in either alpha bias, magnify-ing existing differences, or beta bias, downplaying existing differences. It is also due to the imperfect nature of the research evidence.

Gender differences influence how people react to others' behavior in work settings. Some gender differences represent beliefs that are held by a large pro-portion of the population. For example, males are commonly believed to be high in "masculine" traits such as independence, aggressiveness, and domi-nance, and females are commonly believed to be high in "feminine" traits such as gentleness, sensitivity to the feelings of others, and tactfulness. Although others have used the terms "sex role stereotypes" or "sex stereotypes," we will refer to *gender stereotypes* as shared beliefs about the psychological traits that are characteristic of each sex. Gender stereotypes have been generally stable over time. Other gender differences represent beliefs about the roles that males and females should play in the workplace and society at large. We will refer to *gender roles* as norms that prescribe the activities and behaviors con-sidered appropriate for each sex. The attitudes of both women and men toward gender roles have become less traditional and more egalitarian in recent years. However, men's attitudes are less egalitarian than women's atti-tudes, especially those of younger, highly educated women with highly educated working mothers.[2]

This chapter examines general sex and gender differences in society that influence male/female interactions in the workplace. First, research evidence about sex differences is presented. Next, the nature of gender stereotypes and different types of sexist attitudes is examined. The concepts of gender identity and psychological androgyny are introduced. The influence of nature and nurture on individuals' behavior is considered, and the ways in which gender role expectations are conveyed to children are examined. Finally, the chapter considers how gender stereotypes and roles unduly restrict adult behavior.

Sex Differences

The study of sex differences is an international preoccupation. Many research studies have been conducted on the topic of sex differences. The first major review of research on the psychology of sex differences was published in 1974 by Eleanor Maccoby and Carole Nagy Jacklin. Maccoby and Jacklin's review of over 1,400 published studies was then the most complete work of its kind ever published. Since that time, more than 50,000 studies on the topic of sex differences have been published by scholars around the world. This topic is not simply "hot" in the sense of being fashionable; it is also inflammatory. Many people have strong beliefs about male and female similarities and differences in basic interests, abilities, attitudes, and behaviors.[3] In this section of the chapter, we first consider sex differences in children's interests and activities; then we consider sex differences in cognitive abilities, moral judgments, and social behavior.

CHILDREN'S INTERESTS AND ACTIVITIES

Starting at an early age, the interests and activities of boys and girls differ greatly. A sex difference in toy preferences emerges at about 2 years of age. Boys are more likely than girls to prefer action figures, toy guns, sports collectibles, and remote-controlled sports cars and trucks. For example, the G.I. Joe product line, introduced in 1964, is marketed to boys as its name suggests. Boys may choose from action figures representing soldiers from various countries (e.g., U.S. Army Infantry, British SAS, French Foreign Legion), intergalactic warriors, generals, astronauts, football players, and wrestlers; vehicles such as tanks, land assault vehicles, and motorcycles; and accessories such as rifles, bomber jackets, and emergency ration kits. Until 1997, when a female helicopter pilot was introduced, the only female action figure in the G.I. Joe line was (of course) a nurse.[4]

In contrast, girls are more likely than boys to prefer dolls, dollhouses, play kitchens, and housekeeping toys. As noted in the passage at the beginning of the chapter, Barbie dolls offer an image of emphatic (exaggerated) femininity. Introduced in 1959, more than 1 billion Barbie dolls have been sold in 150 countries. Girls may choose Barbie dolls, now available in White, Black, Asian, and Hispanic versions, that emphasize beauty, celebrity, fantasy, sportiness, trendiness, and various activities such as putting a baby to bed, dating her boyfriend Ken, caring for her cat Marshmallow, and being a children's doctor. For their dolls, they may choose various types of Barbie apparel (e.g., pink rain boots and rain coats), accessories (e.g., jewelry, nail kit, rolling luggage), electronic toys (e.g., phone, laptop computer, boom box), houses, furniture, play sets (e.g., wedding party set), pets, vehicles, and household items (e.g., vacuum, blender, hand mixer, recipe box, and timer). Girls may also choose the same types of Barbie products for themselves.[5]

Boys prefer a more physically aggressive rough-and-tumble style of play than do girls, including both fighting and mock fighting. They welcome a physically active style of play with both parents. However, due to a sex difference in parental preferences for this style of play, boys engage in it more with their fathers than with their mothers. Boys spend more time watching television and participating in sports, whereas girls spend more time reading. The sex difference in play interests is seen on doorsteps on Halloween. Boys are more likely to dress as villainous characters, monsters, or symbols of death, whereas girls are more likely to dress as princesses, beauty queens, and other examples of traditional femininity.[6]

Sex differences are also exhibited in interest in computer games and use of computers. Boys are more likely to play interactive video games on home computers and to crowd around video game machines in public settings. Compared with girls, boys are much more involved with the many possible uses of computers. One of the strongest adolescent male stereotypes is that of the "hacker," who spurns involvement with the real world (including girls) and becomes excessively involved with the world of computers.[7]

Mattel, the maker of Barbie dolls and related products, sensed an opportunity in this sex difference. It marketed a pink-flowered Barbie computer and several interactive computer games for girls, including Barbie Fashion Designer, Barbie Magic Hair Styler, Barbie Nail Designer, Barbie Digital Makeover, Barbie Pet Rescue, Detective Barbie, Barbie Magic Genie, Barbie as Sleeping Beauty, and Barbie as Princess Bride. Mattel quickly captured the lioness' share of the girls' computer game market, thereby promoting computer usage by girls. Note the emphatically feminine nature of most of the activities in which the software Barbie is engaged.[8]

Although there is variation across cultures, boys and girls exhibit considerable differences in how they spend their time.[9] In Western cultures, it is believed that play is the work of children; play is culturally sanctioned. However, boys have more time to play than do girls because they do not have to devote as much time to household chores. Boys and girls also differ in the types of household chores they perform. Boys perform more tasks outside the home, including yard work and outdoor errands. Girls perform more tasks inside the home, including taking care of younger children, cleaning, and preparing food.

As they move into adolescence, girls and boys in Western cultures devote similar amounts of time to paid labor. Adolescent employment is particularly encouraged in the United States as a way to learn self-sufficiency and responsibility. However, girls and boys are employed in different kinds of activities. Girls are likely to be babysitters, waitresses, and food counter workers, whereas boys are likely to be gardeners, busboys, and manual laborers.

Overall, girls show more interest in activities associated with boys than vice versa. Toy retailers assume that they can sell a "boy" product to a girl but not the reverse. Although boys as well as girls might enjoy playing at rescuing pets and being detectives, no boy would want to be caught by his peers using Barbie-oriented computer games to do so. Girls who are interested in activities that are considered more typical of boys than of girls are labeled "tomboys," whereas boys who are interested in activities associated with girls are labeled "sissies." Sissies are more negatively evaluated than tomboys, especially by males. Tomboys are seldom rejected by their peers because of their interest in activities associated with boys; they can always return to playing with other girls. However, boys have less freedom of choice and run a greater risk of being taunted by other boys for showing any interest in girls' activities. Most tomboy activity stops at puberty, when pressures on girls to adhere to the female gender roles become particularly intense. However, former or would-be tomboys now have more alternative outlets for their interests, such as female athletic teams at all levels of education. In fact, female undergraduates who participate in varsity athletics are more likely than nonathletes to describe themselves as having been tomboys.[10]

As children grow up and progress through adolescence, they exhibit considerable sex differences in activities and interests. Girls, however, engage more in activities typically associated with boys than the opposite. As we discuss later in the chapter, the ways parents socialize girls and boys contribute greatly to sex differences in children's activities.

COGNITIVE ABILITIES

The field of cognitive psychology is concerned with how people think, learn, and remember. People who are better at thinking, learning, and remembering are generally regarded as more intelligent. At the beginning of the 20th century, intelligence was viewed by test designers such as the French psychologist Alfred

Binet as a universal concept. Tests were designed to yield a single score called an "intelligence quotient," or IQ, for every individual. However, IQ tests were designed to equalize the average scores of males and females because Binet, surprisingly for his times, believed that there was no sex difference in general intelligence.[11] Most psychologists now regard intelligence as consisting of different types of abilities, such as verbal, visual-spatial (that is, the ability to visualize figures or objects in space and how they are related), and mathematical or quantitative.

Diane Halpern reviewed the evidence from thousands of research studies regarding sex differences in verbal, visual-spatial, and mathematical abilities, each of which may be divided into more specific types of abilities. She found that sex differences in cognitive abilities tend to be stable across national cultures, even though there are large between-country differences that affect both sexes. For example, students of both sexes are better at math in some countries than in others. Halpern's conclusions are briefly summarized.[12]

Verbal abilities include all uses of language: word fluency (the ability to generate words), grammar, spelling, reading, writing, verbal analogies, vocabulary, and oral comprehension. Females have the advantage in most types of verbal abilities from birth to death. The only type of verbal ability at which males have an advantage is in solving verbal analogies.

Visual-spatial abilities include spatial perception (the ability to see objects as horizontal or vertical), mental rotation (the ability to rotate mentally a three-dimensional object pictured in two dimensions), spatial visualization (the ability to visualize a simpler figure in a more complex figure), spatiotemporal ability (the ability to respond to moving visual displays), and generation and maintenance of verbal images (the ability to commit visual images to memory and to use them later to perform a task). Sex differences favor males in four of the five types of visual-spatial abilities. There is no sex difference in spatial visualization. Visual-spatial abilities decline considerably with age, but the overall sex difference favoring males remains.

Mathematical, or quantitative, abilities include computation, understanding of mathematical concepts, and problem solving (the application of math concepts to new situations). Girls are superior in computation in elementary school, with males displaying superiority in problem solving. However, sex differences increasingly favor males during adolescence. There is no sex difference in the understanding of math concepts.

Some evidence suggests that sex differences in cognitive abilities have diminished over time. There has been such a trend in tests of verbal abilities, visual-spatial abilities, and math abilities.[13] However, for several reasons, it is difficult to reach firm conclusions about whether such trends reflect actual reductions in sex differences. First, test designers only recently began to avoid questions that are based more on the experiences of one sex than that of the other. Second, the proportions of male and female students taking such tests have become more similar over time, making it difficult to reach firm conclusions about sex differences in test results at different times. Third, research methods used in reviews of studies of sex differences have evolved. Maccoby and Jacklin, in their early review of research studies on the topic, used what may be called a vote counting technique. That is, they simply tallied the number of studies on a given topic that found significant differences favoring females, significant differences favoring males, or no significant sex differences and then reached conclusions based on the "vote." A statistical method called *meta-analysis* is commonly used now. Meta-analysis uses sophisticated quantitative methods to synthesize statistical evidence from numerous studies. It yields results that are typically more complex and often different from those yielded by vote counting.[14]

In conclusion, sex differences favor males in some types of cognitive abilities and females in other types of cognitive abilities, whereas sex similarities prevail in still other types of cognitive abilities. The magnitude of sex differences varies over the life span and may have decreased over time.

MORAL JUDGMENTS

The most celebrated research study on the topic of sex differences is Carol Gilligan's *In a Different Voice*. Gilligan examined sex differences in moral judgments. She distinguished between males' and females' approaches to morality. Males tend to use a *justice orientation*, which is concerned with principles of equality and fairness. In contrast, females tend to use a *care orientation*, which is concerned with maintaining relationships, being sensitive to the needs of others, and avoiding harm to others. Thus, when asked whether it is right for a man to steal a drug he cannot afford to keep his wife from dying, boys tend to answer no, citing principles of justice, and girls tend to answer yes, citing human compassion.[15]

According to Lawrence Kohlberg's theory of moral development, which prevailed at the time of Gilligan's study, individuals who exhibit a care orientation are at a lower and earlier stage of moral development than those who exhibit a justice orientation. However, Kohlberg's theory was based on observations of an all-male sample. Gilligan pointed out the bias inherent in basing a theory for both sexes on observation of only one sex and argued that the "different voice" associated with females in her study was just as legitimate as that associated with males. *Time* named Carol Gilligan as one of the 25 most influential Americans for her landmark study, noting that "Gilligan's work has changed the voice of psychology." A meta-analysis of later studies confirmed the existence of the sex difference in moral judgments originally reported by Gilligan, although other factors such as the nature of the moral dilemma at hand also play an important role in moral judgments.[16]

SOCIAL BEHAVIOR

Sex differences have been examined in many types of social behavior, including aggression, altruism, influenceability, and nonverbal communications. Aggression, or behavior that is intended to hurt someone else, may be physical, verbal, or indirect. Males are more likely to engage in physical aggression that produces pain or physical injury than are females. However, this does not necessarily mean that males are the more aggressive sex. Because females are on average physically weaker than males, they may learn to avoid physical aggression and to adopt other ways to bring about psychological or social harm. For instance, they may use their superior verbal skills for aggressive purposes; the sex difference in aggression favoring males is less pronounced for verbal than for physical aggression.[17]

Females may also engage in indirect aggression by trying to hurt others without being identified by their victims. For example, on Bellona, an island in the Pacific Ocean, the society was characterized until recent times by extreme male violence and physical dominance. Women were to respond quickly and unquestioningly to the demands of men, especially their husbands, or expect to be beaten. However, women found creative ways to get back at men. One approach was to compose a "mocking song" to humiliate the offending man. As the song was circulated around the island, the subject was stigmatized in the eyes of his fellow men. The mocking song is a form of indirect aggression.[18]

Women and men exhibit similarities and differences in altruism, or behavior that is intended to help someone else. Although both females and males behave altruistically, they do so differently. Males are more likely to offer heroic or chivalrous help in areas where they feel most competent, such as helping a motorist with a flat tire at the side of a dangerous highway. In contrast, females are more likely to offer nurturant or caring help in areas where they feel most competent, such as volunteering to spend time with a sick child. These differences are also seen in occupational roles: Women are particularly well represented in occupations that involve some type of personal service, such as nurse and teacher, whereas men are especially well represented in occupations that call for placing one's life in jeopardy to help others, such as firefighter and law enforcement officer.[19]

In addition, studies of sex differences in influenceability in social settings have found that men tend to be more influential and women more easily influenced, especially when there is group pressure to conform. This difference may be due to differences in men's and women's status in organizations. As we noted in Chapter 2, men are more likely to hold the higher-level positions in the organization. Male-intensive occupations (e.g., physician) also typically have greater power and status than female-intensive occupations (e.g., nurse). Sex differences in influenceability, when exhibited in work settings, may simply reflect the fact that more powerful people are more influential than are less powerful people.[20]

Status differences between women and men may also play an important role in nonverbal communication skills and behavior. Nonverbal communication skills include the ability to express oneself accurately using the face, body, and voice; to assess the meaning of nonverbal cues from others; and to recall having met or seen people. Females have higher skills than do males in all three areas, perhaps because they tend to have lower status. They may be better able to interpret nonverbal cues because they are in weaker positions and constantly have to monitor others' reactions to themselves.[21]

In conclusion, this is a selective review of some of the major findings about sex similarities and differences obtained from psychological research. This review suggests that there are both sex differences and sex similarities. Some sex differences, such as those in cognitive activities, may have diminished over time and may be attributable to factors other than sex. Other sex differences, such as those in children's interests and activities, remain strong. Now that we have reviewed the evidence about sex differences, we turn to traditional beliefs about sex differences.

Gender Differences

As we noted in Chapter 1, gender differences are manifested in stereotypes, prejudice, and discrimination. In this section of the chapter, we focus on gender stereotypes and sexism, or prejudicial attitudes displayed toward individuals based on their sex. In subsequent chapters, we identify different ways in which workplace discrimination based on sex may occur, as well as how to prevent it and how to respond to it.

GENDER STEREOTYPES

Before we discuss gender stereotypes, try the following exercise. Create a mental image of the "typical woman"; then create a mental image of what most people would consider the typical woman. Next, complete these two sentences with five different adjectives or phrases: (1) I think the typical woman is _____. (2) Most other people think the typical woman is

_____. Now repeat the exercise, this time thinking about the "typical man."[22]

Now consider your responses. You probably feel that most people would answer in a more biased manner than you, invoking gender stereotypes of the two sexes. But, have you noticed the bias of the exercise itself? It is likely to have led you to focus on the differences between the sexes, when, in fact, there is considerable overlap and similarity between their characteristics.

One of the earliest and best known studies of gender stereotypes was conducted in this manner. Inge Broverman and her colleagues asked a group of college students to list characteristics, attitudes, and behaviors in which they believed women and men differ; these students compiled a list of 122 items. A second group of college students rated the extent to which they agreed that these 122 items were typical of an adult man or an adult woman. Analysis of these results yielded 41 items that were believed to differentiate between men and women. The men and women who responded to the survey were in almost complete agreement on the items, which fell into two clusters. Men were seen as more instrumental or competent at tasks than were women, rating higher on items such as "very skilled in business," "can make decisions easily," and "almost always acts as a leader." In contrast, women were seen as more expressive and sensitive to the needs of others than were men, rating higher on items such as "very aware of feelings of others," "very talkative," and "easily expresses tender feelings."[23]

Subsequent research studies have found little change in the gender stereotypes originally documented by Broverman et al. Beliefs about sex differences have remained essentially the same since the 1970s despite considerable change in the roles of women and men in the workplace. Moreover, there is consensus in beliefs about the personal attributes of females and males across cultures. A study of gender stereotypes in 30 different nations found evidence for common male and female stereotypes. Across cultures, the male stereotype was seen as stronger and more active than the female stereotype. The male stereotype was characterized by high needs for dominance, autonomy, aggression, and achievement, whereas the female stereotype was characterized by high needs for deference, nurturance, and affiliation.[24]

More specific stereotypes may also be applied to members of each sex. For example, women have been further stereotyped as falling into one of five categories: sex object, career woman, housewife, athlete, and feminist. Men have been similarly categorized into four distinct types: businessman, athletic man, blue-collar working man, and macho man.[25]

Why have gender stereotypes remained essentially stable over time in different cultures in the face of dramatic societal changes in the roles of women and men? Stereotypes of all kinds tend to be durable over time. People evidently like to categorize themselves and others into groups along primary and secondary dimensions of diversity and then identify ways in which their own group is better than and different from other groups. When these beliefs act as self-fulfilling prophecies, there is little reason for them to change. Also, girls and boys tend to learn stereotypes of different groups in their formative years from parents, teachers, other adults, and the media. By the time they become adults themselves, their stereotypes of various groups are mostly fixed. People are reluctant to give up a long-held stereotype unless it is thoroughly discredited, and even then they may still hold onto it. After all, using stereotypes saves us mental work in identifying and categorizing others. More thought is required to judge another person without using a stereotype. It is easier for people to maintain a stereotype than to change it; hence, gender stereotypes prevail.[26]

SEXISM

The term *sexism* refers to prejudice displayed toward members of one sex, typically women. Sexism, like prejudice in general, is usually assumed to represent a negative attitude. However, some researchers have distinguished between *hostile sexism* and *benevolent sexism* (also known as "subtle sexism"). Hostile sexists, as the label suggests, display blatantly negative attitudes toward women as a group. In contrast, benevolent sexists display more positive attitudes of protective paternalism, idealization of women as wonderful and pure creatures, and affection toward women for making men's lives complete. Benevolent sexists may seem less offensive than hostile sexists because they essentially put women on pedestals. They do so, however, to justify women's subordination to men. Thus, both hostile and benevolent sexism may be used as justifications for sex inequalities in the workplace.[27]

A research study by Peter Glick, Susan Fiske, and their many colleagues in 19 countries examined sex differences in hostile sexism and benevolent sexism across cultures. Men scored significantly higher in hostile sexism than did women in all 19 countries. The sex difference in benevolent sexism was much less than the sex difference in hostile sexism. Overall, women rejected hostile sexism outright but often accepted benevolent sexism, believing that they needed to be protected by men.[28]

Similarly, people may display hostile and benevolent sexism toward men as a group. For example, women may exhibit hostile attitudes by criticizing men's greater power and status in society, sexist attitudes, and manner of asserting control. Women also may display the benevolent attitudes of protective maternalism, admiration for men's competence, and appreciation of men's roles in making women's lives complete. Women score higher than men on hostility toward men and lower on benevolence toward men.[29]

A distinction may also be made between *old-fashioned sexism* and *modern sexism*. Old-fashioned sexism, like hostile sexism, is blatant; it is associated with endorsement of traditional male and female roles in the workplace and of laws and societal norms that promote adherence to these roles. In contrast, modern sexism is associated with denial of the existence of sex discrimination, antagonism toward women's demands that alleged sex discrimination be discontinued, and lack of support for programs that are intended to help women in the workplace.[30]

The old-fashioned sexist says, "Women cause problems in the workplace when they don't stick to their proper roles." The modern sexist says, "Women cause problems in the workplace when they complain too much about alleged problems they face." Both statements reflect sexist attitudes, but in different ways. The old-fashioned sexist is prejudiced against women who seek to play nontraditional roles in the workplace, whereas the modern sexist expresses prejudice against women who claim that there are barriers to their performing such roles. The modern sexist, in denying the existence of barriers to women's full participation in the workplace, ignores a vast body of evidence on disparities in the organizational status and pay of women and men.

Women are more likely to perceive gender inequalities in the workplace and support efforts to combat them than are men, suggesting that women are less inclined to be modern sexists. In addition, Blacks, because of their greater experience as targets of racism, may be more aware of gender inequalities and be more supportive of efforts to combat them than are Whites.[31]

The distinction between old-fashioned and modern sexism is similar to one that has been made between old-fashioned and modern racism (also known as "aversive racism" and "symbolic racism"). Racism and sexism, however, differ in basic ways in how they are learned and experienced. Women are not statistically in the minority in Western societies, whereas members of most racial and ethnic groups other than non-Hispanic Whites are. The socialization of males and females takes place in the presence of the other, whereas races are far more separate in society. Thus, non-Hispanic White males may view racism as a problem affecting a small group of "outsiders" (i.e., non-Whites), whereas they may be more concerned with sexism, especially the hostile or old-fashioned kind, because they can directly observe its effects on their mothers, wives, sisters, and daughters.[32]

Open displays of negative sexist attitudes, at least in public settings, have diminished over the years. It is now less fashionable to be a hostile or old-fashioned sexist (i.e., to be blatantly prejudiced against women as a group) than it is to be a benevolent or modern sexist.

Gender Identity

Until the beginning of the women's movement, masculinity and femininity generally were believed to be opposites. If a person was high in masculinity, he or she was regarded as low in femininity, and vice versa. It was considered appropriate for an individual to conform to his or her gender stereotype. Males were supposed to be masculine, females were supposed to be feminine, and anyone who fell in the middle or at the "wrong" end of the scale was considered to be maladjusted and in need of intensive therapy.[33]

Sandra Bem challenged these assumptions and beliefs. As others had done, she labeled traits as masculine or feminine based on whether they were typically seen as desirable for men or for women. However, unlike earlier researchers, Bem defined masculinity and femininity as independent dimensions rather than opposite ends of a single dimension. Instead of classifying each trait on a single scale ranging from masculine at one end to feminine at the other end, she classified masculine and feminine traits on two separate scales. Masculine items were evaluated on a scale ranging from "high in masculinity" at one end and "low in masculinity" at the other end, and feminine items were evaluated on a scale ranging from "high in femininity" at one end to "low in femininity" at the other. Bem used data from this procedure to choose the items that were included in the Bem Sex-Role Inventory (BSRI).[34]

The BSRI contained 20 masculine items, 20 feminine items, and 20 filler items to disguise the purpose of the instrument. Individuals were asked to rate the extent to which they thought each item was characteristic of themselves. Masculinity and femininity scores were calculated by averaging individuals' self-ratings for the respective items. Rather than measuring beliefs about others, the BSRI measured beliefs about oneself in relation to traditional concepts of masculinity and femininity. Although Bem called these beliefs an individual's "sex role identity," we use the term *gender identity.* She adopted a four-quadrant classification scheme for gender identity as shown in Figure 3.1.[35]

Bem introduced the concept of psychological androgyny, representing high amounts of masculinity and femininity, and a means of measuring it. The term *androgyny* comes from the Greek words "andr" (man) and "gyne" (woman), meaning both masculine and feminine. An androgynous gender identity was found by Bem and others to be associated with higher self-esteem, a more flexible response to situations that seemed to call for either feminine or masculine behaviors, and a host of other positive factors. The individual who adheres to gender stereotypes no longer seemed the ideal of psychological health. Instead, the androgynous individual, whose self-image and behavior are less narrowly restricted, was seen as more ready to meet the complex demands of society. In short, androgyny was proposed as an ideal combination of the "best of both worlds," both highly valued masculine behaviors and highly valued feminine behaviors.[36]

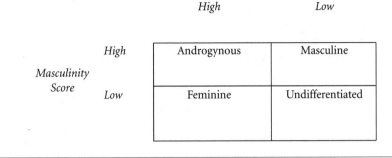

Figure 3.1   Classification of Gender Identity Based on the Four-Quadrant
Classification Scheme

Bem later reflected on the implications of the concept of androgyny:

As I saw it at the time, and as I still see it today, the concept of androgyny challenged gender polarization in psychology and in the American culture as almost nothing up to that time had done. Whereas it had earlier been assumed that masculinity and femininity were core dimensions of the human personality, now it was being suggested that masculinity and femininity were merely cultural stereotypes to which people conformed at their peril. Whereas it had earlier been assumed that mental health required men to be masculine and women to be feminine, now it was being suggested not only that everyone could be both masculine and feminine but, even more important, that standards of mental health should be genderless. Finally, whereas it had earlier been assumed that sex should determine the kind of self-concept an individual should develop and the kind of behavior she or he should engage in, now it was being suggested not only that an individual should be free to her or his own unique blending of temperament and behavior but, even more important, that the very division of attributes and behaviors into the two categories of masculine and feminine was somewhere between problematic and immoral.[37]

The revolutionary nature of the concept of androgyny in the field of psychology matched the feminist spirit of the women's movement. However, not surprisingly given the emotions stirred by the same spirit, the concept of androgyny came under severe attack almost as quickly as it was idealized. Some criticized Bem for poor science because her beliefs in what is "right" for individuals were made so obvious. This is not a valid argument. Although *all* scientific research is value-laden, most researchers are not as explicit as Bem in stating their values. More meaningful criticism was made of the items that comprised the BSRI. Here, Bem appears to have been victimized by her original methodology. The average desirability of the masculine items in the BSRI for a man was similar to the average desirability of the feminine items for a woman, but the desirability of the various items had not been assessed for an adult in general. Other researchers found that masculine characteristics were more desirable overall than feminine characteristics when rated for an adult of unspecified sex. Bem accepted this criticism, and developed an alternative instrument, the Short BSRI, that eliminated most of the items regarded as undesirable for adults.[38]

Some researchers have maintained that the masculinity and femininity components of androgyny do not equally contribute to psychological well-being, flexibility, and adjustment. According to this argument, masculinity rather than androgyny yields positive outcomes for individuals, with femininity making no difference. For example, masculinity has a far greater influence on self-esteem than does femininity. However, research evidence does not consistently demonstrate that masculinity is superior to androgyny. Many studies have suggested that being androgynous yields benefits for individuals above and beyond those gained from their being highly masculine.[39]

Other researchers have argued that masculinity and femininity may be further divided into independent concepts. For example, masculinity could consist of separate characteristics pertaining to dominance or aggressiveness and to autonomy or independence. Bem counterargued that strong beliefs about sex differences suggest that the terms masculinity and femininity refer to meaningful concepts, even if the concepts themselves can be broken down further. She acknowledged that her early results had generated inappropriate goals and subsequently proposed the elimination of society's dependence on gender as the primary means of classifying people. She then advocated the development of an environment where everyone is free to be themselves rather than being expected to live up to any standard of psychological health.[40]

Although masculinity and femininity as measured by the BSRI represent individual characteristics, Geert Hofstede used the same terms to distinguish between national cultures. Hofstede characterized national cultures along five dimensions, one of which was masculinity-femininity. He treated masculinity and femininity as opposite ends of a single dimension. Highly masculine cultures distinguish between the emotional roles of males and females; males are expected to be assertive, tough, and focused on material success, whereas females are expected to be modest, tender, and focused on the quality of life. In contrast, in highly feminine cultures, both females and males are expected to be modest, tender, and focused on the quality of life. In a study of 50 nations and three regions of the world, Japan ranked highest in masculinity (lowest in femininity) and Sweden ranked highest in femininity (lowest in masculinity). Hofstede regarded neither a masculine culture nor a feminine culture as ideal. In acknowledging Bem's work, he conceded that individuals from a given culture could be high or low in both masculinity and femininity. However, his analysis found that national cultures tended toward being either masculine or feminine. Supporting a linkage between individual and cultural scores, BSRI masculinity scores were found to be higher for U.S. males than for Israeli males, consistent with Hofstede's ranking of the American culture as more masculine overall than the Israeli culture.[41]

The BSRI and other inventories of masculine and feminine characteristics do not acknowledge cultural differences in definitions of desirable male and female behavior. The BSRI does a good job of capturing definitions of masculinity and femininity held by Whites and Hispanics, even though exaggerated masculinity and femininity have historically been associated with Hispanic cultures. However, it does not do as good a job of capturing Blacks' definitions of masculinity and femininity.[42]

The debate over androgyny continues. Several conceptions of what females and males should be like have been proposed. One view argues for conformity with gender stereotypes. A second view argues that people should break free from gender stereotypes and pursue an androgynous ideal. A third view argues that there should be no standard conception of ideal behavior for females and males and that people should simply be themselves, whatever that may be; as Sandra Bem put it, "*behavior* should have no gender."[43] Finally, a fourth view suggests that standards of behavior are dependent on the culture of the particular nation or racial/ethnic group; cultures are not right or wrong, but merely different.

While scholars, political groups, and individual citizens have been debating the merits of these four views, women's and men's gender identities have been changing. BSRI scores for females as a whole and males as a whole have changed since the instrument was developed in the 1970s. Among U.S. undergraduates, females' masculinity scores have increased considerably and femininity scores have remained stable. Males' masculinity and femininity scores have both increased, but the changes for males have been fairly small. As a result, U.S. undergraduate women have shown a greater increase in androgyny over time, and men have shown a lesser increase. The average female college student seems to be closer to exemplifying the androgynous ideal.[44]

Nature and Nurture

Numerous complex theories have been offered for why sex differences occur in the first place. These theories focus on two competing explanations: biological factors (nature) and social-environmental factors (nurture). The following question is often posed: What ultimately determines individual behavior, nature or nurture? To understand the effects of nature and nurture, we need to consider the basic arguments concerning how biological and social-environmental factors lead to sex differences.[45]

Those who focus on the effects of *biological* factors argue that sex differences in adults and children are determined mostly by biological sex. According to this argument, boys behave the way they do simply because they are male, and girls behave as they do because they are female, although the underlying reasons proposed for biological effects differ. For example, the creationist perspective attributes male-female differences to distinct acts of creation by God. Others argue that sex differences in levels of hormones such as testosterone and androstenedione during critical stages of development (prenatal, after birth, after puberty) cause sex differences in behaviors such as aggressiveness and nurturance, or act as constraints on the effects of other influences on male and female behavior.[46]

Another prominent biological view focuses on the effects of evolution on men's and women's genes and subsequent behavior. Evolutionary psychologists, following the famed 19th century scientist Charles Darwin, suggest that sex differences in behavior reflect adaptations to the differential demands of the environment on males and females during prehistoric times. According to evolutionary theory, men and women coexisted in hunting-and-gathering groups at the beginning of civilization, with men doing most of the hunting of food, being the physically stronger sex, and women doing most of the food gathering. This ancestral division of labor between the sexes favored men and women who were the most psychologically prepared for their assigned roles. Effective adaptations to these environmental demands were then incorporated into the genetic makeup of humans and inherited by future generations. Thus, different psychological mechanisms evolved in males and females over time, leading to the sex differences in behavior that we observe today.[47]

Others argue that *social-environmental* factors (e.g., family, peers, media, schools, cultural groups) cause sex differences in behavior. According to this view, the present-day environment influences the behavior of girls and boys by rewarding them for engaging in the "right" behaviors (i.e., behaviors consistent with their gender stereotypes and roles) and by punishing them for engaging in the "wrong" behaviors. The modern division of labor between the sexes, as reflected in differences in women's and men's domestic and occupational roles (see Chapter 2), leads to the formation of gender roles that dictate the behaviors appropriate for each sex. Children are expected to behave in accordance with these gender roles. Boys are socialized to behave in a masculine manner and girls in a feminine manner. Parents play a large role in shaping their sons' and daughters' behavior, but other people and institutions have a considerable effect as well. Children's contacts with their peers, especially same-sex peers, are important in the development of gender roles. Children actively exchange knowledge about gender roles and reinforce each other's adherence to these roles.[48]

In conclusion, good arguments may be made for the influence of both biological forces (nature) and social-environmental forces (nurture) on the development of children and subsequent behavior of adults. No agreement has been reached as to whether nature or nurture is more important, but both seem to have some effect. In fact, their effects are so intertwined that it is difficult to separate them. Because biological forces are less amenable to change, we focus in the next section of the chapter on the influence of social-environmental forces.

Gender Role Socialization

Although the concept of androgyny offers a vision of a society free of the influence of gender roles and stereotypes, that society has not yet arrived. Boys grow up under the heavy influence of the male gender role and girls under the influence of the female gender role. To explain the effects of these influences, we need to examine how young males and females are socialized to live up to the expectations of the appropriate gender role. Although many social-environmental factors contribute to children's socialization into gender roles, we will focus on the influence of parents, schools, and the mass media.

PARENTS

Parents are in a position to have a special effect on child development. They provide the opportunity for imitation of their own behavior and reinforcements for their children's behavior. Children imitate same-sex models more than opposite-sex models, although they could presumably imitate any adult to whom they were exposed. Because parents are highly available and powerful, they are the role models children are most likely to copy, particularly during the preschool years. Parents who are absent, however, are unavailable to serve as role models; 27% of U.S. children live in households with only one parent, a proportion that has been increasing over time.[49]

Parents' attitudes toward gender roles affect how they raise their children. Parents who believe that opportunities for both sexes should be equal in the adult world are more likely to encourage their children to deviate from gender stereotypes than are parents who advocate separate roles for women and men.

Parents' beliefs about their children's abilities also affect how those children view their own abilities. In a provocative study of attitudes toward math, Jacquelynne Eccles and Janis Jacobs found that students' math performance was affected by their estimates of their mathematical abilities, their perceptions of the value of math courses, and their levels of math anxiety. These beliefs and anxiety levels were, however, strongly influenced by their mothers' beliefs concerning the difficulty of mathematics for them.[50]

Eccles and Jacobs had the unexpected opportunity to assess the effects of media reports concerning sex differences in math ability on mothers' expectations for their own children's math performance. They were in the midst of a long-term study of the effects of socialization by parents on girls' and boys' attitudes toward math. While they were conducting their study, a study published in *Science* argued in favor of superior male mathematical ability as the cause of general sex differences in both mathematical achievement and attitudes toward math; this study received considerable media attention.[51] Three months later, Eccles and Jacobs asked parents whether they had heard of the study and compared the attitudes of mothers who were aware of it (called "misinformed"—you can see their bias) with those who had not heard of it (called "uninformed"). Uninformed mothers believed that the math ability of their daughters and sons was equivalent. Misinformed mothers of girls felt that math was more difficult for their daughters than misinformed mothers of boys thought it was difficult for their sons. Thus, mothers' perceptions of their children's competence in math were influenced by their beliefs about sex differences in math ability, independent of their children's actual performance in math. These beliefs, fueled by the media campaign, may have led to a self-fulfilling prophecy. Whether or not there are sex differences in cognitive abilities, many parents believe there are and act accordingly.

Parents' employment also affects how they raise their children. In particular, the effect of maternal employment on children's development has been hotly debated. Defenders of traditional gender roles perceive a backlash against stay-at-home mothers, whereas those who decry the limitations of traditional gender roles perceive a backlash against working mothers. Research suggests that daughters of mothers who work outside of the home have more egalitarian attitudes toward gender roles than daughters of mothers who are not employed outside of the home. This may be because employed mothers play a less stereotypical role than do stay-at-home mothers. It may also be because husbands of employed mothers devote more time to household labor and child care activities than do husbands of stay-at-home mothers, giving their daughters another example of deviation from traditional gender roles. Maternal employment has less influence on sons' attitudes toward gender roles, primarily because sons are less likely than daughters to use their mothers as role models and sources of identification. However, all children benefit from the income that their mothers, as well as their fathers, earn; increased family income has a positive effect on children's academic performance and reduces behavioral problems.[52]

In addition, parents' workplace experiences influence their moods and parenting behaviors, which in turn influence how their children behave. Mothers and fathers whose jobs put them in a bad mood are more likely to punish their children, which negatively influences their children's motivation and academic performance and increases their behavioral problems at school. However, stay-at-home mothers whose family roles put them in a bad mood also are more likely to engage in punishing behavior, thereby contributing to their children's behavioral problems. Happier parents, no matter what roles they play in the household and workplace, tend to raise happier, better-adjusted sons and daughters.[53]

We should acknowledge that children also affect their parents' moods. Parents of happier children are likely to be happier in their own lives. In Chapter 8, we examine how the presence of children influences the lives of working parents as we address issues related to the balancing of work and family.

A meta-analysis of studies on childhood socialization found few differences in parents' actual treatment of boys and girls. There are minimal differences in amounts of interaction, encouragement of achievement, warmth and nurturance, encouragement of dependency or independence, and disciplinary strictness displayed toward sons and daughters of all ages. However, parents, especially fathers, show a strong tendency to encourage gender stereotypical activities in their children.[54]

This tendency is seen in such diverse areas as parents' assignments of household labor responsibilities and preferred style of play with their children. In addition, parents offer their sons and daughters different types of toys, physical environments, and experiences. Boys are provided with more sports equipment, tools, and vehicles. Girls are provided with more dolls (including, of course, Barbie), jewelry, and children's furniture. More pink and less blue is seen in girls' rooms.[55]

Encouragement of gender stereotypical activities in children contributes to other behavioral differences. For example, a study of 11 cultures found similarity in the way girls and boys respond to "lap children" (those from birth to 1 year). Lap children draw positive responses and nurturing behavior from children as young as 2 years, as well as from adults. However, girls are more often assigned by parents to take care of lap children than are boys. As a result, girls develop greater nurturing skills, and nurturance becomes both familiar and enjoyable to them. The researchers suggested that if boys were assigned greater care of lap children, they would develop greater nurturing tendencies and skills.[56]

In conclusion, in parents' encouragement or discouragement of activities, beliefs about their sons' and daughters' abilities, creation of household environments, and general parenting behavior, they contribute to the arousal of different interests and development of different abilities in their children. In so doing, they both convey and reinforce the message that girls and boys are different. The same theme emerges as we consider children's experiences in schools.

SCHOOLS

Once they enter school systems, children are subject to the influence of additional authority figures other than their parents. They have more adult role models from which to choose, and they have more occasion to be rewarded or punished for their behavior. One of the first messages that children receive at school is the sex segregation of positions in the school system itself. In countries around the world, men typically run the system in which women teach. Women are not represented in educational administration in equal proportion to their representation in teaching. The older the child and the higher the grade, the fewer women administrators and teachers. When women become school administrators, it is more likely to be in primary schools than at higher levels.[57]

Within schools, there is a consistent sex difference in children's academic performance: Girls get better grades than do boys. This sex difference holds for all ethnic groups, subject areas (including the traditional male preserves of math and science), ages, and levels of education beginning with the earliest school years and extending through college. However, this does not necessarily mean that girls are smarter than boys; recall the inconsistent pattern of sex differences in cognitive abilities. Better grades are earned by students with good work habits and study skills. Females tend to be more disciplined, organized, orderly, and respectful of rules and regulations than are males (i.e., they do as they are told), all of which contributes to their getting good grades. These characteristics are more associated with the feminine than with the masculine gender role. In addition, boys are more likely than are girls to exhibit seriously dysfunctional school behaviors, including cutting classes, disobeying rules, and being suspended or transferred to other schools for disciplinary reasons, all of which interferes with their getting good grades.[58]

Even though girls get better grades, boys get more attention from teachers in the classroom. Teachers seldom see themselves as feeling differently toward girls and boys or treating them differently. However, classroom observations at all grade levels reveal considerable differences in both male and female teachers' interactions with students. Boys receive more positive and negative attention than do girls. Boys are questioned more, criticized more, and have more ideas accepted and rejected. Girls volunteer more often but are not called upon as often and are given less time to answer. When teachers give more attention and "airtime" to boys than to girls, whether consciously or unconsciously, they convey a message that boys as a group deserve more attention.[59]

This message contributes to lower self-esteem in girls. Males have higher self-esteem throughout the life span, but the sex difference in self-esteem peaks during the adolescent years (15–18 years of age). Moreover, adolescent girls are less confident than adolescent boys that they will be able to find employment in the occupation of their choice.[60] These sex differences could be due to societal forces other than school systems, such as parents' differential treatment of their sons and daughters and media portrayals of males and females. However, the pattern of teacher-student interactions clearly undermines girls' sense of competence.

Girls' self-esteem influences their choice of courses, fields of study, and eventual employment. For example, in high school, girls tend to avoid advanced mathematics and science courses, even though girls earn higher grades in such courses than do boys. Even when girls are specifically identified as being highly gifted in math and science, they have lower academic self-esteem and show less interest in pursuing math and science careers than do their male counterparts. As a result, although women have more access to college education than ever before, female undergraduates are less likely than male undergraduates to major in math and science fields. After their undergraduate schooling, women are less likely to pursue graduate degrees and seek employment in these areas.[61]

In summary, despite getting better grades, girls emerge from their school years with lower self-esteem than do boys, a sex difference with lasting consequences. Girls may be both rewarded with good grades in the short run and punished in the long run by their experiences in schools.

THE MASS MEDIA

The mass media, particularly television, influence children's development by providing a view (whether real or distorted) of the outside world. Television is the most popular source of information and entertainment worldwide, partly because it is so accessible and easy to use. Unlike the print media, TV watching does not require literacy. Unlike the movies, theater, and concerts, TV is always running and available; it comes directly into the home. Television is the first centralized cultural influence in the earliest years of life. Children begin to watch TV before they can walk or talk. By the time they begin school, they will have spent more time watching TV than they will ever spend in a college classroom. Across cultures, children spend more time watching TV than in using any other type of media, averaging 1.5 to 2.5 hours per day. Boys spend more time watching TV than do girls, primarily due to their greater interest in sports and action programs. However, the amount of TV viewing is high among children of both sexes.[62]

TV can have beneficial effects for children. For example, educational programming, although not a major part of most children's TV viewing, has a positive effect on their academic performance. However, TV watching in general is characterized by mental and physical passivity. Children who watch more than 3 hours per day of TV are more likely to experience negative side effects such as obesity and poor academic performance. Furthermore, children who watch more hours of TV violence, especially boys, are more likely to exhibit aggressive behavior. Thus, TV watching has a strong influence on children's development.[63]

TV has been described as the great socializer. It teaches children what is important and how to behave. It also teaches gender stereotypes and roles. Stereotypical portrayals of females and males have been the norm in most television programming. In prime-time TV programs, despite the fact that women comprise more than half the population, male characters outnumber female characters. Also, despite the fact that the average woman is older than the average man, female characters are younger than male characters, conveying the message that a woman's value is in her youthfulness. More women are depicted working outside the home than in the past, and the jobs they hold are more likely to be in male-intensive occupations such as law and medicine. However, prime-time TV programs focus on male-intensive occupations more than sex-neutral or female-intensive occupations. As a result, television is still primarily a man's world, and secondarily a young woman's world.[64]

Over time, television programs have been aimed less at a mass audience and more at specific demographic groups differing in race, ethnicity, and sex. Prime-time TV programs, especially situation comedies that focus primarily on family life, tend to show members of a single race or ethnic group. To find any celebration of diversity on television, we need to turn to science-fiction programming such as the popular *Star Trek* series and its successors (*The Next Generation, Deep Space Nine, Voyager, Enterprise*) in which the universe is full of races of different kinds of beings. *Star Trek* assumes not only the existence of other life in the universe, but the existence of compatible life. Thus, other kinds of beings are never viewed as completely alien. The challenge then becomes to understand, communicate, and get along with other races in the universe. The original crew of the *U.S.S. Enterprise* was all-inclusive. Although the crew had a White male captain, it had Black, Asian, Russian, Scottish, Anglo-Saxon, and Vulcan members. *Star Trek's* portrayal of members of different races as well as members of both sexes in key positions of responsibility was rare in television at the time (the 1960s). According to George Takei, the

Japanese American actor who played Mr. Sulu in the original *Star Trek* series, "True Trekkies embrace diversity."[65] Television programming as a whole, however, does not.

Depictions of female and male characters differ in TV commercials. There are fewer female characters in TV commercials, and they are more likely to be shown in families, less likely to hold jobs, and less likely to exercise authority. On the rare occasions when men are shown in family situations, they are less likely to cook, clean, wash dishes, or shop. They are seldom shown changing a diaper or taking care of a sick child. Men are more often shown reading, talking, eating, and playing with children.[66]

Male and female characters in TV commercials differ in the kinds of products they sell. Females are more likely to promote products used in the home, such as foods, cleaning products, and home remedies. In contrast, males are more likely to promote products used outside the home, such as cars, trucks, and cameras. Commercials often make different types of appeals to women and men. In commercials for jeans, the emphasis for men is on being an individual and doing your own thing, whereas the emphasis for women is on enhancing one's appearance to get a man. In beer commercials, the goal seems to be to appeal to men's masculinity. Men are promised sex and fun if they drink the right brand of beer. In these ads, male characters are physically active and spend their time either outdoors or in bars. If women are pictured, they are admiring onlookers. Some beer commercials portray mixed-sex bar scenes where the focus is on women's bodies (for male viewers to admire) and men's faces (as they admire the women's bodies).[67]

TV commercials also differ in their portrayals of stereotypes associated with different combinations of race and sex. For example, TV commercials tend to depict White men as powerful, White women as sex objects, Black men as aggressive, and Black women as having no distinctive presence. White infants and small children are depicted as go-getters, whereas Black children are more likely to be passive observers. White children may be pictured with Black children playing in public settings, such as schools, but family scenes are totally segregated by race. Hispanics, Asians, and Native Americans of both sexes and all ages are included less in TV commercials.[68]

Other types of media such as video games, newspaper comic strips, magazines, and movies convey images of gender roles that have been updated slightly for females and little for males.[69] However, because people of all ages spend so much time watching TV, none of these media has as much impact as television.

What is the ultimate impact on children of TV portrayals of gender roles? Many studies suggest that television viewing affects perceptions of social reality. The more time people spend watching TV, the more likely they are to perceive the real world in ways that reflect what they have seen on TV. Children and adolescents who watch more TV are more aware of gender stereotypes and hold more traditional attitudes toward gender roles. For example, children who watch more TV are more likely to say that only girls should do household chores traditionally associated with women and only boys should do chores traditionally associated with men.[70]

However, television viewing does not always reinforce gender stereotypes. One study found that public perceptions of the proportion of women in nine different occupations, including physician, nurse, lawyer, college teacher, and grade school teacher, differed from U.S. census data and also from the proportion of women seen in these occupations in prime-time television programming. Respondents erred consistently in the direction of sex neutrality in the chosen professions. That is, their estimates were closer to a 50–50 split of women and men in occupations than was really the case. They may have learned from TV news shows about trends toward a more equal distribution of men and women in different types of jobs, and then confused those trends with the status quo.[71]

In conclusion, television and other mass media now portray women and men in roles that are somewhat less stereotypical than they have in the past. However, their overall depiction of men and women in and outside the workplace largely conveys and reinforces traditional gender stereotypes and roles. Given how much time children spend watching TV, it has enormous potential to influence their perceptions of reality.

Limitations of Gender Stereotypes and Roles

With the assistance of their peers, parents, schools, and the mass media, children learn about gender stereotypes, or the traits that members of each sex are believed to possess, and gender roles, or the activities and behaviors that are considered appropriate for each sex. However, children eventually face hazards as adults if they learn these lessons too well. In this section, we consider the limitations associated with strict belief in gender stereotypes and strict adherence to gender roles.

Stereotyping, or the cognitive activity of sorting people into different groups based on some personal characteristic or characteristics and then assigning traits to members of each group, is a pervasive human phenomenon that may seem harmless at first glance. Several types of problems may result from an overreliance on stereotypes, in this case, gender stereotypes. First, without stereotyping, prejudice and discrimination would be less likely to take place. If people did not stereotype one another, perhaps they would exhibit less prejudice and discrimination toward each other.[72]

Second, although a given stereotype may accurately describe the average member of a group, it rarely applies to all group members. For example, when the Short BSRI is administered to undergraduates, males as a group are more likely than females as a group to be classified as masculine and less likely to be classified as feminine in gender role identity.[73] Thus, gender stereotypes of males as masculine and females as feminine hold for this population. This does not mean that every male undergraduate is masculine and every female undergraduate is feminine. Male undergraduates may be androgynous, undifferentiated, or feminine, as well as masculine in gender identity. Similarly, female undergraduates may be androgynous, undifferentiated, or masculine, as well as feminine in gender identity. Thus, when we stereotype people on the basis of sex (or any other dimension of diversity), we may overlook who they really are as individuals.

Third, stereotypes imply that differences between members of different groups are a result of their group membership. This is virtually impossible to prove. When we examine whether a sex difference is present in some type of ability, attitude, or behavior, we need to distinguish between two questions: "Is there a difference *between* the sexes?" and "Is there a difference *on account of* sex?"[74] Answering the first question is relatively simple; it involves only testing and comparing male and female populations. Answering the second question is much more difficult. It requires demonstrating that a difference is innate and due to biological sex alone, which involves testing and comparing male and female populations who have been living under identical environmental conditions. Due to differences in the socialization of girls and boys, these conditions are not present in any culture. Thus, people need to be cautious in what they conclude from sex differences in individuals' abilities, attitudes, and behavior. Such differences are unlikely to be caused entirely by biological differences between the sexes. Instead, they may be caused in part by differences in the environments that males and females experience.

Different types of problems result from strict adherence to gender roles. Neither the female nor the male gender role offers an ideal prescription for an emotionally satisfying and rewarding life. A rigid adherence to either role may be hazardous to one's mental and physical health.[75]

The female gender role is generally lower in status than is the male gender role in Western societies. Thus, adherence to the female role means being dependent on others and surrendering to others' control over many aspects of one's life. Reactions to this lack of control may be manifested in depression and other forms of illness. However, the female gender role places an emphasis on self-awareness, which could lead women to be more aware than men of symptoms of ill health, even if they were no less healthy. This role also encourages expression of feelings, including admission of difficulties, which can lead people to seek help from others.[76]

In contrast, the male gender role encourages aggressiveness and competitiveness, which can lead men to put themselves in dangerous situations. This role is also associated with emotional inexpressiveness, which may cause psychosomatic and other health problems. Lack of self-awareness keeps men from being sensitive to signals that all is not well with them. Adherence to the male gender role means suppressing one's feelings and always striving (or pretending) to be in control of one's own life. The effects of this unbridled push for dominance may take a toll on men, even though it may seem better to dominate than to be dominated.[77]

One way to shed light on the effects of adherence to gender roles is to examine sex differences in various measures of mental and physical health. We need to proceed with caution in using this approach because pressure to conform to gender roles is only one of many factors that could influence behavior and health.

Mortality statistics are striking. In 1900, the expectation of longevity at birth for the U.S. population was 48 years for women and 46 years for men. Since then, these expectations have risen to 79 years for women and 74 years for men. The sex difference in mortality favoring women is present for individuals of all races and ethnic groups. Males die at a higher rate than females at all ages, ranging from birth to 85 years and older. Life expectancy has increased substantially for women and men, but the difference favoring women has also increased.[78]

Health statistics vary considerably for women and men. Even when illnesses due to reproductive functions are excluded, women suffer more from acute conditions (e.g., infections/parasitic diseases, influenza, digestive conditions) and nonfatal chronic conditions (e.g., varicose veins, anemia, gallbladder conditions, colitis). Women report more visits to physicians, are admitted more to hospitals and require more days of hospital care when admitted, and make greater use of outpatient facilities. Women also report more depression and anxiety disorders and are treated more for mental illness. They report a greater number of physical ailments such as headaches, dizziness, and stomach upsets. Women use more prescription medicines and over-the-counter drugs. They restrict their activities due to health problems more and spend more days per year in bed.[79]

Women also suffer more from eating disorders such as anorexia (an obsession with being thin and intense fear of gaining weight) and bulimia (a "binge-purge" style of eating in which there are recurrent episodes of consuming large amounts of food and then purging them by extreme methods). Females who strive to match Barbie's body shape may be more prone to anorexia and bulimia. For example, women in professions such as modeling, dance, and acting, in which thinness is mandated, are at higher risk for anorexia and bulimia. However, many women outside such professions pursue the objective of extreme thinness out of their own personal interest. The probability that a woman will have a Barbie-like body shape is less than 1 in 100,000, an unattainable objective for virtually all women, even anorexics. The probability that a man will have a body shape resembling that of Ken, Barbie's boyfriend, is about 1 in 50, a more attainable, though still challenging, objective for men.[80]

In contrast, men suffer more from major physical ailments. They suffer more injuries from accidents. They are more susceptible to visual and hearing problems and paralysis than are women at all ages. Men have a higher rate of alcohol and drug disorders and are more likely to take their own lives. They are more likely to exhibit the Type A behavior pattern, characterized by extreme competitiveness, striving for achievement, aggressiveness, hastiness, impatience, and feelings of being under pressures of time and responsibility, that contributes to coronary heart disease. Men also suffer more from life-threatening diseases such as atherosclerosis and emphysema. They experience more overall long-term disability due to chronic health problems.

In summary, women experience more frequent illness and short-term disability, but their problems typically do not endanger their lives, and they take more actions to address their problems. In contrast, men suffer from more life-threatening diseases that cause permanent disability and earlier death. Women are "sicker" in the short run, but men are "sicker" in the long run. At least part of the reason for these differences may be the adherence of women and men to gender roles.[81]

Does androgyny offer a better prescription for living a satisfying and rewarding life than that offered by traditional gender roles? Not necessarily, if androgyny is considered just another role with standards for behavior. The underlying problem with advocating a particular role for any group of people is that it cannot possibly match all group members' interests and preferences. Some people may be content to fulfill the prescribed role. Other people, however, feel confined by the role, and there seems to be no good reason for them to experience such confinement.

Influencing Gender Stereotypes and Roles

We began this chapter by posing several questions about the existence of sex differences, gender differences, and their causes and effects. We suggest that although there are both similarities and differences between the sexes, most people believe that there are substantial differences. These beliefs are reflected in persistent gender stereotypes and sometimes in sexist attitudes. Women and men are expected to adopt roles that are consistent with gender stereotypes. However, individuals develop their own gender identities, or beliefs about themselves in relation to traditional definitions of masculinity and femininity. Individual behavior is influenced by a combination of biological and social-environmental factors. Parents, schools, and the mass media shape children's behavior in a manner consistent with traditional notions of masculinity and femininity. Unfortunately, strict adherence to traditional gender roles escalates stereotyping and prejudice and can be hazardous to the mental and physical health of adults. As Sandra Bem suggested, we believe that the solution to these problems is to allow people to simply be themselves.

Given the persistence of gender stereotypes and roles, is it possible to create settings in which behavior is not linked to gender? We believe that change is possible. Existing influences do not have to be taken for granted. Parents, teachers, the media, and society at large must change the way they view gender-related issues. Parents and teachers need to be made aware of the powerful effect of their expectations on children's learning. Institutions that provide teacher training can ensure that teachers are aware of how their own expectations and interactions with students affect student performance. The media can improve its presentation of factual information to children and adults about individual abilities and social forces. The media have a responsibility to inform the public accurately about gender-related issues.

If the opening passage of the chapter provides any indication, change will be difficult. Toys such as Barbie are firmly entrenched in popular culture. In fact, one of your authors has fond memories of playing with Barbie and her boyfriend Ken. We won't say which author, but you should be able to guess.

What societal changes would reduce adherence to prescribed gender roles? Dolls such as female warriors and male nurses marketed to boys? Video games in which females rescue males, or in which women in danger muster their own resources and rescue themselves? Male child care providers? A female president of the United States to go along with the increase in female political leaders in other countries?[82] More female CEOs and senior executives? We hope to get the chance to find out.

Notes

1. Rogers, M. F. (1999). *Barbie culture*. London: Sage, pp. 11, 14–15; Connell, R. W. (1987). *Gender and power.* Stanford, CA: Stanford University Press.

2. Broverman, I. K., Vogel, S. R., Broverman, D. M., Clarkson, F. E., & Rosenkrantz, P. S. (1972). Sex role stereotypes: A current appraisal. *Journal of Social Issues, 28* (2), 59–78; Eagly, A. H., Wood, W., & Diekman, A. B. (2000). Social role theory of sex differences and similarities: A current appraisal. In T. Eckes & H. M. Trautner (Eds.), *The developmental social psychology of gender* (pp. 123–174). Mahwah, NJ: Erlbaum; Eagly, A. H. (1987). *Sex differences in social behavior: A social-role interpretation.* Hillsdale, NJ: Erlbaum; Deaux, K., & LaFrance, M. (1998). Gender. In D. T. Gilbert, S. T. Fiske, & G. Lindzey (Eds.), *The handbook of social psychology,* 4th ed., Vol. 1

(pp. 788–827). Boston: McGraw-Hill; Harris, H. J., & Firestone, J. M. (1998). Changes in predictors of gender role ideologies among women: A multivariate analysis. *Sex Roles, 38,* 239–252; McBroom, W. H. (1987). Longitudinal change in sex role orientations: Differences between men and women. *Sex Roles, 16,* 439–452.

3. Maccoby, E. E., & Jacklin, C. N. (1974). *The psychology of sex differences.* Stanford, CA: Stanford University Press; Halpern, D. F. (2000). *Sex differences in cognitive abilities* (3rd ed.), Mahwah, NJ: Erlbaum.

4. Goldstein, J. H. (1992). Sex differences in aggressive play and toy preference. In K. Björkqvist & P. Niemelä (Eds.), *Of mice and women: Aspects of female aggression* (pp. 65–76). San Diego, CA: Academic Press; Bannon, L. (2000, February 14). Why girls and boys get different toys. *Wall Street Journal,* pp. B1, B4; Hasbro, Inc. (2002). *History of G.I. Joe.* Retrieved April 30, 2002, from http://www.gijoe.com; Hasbro, Inc. (2002). *G.I. Joe: Toys.* Retrieved April 30, 2002, from http://www.gijoe.com

5. Mattel, Inc. (2001). *Barbie.com: Activities and games for girls online!* Retrieved June 28, 2001, from http://www.barbie.com; Rogers; Frey, J. (2002, April 30). The doll with a life of its own. *Washington Post.* Retrieved April 30, 2002, from http://www.washingtonpost.com

6. Roos, H., & Taylor, H. (1989). Do boys prefer Daddy or his physical style of play? *Sex Roles, 20,* 23–33; Goldstein; Larson, R. W., & Verma, S. (1999). How children and adolescents spend time across the world: Work, play, and developmental opportunities. *Psychological Bulletin, 125,* 701–736; Nelson, A. (2000). The pink dragon is female: Halloween costumes and gender markers. *Psychology of Women Quarterly, 24,* 137–144.

7. Markoff, J. (1989, February 13). Computing in America: A masculine mystique. *New York Times,* pp. A1, B10.

8. Gahr, E. (1998, October 30). Computers are for girls. *Wall Street Journal,* p. W11; Mattel.

9. Larson & Verma.

10. Bannon; Maccoby, E. E. (1998). *The two sexes: Growing up apart, coming together.* Cambridge, MA: Belknap Press of Harvard University Press; Burn, S. M., O'Neil, A. K., & Nederend, S. (1996). Childhood tomboyism and adult androgyny. *Sex Roles, 34,* 419–428; Martin, C. L. (1990). Attitudes and expectations about children with nontraditional and traditional gender roles. *Sex Roles, 22,* 151–165; Giuliano, T. A., Popp, K. E., & Knight, J. L. (2000). Footballs versus Barbies: Childhood play activities as predictors of sport participation by women. *Sex Roles, 42,* 159–181.

11. Hyde, J. S. (1990). Meta-analysis and the psychology of gender differences. *Signs, 16,* 55–73.

12. Halpern.

13. Feingold, A. (1988). Cognitive gender differences are disappearing. *American Psychologist, 43,* 95–103; Brody, N. (1992). Group differences in intelligence. In *Intelligence* (2nd ed. pp. 280–328). San Diego, CA: Academic Press; Hyde, J. S., & Linn, M. C. (1988). Gender differences in verbal ability: A meta-analysis. *Psychological Bulletin, 104,* 53–69; Voyer, D., Voyer, S., & Bryden, M. P. (1995). Magnitude of sex differences in spatial abilities: A meta-analysis and consideration of critical variables. *Psychological Bulletin, 117,* 250–270; Hyde, J. S., Fennema, E., & Lamon, S. J. (1990). Gender differences in mathematics performance: A meta-analysis. *Psychological Bulletin, 107,* 139–155.

14. Halpern; Maccoby & Jacklin; Hyde, J. S., & Frost, L. A. (1993). Meta-analysis in the psychology of women. In F. L. Denmark & M. A. Paludi (Eds.), *Psychology of women: A handbook of issues and theories* (pp. 67–103). Westport, CT: Greenwood; Eagly, A. H., & Wood, W. (1991). Explaining sex differences in social behavior: A meta-analytic perspective. *Personality and Social Psychology Bulletin, 17,* 306–315; Hyde, J. S., & Linn, M. C. (1986). *The psychology of gender: Advances through meta-analysis.* Baltimore: Johns Hopkins University Press.

15. Gilligan, C. (1982). *In a different voice: Psychological theory and women's development.* Cambridge, MA: Harvard University Press.

16. Kohlberg, L. (1976). Moral stages and moralization: The cognitive-developmental approach. In T. Lickona (Ed.), *Moral development and behavior: Theory, research, and social issues*

(pp. 31–53). New York: Holt, Rinehart, & Winston; *Time*'s 25 most influential Americans. (1996, June 17). *Time*, 66; Jaffee, S., & Hyde, J. S. (2000). Gender differences in moral orientation: A meta-analysis. *Psychological Bulletin, 126,* 703–726.

17. Howard, J. A., & Hollander, J. (1997). Altruism and aggression: Gendered dynamics of helping and harming others. In *Gendered situations, gendered selves: A gender lens on social psychology* (pp. 117–148). Thousand Oaks, CA: Sage; Eagly, A. H., & Steffan, V. J. (1986). Gender and aggressive behavior: A meta-analytic review of the social psychological literature. *Psychological Bulletin, 100,* 309–330; Björkqvist, K. (1994). Sex differences in physical, verbal, and indirect aggression: A review of recent research. *Sex Roles, 30,* 177–188.

18. Kuschel, R. (1992). "Women are women and men are men": How Bellonese women get even. In K. Björkqvist & P. Niemelä (Eds.), *Of mice and women: Aspects of female aggression* (pp. 173–185). San Diego, CA: Academic Press.

19. Howard & Hollander; Eagly, A. H., & Crowley, M. (1986). Gender and helping behavior: A meta-analytic review of the social psychological literature. *Psychological Bulletin, 100,* 283–308; Piliavin, J. A., & Unger, R. K. (1985). The helpful but helpless female: Myth or reality? In V. E. O'Leary, R. K. Unger, & B. S. Wallston (Eds.), *Women, gender, and social psychology* (pp. 149–189). Hillsdale, NJ: Erlbaum.

20. Eagly, A. H., & Wood, W. (1985). Gender and influenceability: Stereotype versus behavior. In V. E. O'Leary, R. K. Unger, & B. S. Wallston (Eds.), *Women, gender, and social psychology* (pp. 225–256). Hillsdale, NJ: Erlbaum; Eagly, A. H., & Carli, L. L. (1981). Sex of researchers and sex-typed communications as determinants of sex differences in influenceability: A meta-analysis of social influence studies. *Psychological Bulletin, 90,* 1–20; Eagly (1987).

21. Hall, J. A. (1987). On explaining gender differences: The case of nonverbal communication. In P. Shaver & C. Hendrick (Eds.), *Sex and gender: Review of personality and social psychology,* Vol. 7 (pp. 177–200). Newbury Park, CA: Sage; Hall, J. A. (1998). How big are nonverbal sex differences? The case of smiling and sensitivity to nonverbal cues. In D. J. Canary & K. Dindia (Eds.), *Sex differences and similarities in communication: Critical essays and empirical investigations of sex and gender in interaction* (pp. 155–177).

22. Larwood, L., & Wood, M. M. (1977). *Women in management.* Lexington, MA: Lexington Books, p. 33.

23. Broverman et al.

24. Deaux & LaFrance; Deaux, K., & Kite, M. (1993). Gender stereotypes. In F. L. Denmark & M. A. Paludi (Eds.), *Psychology of women: A handbook of issues and theories* (pp. 107–139). Westport, CT: Greenwood; Ruble, D. N., & Ruble, T. L. (1982). Sex stereotypes. In A. G. Miller (Ed.), *In the eye of the beholder: Contemporary issues in stereotyping* (pp. 188–252). New York: Praeger; Williams, J. E., & Best, D. L. (1990). Pancultural similarities. In *Measuring sex stereotypes: A multination study* (Rev. ed. pp. 225–245). Newbury Park, CA: Sage; Best, D. L., & Williams, J. E. (1998). Masculinity and femininity in the self and ideal self descriptions of university students in 14 countries. In G. Hofstede (with W. A. Arrindell, D. L. Best, M. De Mooij, M. H. Hoppe, E. Van de Vliert, J. H. A. Van Rossum, J., et al.), *Masculinity and femininity: The taboo dimension of national cultures* (pp. 106–116). Thousand Oaks, CA: Sage.

25. Deaux, K. (1995). How basic can you be? The evolution of research on gender stereotypes. *Journal of Social Issues, 51* (1), 11–20; Noseworthy, C. M., & Lott, A. J. (1984). The cognitive organization of gender-stereotypic categories. *Personality and Social Psychology Bulletin, 10,* 474–481; Deaux, K., Winton, W., Crowley, M., & Lewis, L. L. (1985). Level of categorization and content of gender stereotypes. *Social Cognition, 3,* 145–167; Six, B., & Eckes, T. (1991). A closer look at the complex structure of gender stereotypes. *Sex Roles, 24,* 57–71; Ashmore, R. D., Del Boca, F. K., & Wohlers, A. J. (1986). Gender stereotypes. In R. D. Ashmore & F. K. Del Boca (Eds.), *The social psychology of female-male relations: A critical analysis of central concepts* (pp. 69–119). Orlando: Academic Press.

26. Fiske, S. T. (1998). Stereotyping, prejudice, and discrimination. In D. T. Gilbert, S. T. Fiske, & G. Lindzey (Eds.), *The handbook of social psychology,* Vol. 2 (4th ed. pp. 357–411). Boston:

McGraw-Hill; Hamilton, D. L., & Sherman, J. W. (1994). Stereotypes. In R. S. Wyer, Jr. & T. K. Srull (Eds.), *Handbook of social cognition* (2nd. ed.), Vol. 2: Applications (pp. 1–68). Hillsdale, NJ: Erlbaum; Hilton, J. L., & von Hippel, W. (1996). Stereotypes. In J. T. Spence, J. M. Darley, & D. J. Foss (Eds.), *Annual review of psychology,* Vol. 47 (pp. 237–271). Palo Alto, CA: Annual Reviews.

27. Benokraitis, N. V. (Ed.). (1997). *Subtle sexism: Current practice and prospects for change.* Thousand Oaks, CA: Sage; Unger, R., & Saundra. (1993). Sexism: An integrated perspective. In F. L. Denmark & M. A. Paludi (Eds.), *Psychology of women: A handbook of issues and theories* (pp. 141–188); Glick, P., & Fiske, S. T. (1996). The Ambivalent Sexism Inventory: Differentiating hostile and benevolent sexism. *Journal of Personality and Social Psychology, 70,* 491–512; Glick, P., & Fiske, S. T. (2001). An ambivalent alliance: Hostile and benevolent sexism as complementary justifications for gender inequality. *American Psychologist, 56,* 109–118.

28. Glick, P., Fiske, S. T., Mladinic, A., Saiz, J. L., Abrams, D., Masser, B., et al. (2000). Beyond prejudice as simple antipathy: Hostile and benevolent sexism across cultures. *Journal of Personality and Social Psychology, 79,* 763–775.

29. Glick, P., & Fiske, S. T. (1999). The Ambivalence toward Men Inventory: Differentiating hostile and benevolent beliefs about men. *Psychology of Women Quarterly, 23,* 519–536.

30. Swim, J. K., Aikin, K. J., Hall, W. S., & Hunter, B. A. (1995). Sexism and racism: Old-fashioned and modern prejudices. *Journal of Personality and Social Psychology, 68,* 199–214.

31. Davis, N. J., & Robinson, R. V. (1991). Men's and women's consciousness of gender inequality: Austria, West Germany, Great Britain, and the United States. *American Sociological Review, 56,* 72–84; Kane, E. W. (2000). Racial and ethnic variation in gender-related attitudes. In K. S. Cook & J. Hagan (Eds.), *Annual review of sociology,* Vol. 26 (pp. 419–439). Palo Alto, CA: Annual Reviews.

32. McConahay, J. B. (1986). Modern racism, ambivalence, and the Modern Racism Scale. In J. F. Dovidio & S. L. Gaertner (Eds.), *Prejudice, discrimination, and racism* (pp. 91–125). Orlando, FL: Academic; Gaertner, S. L., & Dovidio, J. F. (1986). The aversive form of racism. In J. F. Dovidio & S. L. Gaertner (Eds.), *Prejudice, discrimination, and racism* (pp. 61–89). Orlando, FL: Academic; Sears, D. O. (1988). Symbolic racism. In P. A. Katz & D. A. Taylor (Eds.), *Eliminating racism: Profiles in controversy* (pp. 53–84). New York: Plenum; Reid, P. T. (1988). Racism and sexism: Comparisons and conflicts. In P. A. Katz and D. A. Taylor (Eds.), *Eliminating racism: Profiles in controversy* (pp. 203–221). New York: Plenum.

33. Constantinople, A. (1973). Masculinity-femininity: An exception to a famous dictum? *Psychological Bulletin, 80,* 389–407.

34. Bem, S. L. (1974). The measurement of psychological androgyny. *Journal of Consulting and Clinical Psychology, 42,* 155–162. Another instrument developed at about the same time, the Personal Attributes Questionnaire (PAQ), also presented independent measures of masculinity and femininity; see Spence, J. T., & Helmreich, R. L. (1978). *Masculinity and femininity: Their psychological dimensions, correlates, and antecedents.* Austin: University of Texas Press.

35. Bem, S. L. (1977). On the utility of alternative procedures for assessing psychological androgyny. *Journal of Consulting and Clinical Psychology, 45,* 196–205.

36. Lenney, E. (1979). Androgyny: Some audacious assertions toward its coming of age. *Sex Roles, 5,* 703–719; Cook, E. P. (1985). *Psychological androgyny.* New York: Pergamon Press; Korabik, K. (1999). Sex and gender in the new millennium. In G. N. Powell (Ed.), *Handbook of gender and work* (pp. 3–16). Thousand Oaks, CA: Sage.

37. Bem, S. L. (1993). *The lenses of gender: Transforming the debate on sexual inequality.* New Haven, CT: Yale University Press, pp. 120–121.

38. Pedhazur, E. J., Tetenbaum, T. J. (1979). Bem Sex Role Inventory: A theoretical and methodological critique. *Journal of Personality and Social Psychology, 37,* 996–1016; Bem, S. L. (1981). *Bem Sex-Role Inventory: Professional manual.* Palo Alto, CA: Consulting Psychologists Press. Although Bem intended the Short BSRI to replace the original version of the BSRI in future research, the original version continues to be widely used.

39. Markstrom-Adams, C. (1989). Androgyny and its relation to adolescent psychosocial well-being: A review of the literature. *Sex Roles, 21,* 325–340; Taylor, M. C., & Hall, J. A. (1982).

Psychological androgyny: Theories, methods, and conclusions. *Psychological Bulletin, 92,* 347–366; Whitley, B. E., Jr. (1983). Sex role orientation and self-esteem: A critical meta-analytic review. *Journal of Personality and Social Psychology, 44,* 765–778.

40. Bem (1993).

41. Hofstede, G. (with Arrindell, W. A., Best, D. L., De Mooij, M., Hoppe, M. H., Van de Vliert, E., Van Rossum, J. H. A., et al.). (1998). *Masculinity and femininity: The taboo dimension of national cultures.* Thousand Oaks, CA: Sage; Hofstede, G. (2001). *Culture's consequences: Comparing values, behaviors, institutions, and organizations across nations,* (2nd ed.) Thousand Oaks, CA: Sage; Maloney, P., Wilkof, J., & Dambrot, F. (1981). Androgyny across two cultures: United States and Israel. *Journal of Cross-Cultural Psychology, 12,* 95–102.

42. Harris, A. C. (1994). Ethnicity as a determinant of sex role identity: A replication study of item selection for the Bem Sex Role Inventory. *Sex Roles, 31,* 241–273.

43. Bem, S. L. (1978). Beyond androgyny: Some presumptuous prescriptions for a liberated sexual identity. In J. A. Sherman & F. L. Denmark (Ed.), *The psychology of women: Future direction in research* (pp. 1–23). New York: Psychological Dimensions, p. 19.

44. Twenge, J. M. (1997). Changes in masculine and feminine traits over time: A meta-analysis. *Sex Roles, 36,* 305–325.

45. Lippa, R. A. (2002). *Gender, nature, and nurture.* Mahwah, NJ: Erlbaum; Jacklin, C. N. (1989). Female and male: Issues of gender. *American Psychologist, 44,* 127–133; Lewis, M., & Weinraub, M. (1979). Origins of early sex-role development. *Sex Roles, 5,* 135–153; Stockard, J. (1999). Gender socialization. In J. S. Chafetz (Ed.), *Handbook of the sociology of gender* (pp. 215–227). New York: Kluwer Academic/Plenum.

46. Udry, J. R. (2000). Biological limits of gender construction. *American Sociological Review, 65,* 443–457; Lippa.

47. Archer, J. (1996). Sex differences in social behavior: Are the social role and evolutionary explanations compatible? *American Psychologist, 51,* 909–917; Buss, D. M. (1995). Evolutionary psychology: A new paradigm for psychological science. *Psychological Inquiry, 6,* 1–30; Buss, D. M. (1995). Psychological sex differences: Origins through sexual selection. *American Psychologist, 50,* 164–168; Tiger, L., & Fox, R. (1971). *The imperial animal.* New York: Holt, Rinehart, & Winston; Darwin, C. (1871). *The descent of man, and selection in relation to sex.* New York: Murray; Lippa.

48. Eagly, A. H., & Wood, W. (1999). The origins of sex differences in human behavior: Evolved dispositions versus social roles. *American Psychologist, 54,* 408–423; Eagly, A. H. (1993). Sex differences in human social behavior: Meta-analytic studies of social psychological research. In M. Haug, R. E. Whalen, C. Aron, & K. L. Olsen (Eds.), *The development of sex differences and similarities in behavior* (pp. 421–436). Dordrecht, The Netherlands: Kluwer Academic; Eagly (1987); Maccoby (1998); Maccoby, E. E. (1990). Gender and relationships: A developmental account. *American Psychologist, 45,* 513–520; Harris, J. R. (1998). *The nurture assumption: Why children turn out the way they do.* New York: Free Press; Harris, J. R. (1995). Where is the child's environment? A group socialization theory of development. *Psychological Review, 102,* 458–489; Stockard; Larson & Verma; Lippa.

49. Maccoby & Jacklin; U.S. Department of Commerce, Bureau of the Census. (2002). *Families and living arrangements* (computed from Table CH-1). Retrieved May 1, 2002, from http://www.census.gov

50. Antill, J. K. (1987). Parents' beliefs and values about sex roles, sex differences, and sexuality: Their sources and implications. In P. Shaver & C. Hendrick (Eds.), *Sex and gender: Review of personality and social psychology,* Vol. 7 (pp. 294–328). Newbury Park, CA: Sage; Eccles, J. S., & Jacobs, J. E. (1986). Social forces shape math attitudes and performance. *Signs, 11,* 367–380; Eccles, J. S., Jacobs, J. E., & Harold, R. D. (1990). Gender role stereotypes, expectancy efforts, and parents' socialization of gender differences. *Journal of Social Issues, 46* (2), 183–201.

51. Benbow, C. P., & Stanley, J. C. (1980). Sex differences in mathematical ability: Fact or artifact? *Science, 210,* 1262–1264.

52. Hoffman, L. W., & Youngblade, L. M. (1999). *Mothers at work: Effects on children's well-being.* Cambridge, UK: Cambridge University Press; Lerner, J. V. (1994). *Working women and their families.* Thousand Oaks, CA: Sage; Harvey, E. (1999). Short-term and long-term effects of early parental employment on children of the National Longitudinal Survey of Youth. *Developmental Psychology, 35,* 445–459; Chira, S. (1998). *A mother's place: Taking the debate about working mothers beyond guilt and blame.* New York: HarperCollins; Peters, J. K. (1997). *When mothers work: Loving our children without sacrificing our selves.* Reading, MA: Addison-Wesley.

53. Stewart, W., & Barling, J. (1996). Fathers' work experiences effect children's behaviors via job-related affect and parenting behaviors. *Journal of Organizational Behavior, 17,* 221–232; MacEwen, K. E., & Barling, J. (1991). Effects of maternal employment experiences on children's behavior via mood, cognitive difficulties, and parenting behavior. *Journal of Marriage and the Family, 53,* 635–644; Barling, J., MacEwen, K. E., & Nolte, M-L. (1993). Homemaker role experiences affect toddler behaviors via maternal well-being and parenting behavior. *Journal of Abnormal Child Psychology, 21,* 213–229.

54. Lytton, H., & Romney, D. M. (1991). Parents' differential socialization of boys and girls: A meta-analysis. *Psychological Bulletin, 109,* 267–296.

55. Pomerleau, A., Boldue, D., Malcuit, G., & Cossette, L. (1990). Pink or blue: Environmental gender stereotypes in the first two years of life. *Sex Roles, 22,* 359–367; Silverman.

56. Whiting, B. B., & Edwards, C. P. (1988). *Children of different worlds: The formation of social behavior.* Cambridge, MA: Harvard University Press.

57. Shakeshaft, C. (1999). The struggle to create a more gender-inclusive profession. In J. Murphy & K. S. Louis (Eds.), *Handbook of research on educational administration* (2nd ed. pp. 99–118). San Francisco: Jossey-Bass.

58. Dwyer, C. A., & Johnson, L. M. (1997). Grades, accomplishments, and correlates. In W. W. Willingham & N. S. Cole (Eds.), *Gender and fair assessment* (pp. 127–156). Mahwah, NJ: Erlbaum.

59. Sadker, M., & Sadker, D. (1994). *Failing at fairness: How America's schools cheat girls.* New York: Charles Scribner's Sons; Golombok, S., & Fivush, R. (1994). *Gender development.* Cambridge, UK: Cambridge University Press; American Association of University Women. (1998). *Gender gaps: Where schools still fail our children.* Washington, DC: American Association of University Women; American Association of University Women. (1992). *How schools shortchange girls.* Washington, DC: American Association of University Women; Guttentag, M., & Bray, H. (1977). Teachers as mediators of sex-role standards. In A. G. Sargent (Ed.), *Beyond Sex Roles* (pp. 395–411). St. Paul, MN: West.

60. Kling, K. C., Hyde, J. S., Showers, C. J., & Buswell, B. N. (1999). Gender differences in self-esteem: A meta-analysis. *Psychological Bulletin, 125,* 470–500; Major, B., Barr, L., Zubek, J., & Babey, S. H. (1999). Gender and self-esteem: A meta-analysis. In W. B. Swann, Jr., J. H. Langlois, & L. A. Gilbert (Eds.), *Sexism and stereotypes in modern society: The gender science of Janet Taylor Spence* (pp. 223–253). Washington, DC: American Psychological Association; Marini, M. M., & Brinton, M. C. (1984). Sex typing in occupational socialization. In B. F. Reskin (Ed.), *Sex segregation in the workplace: Trends, explanations, remedies* (pp. 192–232). Washington, DC: National Academy Press.

61. Dwyer & Johnson; Lubinski, D., & Benbow, C. P. (1994). The Study of Mathematically Precocious Youth: The first three decades of a planned 50-year study of intellectual talent. In R. F. Subotnik & K. D. Arnold (Eds.), *Beyond Terman: Contemporary longitudinal studies of giftedness and talent* (pp. 255–281). Norwood, NJ: Ablex; Arnold, K. D. (1994). The Illinois Valedictorian Project: Early adult careers of academically talented male high school students. In R. F. Subotnik & K. D. Arnold (Eds.), *Beyond Terman: Contemporary longitudinal studies of giftedness and talent* (pp. 24–51). Norwood, NJ: Ablex; Jacobs, J. A. (1996). Gender inequality and higher education. In J. Hagan & K. S. Cook (Eds.), *Annual review of sociology,* Vol. 22 (pp. 153–185). Palo Alto, CA: Annual Reviews.

62. Gerbner, G., & Gross, L. (1976). Living with television: The violence profile. *Journal of Communications, 26* (2), 172–199; Larson & Verma.

63. Davis, D. M. (1990). Portrayals of women in prime-time network television: Some demographic characteristics. *Sex Roles, 23,* 325–332; Larson & Verma.

64. Signorielli, N., & Bacue, A. (1999). Recognition and respect: A content analysis of prime-time television characters across three decades. *Sex Roles, 40,* 527–544.

65. Grove, L. (1999, September 16). Captain's Log, Stardate 1999: Mr. Sulu pushes diversity on TV. *Washington Post.* Retrieved September 16, 1999, from http://www.washingtonpost.com; Paramount Pictures. (2002). *STARTREK.COM: Biographies.* Retrieved May 3, 2002, from http://www.startrek.com; Richards, T. (1997). *The meaning of Star Trek.* New York: Doubleday.

66. Coltrane, S., & Adams, M. (1997). Work-family imagery and gender stereotypes: Television and the reproduction of difference. *Journal of Vocational Behavior, 50,* 323–347; Kaufman, G. (1999). The portrayal of men's family roles in television commercials. *Sex Roles, 41,* 439–458.

67. Bartsch, R. A., Burnett, T., Diller, T. R., & Rankin-Williams, E. (2000). Gender representation in television commercials: Updating an update. *Sex Roles, 43,* 735–743; Hall, C. C. I., & Crum, M. J. (1994). Women and "body-isms" in television beer commercials. *Sex Roles, 31,* 329–337; Strate, L. (1992). Beer commercials: A manual on masculinity. In S. Craig (Ed.), *Men, masculinity, and the media* (pp. 78–92). Newbury Park, CA: Sage; Ogletree, S. M., Williams, S. W., Raffeld, P., Mason, B., & Fricke, K. (1990). Female attractiveness and eating disorders: Do children's television commercials play a role? *Sex Roles, 22,* 791–797

68. Coltrane, S., & Messineo, M. (2000). The perpetuation of subtle prejudice: Race and gender imagery in 1990s television advertising. *Sex Roles, 42,* 363–389; Seiter, E. (1995). Different children, different dreams: Racial representation in advertising. In G. Dines & J. M. Humez (Eds.), *Gender, race and class in media: A text-free reader* (pp. 99–108). Thousand Oaks, CA: Sage.

69. Dietz, T. L. (1998). An examination of violence and gender role portrayals in video games: Implications for gender socialization and aggressive behavior. *Sex Roles, 38,* 425–442; Brabant, S., & Mooney, L. A. (1997). Sex role stereotyping in the Sunday comics: A twenty year update. *Sex Roles, 37,* 269–281; Willemsen, T. M. (1998). Widening the gender gap: Teenage magazines for girls and boys. *Sex Roles, 38,* 851–861; Peirce, K. (1993). Socialization of teenage girls through teen-magazine fiction: The making of a new woman or an old lady? *Sex Roles, 29,* 59–68.

70. Morgan, M. (1982). Television and adolescents' sex role stereotypes: A longitudinal study. *Journal of Personality and Social Psychology, 43,* 947–955; McGhee, P. E., & Frueh, T. (1980). Television viewing and the learning of sex-role stereotypes. *Sex Roles, 6,* 179–188; Signorielli, N., & Lears, M. (1992). Children, television, and conceptions about chores: Attitudes and behaviors. *Sex Roles, 27,* 157–170; Gertner & Gross.

71. McCauley, C., Thangavelu, K., & Rozin, P. (1988). Sex role stereotyping of occupations in relation to television representations and census facts. *Basic and Applied Social Psychology, 9,* 197–212.

72. Fiske.

73. Powell, G. N., Butterfield, D. A., & Parent, J. D. (2002). Gender and managerial stereotypes: Have the times changed? *Journal of Management, 28,* 177–193.

74. These two questions were suggested by James Jones, who posed similar questions about race; Jones, J. M. (1991). Psychological models of race: What have they been and what should they be? In J. D. Goodchilds (Ed.), *Psychological perspectives on human diversity in America* (pp. 3–46). Washington, DC: American Psychological Association.

75. Burn, S. M. (1996). *The social psychology of gender.* New York: McGraw-Hill.

76. Travis, C. B. (1993). Women and health. In F. L. Denmark & M. A. Paludi (Eds.), *Psychology of women: A handbook of issues and theories* (pp. 283–323). Westport, CT: Greenwood; Russo, N. F., & Green, B. L. (1993). Women and mental health. In F. L. Denmark & M. A. Paludi (Eds.), *Psychology of women: A handbook of issues and theories* (pp. 379–436). Westport, CT: Greenwood.

77. Sabo, D., & Gordon, D. F. (Eds.). (1995). *Men's health and illness: Gender, power, and the body.* Thousand Oaks, CA: Sage; Pleck, J. H. (1981). *The myth of masculinity.* Cambridge, MA: MIT

Press; Lippa, R. A., Martin, L. R., & Friedman, H. S. (2000). Gender-related individual differences and mortality in the Terman longitudinal study: Is masculinity hazardous to your health? *Personality and Social Psychology Bulletin, 26,* 1560–1570.

78. U. S. National Center for Health Statistics. (2002). *Health, United States, 2001,* Tables 28 and 36. Retrieved May 1, 2002, from http://www.cdc.gov/nchs

79. Verbugge, L. M. (1985). Gender and health: An update of hypotheses and evidence. *Journal of Health and Social Behavior, 26,* 156–182; Tavris; Russo & Green.

80. Russo & Green; Norton, K. I., Olds, T. S., Olive, S., & Dank, S. (1996). Ken and Barbie at life size. *Sex Roles, 34,* 287–294.

81. Verbrugge.

82. Adler, N. J. (1999). Global leaders: Women of influence. In G. N. Powell (Ed.), *Handbook of gender and work* (pp. 239–261). Thousand Oaks, CA: Sage.

4

Making Employment Decisions

Out of Sight Keeps Women in Mind

Women have better luck auditioning for the major U.S. orchestras if they can be heard and not seen.

That is the conclusion of a study by Claudia Goldin of Harvard University and Cecilia Rouse of Princeton University. They found that when musicians auditioned behind a heavy cloth suspended from the ceiling so judges can't see their gender—or race or age—it boosts by 50% the odds that a woman will make it past preliminary rounds and by several-fold the odds that she will get the job. . . .

Blind screens are "the only way to assure a fair audition," says Catherine Pickar, a spokeswoman for the International Alliance for Women in Music in Washington.

Sylvia Alimena is certain that performing incognito played at least some role in her hiring 12 years ago to play the French horn—still overwhelmingly a male-dominated instrument—for the National Symphony Orchestra in Washington. She recalls taking off her high heels to walk to her place behind the screen so she wouldn't make the tell-tale clip-clop noises, then slipping them back on her short legs so her five-foot stature would touch the floor.

"The screen assures you that you're going to be taken seriously,"
says Ms. Allimena, one of two female French horn players at
the NSO.

—Christina Duff[1]

Like symphony orchestras, many of today's organizations utilize hiring
practices designed to prevent sex discrimination, as well as other types of
discrimination. Although some organizations have embraced nondiscriminatory practices in order to hire the best talent available, others have been motivated by legal requirements. As we noted in Chapter 2, equal rights laws in
some countries require organizations to implement nondiscriminatory hiring
practices. Penalties for violating equal rights laws vary by country, but can be
quite severe. For instance, Home Depot, the U.S.–based retail building supply
chain, settled a sex-discrimination suit by paying $87 million to over 6,000
women and their attorneys for alleged discriminatory hiring, pay, and promotion practices. Home Depot also earmarked $15 million to improve its employ-
ment programs and settle two other discrimination suits.[2]

Because most employers have substantial motivation to avoid sex discrimination in their employment practices, one might assume that the Home Depot
case is a rare event and that sex and gender have little effect on employment
decisions. Unfortunately, this assumption is incorrect. Both job seekers and
organizations make employment decisions. Job seekers identify and apply for
relevant opportunities, complete job interviews and tests, accept or reject job
offers, and negotiate starting salaries. At the same time, organizations promote
job openings, evaluate applicants, make job offers, and determine job assignments and starting salaries. As we will see, sex and gender influence the decisions of both job seekers and organizations.[3]

Decisions by Individuals

The decisions of individual job seekers during the job search process are called
self-selection decisions. In self-selection decisions, individuals actively choose
which opportunities to pursue and which job offers to accept. Of course, job
seekers' self-selection decisions affect the nature of the jobs that they obtain.
Self-selection decisions, however, also affect organizations. If highly qualified
job seekers do not apply for jobs or do not complete the selection process,
organizations may experience shortages of qualified workers. If women and
people of color remove themselves from consideration for particular jobs,

organizations may be unable to meet diversity goals and to comply with legal requirements.[4]

During the self-selection process, job seekers look for a fit or match between themselves and job opportunities. Individuals' evaluations of the fit between themselves and specific job opportunities are based on the nature of the job and the organization. Sex differences in fit evaluations and, ultimately, self-selection decisions occur when women and men react differently to jobs and organizations.[5]

Sex differences in self-selection decisions also result from differences in the techniques that men and women use to find employment. Men and women may obtain different types of employment because their job search methods are dissimilar. We now examine how sex differences in self-selection decisions arise from differences in men's and women's reactions to jobs and organizations and in their job search behavior.

REACTIONS TO JOBS

As women and men seek job opportunities that fit their own characteristics, they may seek different kinds of jobs. Differences in women's and men's desired jobs could occur if the gender socialization processes described in Chapter 3 lead women to prefer jobs that match the expressive feminine stereotype and role, and men to prefer jobs that match the instrumental masculine stereotype and role. It is also possible that women's desired jobs simply reflect the jobs that are available to them. Sex discrimination may lead women to lower their aspirations to comply with workplace realities. Given the increased labor force participation of women worldwide, do gender stereotypes and roles continue to dictate women's desired jobs? Are there sex differences in preferences for job attributes, as well as for specific work activities and occupations?[6]

Preferences for Job Attributes. We use the term *job attributes* to refer to the qualities and outcomes of paid work. Job attributes are general characteristics of jobs, such as working hours, geographic location, advancement opportunities, salary, benefits, relationships with coworkers, and opportunities for using skills and abilities. The term job attribute preferences refers to the degree to which an individual views specific job attributes as desirable.[7]

Sex differences in job attribute preferences are prevalent. Most of these differences align with gender roles and stereotypes, but others do not. Women are more concerned with job attributes that allow them to meet demands of the homemaker role (e.g., good hours, easy commute) and the feminine stereotype than are men. The opportunity for positive interpersonal relations (e.g., working with people, opportunity to help others, opportunity to make friends) is especially important to women. However, job attributes normally associated with the masculine breadwinner role and the masculine stereotype are not uniformly endorsed to a greater extent by men than by women. Although men consider income, autonomy, the opportunity to exercise leadership and power, challenging work, and promotion opportunities to be more important than do women, women consider job benefits, the availability of job openings, and feelings of accomplishment as more important. There are no sex differences in the extent to which women and men seek jobs that provide high status, recognition for good performance, meaningful work, and responsibility.[8]

Job attributes may be classified as intrinsic or extrinsic. Intrinsic job characteristics pertain to the nature of the job; variety, opportunity for achievement and challenge, and level of responsibility are all intrinsic job characteristics. Extrinsic job characteristics are unrelated to the work itself; they include pay, promotion opportunities, working conditions, peers, supervision, and recognition for good work. In influential research in the 1950s, Frederick Herzberg and his colleagues suggested that males place more importance on intrinsic job characteristics and less importance on extrinsic characteristics than do females. However, recent evidence suggests that neither intrinsic nor extrinsic job attributes are associated exclusively with one sex. Men are more likely than women to value intrinsic (e.g., solitude, autonomy, opportunity to lead and exercise authority) and extrinsic (e.g., promotion opportunities, earnings) attributes that confer independence, power, prestige, and money. In contrast, women value intrinsic attributes that create a sense of enjoyment and accomplishment (e.g., interesting work, feelings of accomplishment and self-fulfillment, opportunity to use one's education and abilities), and extrinsic job attributes that enhance interpersonal relationships at work (e.g., good coworkers, good supervisor) or address personal needs (e.g., benefits, short commute).[9]

Sex differences in job attribute preferences may be influenced by cultural factors. For example, in Japan, where women typically serve as clerks and leave the workforce after marriage, female employees attach more importance to factors such as working hours, commute, location, salary, benefits, and job security than do male employees. In contrast, male employees are more concerned about their future prospects for advancement with the organization. Lengthy commutes and long working hours are common in Japan. Because Japanese women, unlike Japanese men, do not expect to remain with their employers, they may be more concerned with factors that reduce the everyday stresses of their work schedules than with their long-term prospects with the organization.[10]

In summary, job attributes that are linked to the feminine stereotype and role, especially positive interpersonal relations, are preferred more by women than by men. Attributes that are linked to the masculine stereotype and role are not consistently preferred by one sex or the other.

Preferences for Activities and Occupations. Men and women differ in the type of activities that they want to perform in their jobs. Generally, these differences are consistent with gender stereotypes and roles. Young women are more interested in activities that involve people (e.g., taking care of people, performing community service), while young men are more interested in activities that involve things (computers, machines, tools). Young men and women also differ in their interests in Holland's six occupational types. Holland classified individuals based on their interests in six activities: realistic (e.g., manipulation of objects, tools, machines, and animals), investigative (e.g., examination of physical, biological, and cultural phenomena), artistic (e.g., creation of art forms and products), social (e.g., informing, training, and developing others), enterprising (e.g., influencing others to attain goals), and conventional (e.g., administrative) activities. Sex differences in preferences for enterprising and conventional activities appear to be small, with young men preferring enterprising and conventional activities somewhat more than do young women. However, sex differences for the other four types of activities are more substantial. Young women are more interested in artistic and social activities than are men, while men are more interested in realistic and investigative activities.[11]

Sex differences in occupational preferences are also of interest. As the labor force participation of women has increased, young women have become somewhat less interested in pursuing female-intensive occupations (e.g., elementary school teacher) and somewhat more interested in pursuing male-intensive occupations (e.g., business). However, during the same time, the occupational interests of young men have changed very little. As a result, sex differences in occupational preferences have diminished but still remain. Stereotypically masculine occupations such as building contractor, racecar driver, stockbroker, and professional athlete are more likely to be preferred by men than by women. In contrast, the occupations of social worker, bank teller, dietician, elementary school teacher, and registered nurse are more likely to be preferred by women.[12]

Why do individuals continue to prefer jobs that are regarded as appropriate for members of their sex? Gender socialization processes certainly contribute to sex differences in occupational preferences. The sex segregation of occupations, described in Chapter 2, may also lead job seekers to restrict their occupational choices. People assume generally that individuals possess the characteristics needed for their current work roles. Thus, women are assumed to possess the attributes needed in female-intensive jobs while men are assumed to possess those attributes appropriate for male-intensive jobs. People also believe that success in female-intensive jobs requires feminine personality traits and physical characteristics while success in male-intensive jobs requires masculine personality traits and physical characteristics.[13]

The notion that success in the occupations dominated by one sex requires the personal characteristics associated with that sex is likely to have a chilling effect on job seekers. Job seekers may believe that they cannot succeed in occupations that are numerically dominated by the other sex and look elsewhere for employment. Both women and men suffer when they restrict their occupational choices to those that seem suitable for members of their sex. However, women are more likely to suffer financially because female-intensive occupations pay less than male-intensive occupations. In fact, sex differences in occupational choice contribute to the lower pay of women even when we account for differences in the job-related skills and credentials that men and women bring to their jobs.[14]

Job seekers' preferences for work activities and occupations are not a function of their sex only. For example, race may influence women's occupational preferences; Black college women are more interested in pursuing male-intensive occupations than are White college women. Gender identity also plays an important role in individuals' interests and occupational preferences. Individuals differ in the extent to which they internalize the lessons of gender socialization and embrace the gender roles prescribed for members of their sex. Individuals who embrace the masculine gender role and stereotype are more likely to prefer working with things and to choose male-intensive occupations, while individuals who embrace the feminine gender role and stereotype are more likely to prefer working with people and to choose female-intensive occupations. College men who endorse anti-femininity and toughness norms are more likely to pursue male-intensive occupations such as computer science, engineering, and construction technology, while those who reject these norms are more likely to pursue female-intensive occupations such as nursing, counseling, and elementary education.[15]

In addition, gender identity affects whether men and women aspire to positions in top management. Gary Powell and Tony Butterfield examined undergraduate and graduate business students' managerial aspirations and gender identities. Men were more likely to aspire to top management positions than were women. However, sex differences in managerial aspirations were a function of sex differences in gender identity. Masculine individuals, typically men, were most likely to aspire to top management.[16]

In sum, sex differences in preferences for specific work activities and occupations are substantial. As individuals make choices about the occupations in which they would like to work, they are influenced by their own socialization experiences and by the distribution of male and female workers across occupations. Individuals tend to seek jobs that are viewed as appropriate for members of their sex, thereby reinforcing the sex segregation of the workforce.

REACTIONS TO ORGANIZATIONS

Sex differences in self-selection decisions may also be due to differences in women's and men's reactions to organizations. Human resource management programs and practices serve as signals for underlying organizational values. Job seekers use these signals to assess the fit between their own values and those of the organization. For women and people of color, initiatives such as diversity and work-family programs may be important signals concerning the value that the organization places on maintaining a diverse workforce and the likelihood of their own fit within the organization. Selection processes, especially the demographic characteristics and behavior of the recruiter and the nature of the procedures used, serve as further signals about working conditions in the organization.[17]

Inclusive diversity policies make it easier for organizations to attract applicants. Organizations that declare their commitment to hiring and promoting women and people of color in recruitment advertisements increase their attractiveness to all job seekers, regardless of the job seeker's sex or race. Nonetheless, women and people of color pay closer attention to a prospective employer's diversity management practices than do men and Whites. Policies concerning affirmative action and the promotion of women and people of color into the managerial and executive ranks are more important to women and people of color, who are more likely to benefit from them.[18]

The presence of work-family initiatives such as flextime, reduced hours, and on-site day care also seems to increase organizational attractiveness for all employees. Even individuals who pursue traditional career paths prefer flexible organizations that allow all workers to balance work and family. Flexible organizations may be favored because they are seen as more humane and modern. Nonetheless, as we discuss further in Chapter 8, family-friendly policies are most important to individuals who are experiencing work-family conflict. As individuals devote more time to child rearing and household activities, they seek jobs with organizations that provide more flexibility. Because gender socialization may lead women to emphasize family roles to a greater extent than men, work-family initiatives may be especially attractive to women.[19]

The demographic characteristics of the recruiter could differentially affect men's and women's evaluations of the organization's attractiveness. For instance, applicants could see job opportunities as less attractive when they are interviewed by female rather than male recruiters. Because females typically have less power and status in their organizations, job seekers who are interviewed by female recruiters may infer that the jobs for which they are interviewing are low in status. They may also believe that female recruiters have little say in the decision-making process. In addition, sex similarity between the job seeker and the recruiter could affect the job seeker's attraction to the organization. Sex similarity may lead to perceived similarity in attitudes and values, which in turn leads to interpersonal attraction or liking and more positive evaluations of the other party. Sex similarity may also enhance communication between the applicant and the recruiter. Because individuals are more open to influence from similar others, applicants may be more easily sold on a job by same-sex than by opposite-sex recruiters. The presence of a same-sex recruiter may also serve as a signal that individuals similar to the job seeker are valued at the organization. According to the evidence, neither recruiter sex nor sex similarity between the recruiter and the applicant have consistent effects on men's or women's evaluations of the attractiveness of job opportunities.[20]

Although recruiter sex and sex similarity do not lead to predictable sex differences in reactions to job opportunities, recruiter behavior does lead to such differences. Sara Rynes, Robert Bretz, and Barry Gerhart obtained rich evidence on this issue from intensive interviews with 41 diverse undergraduate and graduate students throughout their job searches. In the interviews, the researchers tried to understand why students pursued or rejected various job opportunities. Despite the fact that the researchers asked no questions about sex discrimination, half of the women in their sample mentioned a negative experience that might be a sign of such discrimination. For instance, corporate representatives commented on women's personal appearances, asked women to interview in men's hotel rooms, or told women that they would not advance as quickly as men. In addition, when students described why they became more negative or positive about particular organizations during their job searches, women were much more likely than men to cite their interactions with recruiters and other organizational representatives. Given the negative experiences of women, it is logical to assume that their evaluations of job opportunities are more affected by their interactions with organizational representatives. It is rational for women to base their assessments of the environment for women and the likelihood of their own success in the organization on their interactions with organizational representatives.[21]

Men and women also differ in their evaluations of the fairness of selection procedures. The use of structured selection procedures designed to avoid sex discrimination appears to be more important to women than to men, at least among applicants for entry-level positions. Advertising every open position, using panels of interviewers of both sexes, ensuring equal opportunity regardless of sex, age, or race, and avoiding the use of appearance as a selection criterion are more important in determining the fairness of selection procedures for women. In contrast, men are more likely than women to believe that the use of job-related competence is important for fair selection decisions. These sex differences in reactions to selection procedures may arise from differences in men's and women's actual interview experiences. If women commonly experience the discrimination discovered by Rynes and her colleagues, they may feel that formal procedures are needed to reduce sex discrimination.[22]

In sum, human resource management programs and practices differentially affect men's and women's attraction to job opportunities. Although both women and men view organizations with diversity and work-family programs in a positive light, these characteristics are especially important to females. In addition, women often experience offensive behavior in their interactions with organizational representatives. As a result, these interactions are more important in women's than in men's job choice decisions. Women also endorse the use of nondiscriminatory selection procedures to a greater extent than do men. Overall, these findings suggest that organizations that want to attract women need to consider the signals conveyed by their diversity and work-family initiatives, and their selection processes.

JOB SEARCH BEHAVIOR

Sex differences in job search behavior are likely to influence the kinds of jobs that men and women obtain. Men may devote more time and effort to their searches. According to traditional gender roles, men, who are envisioned as the primary wage earners, should work harder at finding employment than do women. Men also may have more time available to devote to their job searches because they have fewer household responsibilities. If men devote more time and effort to job seeking, they may have better alternatives from which to choose. Evidence supports the notion that men and women differ in the amount of time they devote to job searches. According to a study of the job search efforts of a broad group of job seekers, women spend less time (4 weeks) searching for jobs than do men (10 weeks). However, women in male-intensive occupations spend much more time (12 weeks) searching for jobs than women in other occupations (4 weeks). Not surprisingly, individuals who search longer find higher-paying jobs.[23]

Men and women also differ in the methods they use to find jobs. Job search methods may be formal or informal. Formal methods include obtaining referrals from employment agencies, labor unions, and school placement officers and responding to newspaper ads and help-wanted signs. Informal methods consist of referrals from networks of friends, family members, and business associates. Although both methods are useful in the job search process, informal methods are a frequent mechanism for finding employment. In fact, many individuals who find new jobs are not even actively engaged in job searches. Instead, they "fall into" jobs that they hear about through their social networks.[24]

Men's and women's networks differ substantially. Women's networks are more kin-centered and men's networks are more work-centered. Women tend to have networks that are more concentrated in the local community and comprised of friends and relatives than are men's, perhaps because of women's greater domestic responsibilities and lower status positions. Men, who typically have fewer domestic responsibilities and higher status positions, have more geographically dispersed, diverse networks containing a greater number of business contacts and high-status individuals. When men and women use their networks to identify desirable jobs, they tend to rely on same-sex contacts. Same-sex contacts restrict the job choices of women compared to those of men, funneling them to female-intensive jobs in their local communities with less status and lower pay than male-intensive jobs. As a result, women benefit less from their social networks during the job search process.[25]

Once they hold jobs, men and women differ in the strategies they use to obtain new jobs and the benefits derived from their chosen strategy. Women often adopt an internal labor market strategy, seeking promotions and earnings growth within a single organization. In contrast, men tend to use an external labor market strategy, seeking advancement by searching for jobs with new employers while continuing to work for their present employers. Because using an external labor market strategy increases individuals' compensation more than using an internal labor market strategy, sex differences in the strategy used contribute to the pay differential between men and women. Moreover, even when women seek external employment, it yields them little benefit. The primary beneficiaries of an external labor market strategy are White males. Women and people of color who change companies do not increase their pay compared to those who stay with their companies, perhaps because of discrimination in employment systems.[26]

When negotiating with potential employers about job opportunities, sex differences in job seekers' perceptions of appropriate pay may lead to sex differences in actual wages. Because women expect and accept less pay than men, they may request and receive less pay than men in equivalent positions. For almost all occupations, young women have lower expectations regarding both their entry pay and their pay at the peaks of their careers than do young men. Young women in the U.S. expect to earn salaries that are $1,238 less at career entry and $18,659 less at career peak than young men. The sex difference in pay expectations is especially striking for male-intensive occupations such as engineering; female engineering students expect to earn $35,000 less at career peak than do male engineering students. Sex differences in pay expectations occur even when individuals estimate a fair salary for a particular job. Compared to men, women actually see lower pay as "fair pay."[27]

Several factors account for sex differences in pay expectations. First, women's lower pay expectations may be realistic. As victims of past discrimination in salary decisions, women simply may have lower pay standards.

Second, as we noted in our discussion of sex differences in job attribute preferences, pay is more important to men than to women. Women may be less concerned about pay and more concerned about other aspects of work, such as interpersonal relations and convenience. Third, men and women use different reference groups in determining pay expectations. Women usually base their pay expectations on the pay of other women, whereas men base their pay expectations on the pay of other men. Because men are likely to be more highly paid, this tendency to develop pay expectations based on same-sex comparisons may lead to sex differences in pay expectations. Finally, because of their limited business contacts, women's knowledge of pay levels may be less accurate.[28]

Differences in women's and men's job search methods contribute to differences in the jobs available to them and the salaries they receive. Men devote more time to their searches and have more access to beneficial contacts than do women. As a result, men identify more and better job opportunities. Further, even when men and women find equivalent jobs, women's salaries may be lower. Compared to men, women are less likely to obtain wage increases by changing employers. Women appear to have lower pay expectations than men in the same occupation, putting them at a disadvantage when negotiating salaries.

In summary, male and female job seekers make different job choice decisions. Women generally prefer jobs in female-intensive occupations, while men seek jobs in male-intensive occupations. Sex differences in job search behaviors contribute to the continued segregation of women into jobs that are female-intensive and lower paid. Further, women may be more affected than men by the organization's human resource management programs and practices. Organizations with policies that emphasize managing diversity and balancing work-family will be more attractive to women. Also, women will be more attracted to organizations when they view selection procedures as fair and have positive, nondiscriminatory interactions with recruiters.

Decisions by Organizations

Although the selection decisions of organizations are based primarily on applicants' qualifications, sex discrimination does occur. How big of a problem is sex discrimination? Despite a wealth of research on sex discrimination in the employment interview, there is no definitive answer to this question. Some studies suggest that women are evaluated less favorably, hired less often, and paid less than men. For instance, one study asked a sample of academic psychologists to evaluate the résumé of a male or a female biopsychologist. Although the two résumés were identical, the psychologists evaluated the qualifications of the male candidate more highly and viewed him as more suitable for hire. This finding is particularly disturbing because psychologists are likely to have been exposed to material on sex bias. Another study tracked selection decisions regarding over 5,000 applicants for entry-level professional positions (customer service representative, mortgage consultant, personal banker, business banker) at a retail bank over a 2-year period. The results indicated that women and men were equally likely to be interviewed but that men were more likely to get job offers. A study of pay decisions for employees in professional, managerial, sales, and technical positions during a 10-year period at a large diversified company found that women received lower starting salaries, even after accounting for the influence of such factors as experience, college major, and job title.[29]

Other studies have revealed either favoritism toward women or no effects of applicant sex. A study of hiring decisions regarding over 4,000 applicants for customer service positions at a credit card phone center found that women were more likely to be interviewed and receive job offers. A study of over 30,000 applicants who applied for employment at a large technology company found no sex differences in job offers or starting salaries after accounting for factors such as age and education.[30]

The findings described above represent just a small sampling of existing research evidence on sex discrimination in selection decisions. There is no question that sex discrimination occurs in the selection process. However, the issue of discrimination is extremely complex. Sex discrimination is a function of the situation, the organizational representatives, and the applicants. Instead of attempting to assess the extent of sex discrimination overall, we need to consider how and when it occurs and who discriminates against whom.[31]

HOW AND WHEN DOES SEX DISCRIMINATION OCCUR?

To understand how and when sex discrimination occurs, it is helpful to examine how organizational representatives make selection decisions. Organizational decision makers use a matching process to assess applicants. Decision makers form *mental prototypes* or images of the ideal applicant. These prototypes define the traits and behaviors that are required for success in a particular job. As decision makers evaluate applicants, they favor applicants whose attributes come closest to matching this prototype.[32]

Sex discrimination may arise from decision makers' prototypes of the ideal applicant. Decision makers' prototypes may include traits that are specifically linked to one sex. When the tasks required for job performance are mostly masculine, the prototype will be masculine and men will be seen as more likely to succeed. For example, the requirements of managerial positions may include stereotypically masculine behaviors such as making tough decisions or competing for scarce organizational resources. As a result, decision makers' prototypes for such positions may emphasize masculine traits and male applicants may be seen as better suited for the job. On the other hand, if the prototype for a job (e.g., day care worker) includes feminine traits, females will be seen as more suitable.[33]

In some cases, decision makers' prototypes explicitly specify the sex of the jobholder. When job incumbents or job applicants are predominantly from one sex, organizational decision makers' prototypes specify the sex of the ideal applicant; applicants whose sex matches the prototype will be seen as more qualified and will be favored in the selection process. Among applicants for female-intensive jobs (e.g., day care worker, counselor, receptionist/secretary), female applicants are likely to be rated as more qualified, offered higher starting salaries and more challenging job assignments, and hired more often than males. In contrast, male applicants are likely to be preferred over females for male-intensive jobs (e.g., firefighter, surgeon, finance officer). Decision makers do not hire blatantly unqualified applicants of the "correct" sex over qualified applicants of the "wrong" sex. However, they may hire moderately qualified applicants of the correct sex over slightly more qualified applicants of the other sex. This phenomenon provides a possible explanation for the sex discrimination suit against Home Depot mentioned earlier; women may experience discrimination at companies such as Home Depot because they are the wrong sex for jobs in the male-intensive building supply industry.[34]

An example from the restaurant industry demonstrates the use of sex as an explicit element of decision makers' ideal applicant prototypes. Imagine going to the most elegant restaurant in a large city to celebrate your birthday. This particular birthday is a significant milestone and you are sparing no expense to enjoy an incredible dining experience. Look around your restaurant. What sex are the servers? They are probably mostly or entirely male. Now, imagine going to the nearest sandwich shop or ice cream parlor, which would provide a less elegant dining experience. What sex are the servers? They are probably mostly female. One possible explanation for this phenomenon is that women prefer the limited tips earned in inexpensive restaurants and men prefer the more generous tips in expensive restaurants. Another is that men are more qualified to serve expensive food and women more qualified to serve inexpensive food. A more likely explanation is that managers of expensive restaurants possess ideal applicant prototypes that specify that servers should be male, while managers of inexpensive restaurants have prototypes that specify that servers should be female. A recent study suggests that this is indeed the case.

In the study, two male and two female students in an undergraduate economics course applied for jobs as servers at selected restaurants in Philadelphia. One male and one female student dropped off equivalent résumés at each restaurant. The students visited 23 high-priced restaurants and received a total of 13 job offers from these restaurants. Eleven of these 13 job offers were made to men. The students visited 21 low-priced restaurants and received a total of 10 offers for jobs from these restaurants. Women received 8 of the 10 offers. Thus, male applicants were preferred at expensive restaurants and female applicants were preferred at inexpensive restaurants. The preference for male servers at high-priced restaurants seems to be due to the managers' beliefs about the preferences of patrons in these restaurants, who are more likely to be male than are the patrons in low-priced restaurants. Restaurant managers, regardless of their own sex, prefer servers whose sex matches patrons' expectations. Thus, restaurant managers' ideal applicant prototypes specify the sex of the jobholder.[35]

Sex discrimination also arises in the selection process because decision makers have a general tendency to devalue the qualifications of female applicants. In society, individuals are assigned status or esteem based on the demographic groups to which they belong; Whites and men are typically ascribed higher status than women and people of color. Judgments of individuals' task competence are based, in part, on the status assigned to members of their demographic group. Individuals who belong to high-status groups are viewed as more competent than those of low-status groups. Because females are typically ascribed less status or esteem in society, decision makers may believe that women are less qualified than men. As a result, male applicants are valued more than identically qualified female applicants. Moreover, to be seen as qualified, female applicants must provide more evidence of their ability than similarly qualified male applicants.[36]

Thus, sex discrimination in the selection process may lead women to be preferred for jobs that are female-intensive or require feminine traits and men to be preferred for jobs that are male-intensive or require masculine traits. However, if men are generally seen as more qualified than women, men who apply for female-intensive jobs (e.g., male applicant for nursing position) may suffer less discrimination than women who apply for male-intensive jobs (e.g., woman applicant for firefighter position).

Sex discrimination is most likely to occur when jobs are associated with one sex, either because the traits required for the job are stereotypically masculine or feminine or because the job is dominated by members of one sex. However, the presence of sex discrimination is also influenced by other situational factors, especially the amount of information available about applicants and the conspicuousness of the applicant's sex. Recruiters and managers often have insufficient information on which to base their selection decisions. For instance, the initial screening of applicants is typically based on résumés or application forms, which present little information about applicants' personal qualities.

When recruiting is conducted on college campuses, decisions about which applicants to consider further are based on interviews of no more than 20 to 30 minutes. These interviews lead to quickly formed impressions that present only a glimpse of the applicant. Follow-up interviews provide more information about applicants, but not so much that employers can be sure that they are making the right choice or offering an appropriate salary.[37]

Insufficient information increases the likelihood that discrimination will occur. In the absence of information, decision makers have no reliable way to evaluate an applicant's potential productivity. They are likely to rely on gender stereotypes and status judgments to form impressions of applicants. Decision makers assume that applicants possess attributes associated with their sex and use these attributes to assess the fit of the applicants with the prototype of the ideal applicant. As a result, when decision makers with limited information evaluate applicants, women are less likely than men to advance into the final applicant pool and to receive job offers. Women also are likely to receive lower starting salaries. On the other hand, when decision makers have access to extensive information about applicants' abilities, sex discrimination is less likely to occur.[38]

Although information about applicant qualifications may reduce discrimination, information about applicants' personality traits may not. We would expect that providing information about the candidate's personality would reduce decision makers' reliance on gender stereotypes and status judgments, and, therefore, eliminate sex discrimination. The results of studies that require students or business professionals to evaluate bogus résumés suggest that this may not be the case. When decision makers receive résumés indicating that the applicant's personality (i.e., masculinity, femininity) is inconsistent with his or her sex, they form nonstereotypical impressions of the applicant. Nonetheless, they still select the applicant whose sex matches the sex of the typical job-holder. Females are still preferred for female-intensive jobs and males are still preferred for male-intensive jobs. Thus, supplying stereotype-inconsistent information on résumés may not reduce sex discrimination.[39]

Sex discrimination also seems to occur when the situation calls attention to the sex of the applicant. When applicant sex is highly conspicuous, decision makers are likely to access their gender stereotypes and status judgments, thereby increasing the chance of sex discrimination. Numerous factors increase the conspicuousness of applicant sex. Applicant sex is likely to be conspicuous when decision makers encounter applicants whose sex is atypical among applicants or job incumbents. Aspects of the applicant's appearance (e.g., a very femininely dressed woman) may also increase attention to the applicant's sex.[40]

Perhaps the most striking demonstration of the importance of the conspicuousness of applicant sex comes from Claudia Goldin and Cecilia Rouse's research on the effect of screens on sex discrimination in the selection decisions made by major symphony orchestras. Elite symphonies historically have discriminated against female musicians. In fact, some conductors of major orchestras have been known to make public comments such as "I just don't think women should be in an orchestra," or "the more women in an orchestra, the smaller the sound." Because women musicians are underrepresented in major symphonies, sex is likely to be an explicit aspect of decision makers' prototypes of the ideal applicant and applicant sex is likely to be conspicuous. The use of screens in orchestra auditions reduces the conspicuousness of applicant sex; in fact it makes applicant sex invisible. Thus, by comparing the amount of sex discrimination with and without screens, we can get an idea of how conspicuousness affects the occurrence of discrimination. As we saw in the introductory passage to the chapter, using screens substantially reduces discrimination against women. This finding reinforces the notion that the conspicuousness of applicant sex is an important factor in determining whether sex discrimination occurs.[41]

In most cases, the processes described above probably operate at an unconscious level. With perhaps the exception of symphony conductors, most decision makers probably do not say to themselves, "Women simply aren't qualified for this job" or "I will act on my belief in gender stereotypes in evaluating applicants" or "I must hire a man for this position because this job is usually filled by men." However, some decision makers may consciously use what they believe are other peoples' biases as the basis for their decisions about applicants. If they think, for example, that employees or customers will feel uncomfortable with a female engineer or a male secretary, they may defer to that attitude in their hiring decisions even if they do not share it. For instance, a study of law firms found that many were reluctant to hire female attorneys because the firms' partners believed that clients preferred male attorneys. Elegant restaurants may hire only male servers because they believe that their patrons prefer to be waited on by male servers. Discrimination on the basis of customer preferences is illegal according to U.S. law, as we discuss further in Chapter 9, but it does occur.[42]

Our attention has been on the "how and when" of sex discrimination in selection decisions. However, other factors as age, race, ethnic group, class, religion, nationality, sexual orientation, and physical abilities/disabilities are also sources of discrimination. The processes by which these other dimensions of diversity influence decision makers are similar to those described above. Decision makers may reject applicants with certain demographic characteristics (e.g., those who are older, non-White, or disabled) because these characteristics violate decision makers' prototypes of the ideal applicant or are associated with low societal status. Moreover, insufficient information and conspicuousness increase the likelihood of discrimination on the basis of all dimensions of diversity, not just sex.

WHO DISCRIMINATES AGAINST WHOM?

Although sex discrimination in selection decisions is influenced by the sex composition of jobholders, the amount of information available, and the conspicuousness of applicant sex, it also is a function of the personal characteristics of the decision maker and of the applicant. It is important to examine who discriminates against whom.

One notion that has received attention is that interviewers favor applicants of the same sex over applicants of the opposite sex. As noted in our discussion of job seekers' self-selection decisions, sex similarity between the interviewer and the applicant may enhance interviewer-applicant liking and facilitate communication in the interview. This not only may increase the applicant's attraction to the job, but also may enhance the interviewer's evaluation of the applicant. In same-sex dyads, greater mutual understanding and ease of communication may lead applicants to share more information about themselves, thereby providing interviewers a better understanding of what they have to offer. In addition, increased liking may lead interviewers to conduct more positive interviews and focus on positive information when forming their judgments of applicants. The effects of sex similarity may even apply to situations where organizational representatives are simply evaluating résumés or application forms. Individuals have a general bias toward individuals who are like themselves, and therefore, may positively evaluate similar others even when they do not interact with them.[43]

However, research findings provide inconsistent support for the idea that sex similarity between the interviewer and the applicant leads to more favorable evaluations of applicants. Although some studies have found that both men and women favor applicants of their own gender, many have found no effect of sex similarity on evaluations of applicants or reported sex similarity effects for only male or female recruiters. Some of our own research demonstrates the inconsistency of sex similarity effects. We collected data from campus recruiters who conducted interviews at a university placement facility at two different points in time: 1983 to 1985 and 1990 to 1991. The earlier data indicated that female recruiters saw male applicants as more similar to themselves, more likeable, and more hirable than female applicants. The later data focused on slightly different variables but found that female recruiters preferred female over male applicants. At both points in time, male recruiters did not favor one sex over the other, perhaps because they were sensitized to concerns about sex discrimination. Our data did not provide an explanation for the differences in the results for female recruiters across the two points in time. However, status disparities between men and women in organizations determine whether women identify with and support other women or choose to derogate them. Women are more likely to identify with and support other women when status disparities between men and women are small. Thus, one possible explanation for our disparate findings is that the status of the female recruiters improved over time such that recruiters in the earlier sample derogated women and recruiters in the later sample favored women. The diversity initiatives undertaken by the recruiters' organizations during the late 1980s may have improved the status of female recruiters. We conclude that sex similarity effects are just as complex as applicant sex effects.[44]

Decision makers' personalities may be more useful than their demographic characteristics in predicting whether they will engage in sex discrimination. The extent to which decision makers endorse traditional gender roles and stereotypes seems to be especially important. Decision makers who adhere to traditional, rather than nontraditional, gender roles and stereotypes are likely to discriminate against women who apply for male-intensive positions. However, even those individuals who reject traditional gender stereotypes may engage in discrimination by favoring women over men.[45]

We have looked at how the characteristics of the recruiter affect the occurrence of sex discrimination. Another important issue is whether sex discrimination differs as a function of the applicant's race, sexual orientation, physical abilities/disabilities, age, or other characteristics. To date, researchers have focused primarily on the combined effects of applicant sex and race. Competing arguments have been offered regarding these effects. One line of thinking suggests that women of color are doubly advantaged when they look for jobs because they are beneficiaries of affirmative action for women and for people of color. Another position is that women of color are doubly disadvantaged by the negative stereotypes of and prejudicial attitudes toward women and people of color. Although results have been inconsistent, there is little evidence to support the notion that women of color are advantaged in selection decisions by their dual status as women and as people of color.[46]

The applicant's physical appearance may also affect the occurrence of sex discrimination in selection decisions. In most cultures, children and adults with attractive faces are judged more positively, treated more positively, and achieve more success. Further, attractive adults are judged as having higher levels of occupational competence, and experience more career success, as measured by advancement and income, than less attractive adults. In job interviews, physically attractive applicants are seen as more likeable and ultimately as being more suitable for hiring. Candidates with attractive facial features are preferred over unattractive candidates and normal-weight applicants are preferred over overweight candidates. However, appearance may be more important in the evaluation of female than of male job seekers. Women with unattractive faces are extremely likely to be viewed as unsuitable for hire. Likewise, overweight women are less likely to be selected than overweight men. Thus, unattractive and overweight women may be especially likely to be devalued.[47]

Style of dress may also affect decision makers' perceptions of applicants' suitability. Because appropriate business attire is less defined for women than for men, female applicants typically have more flexibility in their interview attire. The clothing choices of female applicants may affect how they are evaluated, especially for managerial positions. Female applicants for middle management positions who wear more masculine dress (e.g., emphasis on vertical and angular lines, straight silhouettes, large-scale details, dark or dull colors, and heavy textures) are seen as more forceful, self-reliant, dynamic, and aggressive and receive more favorable hiring recommendations than those with more feminine dress (e.g., emphasis on horizontal and curved lines, rounded silhouettes, small-scale details, light colors, and soft details). Women who dress in a more masculine style may be seen as having more of the traits associated with managerial jobs than those who dress in a more feminine style.[48]

The effects of appearance on hiring decisions are disturbing because they emphasize appearance rather than qualifications. People have little control over their attractiveness. Applicants have more control over their dress than over their basic appearance, but dress is a frivolous means for deciding whom to hire for a managerial position. Some executives claim, however, that if an applicant wears an outfit judged by others to be inappropriate to an employment interview, he or she does not understand the realities of the work world and would be an ineffective performer.

In summary, organizations have considerable opportunity to engage in sex discrimination during the selection process. Selection decisions are based on a largely unconscious, subjective process in which decision makers determine whether there is a match between their perceptions of the applicant and their notions about the job requirements. During this process, decision makers seek a match between the sex of the applicant and the sex of the typical job holder such that women are preferred for female-intensive jobs and men are preferred for male-intensive jobs. The qualifications of women may be devalued due to gender stereotypes and women's lower status in society. Sex discrimination in selection decisions is highly complex and varies as a function of the characteristics of the situation, the decision makers, and the applicants. Sex discrimination is especially likely to occur when there is little information about applicants and when applicant sex is conspicuous. The decision maker's belief in traditional gender roles, as well as the race and appearance of the applicant, may also determine whether sex discrimination occurs. Further research on sex discrimination in the interview is needed before we fully understand how and when it occurs and who discriminates against whom. However, we certainly know enough to conclude that organizations need to guard against sex discrimination in selection decisions.

Improving Employment Decisions

We have painted a picture of how job seekers and organizations make employment decisions that heavily emphasizes the influence of sex and gender. In this section, we consider (1) what individual job seekers can do to improve their prospects for attaining a satisfying and rewarding job and (2) what organizations can do to improve their recruitment activities and how they make selection decisions.

TAKING CHARGE OF SELF-SELECTION DECISIONS

Although organizational selection processes have a great impact on the jobs that individuals obtain, individuals can increase the likelihood of obtaining a satisfying and rewarding job by devoting substantial attention to identifying their own interests and to conducting job searches. First, job seekers should engage in self-exploration exercises to identify preferred occupations and job attributes. Career counselors, often available at universities and high schools, may be helpful in this process. Self-help books such as the popular *What Color Is Your Parachute?* may also be useful. Individuals should identify preferred activities and then determine the occupations that will allow them to pursue these activities. Given the influence of the sex segregation of work on occupational preferences, job seekers need to ensure that they do not limit their choices to those that are dominated by their own sex. For instance, females with an interest in medicine might consider becoming surgeons and males with an interest in medicine might explore careers in nursing. Job seekers also should consider their own preferences for specific job attributes. They might rank their preferences for the following job attributes: earnings, benefits, promotion opportunities, job security, prestige, recognition, physical work environment, good coworkers, good supervisor, good hours, easy commute, geographical location, company reputation, working with people, opportunities to lead, opportunities to help others, power/influence/authority, freedom/ autonomy, opportunity for growth/development, challenge, opportunity to use abilities, variety of duties, responsibility, task significance or importance, and feelings of accomplishment. Making such a list clarifies the specific kinds of positions within an occupation that may be suitable for the individual.[49]

Second, job seekers need to devote considerable time and effort to their job searches and to use a broad range of job search methods, both formal and informal. This will allow them to identify more and better alternatives from which to choose. As we noted earlier, informal referrals are especially important in the job search process. Women may have fewer business contacts than do men, and may need to make special efforts to establish a broader range of social contacts. For instance, women might want to consider joining local professional or business-related organizations to increase the diversity of their contacts.

Third, applicants should be prepared to make good impressions in their interviews. The research results discussed earlier are relevant—it is important to dress the part. To reduce the chances of stereotyping, job seekers should provide as much information as possible to potential employers about their qualifications. Applicants need to make known their positive qualities, both in their paper credentials and in their interactions with employers. Also, job seekers benefit from attending job interview training workshops or holding practice interviews with friends.[50]

Fourth, applicants should carefully assess the merits of each potential employer. During the initial employment interview, applicants should not expect to get much information other than whether there might be a potential match. If job seekers proceed to further discussions with an employer, they need additional information to make a good decision. Such information can be difficult to obtain, but it is available if the right questions are asked at the right time of the right people in a sensitive manner. It may be worthwhile for female applicants to consider the signals provided by recruiter behavior, as well as organizational policies with respect to work-family and managing diversity, in evaluating the extent to which women are valued by the organization. Female applicants also may benefit from consulting published information about companies that develop and promote women.[51]

Finally, applicants should select the job that best matches their preferred job attributes and be ready to negotiate their starting salary. All job seekers should become informed about actual pay levels for the jobs that they are seeking so that they can negotiate fair starting salaries. This is particularly important for women, some of whom may have lower pay expectations than men. Applicants who follow all of these steps will increase their chances of obtaining a satisfying and rewarding job.

IMPROVING ORGANIZATIONAL SELECTION DECISIONS

One key source of sex segregation in today's organizations is the sex difference in occupational preferences. Individuals' occupational preferences are formed at a very young age and typically reflect societal notions about "women's work" and "men's work." If organizations want to lower the level of sex segregation in the workplace, they need to influence the formation of children's occupational expectations.

How can organizations influence the development of occupational preferences? Many organizations distribute materials about careers to high school guidance counselors. These materials portray women and men in a greater variety of occupations than ever before. However, high school is not the place to start. If organizations expect to have an appreciable effect on the development of occupational preferences, they need to direct activities toward younger children, such as by sending speakers to elementary schools, Cub Scout and Brownie troops, and other places where young children congregate, to talk about opportunities in their industries and workplaces. The best speakers are members of the sex least represented in the occupations being discussed, or mixed-sex teams that demonstrate that both sexes belong in the occupations. A female engineer who succeeded despite the admonishments of others would be an ideal speaker on opportunities in the engineering professions. Films that are distributed to schools and youth groups can convey similar themes.

Organizations also need to reduce the sex segregation of jobs in their midst and devote more attention to their procedures for attracting and selecting applicants. First, they need to reduce the perception that particular jobs are appropriate for members of one sex. Many jobs require tasks associated with both women's and men's traditional roles. For instance, managerial jobs, which are seen as demanding masculine traits, often require interpersonal tasks regarded as feminine, such as handling conflicts and dealing with subordinates' problems. The full range of activities associated with managerial and other jobs should be included in job descriptions. Organizations may also publicize employees who have been successful in positions that are atypical for their sex. Finally, the leaders of organizations may be a very powerful force in changing perceptions of jobs. If key leaders repeatedly select individuals whose sex is "incorrect" for a particular job, the organization's own employees' perceptions may be changed.[52]

Second, organizations need to examine how they solicit applications. Most job seekers obtain jobs through informal contacts of the same sex, and most organizations rely heavily on referrals from employees to make new hires. Organizations must ensure that reliance on referrals does not promote the sex segregation of work. They need to consider alternative sources of applicants (e.g., internet postings, newspaper advertisements, employment agencies, campus placement centers) if reliance on referrals is limiting the diversity of new hires.

Third, organizations need to screen and train recruiters and other decision makers. Screening of recruiters should include assessments of their beliefs in rigid gender stereotypes and roles to exclude those who are biased. Training of all those involved in the selection process is critical. A survey of *Fortune* 1000 companies found that less than half offered a standardized training program for recruiters. Given the negative experiences of female applicants in the selection process, employers need to do a better job of training the people who attract and select applicants. Organizations should train individuals to avoid discriminatory behaviors and to be aware of the potential influences of gender stereotypes and the sex segregation of work.[53]

Fourth, organizations can reduce the likelihood of sex discrimination by formalizing and standardizing selection practices. Many organizations rely primarily on employment interviews to make hiring decisions. In the typical interview, interviewers ask vague questions about applicants' opinions and attitudes, goals and aspirations, and self-evaluations. Interview judgments based on such questions are highly subjective, and, as a result, are susceptible to bias from gender and racial stereotypes. Unlike symphony orchestras, most organizations cannot solve the problem by putting screens between applicants and decision makers. Organizations, however, can implement structured interviews that are less susceptible to bias than traditional interviews. In structured interviews, the content of the interview and the evaluation process are standardized. Specific, job-related interview questions are asked of all applicants. Further, interviewers evaluate each applicant on multiple scales with well-defined descriptions anchoring each level of each scale. These structured procedures force interviewers to obtain and to process information about the applicants' qualifications in a systematic and detailed manner, thereby reducing their reliance on stereotypes. In addition, the use of multiple interviewers with different viewpoints may reduce sex discrimination by offsetting the idiosyncratic biases of a single interviewer. A review of court cases involving employment discrimination should motivate organizations to devote time and money to structuring interviews. The review found that organizations are more likely to win discrimination suits when they use structured interviews.[54]

Fifth, organizations need to monitor selection practices to enhance their effectiveness and ensure that sex discrimination does not occur. Many organizations do poor jobs of assessing the effectiveness of their selection decisions. Recruiter performance is most often evaluated on procedural grounds, such as whether the recruiter kept appointments and filed necessary reports, rather than on actual results. Recruiter performance is seldom tied to rewards, especially for recruiters who are line managers. To assess the effectiveness of selection processes, organizations should track the performance, satisfaction, turnover rate, and subsequent success of new hires. Assessment should also include measurement of the demographic composition of the applicant pool, the demographic composition of new hires, and differences in starting salaries and initial assignments as a function of sex and race. Attention to these measures helps organizations identify discriminatory selection processes. Moreover, organizations should make performance appraisals and rewards contingent on the extent to which selection processes are effective and bias-free.[55]

Finally, organizations that are serious about attracting a diverse workforce should ensure that their policies and procedures are consistent with this goal. They should examine diversity and work-family policies to ensure that these policies enhance organizational attractiveness and do not lead some individuals to self-select out of the selection process. Policies that signal the organization's commitment to diversity will help attract women and people of color.[56]

In summary, organizations need to take actions to reduce the perception that certain jobs are appropriate for members of only one sex, both among young people and in their own midst. They need to ensure that their hiring process allows them to attract and select the most qualified applicants regardless of sex, race, or any other irrelevant personal characteristics.

The sex segregation of work is a powerful phenomenon and has a great influence on both job seekers and organizations. Individuals' occupational preferences are consistent with the sex composition of jobs. Similarly, organizational representatives are likely to seek a match between the sex of the applicant and the sex of the typical job holder. Job seekers' and organizations' methods of finding and evaluating one another exacerbate the differential status of men and women in organizations. Given these tendencies, it is a wonder that any change has occurred in the amount of sex segregation in any occupation. Some individuals and organizations, however, have made substantial changes. Otherwise, the National Symphony Orchestra in Washington would have no female French horn players.[57]

Notes

1. Duff, C. (1997, March 7). Out of sight keeps women in mind for U.S. orchestra spots, study finds. *Wall Street Journal,* p. B9A. WALL STREET JOURNAL CLASSROOM EDITION (STAFF PRODUCED COPY ONLY) by C. DUFF. Copyright 1997 by DOW JONES & CO INC. Reproduced with permission of DOW JONES & CO INC. in the format Textbook via Copyright Clearance Center.

2. Laabs, J. J. (1998). Judge approves Home Depot's sex-discrimination settlement. *Workforce, 77*(4), 13–14.

3. Gupta, N. D. (1993). Probabilities of job choice and employer selection and male-female occupational differences. *American Economic Review, 83*(2), 57–61; Barber, A. E. (1998). *Recruiting employees: Individual and organizational perspectives.* Thousand Oaks, CA: Sage.

4. Ryan, A. M., Sacco, J. M., McFarland, L. A., & Kriska, S. D. (2000). Applicant self-selection: Correlates of withdrawal from a multiple hurdle process. *Journal of Applied Psychology, 85,* 163–179; Schmit, M. J., & Ryan, A. M. (1997). Applicant withdrawal: The role of test taking attitudes and racial differences. *Personnel Psychology, 50,* 855–876.

5. Rynes, S. L., Bretz, R. D., & Gerhart, B. (1991). The importance of recruitment in job choice: A different way of looking. *Personnel Psychology, 44,* 487–521; Judge, T. A., & Bretz, R. D. (1992). Effects of work values on job choice decisions. *Journal of Applied Psychology, 77,* 261–271.

6. Konrad, A. M., Corrigall, E., Lieb, P., & Ritchie, J. E., Jr. (2000). Sex differences in job attribute preferences among managers and business students. *Group and Organization Management, 25* (2), 108–131.

7. Konrad, A. M., Ritchie, J. E., Jr., Lieb, P., & Corrigall, E. (2000). Sex differences and similarities in job attribute preferences: A meta-analysis. *Psychological Bulletin, 126,* 593–641; Konrad, Corrigall, Lieb, & Ritchie.

8. Konrad, Ritchie, Lieb, & Corrigall; Tolbert, P. S., & Moen, P. (1998). Men's and women's definitions of good jobs. *Work and Occupations, 25,* 168–194; Gati, I., Osipow, S. H., & Givon, M. (1995). Gender differences in career decision making: The content and structure of preferences. *Journal of Counseling Psychology, 42,* 204–216.

9. Herzberg, F., Mausner, B., Peterson, R. O., & Capwell, D. F. (1957). *Job attitudes: Review of research and opinion.* Pittsburgh, PA: Psychological Service of Pittsburgh; Konrad, Ritchie, Lieb, & Corrigall; Tolbert & Moen.

10. Yamauchi, H. (1995). Factor structure of preferences for job attributes among Japanese workers. *Psychological Reports, 77,* 787–791; Browne, B. A. (1997). Gender and preferences for job attributes: A cross-cultural comparison. *Sex Roles, 37,* 61–71; Chew, I., & Teo, A. (1993). Job attribute preferences: The effect of gender in job choice of undergraduates. *Women in Management Review, 8* (5), 15–23.

11. Lippa, R. (1998). Gender-related individual differences and the structure of vocational interests: The importance of the people-things dimension. *Journal of Personality and Social Psychology, 74,* 996–1009; Holland, J. L. (1985). *Making vocational choices: A theory of vocational personalities and work environments* (2nd ed.). Englewood Cliffs, NJ: Prentice-Hall; Aros, J. R., Henly, G. A., & Curtis, N. T. (1998). Occupational sextype and sex differences in vocational preference-measured interest relationships. *Journal of Vocational Behavior, 53,* 227–242; Gati, Osipow, & Givon.

12. Jacobs, J. A. (1999). The sex segregation of occupations: Prospects for the 21st century. In G. N. Powell (Ed.), *Handbook of gender and work* (pp. 125–141). Thousand Oaks, CA: Sage; Jacobs, J. A. (1989). *Revolving doors: Sex segregation and women's careers.* Stanford, CA: Stanford University Press; Aros, Henly, & Curtis.

13. Eagly, A. H. (1987). *Sex differences in social behavior: A social-role interpretation.* Hillsdale, NJ: Lawrence Erlbaum; Cejka, M. A., & Eagly, A. H. (1999). Gender-stereotypic images of occupations correspond to the sex segregation of employment. *Personality and Social Psychology Bulletin, 25,* 413–423; Cleveland, J. N., & Smith, L. A. (1989). The effect of job title and task composition on job and incumbent perceptions. *Journal of Applied Social Psychology, 19,* 744–757.

14. Cejka & Eagly; Lapan, R. T., Shaughnessy, P., & Boggs, K. (1996). Efficacy expectations and vocational interests as mediators between sex and choice of math/science college majors: A longitudinal study. *Journal of Vocational Behavior, 49,* 277–291; Matsui, T. (1994). Mechanisms underlying sex differences in career self-efficacy of university students. *Journal of Vocational Behavior, 45,* 177–184; Subich, L. M., Barrett, G. V., Doverspike, D., & Alexander, R. A. (1989). The effects of sex-role related factors on occupational choice and salary. In R. T. Michael, H. I. Hartman, & B. O'Farrell (Eds.), *Pay equity: Empirical inquiries* (pp. 91–104). Washington, DC: National Academy Press; Marini, M. M., & Fan, P. (1997). The gender gap in earnings at career entry. *American Sociological Review, 62,* 588–604.

15. Murrell, A. J., Frieze, I. H., & Frost, J. L. (1991). Aspiring to careers in male- and female-dominated professions: A study of black and white college women. *Psychology of Women Quarterly, 15,* 103–126; Subich, Barrett, Doverspike, & Alexander; Lippa; Jome, L. M., & Tokar, D. M. (1998). Dimensions of masculinity and major choice traditionality. *Journal of Vocational Behavior, 52,* 120–134.

16. Powell, G. N., & Butterfield, D. A. (August, 2002). *As the millennium turns: Gender and aspirations to top management.* Paper presented at the meeting of the Academy of Management, Denver, CO.

17. Bretz, R. D., & Judge, T. A. (1994). The role of human resource systems in job applicant decision processes. *Journal of Management, 20,* 531–551; Judge & Bretz; Marrs, M. B., Turban, D. B., Dougherty, T. W., & Roberts, R. (April, 1996). *Applicant attraction to demographically diverse firms: A person-organization fit perspective.* Paper presented at the meeting of the Society for Industrial and Organizational Psychology, San Diego, CA; Rynes, S. L. (1991). Recruitment, job choice, and post-hire consequences: A call for new directions. In M. D. Dunnette & L. M. Hough (Eds.), *Handbook of industrial and organizational psychology: Vol. 2.* (2nd ed. pp. 399–444). Palo Alto, CA: Consulting Psychologists Press; Rynes, Bretz, & Gerhart.

18. Williams, M. L., & Bauer, T. N. (1994). The effect of a managing diversity policy on organizational attractiveness. *Group and Organization Management, 19,* 295–308; Saks, A. M., Leck, J. D., & Saunders, D. M. (1995). Effects of application blanks and employment equity on applicant reactions and job pursuit intentions. *Journal of Organizational Behavior, 16,* 415–430; Marrs, Turban, Dougherty, & Roberts; Thomas, K. M., & Wise, P. G. (1999). Organizational attractiveness and individual differences: Are diverse applicants attracted by different factors? *Journal of Business and Psychology, 13,* 375–390; Barber, A. E., & Roehling, M. V. (1993). Job postings and the decision to interview: A verbal protocol analysis. *Journal of Applied Psychology, 78,* 845–856.

19. Bretz, R. D., Boudreau, J. W., & Judge, T. A. (1994). Job search behavior of employed managers. *Personnel Psychology, 47,* 275–301; Bretz & Judge; Honeycutt, T. L., & Rosen, B. (1997). Family friendly human resource policies, salary levels, and salient identity as predictors of organizational attraction. *Journal of Vocational Behavior, 50,* 271–290; Konrad, A. M., & Corrigall, E. (May, 2000). *Impact of family demands on the job attribute preferences of women and men.* Paper presented at the meeting of the Eastern Academy of Management, Danvers, MA; Kulik, L. (2000). Jobless men and women: A comparative analysis of job search intensity, attitudes toward unemployment, and related responses. *Journal of Occupational and Organizational Psychology, 73,* 487–500; Tolbert & Moen; Wiersma, U. J. (1990). Gender differences in job attribute preferences: Work-home role conflict and job level as mediating variables. *Journal of Occupational Psychology, 63,* 231–243.

20. Barber; Connerly, M. L., & Rynes, S. L. (1997). The influence of recruiter characteristics and organizational recruitment support on perceived recruiter effectiveness: Views from applicants and recruiters. *Human Relations, 50,* 1563–1587; Taylor, M. S., & Bergmann, T. J. (1987). Organizational recruitment activities and applicants' reactions at different stages of the recruitment process. *Personnel Psychology, 40,* 261–285; Turban, D. B., & Dougherty, T. W. (1992). Influences of campus recruiting on applicant attraction to firms. *Academy of Management Journal, 35,* 739–765; Cable, D. M., & Judge, T. A. (1996). Person-organization fit, job choice decisions, and organizational entry. *Organizational Behavior and Human Decision Processes, 67,* 294–311; Graves, L. M. & Powell, G. N. (1995). The effect of sex similarity on recruiters' evaluations of actual applicants: A test of the similarity-attraction paradigm. *Personnel Psychology, 48,* 85–98; Graves, L. M., & Powell, G. N. (1996). Sex similarity, quality of the employment interview and recruiters' evaluation of actual applicants. *Journal of Occupational and Organizational Psychology, 69,* 243–261; Mauer, S. D., Howe, V., & Lee, T. W. (1992). Organizational recruiting as marketing management: An interdisciplinary study of engineering graduates. *Personnel Psychology, 45,* 807–833.

21. Rynes, Bretz, & Gerhart.

22. Singer, M. (1990). Determinants of perceived fairness in selection practices: An organizational justice perspective. *Genetic, Social, and General Psychology Monographs, 116,* 475–494.

23. Hanson, S., & Pratt, G. (1991). Job search and the occupational segregation of women. *Annals of the American Association of Geographers, 81,* 229–253; Kulik (2000); Leana, C. R., & Feldman, D. C. (1991). Gender differences in responses to unemployment. *Journal of Vocational*

Behavior, 38, 65–77; Jones, S. R. G. (1989). Job search methods, intensity, and effects. *Oxford Bulletin of Economics and Statistics, 51,* 277–296; Kulik, L. (2001). Impact of length of unemployment and age on jobless men and women: A comparative analysis. *Journal of Employment Counseling, 38,* 15–27; Malen, E. A., & Stroh, L. K. (1998). The influence of gender on job loss coping behavior among unemployed managers. *Journal of Employment Counseling, 35,* 27–39; Wanberg, C. R., Watt, J. D., & Rumsey, D. J. (1996). Individuals without jobs: An empirical study of job-seeking behavior and reemployment. *Journal of Applied Psychology, 81,* 76–87.

24. Drentea, P. (1998). Consequences of women's formal and informal job search methods for employment in female-dominated jobs. *Gender & Society, 12,* 321–338; Hanson & Pratt; Huffman, M. L. & Torres, L. (2001). Job search methods: Consequences for gender-based earnings inequality. *Journal of Vocational Behavior, 58,* 127–141; Leicht, K. T., & Marx, J. (1997). The consequences of informal job finding for men and women. *Academy of Management Journal, 40,* 967–987; Mencken, F. C. & Winfield, I. (2000). Job search and sex segregation: Does sex of social contact matter? *Sex Roles, 42,* 847–864.

25. Drentea; Hanson & Pratt; Huffman & Torres; Mencken & Winfield; Straits, B. C. (1998). Occupational sex segregation: The role of personal ties. *Journal of Vocational Behavior, 52,* 191–207; Petersen, T., Saporta, I., & Seidel, M. L. (2000). Offering a job: Meritocracy and social networks. *American Journal of Sociology, 106,* 763–816.

26. Keith, K., & McWilliams, A. (1999). The return to mobility and job search by gender. *Industrial and Labor Relations Review, 52,* 460–477; Lyness, K. S., & Judiesch, M. K. (1999). Are women more likely to be hired or promoted into management positions? *Journal of Vocational Behavior, 54,* 158–173; Brett, J. M., & Stroh, L. K. (1997). Jumping ship: Who benefits from an external labor market career strategy? *Journal of Applied Psychology, 82,* 331–341; Dreher, G. F., & Cox, T. H., Jr. (2000). Labor market mobility and cash compensation: The moderating effects of race and gender. *Academy of Management Journal, 43,* 890–900.

27. Jackson, L. A., Gardner, P. D., & Sullivan, L. A. (1992). Explaining gender differences in self-pay expectations: Social comparison standards and perceptions of fair pay. *Journal of Applied Psychology, 77,* 631–663; Jackson, L. A., & Grabski, S. V. (1988). Perceptions of fair pay and the gender wage gap. *Journal of Applied Social Psychology, 18,* 606–625; Major, B., & Konar, E. (1984). An investigation of sex differences in pay expectations and their possible causes. *Academy of Management Journal, 27,* 777–792; Summers, T. P., Sightler, K. W., & Stahl, M. J. (1992). Gender differences in preference for over-reward and tolerance for over-reward. *Journal of Social Behavior and Personality, 7,* 177–188.

28. Barber, A. E., & Daly, C. L. (1996). Compensation and diversity: New pay for a new workforce? In E. E. Kossek and S. A. Lobel (Eds.), *Managing diversity: Human resource strategies for transforming the workplace* (pp. 194–216). Cambridge, MA: Blackwell; Haberfeld, Y. (1992). Pay, valence of pay and gender: A simultaneous equation model. *Journal of Economic Psychology, 13,* 93–109; Konrad, Ritchie, Lieb, & Corrigall; Major & Konar; Summers, Sightler, & Stahl; Witt, L. A., & Nye, L. G. (1992). Gender and the relationship between perceived fairness of pay or promotion and job satisfaction. *Journal of Applied Psychology, 77,* 910–917; Zanna, M. P., Crosby, F., & Lowenstein, G. (1987). Male reference groups and discontent among female professionals. In B. A. Gutek and L. Larwood (Eds.), *Women's career development* (pp. 28–41). Newbury Park, CA: Sage; McFarlin, D. B., Frone, M. R., Major, B., & Konar, E. (1989). Predicting career-entry pay expectations: The role of gender-based comparisons. *Journal of Business and Psychology, 3,* 331–340; Martin, B. A. (1989). Gender differences in salary expectations when current salary information is provided. *Psychology of Women Quarterly, 13,* 87–96.

29. Olian, J. D., Schwab, D. P., & Haberfeld, Y. (1988). The impact of gender compared to qualifications on hiring recommendations. *Organizational Behavior and Human Decision Processes, 41,* 180–195; Steinpreis, R. H., Anders, K. A., & Ritzke, D. (1999). The impact of gender on the review of the curricula vitae of job applicants and tenure candidates: A national empirical study. *Sex Roles, 41,* 509–528; Fernandez, R. M., & Weinberg, N. (1997). Sifting and sorting: Personal contacts and

hiring in a retail bank. *American Sociological Review, 62,* 883–902; Gerhart, B. (1990). Gender differences in current and starting salaries: The role of performance, college major, and job title. *Industrial and Labor Relations Review, 43,* 418–433.

30. Fernandez, R. M., Castilla, E.J., & Moore, P. (2000). Social capital at work: Networks and employment at a phone center. *American Journal of Sociology, 105,* 1288–1356; Petersen, Saporta, & Seidel.

31. Hitt, M. A., & Barr, S. H. (1989). Managerial selection decision models: Examination of configural cue processing. *Journal of Applied Psychology, 74,* 53–61; Perry, E. L., Davis-Blake, A., & Kulik, C. T. (1994). Explaining gender-based selection decisions: A synthesis of contextual and cognitive approaches. *Academy of Management Review, 19,* 786–820.

32. Graves, L. M. (1993). Sources of individual differences in interviewer effectiveness: A model and implications for future research. *Journal of Organizational Behavior, 14,* 349–370; Perry, Davis-Blake, & Kulik; Heilman, M. E. (1983). Sex bias in work settings: The lack of fit model. In L. L. Cummings & B. M. Staw (Eds.), *Research in organizational behavior: Vol. 5* (pp. 269–298). Greenwich, CT: JAI.

33. Heilman (1983); Perry, Davis-Blake, & Kulik; Glick, P. (1991). Trait-based and sex-based discrimination in occupational prestige, occupational salary, and hiring. *Sex Roles, 25,* 351–378; Cleveland & Smith; Van Vianen, A. E. M., & Willemsen, T. M. (1992). The employment interview: The role of sex stereotypes in the evaluation of male and female job applicants in the Netherlands. *Journal of Applied Social Psychology, 22,* 471–491; Pratto, F., Stallworth, L. M., Sidanius, J., & Siers, B. (1997). The gender gap in occupational role attainment: A social dominance approach. *Journal of Personality and Social Psychology, 72,* 37–53; Van Vianen, A. E. M., & Van Schie, E. C. M. (1995). Assessment of male and female behavior in the employment interview. *Journal of Community & Applied Social Psychology, 5,* 243–257.

34. Perry, Davis-Blake, & Kulik; Konrad, A. M., & Pfeffer, J. (1991). Understanding the hiring of women and minorities in educational institutions. *Sociology of Education, 64,* 141–157; Katz, D. (1987). Sex discrimination in hiring: The influence of organizational climate and need for approval on decision making. *Psychology of Women Quarterly, 11,* 11–20; Heilman, M. E. (1980). The impact of personnel decisions concerning women: Varying the sex composition of the applicant pool. *Organizational Behavior and Human Decision Processes, 26,* 386–395; Goldin, C., & Rouse, C. (2000). Orchestrating impartiality: The impact of blind auditions on female musicians. *American Economic Review, 90,* 715–741; Atwater, L. E., & Van Fleet, D. D. (1997). Another ceiling? Can males compete for traditionally female jobs? *Journal of Management, 23,* 603–626; Davison, H. K, & Burke, M. J. (2000). Sex discrimination in simulated employment contexts: A meta-analytic investigation. *Journal of Vocational Behavior, 56,* 225–248; Glick, P., Zion, C., & Nelson, C. (1988). What mediates sex discrimination in hiring decisions? *Journal of Personality and Social Psychology, 55,* 178–186; McRae, M. B. (1994). Influence of sex role stereotypes on personnel decisions of black managers. *Journal of Applied Psychology, 79,* 306–309; Perry, E. (1994). A prototype matching approach to understanding the role of applicant gender and age in the evaluation of job applicants. *Journal of Applied Social Psychology, 24,* 1433–1473; Sheets, T. L., & Bushardt, S. C. (1994). Effects of the applicant's gender-appropriateness, and qualifications and rater self-monitoring propensities on hiring decisions. *Public Personnel Management, 23,* 373–382; Zebrowitz, L. A., Tenenbaum, D. R., & Goldstein, L. H. (1991). The impact of job applicants' facial maturity, gender, and academic achievement on hiring recommendations. *Journal of Applied Social Psychology, 21,* 525–548.

35. Neumark, D., Bank, R. J., & Van Nort, K. D. (1996). Sex discrimination in restaurant hiring: An audit study. *Quarterly Journal of Economics, 111,* 915–942.

36. Ridgeway, C. L. (1991). The social construction of status value: Gender and other nominal characteristics. *Social Forces, 70,* 367–386; Jackson, L. M., Esses, V. M., & Burris, C. T. (2001). Contemporary sexism and discrimination: The importance of respect for men and women. *Personality and Social Psychology Bulletin, 27,* 48–61; Biernat, M., & Kobrynowicz, D. (1997).

Gender- and race-based standards of competence: Lower minimum standards but higher ability standards for devalued groups. *Journal of Personality and Social Psychology, 72,* 544–557.

37. Seidel, R. P., & Powell, G. N. (1983). On the campus: Matching graduates with jobs. *Personnel, 61*(4), 66–72.

38. Davison & Burke; Tosi, H. L., & Einbender, S. W. (1985). The effects of the type and amount of information in sex discrimination research: A meta-analysis. *Academy of Management Journal, 28,* 712–723; Gerhart; Nieva, V. F., & Gutek, B. A. (1981). *Women and work: A psychological perspective.* New York: Praeger; Heilman, M. E., Martell, R. F., & Simon, M. C. (1988). The vagaries of sex bias: Conditions regulating the undervaluation, equivaluation, and overvaluation of female job applicants. *Organizational Behavior and Human Decision Processes, 41,* 98–110.

39. Brewer, M. B., & Miller, N. (1984). Beyond the contact hypothesis: Theoretical perspectives on desegregation. In N. Miller & M. B. Brewer (Eds.), *Groups in contact: The psychology of desegregation* (pp. 281–301). Orlando, FL: Academic Press; Glick, Zion, & Nelson; Pratto, Stallworth, Sidanius, & Siers.

40. Perry, Davis-Blake, & Kulik; Davison & Burke.

41. Goldin & Rouse; Seltzer, G. (1989). *Music matters: The performer and the American Federation of Musicians.* Metuchen, NJ: Scarecrow.

42. Epstein, C. F. (1981). *Women in law.* New York: Basic Books; Neumark, Bank, & Van Nort.

43. Graves & Powell (1995); Graves & Powell (1996); Tsui, A. S., Egan, T. D., & O'Reilly, C. A., III. (1992). Being different: Relational demography and organizational commitment. *Administrative Sciences Quarterly, 37,* 549–579.

44. Foster, N., Dingman, S., Muscolino, J., & Jankowski, M. A. (1996). Gender in mock hiring decisions. *Psychological Reports, 79,* 275–278; Davison & Burke; Steinpreis, Anders, & Ritzke; Foschi, M., Larissa, L, & Sigerson, K. (1994). Gender and double standards in the assessment of job applicants. *Social Psychology Quarterly, 57,* 326–339; Graves & Powell (1995); Graves & Powell (1996); Ely, R. (1994). The effects of organizational demographics and social identity on relationships among professional women. *Administrative Sciences Quarterly, 39,* 203–238.

45. Simas, K., & McCarrey, M. (1979). Impact of recruiter authoritarianism and applicant sex on evaluation and selection decisions in a recruitment interview analogue study. *Journal of Applied Psychology, 64,* 483–491; Sharp, C., & Post, R. (1980). Evaluation of male and female applicants for sex-congruent and sex-incongruent jobs. *Sex Roles, 6,* 391–401; Gallois, C., Callan, V. J., & Palmer, J. M. (1992). The influence of applicant communication style and interviewer characteristics on hiring decisions. *Journal of Applied Social Psychology, 22,* 1041–1060.

46. McRae, M. B. (1991). Sex and race bias in employment decisions: Black women considered. *Journal of Employment Counseling, 28,* 91–98; Bell, E. L., Denton, T. C., & Nkomo, S. (1993). Women of color in management: Toward an inclusive analysis. In E. A. Fagenson (Ed.), *Women in management: Trends, issues, and challenges in managerial diversity* (pp. 105–130). Newbury Park, CA: Sage; Kacmar, K. M., Wayne, S. J., & Ratcliff, S H. (1994). An examination of automatic versus controlled processing in the employment interview: The case of minority applicants. *Sex Roles, 30,* 809–828; Cesare, S. J., Dalessio, A., & Tannenbaum, R. J. (1988). Contrast effects for black, white, male, and female interviewees. *Journal of Applied Social Psychology, 18,* 1261–1273.

47. Langlois, J. H., Kalakanis, L., Rubenstein, A. J., Larson, A., Hallam, M., & Smoot, M. (2000). Maxims or myths of beauty? A meta-analytic and theoretical review. *Psychological Bulletin, 126,* 390–423; Raza, S. M., & Carpenter, B. N. (1987). A model of hiring decisions in real employment interviews. *Journal of Applied Psychology, 72,* 596–603; Marlowe, C. M., Schneider, S. L., & Nelson, C. E. (1996). Gender and attractiveness biases in hiring decisions: Are more experienced managers less biased? *Journal of Applied Psychology, 81,* 11–21; Pingatore, R., Dugoni, B. L., Tindale, R. S., & Spring, B. (1994). Bias against overweight job applicants in a simulated employment interview. *Journal of Applied Psychology, 79,* 909–917.

48. Forsythe, S. M. (1990). Effects of applicant's clothing on interviewer's decision to hire. *Journal of Applied Social Psychology, 20,* 1579–1595; Forsythe, S. M. (1988). Effect of clothing

masculinity on perceptions of managerial traits: Does gender of the perceiver make a difference? *Clothing and Textiles Research Journal, 6,* 10–16.

49. Bolles, R. (2000) *What color is your parachute? A practical guide for job-hunters and career changers.* Berkeley, CA: Ten Speed Press; Konrad, Ritchie, Lieb, & Corrigall; Konrad, Corrigall, Lieb, & Ritchie.

50. Dipboye, R. L. (1992). *Selection interviews: Process perspectives.* Cincinnati, OH: Southwestern.

51. Zeitz, B., & Duffy, L. (1988). *The best companies for women.* New York: Simon & Schuster; Himelstein, L., & Forest, S. A. (1997, February 17). Breaking through. *Business Week,* 64–70.

52. Heilman (1983); Perry, Davis-Blake, & Kulik.

53. Rynes, S. L., & Boudreau, J. W. (1986). College recruiting in large organizations: Practice, evaluation, and research implications. *Personnel Psychology, 39,* 729–757.

54. Campion, M. A., Palmer, D. K., & Campion, J. E. (1997). A review of structure in the selection interview. *Personnel Psychology, 50,* 655–702; Dipboye (1992); Williamson, L. G., Campion, J. E., Malos, S. B., Roehling, M. B., & Campion, M. A. (1997). Employment interview on trial: Linking interview structure with litigation outcomes. *Journal of Applied Psychology, 82,* 900–912.

55. Rynes & Boudreau; Graves, L. M. (1989). College recruitment: Removing personal biases from selection decisions. *Personnel, 66*(3), 48–52; Perry, Davis-Blake, & Kulik; Cox, T. H, Jr., & Blake, S. (1991). Managing cultural diversity: Implications for organizational competitiveness. *Academy of Management Executive, 5*(3), 45–56.

56. Cox & Blake.

57. Duff.

5

Working in Teams

Russian space officials have only the highest praise and affection for NASA astronaut Shannon Lucid.

She's spent the past six months aboard their orbiting station and never complained aloud once, even though she's been stuck there an extra 1½ months.

Her assignment is about to end soon.

Space shuttle Atlantis was scheduled to blast off early today to go get her and drop off her replacement, astronaut John Blaha. . . .

"As far as Dr. Shannon Lucid is concerned, I would like to extend my sincerest thanks to the management of the program for making such a selection," Gen. Yuri Glazkov, deputy commander of Russia's cosmonaut training center, said Sunday. . . .

Lucid, 53, a biochemist and mother of three grown children, was supposed to return to Earth in early August. But problems with shuttle booster rockets and two hurricanes stalled Atlantis' trip to the Russian space station Mir.

Every time Lucid was notified of a shuttle delay, she took the news well. In fact, she reacted like Russian cosmonauts do when informed in orbit that their missions are being extended, said Valery Ryumin, a Russian space manager.

The Russians deliberately choose cosmonauts "who are strong enough not to show any feelings when receiving bad news," Ryumin said. "Probably they are shocked, but they never let us understand that," he added.

Lucid did everything she was asked to do aboard Mir, house-keeping included, Glazkov said. Before her flight, he said he was pleased that she was going "because we know that women love to clean."

Glazkov assured reporters Sunday that Lucid's male crew-mates did their share of cleaning, too.

—Marcia Dunn[1]

T he use of work teams is not restricted to space exploration and other extraordinary feats. In fact, many organizations now use work teams to achieve their strategic objectives. Teams produce goods and provide services, design new products, solve organizational problems, and even lead entire organizations. Teams are common across industries as diverse as health care, automobile manufacturing, financial services, and electronics. Although the extent to which teams are used is difficult to assess, estimates suggest that about 70% of *Fortune* 1000 corporations use teams and that about half of the U.S. workforce will soon be working in teams. Moreover, the proliferation of teams is not just a U.S. phenomenon. Global organizations such as IBM, Heineken, BP, and Glaxo-Wellcome use teams to achieve global efficiencies, respond to regional markets, and transfer knowledge throughout their organizations.[2]

As a result of changing workforce demographics (see Chapter 2) and the globalization of business, today's work teams are more diverse in sex, race, and nationality than ever before. What are the implications of this diversity for the effectiveness of work teams? Like U.S. Astronaut Shannon Lucid, are female team members evaluated based on gender stereotypes? Are they expected to "keep house?" What happens in "down to earth" teams? In this chapter, the effects of sex and gender on interpersonal relations in work teams, and the results they achieve, are explored.[3]

We are interested in the effects of sex and gender in both teams and working groups. A *team* is a set of individuals who perform interdependent or interconnected tasks, share responsibility for achieving results, and are viewed by themselves and others as an intact social entity. In contrast, members of a *working group* belong to the same work unit or department but work with more independence. The dynamics that we discuss in this chapter may occur in any small group of employees, whether a team or a working group. Thus, we use the two terms interchangeably throughout the chapter.[4]

There are five sections in this chapter. The initial section explores the nature of sex and gender differences within mixed-sex work teams. Does the behavior of women and men in teams mirror gender roles? The second and third sections explore how the sex composition of the team affects the experiences of male and female members and the team's effectiveness. Do women or men have a more difficult time when they are members of teams composed primarily of the opposite sex? Does diversity on the basis of sex enhance or hinder team performance? The fourth section considers how the circumstances under which mixed-sex teams operate influence their dynamics. The final section outlines the actions team members and organizations can take to ensure that mixed-sex teams are effective.

Sex and Gender Differences in Mixed-Sex Teams

This section examines how sex and gender influence members' interactions in mixed-sex teams. Although behavior in all-male teams may differ from that in all-female teams, sex and gender differences are especially important in mixed-sex teams. When women and men serve on the same team, sex serves as a basis for distinguishing between team members and influences members' interactions. Women's and men's behaviors may differ. Moreover, team members are likely to evaluate the behaviors of males and females differently. Two questions concerning sex and gender differences in mixed-sex teams are addressed below: (1) What explanations have been offered for sex and gender differences? (2) What are the actual differences in how men and women behave and are evaluated?[5]

EXPLANATIONS

Status characteristics theory and social role theory provide complementary explanations for sex and gender differences in mixed-sex teams. *Status characteristics theory* suggests that differences in women's and men's experiences in mixed-sex teams are due to differences in the social status of women and men. As noted in Chapter 4, individuals are assigned status based on their demographic characteristics. High-status individuals view themselves and are viewed by others as more competent than low-status individuals. As a result, high-status individuals are expected to perform at higher levels than low-status individuals. Because women and people of color are generally assigned lower status or worthiness in society than men and Whites, women and people of color are likely to be viewed as less competent with lower performance expectations. These expectations are reflected in group interactions such that high-status men make more task contributions, act more confidently and assertively, receive more positive feedback for their contributions, and are more influential. When low-status women violate performance expectations by making task contributions or acting confidently and assertively, their contributions are likely to be rejected.[6]

Social role theory suggests that differences in the behavior of women and men and how they are evaluated in mixed-sex teams are due to differences in their social roles. As noted in earlier chapters, women and men are typically employed in different types of jobs. Consistent with gender stereotypes, women's jobs require more expressive and subordinate behaviors (e.g., nurturing, caretaking), and men's jobs require more instrumental and dominant behaviors (e.g., leading, directing). As a result, women and men develop different skills and modify their behaviors to be consistent with gender roles. Moreover, people expect, or even demand, that women and men behave differently. Consequently, women in teams might be expected to engage in more expressive and subordinate behavior than do men, while men might be expected to engage in more instrumental and dominant behavior. As astronaut Shannon Lucid's experiences suggest, social roles influence expectations for behavior even in outer space.[7]

Thus, sex differences in status and social roles may lead team members to have very different expectations regarding the roles of women and men in work teams. Women's lower social status may limit their task contributions and assertiveness and diminish evaluations of their performance and influence in the group. Women are expected to specialize in expressive and subordinate roles while men focus on instrumental and dominant roles.[8]

Of course, sex and gender differences do not occur universally and may depend on the overall characteristics of team members and the nature of their task. Each team member's status and subsequent behaviors are based on a broad set of characteristics (e.g., sex, race, age, organizational rank, ability, work experience). If a highly experienced female executive is teamed with an inexperienced male staff accountant, the female executive will probably have higher status than the male accountant by virtue of her experience and organizational rank. Thus, the woman is likely to exhibit high-status behaviors and the man low-status behaviors.[9]

The experiences of male and female team members also depend on the team's task. When the task is one that is typically performed by men, men are awarded higher status, presumed to be more competent, and expected to engage in more instrumental behavior than women. However, if the task is typically performed by women, women are awarded higher status, presumed to have more expertise, and expected to engage in more instrumental behavior. If the task is not clearly associated with men or women, team members' perceptions of the relative status and expertise of males and females are based on societal beliefs concerning the status of two sexes. In the United States, men are viewed as higher in status and competence.[10]

DIFFERENCES

We now consider research evidence on sex and gender differences in mixed-sex teams. Researchers have looked primarily at differences in (1) women's and men's behavior and (2) evaluations of women's and men's performance, influence, and leadership. Much of this research has been conducted on groups of students who met for brief periods of time in laboratory settings. These conditions increase the likelihood of sex and gender differences. Sex and gender differences in ongoing teams in real organizations may be less than those revealed in laboratory studies.[11]

Behavior. Research on sex differences in behavior in teams has focused on both the style and the content of communications. In communication style, two dimensions of behavior appear to be important: (1) self-assertion and dominance and (2) deference and warmth. In general, men display more self-assertion and dominance and women display more deference and warmth. Men talk more, are more powerful and authoritarian, and display more visual dominance (i.e., more eye contact while talking and less eye contact while listening). In contrast, women talk less, are more deferent and warm (e.g., they smile more and lean toward others), and display less visual dominance. As predicted by status characteristics theory, these differences are most likely to occur when the team's task is male-intensive or sex-neutral.[12]

With respect to the content of communication, research focuses on sex differences in task and social behaviors. *Task* (or *instrumental*) *behaviors* contribute directly to the group's task. *Social* (or *expressive*) *behaviors* help maintain the morale and interpersonal relations among team members. In task groups, both women and men devote most of their interactions to task-related communications. About two thirds of women's and three quarters of men's communications are task-related; men devote a somewhat higher percentage of their communications to task behavior and women display a higher percentage of positive social behaviors. These differences may occur because women engage in more socially-oriented behavior than men in general. Women's emphasis on social behaviors in teams is consistent with their desire for positive interpersonal relationships in their jobs (see Chapter 4). Women, more than men, view their teams as families or communities where members nurture and support one another.[13]

Research on sex differences in communication behavior in work teams has focused on the behaviors of White males and females and may not apply to all cultural groups. For example, among Asians of equal status, high levels of self-assertion and dominance are not socially acceptable, perhaps due to Asian cultural values of modesty, self-effacement, and interpersonal harmony. Neither Asian men nor women are likely to display much self-assertion and dominance in a team setting. In addition, there may be few sex differences in communication behaviors among U.S. Blacks. Because Black women have traditionally filled the dual social roles of homemaker and employee, their communication behaviors may not differ substantially from those of Black men. In mixed-race teams, the lower status of people of color in many societies may lead them to engage in low-status behaviors (e.g., deference, low levels of task behavior) regardless of their sex. White team members also may expect people of color to conform to roles dictated by the stereotypes of their particular race and gender groups. For example, Asian women may be expected to play the role of "timid Asian flowers" and Black women may be expected to be "aggressive, Black female mamas."[14]

Evaluations of performance, influence, and leadership. Researchers have also examined differences in evaluations of the performance, influence, and leadership of women and men in mixed-sex teams. Consistent with sex differences in societal status and roles, team members evaluate men's task contributions more positively than women's contributions. Women may even devalue their own performances. Moreover, team members use a higher standard to judge women. Women thus must provide more evidence of their abilities to be seen as competent.[15]

Men have more influence in mixed-sex teams than women. This is not surprising given men's displays of dominance, greater relative proportion of task behavior, and perceived greater competence. In fact, women's influence attempts are ignored. One study of simulated jury decision making found that unique information (i.e., that possessed by a single group member) influenced the group 72% of the time when it was introduced by a man but only 13% of the time when introduced by a woman! Further, women in mixed-sex teams tend to be more easily influenced than men, perhaps because their lower status and less favorable self-evaluations lessen their confidence in their own views.[16]

Men are also more likely than women to emerge as informal leaders in mixed-sex groups that have no assigned leaders. Researchers have measured task leadership, social leadership, and general leadership, in which the exact nature of the leadership behavior is unspecified. Consistent with the explanations outlined above, men are more likely to emerge as general leaders and task leaders than women, and less likely to emerge as social leaders. However, the tendency for men to emerge as general leaders is reduced for tasks that are female-intensive or for tasks that demand longer or more social interaction.[17]

Sex differences in informal leadership may reflect sex differences in gender identity. Masculine and, perhaps, androgynous individuals are most likely to emerge as leaders. This is not surprising because stereotypes of leadership emphasize masculine instrumental behaviors (see Chapter 6). The preference for masculine leaders may result in fewer leadership opportunities for women, who typically are seen as less masculine than are men. However, men who do not display assertive masculine behaviors (e.g., deferential Asian males) also may be excluded from leadership roles.[18]

Women cannot increase evaluations of their competence, influence, and leadership in mixed-sex teams simply by behaving like men. Confident, assertive women are less influential than confident, assertive men. In fact, confident, assertive women may be even less influential than nonassertive women, especially among male team members. Men are *more* influenced by women who use tentative language (e.g., hedges, disclaimers, tag questions) or who express support for the feminine gender role than they are influenced by women who use assertive language or reject the feminine gender role. In contrast, women are more likely to be influenced by assertive or nontraditional women. Confident, assertive women are also often viewed by their teammates as less likeable than confident, assertive men. Nonetheless, assertive women can attain influence and acceptance if they combine assertive behaviors with expressions of interpersonal warmth and a desire to cooperate with the group. Women must be "friendly and nice" in their influence attempts and demonstrate that they care for the good of the group. Such behavior is not required of men.[19]

In summary, sex and gender differences in mixed-sex teams are consistent with differences in the status and social roles assigned to women and men. Women are less assertive, engage less in task behavior and more in social behavior, are evaluated more negatively, and exercise less influence and leadership than men in mixed-sex groups. Women who attempt to increase their influence by behaving like men encounter roadblocks.

Are women really as marginalized in mixed-sex teams as the evidence suggests? Probably not. First, sex differences in communication behaviors and evaluations of competence, influence, and leadership are reduced when team members receive task-related training or have information about the relative competence or organizational rank of team members. In these circumstances, members' behaviors and evaluations reflect their relative abilities, not their sex. Second, research findings may be a function of the use of student samples in experimental studies in which strangers interacted for brief periods of time and had little information about one another. Because stereotyping is most likely to occur when individuals have little information about one another, these findings probably overstate the extent to which sex differences occur. In real teams, members typically possess much more information about one another (e.g., organizational rank, age, expertise, function, etc.), thereby reducing the likelihood that gender stereotypes are used.[20]

Influence of Team Composition on Individual Members

An individual's experience in a team is not a function simply of his or her sex, but is also determined by the sex composition of the team. In her autobiography, Katharine Graham powerfully demonstrates the effects of team composition on individuals. As publisher of the *Washington Post,* Graham was for many years the only woman member of a trade group. When the group met, there was always self-consciousness about Graham's presence. Group members routinely began their comments, accompanied by snickers, with statements such as "Lady and Gentlemen," or "Gentlemen and Mrs. Graham." Graham noted, "It made me extremely uncomfortable, and I longed to be omitted, or at least not singled out."[21]

This section explores how team composition affects women's and men's experiences as team members. For instance, like Katharine Graham, do individuals in teams have more negative experiences when members of their sex are in the minority? Are women who are in the minority (e.g., the only female in a team of engineers) more likely to have negative experiences than men who are in the minority (e.g., the only male in a team of nurses)? First, we examine possible explanations for the effects of the sex composition of the team on male and female team members. Next, we review research evidence on the actual effects of team composition on males and females. Throughout the section, we consider the effect of the team's sex composition on two different individual outcomes: attachment or attraction to the team and task performance.[22]

EXPLANATIONS

There are two competing views concerning the effects of team composition on women and men.[23] One view suggests that the effects of team composition are similar for men and women; the other view suggests that these effects differ for women and men.

According to the first view, both women and men have negative experiences when they are in teams comprised primarily of members of the opposite sex, and their experiences improve as the representation of women and men on the team becomes more equal. In Chapter 4, we noted that sex similarity between the recruiter and applicant may lead each party to evaluate the other more favorably. In the same vein, sex similarity among team members may lead to perceived similarity in attitudes and values and foster openness, trust, and reciprocity. Same-sex team members have more frequent and higher quality interactions and higher levels of interpersonal attraction than do opposite-sex team members. Team members evaluate the competence and performance of same-sex others more highly and may ultimately create more opportunities for same-sex others to contribute to the group's task. As the proportion of women in a group increases, women experience increased attachment to the group and higher levels of performance. Men's levels of attachment and task performance also increase as the proportion of men in the group increases.[24]

When a team is comprised of a clear numerical majority of one sex, the majority has few interactions with the minority and exhibits prejudice and discrimination toward them. In contrast, when a group is made up of a more equal representation of both sexes, the majority finds it difficult to avoid interacting with the minority. Members of the majority begin to view members of the minority as individuals rather than simply as representatives of their sex, resulting in a reduction of prejudice and discrimination toward the minority.[25]

Rosabeth Kanter examined the effects of the team's sex composition on individuals in work groups. Based on her observation of male-female work relationships in a large industrial corporation, she identified four types of groups. *Uniform* groups of all males or all females represent one extreme. By definition, there are no male-female issues in uniform groups. *Balanced* groups of approximately equal numbers of women and men, represent the other extreme. Attributes other than sex influence how individuals interact in balanced groups.[26]

Between these two extremes are skewed and tilted groups. *Skewed* groups have a ratio of one sex to another ranging from about 85:15 to almost 100:0. Members of the sex in abundance in skewed groups are "dominants," because they control the group and its culture. Members of the other sex are "tokens," because they are viewed as representatives of their sex rather than as individuals. *Tilted* groups have less abundance of one sex with the ratio ranging from about 65:35 to about 85:15. In tilted groups, dominants become a majority and tokens a minority. Minority members may become allies and have more effect on group culture in tilted than in skewed groups. They are distinguishable from each other, as well as from the majority type.

Kanter's primary interest was in the experiences of tokens in skewed groups. Kanter chose the term "tokens" for the underrepresented members in a skewed group to highlight the special characteristics associated with that position. Tokens exist only in small numbers, and the rest of the group sees them as representing their sex, whether or not they want to. A token rarely becomes "just another member of the group." Tokens receive special treatment that is detrimental to their performance in, and attachment to, the group in several ways. First, tokens face performance pressures. Because they are highly visible, they get attention that dominants do not. This does not necessarily lead to recognition of their competence; tokens may have to work harder to get their accomplishments recognized. Second, differences between tokens and dominants tend to be exaggerated. Dominants emphasize what they have in common and exclude tokens from social activities. Third, the characteristics of tokens are often distorted or misperceived because of the dominants' tendency to stereotype them. Tokens are expected to behave in a manner consistent with the stereotype of their sex or risk rejection by the team. Although Kanter based her conclusions about the effects of sex composition on analysis of an environment in which men vastly outnumbered women in positions of authority, she assumed that her notions would apply equally to women in male-intensive groups and to men in female-intensive groups.

The second view suggests that the effects of team composition are not identical for men and women. Interactions in mixed-sex teams are driven by individuals' desires to maintain positive self-concepts. According to *social identity theory,* each team member possesses a social identity based on his or her social category memberships (e.g., sex, race, gender, profession, religion, age) and his or her personal attributes (e.g., personality, abilities). Team members categorize themselves and other team members based on multiple social categories (e.g., Asian female clerical worker, Black male engineer). Once team members categorize one another, they identify with and favor individuals who are like themselves.[27]

Sex is especially likely to serve as the basis for categorization and identification; sex is a highly visible and well-learned dimension of diversity. When sex-based categorization occurs, team members may identify with and exhibit positive attitudes and behaviors toward same-sex others. However, the relative status of women and men also affects the social identification process. Because individuals seek to maintain a positive social identity, individuals who belong to low-status groups (e.g., women) sometimes distance themselves from their own group and identify with the high-status group (e.g., men). When women have low status in the organization, both women and men identify with and exhibit favoritism toward men. As a result of this pro-male bias, men have more opportunities to contribute to the team, regardless of which sex is in the majority.[28]

How do social identification processes influence women's and men's attachment to their groups? Men may have low levels of attachment when they are in the numerical minority because they feel that association with lower-status, lower-paid females threatens their own status. In contrast, women in a predominantly male group may feel that association with higher-status, higher-paid males enhances their own status. However, women could experience low levels of attachment when in the minority because the feminine gender role leads to questions about whether they even belong in the workplace. Men's presence in the workplace is more taken for granted.[29]

In addition, competition between women and men for political and economic power may influence behavior in teams. Because men generally control societal resources and particularly value power and authority (see Chapter 4), they may feel that their power is threatened when the percentage of women in the group begins to grow. When the proportion of women in the group is very small, men may perceive little threat from the presence of women and will not challenge them. However, when the percentage of women in the group increases, relations between women and men may deteriorate. Men may exhibit more prejudice and discrimination toward female group members, which jeopardizes women's performance and attachment to the group. Women in the majority may feel less threatened by increasing proportions of males in teams because they place less value on having power and authority.[30]

In sum, there are two different views of the effects of team composition on male and female team members. One suggests that the effects of team composition are similar for men and women and that being in the minority has negative implications for both sexes. The second view suggests that the effects of team composition are not necessarily identical for males and females but depend on the relative social and economic status of each. This view suggests that being in the minority is especially detrimental for low-status team members, typically women. However, having high status may not completely protect team members from the negative effects of being in the minority; high-status men who are members of teams comprised primarily of low-status females may dislike their teams if they believe that their own status is compromised by association with low-status females. Although these two views offer divergent predictions, they generally suggest that being in the numerical minority in a mixed-sex team is not a favorable experience for either women or men.

EXPERIENCES

The publication of Kanter's work in the late 1970s sparked a steady stream of research on the effects of team composition on individuals' experiences in groups. Field studies conducted in the 1970s and 1980s generally found that the effects of being in the minority were different for women and men. Token women experienced increased visibility, social isolation, and stereotyping, especially in male-intensive settings such as the military, law enforcement, and medicine. However, token men in female-intensive settings such as nursing, teaching, and social work did not experience the same negative consequences of numerical imbalance as token women. The visibility that token men received worked to their advantage. For example, a study of police patrol teams and hospital nursing units found that token female police officers reacted with annoyance or resignation to their increased visibility, whereas token male nurses enjoyed the extra attention. Most token male nurses felt that patients attributed a higher status to them than to female nurses, even when they identified themselves as nurses and not physicians. Most also thought that physicians took them more seriously and gave more responsibility to them than to female nurses. On the other hand, 42% of the token female police officers felt that they were the "black sheep" of their teams.[31]

Is being in the minority still more detrimental to women than men? Recent studies of the effect of team composition on individuals' attraction to the teams have yielded highly variable results. Generally, being different from one's teammates has either a detrimental effect or no effect on attraction to the team. As the proportion of team members who are of the same sex as the individual declines, the individual's attraction to the team either declines or remains unchanged. However, the effect of team composition on attraction is not always identical for women and men. In some instances, women suffer more from being different, and, in others, men are more disadvantaged. For example, a study of white-collar workers found that women, but not men, who were in the minority had fewer interactions with members of their work groups. Women in the minority who had higher-status jobs than those of the men in their groups were especially likely to be isolated. Thus, high status did not alleviate the effect of being in the minority; it made it worse. In contrast, a study of symphony orchestras found that men were more sensitive to the effects of team composition. Men's attitudes toward the orchestra (e.g., integrity of orchestra as an ensemble, player involvement) declined sharply as the proportion of women in the orchestra increased; women's views changed very little as the sex composition of the orchestra changed.[32]

The effect of team composition on individual performance as rated by others is different for women and men. Being in the minority is clearly detrimental to women's performance ratings. In contrast, being in the minority may enhance men's performance evaluations. For example, a survey of MBA alumni 14 months after graduation found that men who were dissimilar to their work groups were more likely to have been promoted than dissimilar women or than women and men who were similar to their groups. However, the reverse may be true for individuals' self-evaluations. Men, but not women, view their own competence and creativity less favorably when they are dissimilar to their groups.[33]

In summary, the effects of team composition on women's and men's experiences as team members are quite complex. Dissimilarity between the sex of the individual and the sex composition of the team appears to have either no effect or a negative effect on attachment. Recent research findings are ambiguous concerning whether women or men are less attached to their team when in the minority. Women in the minority receive lower performance evaluations from others than do men in the minority, whereas the opposite is true for self-evaluations. These findings, with the findings of earlier research, mostly support the view that team composition has different effects on women and men. However, the inconsistent nature of the recent findings suggests that the effects of team composition cannot be predicted solely by looking at the numbers of women and men on a team. To fully understand the effects of team composition on individuals, we need to consider the situation in which the team operates. The effects of situational factors are discussed later in the chapter. We next consider how the composition of the team influences its effectiveness.

Influence of Team Composition on Team Effectiveness

The question of whether all-male or all-female teams perform better was the focus of much early research. Generally, the results of these studies suggest that all-male teams perform better than all-female teams. However, all-male teams are better at activities that require a high amount of task behavior, such as brainstorming and generating solutions to a problem. In contrast, all-female teams are better at activities that call for a high amount of social behavior, such as reaching a consensus on the best solution. Women's positive social behaviors, including friendliness and agreement with others, facilitate performance on such activities. These findings are consistent with the sex differences in communication behavior reviewed earlier in the chapter.[34]

However, such research has little practical value today. Same-sex teams are less common now than in the past. Creating all-female or all-male teams is not feasible given the diversity of today's workforce, and managers who attempt to do so will be vulnerable to charges of discrimination. Moreover, assigning all-female and all-male teams to different types of activities is not likely to be effective. The work requirements of real teams (e.g., developing global business strategy or a new product) cannot be easily divided into those demanding task activity and those demanding interpersonal savvy. In addition, real teams interact over extended periods of time, increasing the importance of interpersonal relationships among members. Poor relationships decrease members' attraction to the team and increase the likelihood that they will choose to leave the team.[35]

Understanding the effects of diversity on the effectiveness of mixed-sex teams is of greater practical importance in today's increasingly diverse organizations. Not surprisingly, there are two different views of the general effect of diversity on team effectiveness. One suggests that diversity reduces team effectiveness. According to this view, the effects of similarity and social identification outlined earlier in the chapter cause team members to reject those who are different from themselves. In diverse teams, this leads to the creation of factions (e.g., men vs. women, Asians vs. Whites vs. Blacks, older members vs. younger members), conflict, and communication problems. Ultimately, the performance of the group is impaired and members' satisfaction with and commitment to the group is reduced.[36]

The second view suggests that diversity enhances team effectiveness. In diverse teams, members have different experiences, values, attitudes, and cognitive approaches. They bring varied knowledge and perspectives to the team's task, which will enhance the team's creativity and problem-solving ability. The positive impact of diversity is especially likely to occur on complex tasks such as new-product design and innovation, which require multiple perspectives and varied knowledge. The benefits of diversity also may extend to member attraction to the team. Greater diversity increases the amount of interaction between the two sexes over time and decreases prejudice and discrimination based on sex. This process improves relations among team members and increases member attachment to the team.[37]

Which of these two views better describes what actually occurs in mixed-sex teams? Increasing the sex diversity of the team appears to reduce member attraction to the team. Greater diversity is associated with decreased levels of team cohesion and satisfaction and increased member turnover in settings as varied as hospitals, grocery stores, symphony orchestras, and universities. However, increasing the sex diversity of the team does not influence managers' perceptions of team processes and performance. If diverse teams perform better or worse than homogeneous teams, it is not evident in managers' ratings. In team members' assessments of their own processes and performance, increasing sex diversity has either a negative effect or no effect. Several studies in male-intensive settings (e.g., a predominantly White male state regulatory agency, an elite management school, household moving firms) found that increased sex diversity led to declines in the quality of working relationships and team effectiveness. Other studies in varied settings found that the sex composition of the team was unrelated to members' perceptions of the amount of conflict in the team, the quality of members' interactions, the extent to which the team's interactions supported innovation, and team effectiveness.[38]

Thus, the negative interpersonal dynamics created by sex diversity impair relationships between team members and may even jeopardize team processes and performance. Despite the fact that recent findings are inconsistent, they provide little support for the view that sex diversity enhances team effectiveness. The negative interactions produced by diversity appear to counteract the benefits of having multiple perspectives on the team's task. It is also possible that women and men do not bring different perspectives to the tasks assigned to most work teams. If this is the case, then increasing diversity is unlikely to increase performance.[39]

In conclusion, research on the effects of team composition on team effectiveness provides few firm answers. Early studies suggested that all-male teams perform better than all-female teams. However, all-male teams are better when the task requires high levels of instrumental activity, and all-female teams are better when the task demands high levels of social activity. As noted earlier, this finding has little practical value in today's organizations. How does increasing the sex diversity of a team influence its effectiveness? Although research findings are inconsistent, sex diversity appears to offer few benefits and has the potential to hinder team effectiveness. As teams become more diverse, team performance and team member satisfaction may decline.

The Importance of Situational Factors

Mixed-sex teams are susceptible to serious problems. Women's task contributions may be ignored or devalued, and women and men in the numerical minority may suffer. Also, the effectiveness of the team may decline as its diversity increases. However, these negative consequences are not inevitable. If the conditions under which mixed-sex teams operate de-emphasize the importance of sex as a component of members' identities or create equality between the sexes, negative outcomes may be averted. Several situational factors appear to be important, including characteristics of the team other than its sex composition, the nature of the task, the demographic composition of the organization and its senior officials, the organizational culture, and the societal culture.

The team's overall demographic composition affects interactions among members. The number of subgroups (e.g., young Black males, young White males, young Asian females, middle-aged White females, middle-aged White males) in a mixed-sex team may vary. When there are many subgroups, the sex composition of the team has little effect on outcomes. For example, a team comprised of a 40-year-old White male engineer, a 65-year-old Black female engineer, a 45-year-old Asian male sales representative, and a 20-year-old White female sales representative theoretically could form subgroups based on age, race, occupation, or sex. Because forming subgroups based on any one category (e.g., sex) would lead to differences within the subgroup on other categories (e.g., race, occupation, age), subgroup formation is not likely. However, in a team composed of 2 middle-aged White male engineers and 2 young Black female sales representatives, sex is highly related to age, race, and occupation. There are only two possible subgroups in this team, increasing the likelihood of negative effects.[40]

The team's longevity is critical. As team members interact over extended periods of time, they gain additional information about one another and stereotyping is reduced. Team members may come to see a given female member as "a member of the team" rather than as "a woman." Relationships between members are then formed based on similarity of underlying attitudes, values, and beliefs rather than sex similarity. The greater the team's longevity, the less important its sex composition. However, a great deal of longevity is needed to eliminate the effects of sex composition. According to a study of teams in hospitals and grocery stores, the negative effects of sex diversity disappear only when the average longevity of team members is 3 or more years.[41]

Tasks that are sex-neutral and require cooperation among team members may reduce the negative consequences of diversity in mixed-sex teams. Tasks that are not associated exclusively with women or men and do not create political divisions based on sex should reduce attention to sex differences. In contrast, tasks that are typically performed by members of one sex or the other (e.g., nursing, policing) or create coalitions based on sex (e.g., developing affirmative action plans) increase the likelihood of sex-based categorization. In addition, tasks that require cooperation among team members may be beneficial. When team members must work jointly to achieve collective goals and rewards, they are motivated to form accurate, rather than stereotypical, impressions of one another. Moreover, when cooperation leads the team to form a "team identity" (i.e., view themselves as a team), members categorize themselves as a single group rather than as males and females.[42]

The use of electronic communication media (e.g., e-mail, group decision-making software) also may reduce the extent to which sex-based categorization occurs. Sex differences in evaluations and influence disappear when group members interact electronically. The benefits of electronic exchanges occur even when individuals are aware of the sex of each group member. Electronic exchanges may allow group members to focus on the content of the arguments rather than the individuals who make them. Like the screens used in blind auditions for orchestra positions (see Chapter 4), electronic communication reduces the attention paid to the sex of the participant. The use of electronic media may benefit women more than men. Women appear to experience stronger feelings of inclusion and support in mixed-sex electronic teams than do men. Women in all-female electronic teams are more satisfied than are men in all-male electronic teams. Women's electronic teams engage in higher levels of self-disclosure and agreement, and men's electronic teams display more conflict (i.e., abusive language) and less willingness to change their minds. Perhaps women's relatively greater focus on interpersonal relations enhances their experiences in electronic teams.[43]

The demographic composition of the larger organization also affects relationships between men and women in teams. Sex differences may be less important in organizations where there is a great deal of sex diversity than in organizations where there is little. In highly integrated organizations, team members should be accustomed to differences in sex and should not use sex as the basis for categorization. Moreover, the relative levels of sex and racial integration in an organization may determine whether sex or race is more important to team members. Many organizations have higher levels of sex integration than racial integration. In such organizations, sex differences appear to have much less effect on team members than racial differences, perhaps because sex differences are less noticeable.[44]

Negative outcomes also may be less likely to occur in female-intensive than male-intensive organizations. In female-intensive organizations, increasing sex diversity means that males are added to female teams. In male-intensive organizations, the reverse is true. Because females are more likely to welcome the addition of males to their teams than males are to welcome the addition of females to their teams, increasing diversity may be less problematic in female-intensive organizations.[45]

Further, the sex composition of the organization's senior management affects team members' interactions by determining the relative status of women and men. When women work in organizations with few women in key roles, they are more likely to invoke gender stereotypes, devalue their own abilities, demonstrate less interest in participating in organizational activities, and compete with their female peers. In such organizations, female team members behave as inferiors and male team members behave as superiors. In contrast, when women and men share power at the top of the organization, status differences between women and men in the team should be eliminated or reduced. Although being in the minority still might have a negative effect on women or men, such effects should be lessened by the relative equality of the two sexes.[46]

The organization's culture, especially its values regarding cooperation and diversity, is an important influence on outcomes in mixed-sex teams. Organizations that encourage individuals to focus on their common interests and goals rather than on their demographic differences reduce the deleterious effects of sex diversity. One study assigned diverse teams of MBA students to organizations that had either individualistic (e.g., individual performance valued, individual rewards) or cooperative (e.g., teamwork valued, team-oriented rewards) values. The students who were the most different from their team-mates with respect to sex, race, and nationality combined had fewer interactions with others, regardless of the culture of the organization. They did, however, experience more positive conflict (i.e., conflict over ideas) and more creativity in the cooperative organization than the individualistic organization. This study suggests that an organizational culture that emphasizes cooperation may lessen some of the negative effects of diversity and perhaps even increase the likelihood that diversity enhances performance.[47]

Organizations that have positive diversity cultures also reduce the likelihood of negative consequences in mixed-sex teams. In a *positive diversity culture*, organizational members value efforts to increase the representation of women, people of color, and individuals with disabilities, and view members of these groups as qualified. Equality is stressed, and differences in status based on sex, race, and disability are reduced. Further, in a positive diversity culture, employees acknowledge differences among women and among men, as well as between women and men. Recognition that individual differences are present within each sex allows team members to view each other as distinct persons, not just as representatives of the two sexes. Moreover, organizations that regard the insights, skills, and experiences of individuals from different backgrounds as valuable business resources create a particularly productive environment for diverse teams. In such settings, the input of each individual is valued and respected because of, rather than in spite of, his or her background. We will discuss how organizations can create a positive diversity culture in Chapter 9.[48]

Finally, the societal culture may affect a mixed-sex team. Although there have been few comparisons of mixed-sex teams across cultures, data collected from members of symphony orchestras in Germany are instructive. Women make up a very small proportion of symphony musicians in Germany. Members of symphonies located in the former East Germany believe that male and female orchestra members support one another and work together to achieve common goals. In contrast, in the former West Germany, there is substantial tension over the integration of women into orchestras, and the musicians believe that male and female musicians are treated differently. What might account for this difference? Prior to the unification of Germany, East German women had high rates of workforce participation, and West

German women had very low rates. Differences in societal norms concerning women's participation in the workforce may have led to the disparity in the acceptance of female musicians. As a result, a female in the minority in a symphony in the former West Germany may have many more negative experiences than a female in the minority in a symphony in the former East Germany.[49]

In conclusion, mixed-sex teams experience fewer difficulties when the characteristics of the team, task, organization, and society de-emphasize sex differences and promote equality between the sexes. The negative effects of sex diversity are minimized when extremely diverse teams with significant longevity work together. Tasks that require the cooperation of team members or allow electronic interactions reduce the extent to which sex is an important social category in teams. Finally, mixed-sex teams are likely to encounter fewer problems in organizations, and even in societies, with cooperative, egalitarian values and high levels of sex integration in the workplace.

Making Mixed-Sex Teams Work

We have suggested that mixed-sex teams may experience serious difficulties that impair individual and team effectiveness. Mixed-sex teams, however, are an unavoidable feature of today's workplace. How can organizations ensure that mixed-sex teams are effective? Organizations must create a working environment where all individuals thrive, regardless of sex, race, and other demographic characteristics. As noted above, this environment should include integration of members of both sexes at all levels of the organization, a positive diversity culture, and cooperative values. These conditions create a firm foundation for the work of diverse teams. Team managers and members also need to take action to ensure that mixed-sex teams are effective, whatever the working environment outside of the team.

PROACTIVE MANAGERS

Teamwork is never easy. Some estimates suggest that 7 out of 10 teams fail to achieve the desired results. To ensure team effectiveness, managers must pay attention to the design and development of teams. Throwing a team together and then ignoring it will sabotage any team, even a homogeneous team. Given the difficulties associated with mixed-sex teams, the need for managers to be proactive in designing and developing such teams is intensified. Managers must carefully design mixed-sex teams, train team members, help them get to know one another, and provide ongoing support.[50]

With respect to the design of the team, managers should address three questions: (1) Who will be on the team? (2) How will the task be structured? (3) How will performance be measured and rewarded? In choosing team members, managers should strive for teams that are diverse on a number of demographic characteristics. It is best if demographic characteristics result in numerous subgroups (e.g., women and men, Latinos and Asians, accountants and engineers) with overlapping memberships. Individuals will belong to and identify with many different subgroups, thereby reducing the likelihood of divisions along sex or any other single dimension. Moreover, differences in the organizational status of team members should be minimized, especially if organizational rank is related to sex or some other demographic characteristic. Women's task contributions are likely to be impaired if they have lower organizational status than men. However, managers must achieve a delicate balance between choosing team members for their demographic characteristics and choosing them for their skills. Selecting team members based solely on sex or another visible characteristic may cause more harm than good. When a woman is chosen because of her sex, both the woman and her teammates will question her skills and expertise. Thus, skills and expertise must not be subordinate to demographic characteristics in team formation.[51]

What expertise should managers look for in choosing team members? They must consider whether potential team members have the necessary technical knowledge, skills, and abilities to accomplish the task. They should also select individuals with values and skills that are conducive to teamwork. Individuals who value collaboration over competition and gain pleasure from the achievements of others will be better team players than those who only value competition and personal achievement. Interpersonal skills, such as the abilities to communicate and to resolve differences, are also critical because demographic differences may lead to antagonism in diverse teams.[52]

Once the manager has decided who will be on the team, he or she must consider the task structure, task assignments, and the performance measurement and reward system. Where possible, tasks should be structured to require high levels of cooperation among team members. When group members are dependent on each other and have to make mutual adjustments, they gain valuable experience working together and are less likely to engage in stereotyping. Depending on the task, giving team members access to electronic decision-making software may facilitate the participation of all members. Managers should also ensure that task assignments are not based on the sex of team members. If women and men are assigned tasks consistent with gender stereotypes and roles, sex differences in members' experiences will be accentuated. Rotation of tasks among team members will ensure that tasks are not linked exclusively to one sex and will develop team members for future roles. Finally, goals, performance measurement, and rewards should be determined for the entire team. Encouraging people to cooperate but then assessing and rewarding individual performance does not work. When only individual accomplishment is rewarded, team members have little incentive to cooperate with one another.[53]

It is critical that team members receive training on how to deal with behavioral issues that arise in teams. Because teamwork does not come naturally to many individuals, especially those from individualistic cultures, team members must learn to cooperate with one another. Training in the areas of communication, conflict management, and decision making is valuable. Teams might learn structured decision rules that bring order to team discussions and give all team members a chance to participate. Exposure to electronic decision-making software that allows group members to discuss issues anonymously might also be of value. In addition, team members should be trained to observe and evaluate their own processes. This is particularly important in diverse groups because the lack of interpersonal attraction makes interaction more difficult. Being skilled in process observation will help teams correct problems before there are major breakdowns in team functioning.[54]

Team members should also receive diversity training. Diversity training should make individuals aware of gender stereotypes and the potential effects of these stereotypes on members' interactions. All team members should receive training, not just women or just men. Women can be coached to increase their task contributions and men to elicit and consider women's contributions. Moreover, all team members should be made aware of the possible negative effects of sex dissimilarity on interpersonal liking and performance. Team members can be taught techniques to reduce the lack of interpersonal attraction created by sex dissimilarity. For example, self-disclosure (the sharing of appropriate personal information) tends to create openness, trust, and ease of communication. We will discuss diversity training further in Chapter 9.[55]

Once the team has been designed and members have been trained, the manager should help team members get acquainted so that interactions are based on individuals' underlying attributes, not their sex. When the team is formed, the qualifications and achievements of all group members should be publicized. Identifying the expertise of team members in a formal written communication will prevent team members from making erroneous assumptions about each others' qualifications based on sex. Managers also may provide informal opportunities for team members to interact, such as lunches and other social events. They may also facilitate the exchange of information about personal interests (e.g., hobbies, travel) to help team members identify what they have in common.

As the team tackles its task, the manager must provide ongoing support to the team. The manager should regularly assess the team's effectiveness. The manager can attend meetings and monitor the team's short- and long-term accomplishments. The manager may also administer a team survey that measures how well the team is managing its interpersonal processes. One such survey measures the extent to which diverse teams exclude members, fail to manage differences in perspectives, experience miscommunication and misunderstanding, and treat individuals differently based on sex or race. Managers might use such a survey to identify problems in mixed-sex teams and then to work with team members to develop and implement solutions in a supportive manner.[56]

RESPONSIBLE TEAM MEMBERS

Building effective mixed-sex teams is not only a managerial responsibility. Each team member, male and female, must take responsibility for making the team work. Other than seeking appropriate training, what can team members do? As a first step, each individual must develop an understanding of his or her own social identity. Each team member might ask himself or herself the following questions: (1) What social categories do I use to describe myself and others? (2) How important is each of these categories to my identity? (3) How do I behave toward individuals who are of the opposite sex (or a different race, profession, etc.)? (4) How do I feel about myself when I am in the presence of members of the opposite sex (or a different race, profession, etc.)? (5) How are others' behaviors toward me influenced by my sex (race, profession, etc.)? Answering such questions will give individuals some idea of which social categories are most important to them and how these social categories affect their interactions with others.[57]

Second, team members must hone their ability to evaluate the behaviors of their teammates. Most people are not good at understanding the causes of others' behaviors and are even worse when they evaluate those who are different from them. To address this problem, team members' evaluations of other members' behaviors should be based on careful, repeated observations. Quick judgments, which are likely to be based on gender stereotypes, are to be avoided. Team members also may check the accuracy of their evaluations by comparing them with those of others.[58]

Third, team members should build relationships with other team members. People sometimes feel awkward and uncomfortable working with the opposite sex. To overcome this discomfort, team members should identify common interests that provide a basis for relating. Such interests can be identified through informal conversation about nonwork topics. Observing a teammate's office area (e.g., pictures, plaques, coffee mug) can offer useful clues about his or her interests (e.g., alma mater, travel destinations, family, hobbies) and provide a good starting point for conversation. Identifying common interests eases interactions, contributes to the development of relationships, and, ultimately, reduces stereotyping. Team members also may benefit by sharing appropriate personal information with other team members. As noted earlier, self-disclosure by one team member is likely to lead to self-disclosure by other team members and create an environment of openness and trust.[59]

Fourth, members of skewed or tilted teams need to ensure that both male and female members are fully integrated into the team. Members of the numerical majority should be especially careful to avoid the exclusion of those in the minority. A team member can be assigned to monitor member participation and ensure that all team members have an equal opportunity to contribute. Moreover, members of the majority should include those in the minority in social activities and make them feel welcome.

Those who are in the minority need to take responsibility for their roles in the team. There are several strategies that tokens or others in the numerical minority can adopt to build their power and influence in a team. Tokens can make themselves indispensable to the team by developing special areas of expertise. Other team members then will pay attention to them because of their expertise, not their sex. Tokens should also learn to diagnose power dynamics in teams so that they can maximize their own influence. In a particular situation, they might determine whether they should attempt to influence the assumptions on which decisions are based, the alternatives to be considered, or the information available about alternatives. Tokens also need to ensure that their own gender stereotypes do not dictate the nature of their participation in the team. Individuals sometimes limit their own behaviors to reflect gender stereotypes, even if these stereotypes do not reflect their true selves. Tokens may be especially likely to engage in stereotypical behavior because their numerical status makes gender stereotypes so prominent. Thus, tokens may find it valuable to consider whether their behaviors reflect their true selves or gender stereotypes.[60]

In conclusion, mixed-sex teams face challenges in reaching their full potential. Women's task contributions are often ignored or devalued by other team members. Individuals who are members of teams comprised primarily of the opposite sex have more negative experiences than do individuals who are members of teams comprised primarily of the same sex. Although the effects of being in the minority are not identical for women and men, both men and women are vulnerable to negative experiences when their sex is underrepresented. Moreover, as the level of sex diversity in a team increases, the effectiveness of the team may decline. These effects are not inevitable, but depend on a host of factors, such as the team's characteristics and task, the organization's demographic composition and values, and even the values of the society in which the organization operates. Mixed-sex teams are likely to experience problems in poorly integrated organizations that do not value collaboration and diversity. Although individual managers and team members cannot address all of these problems, there is much that they can do to improve the functioning of a mixed-sex team. Managers must carefully design the team, provide proper training, help team members to get acquainted, and provide continual support to the team. Team members need to understand their own social identities, improve the accuracy of their perceptions, develop relationships with one another, and avoid the dynamics created by a disproportionate representation of one sex. Making any team effective requires a lot of hard work, and mixed-sex teams are no exception.

Above all, managers and team members must be patient. Mixed-sex teams require more time to come together than same-sex teams, and there may be frustrating moments for everyone. However, with appropriate nurturing, mixed-sex teams can be effective—even in outer space.[61]

Notes

1. Dunn, M. (1996, September 15). From Russia, "love" to U.S. female astronaut in space. *The Hartford Courant*, p. A2. Reprinted with permission of The Associated Press.
2. Stewart, G. L., Manz, C. C., & Sims, H. P. (1999). *Teamwork and group dynamics.* New York: Wiley; Lawler, E. E., III, Mohrman, S. A., & Ledford, G. E., Jr. (1995). *Creating high performance organizations: Practices and results of employee involvement and total quality management in Fortune 1000 companies.* San Francisco: Jossey-Bass; Cohen, S. G., & Bailey, D. E. (1997). What makes teams work: Group effectiveness research from the shop floor to the executive suite. *Journal of Management, 23,* 239–290; Snow, C. C., Snell, S. A., Davison, S. C., & Hambrick, D. C. (1996). Use transnational teams to globalize your company. *Organizational Dynamics, 24*(1), 50–66; Marquardt, M. J., & Horvarth, L. (2001). *Global teams: How top multinationals span boundaries and cultures with high-speed teamwork.* Palo Alto, CA: Davies-Black.
3. Jackson, S. E., May, K. E., & Whitney, K. (1995). Understanding the dynamics of diversity in decision making teams. In R. A. Guzzo & E. Salas (Eds.), *Team effectiveness and decision making in organizations* (pp. 204–261). San Francisco: Jossey-Bass.
4. Cohen & Bailey; Katzenbach, J. R., & Smith, D. K. (1993). The discipline of teams. *Harvard Business Review, 71*(2), 110–120.
5. Wagner, D. G., & Berger, J. (1997). Gender and interpersonal task behaviors: Status expectation accounts. *Sociological Perspectives, 40,* 1–32.
6. Wagner & Berger; Ridgeway, C. L. (1991). The social construction of status value: Gender and other nominal characteristics. *Social Forces, 70,* 367–386; Ridgeway, C. L., & Smith-Lovin, L. (1999). Gender and interaction. In J. S. Chafetz (Ed.), *Handbook of the sociology of gender* (pp. 247–274). New York: Kluwer Academic/Plenum; Carli, L. L. , & Bukatko, D. (2000). Gender, communication, and social influence: A developmental perspective. In T. Eckes & H. M. Trautner (Eds.), *The developmental social psychology of gender* (pp. 295–331). Mahwah, NJ: Erlbaum; Carli, L. L., & Eagly, A. H. (1999). Gender effects on social influence and emergent

leadership. In G. N. Powell (Ed.), *Handbook of gender and work* (pp. 203–222). Thousand Oaks, CA: Sage.

7. Eagly, A. H., Wood, W., & Diekman, A. B. (2000). Social role theory of sex differences and similarities: A current appraisal. In T. Eckes & H. M. Trautner (Eds.), *The developmental social psychology of gender* (pp. 123–174). Mahwah, NJ; Erlbaum; Carli & Bukatko; Associated Press.

8. Ridgeway & Smith-Lovin; Wagner & Berger.

9. Wagner & Berger; Ridgeway & Smith-Lovin.

10. Wagner & Berger; Carli, L. L. (2001). Gender and social influence. *Journal of Social Issues, 74*, 725–741; Ridgeway & Smith-Lovin.

11. Carli & Eagly; Carli & Bukatko.

12. Carli & Eagly; Carli & Bukatko; Carli, L. L. (1990). Gender, language, and influence. *Journal of Personality and Social Psychology, 59*, 941–951; Dovidio, J. F., Ellyson, S. L., Keating, C. F., Heltman, K., & Brown, C. E. (1988). The relationship of social power to visual displays of dominance between men and women. *Journal of Personality and Social Psychology, 54*, 233–242; Balkwell, J. W., & Berger, J. (1996). Gender, status and behavior in task situations. *Social Psychology Quarterly, 59*, 273–283.

13. Carli & Eagly; Anderson, L. R., & Blanchard, P. N. (1982). Sex differences in task and social-emotional behavior. *Basic and Applied Social Psychology, 3*(2), 109–139; Wood, W., & Karten, S. J. (1986). Sex differences in interaction style as a product of perceived sex differences in competence. *Journal of Personality and Social Psychology, 50*, 341–347; Carli & Bukatko; Ridgeway & Smith-Lovin; Gerber, G. L. (1996). Status in same-gender and mixed-gender police dyads: Effects on personality attributions. *Social Psychology Quarterly, 59*, 350–363; Gibson, C. B., & Zellmer-Bruhn, M. E. (2001). Metaphors and meaning: An intercultural analysis of teamwork. *Administrative Science Quarterly, 46*, 274–303.

14. Zane, N. W. S., Sue, S., Hu, L., & Kwon, J. (1991). Asian-American assertion: A social learning analysis of cultural differences. *Journal of Counseling Psychology, 38*, 63–70; Filardo, E. K. (1996). Gender patterns in African American and White adolescents' social interactions in same-race, mixed-gender groups. *Journal of Personality and Social Psychology, 71*, 71–82; Ridgeway (1991); Elssass, P. M., & Graves, L. M. (1997). Demographic diversity in decision making groups: The experiences of women and people of color. *Academy of Management Review, 22*, 946–973; Davidson, M. J. (1995). Living in a bicultural world–The role conflicts facing the black ethnic minority woman manager. *International Review of Women and Leadership, 1*, 22–36.

15. Carli & Eagly; Wood & Karten; Carli, L. L. (1991). Gender, status, and influence. In E. J. Lawler, B. Markowvsky, C. Ridgeway, & H. A. Walker (Eds.), *Advances in group processes* (Vol. 8, pp. 89–113). Greenwich, CT: JAI; Cohen, B. P., & Zhou, X. (1991). Status processes in enduring work groups. *American Sociological Review, 56*, 179–188; Foschi, M. (1996). Double standards in the evaluation of men and women. *Social Psychology Quarterly, 59*, 237–254.

16. Carli & Eagly; Carli & Bukatko; Carli (2001); Lockheed, M. E. (1985). Sex and social influence: A meta-analysis guided by theory. In J. Berger & M. Zelditch (Eds.), *Status, rewards, and influence: How expectations organize behavior* (pp. 406–429). San Francisco: Jossey-Bass; Walker, H. A., Ilardi, B. C., McMahon, A. M., & Fennell, M. L. (1996). Gender, interaction, and leadership. *Social Psychology Quarterly, 59*, 255–272; Propp, K. M. (1995). An experimental examination of biological sex as a status cue in decision making groups and its influence on information use. *Small Group Research, 26*, 451–457; Becker, B. J. (1986). Influence again: An examination of reviews and studies of gender differences in social influence. In J. S. Hyde & M. C. Linn (Eds.), *The psychology of gender differences: Advances through meta-analysis* (pp. 178–209). Baltimore: John Hopkins University; Bhappu, A. D., Griffith, T. L., & Northcraft, G. B. (1997). Media effects and communication bias in diverse groups. *Organizational Behavior and Human Decision Processes, 70*, 199–205; Eagly, A. H., & Carli, L. L. (1981). Sex of researchers and sex-typed communications as determinants of sex differences in influenceability: A meta-analysis of social influence studies. *Psychological Bulletin, 90*, 1–20.

17. Eagly, A. H., & Karau, S. J. (1991). Gender and emergence of leaders: A meta-analysis. *Journal of Personality and Social Psychology, 60,* 685–710; Hall, R. J., Workman, J. W., & Marchioro, C. A. (1998). Sex, task, and behavioral flexibility effects on leadership perceptions. *Organizational Behavior and Human Decision Processes, 74,* 1–32; Dobbins, G. H., Long, W. S., Dedrick, E. J., & Clemons, T. C. (1990). The role of self-monitoring and gender on leader emergence: A laboratory and field study. *Journal of Management, 16,* 609–618: Sapp, S. G., Harrod, W. J., & Zhao, L. (1996). Leadership emergence in task groups with egalitarian gender-role expectations. *Sex Roles, 34,* 65–80; Karau, S. J. , & Eagly, A. H. (1999). Invited reaction: Gender, social roles, and the emergence of leaders. *Human Resource Development Quarterly, 10,* 321-327.

18. Eagly & Karau; Karakowsky, L., & Siegel, J. P. (1999). The effects of proportional representation and gender orientation of the task on emergent leadership behavior in mixed-gender work groups. *Journal of Applied Psychology, 84,* 620–631; Kent, R. L., & Moss, S. E. (1994). Effects of sex and gender role on leader role emergence. *Academy of Management Journal, 37,* 1335–1346; Goktepe, J. R., & Schneier, C. E. (1989). Role of sex, gender roles, and attraction in predicting emergent leaders. *Journal of Applied Psychology, 74,* 165–167; Moss, S. E., & Kent, R. L. (1996). Gender and gender-role categorization of emergent leaders: A critical review and comprehensive analysis. *Sex Roles, 35,* 79–96; Cheng, C. (1996). "We choose not to compete": The "merit" discourse in the selection process, and Asian and Asian American men and their masculinity. In C. Cheng (Ed.), *Masculinities in organizations* (pp. 177–200). Thousand Oaks, CA: Sage; Kolb, J. A. (1999). The effect of gender role, attitude toward leadership, and self-confidence on leader emergence: Implications for leadership development. *Human Resource Development Quarterly, 10,* 302–320; Kolb, J. A. (1997). Are we still stereotyping leadership? A look at gender and other predictors of leader emergence. *Small Group Research, 28,* 370–393; Malloy, T. E., & Janowski, C. L. (1992). Perceptions and metaperceptions of leadership: Components, accuracy, and dispositional correlates. *Personality and Social Psychology Bulletin, 18,* 700–708; Karau & Eagly.

19. Carli & Bukatko; Ridgeway & Smith-Lovin; Wagner & Berger; Carli (1990); Carli, L. L., LaFleur, S. J., & Loeber, C. C. (1995). Nonverbal behavior, gender, and influence. *Journal of Personality and Social Psychology, 68,* 1030–1041; Matschiner, M., & Murnen, S. K., (1999). Hyperfemininity and influence. *Psychology of Women Quarterly, 23,* 631–642; Rudman, L. A. (1998). Self-promotion as a risk factor for women: The costs and benefits of counterstereotypical impression management. *Journal of Personality and Social Psychology, 74,* 629–645; Copeland, C. L., Driskell, J. E., & Salas, E. (1995). Gender and reactions to dominance. *Journal of Social Behavior and Personality, 10*(6), 53–68; Butler, D., & Geis, F. L. (1990). Nonverbal affect responses to male and female leaders: Implications for leadership evaluations. *Journal of Personality and Social Psychology, 58,* 48–59; Shackleford, S., Wood, W., & Worchel, S. (1996). Behavioral styles and influence of women in mixed-sex groups. *Social Psychology Quarterly, 59,* 284–293; Ridgeway, C. (1982). Status in groups: The importance of motivation. *American Sociological Review, 47,* 76–88.

20. Lockheed; Wood & Karten; Shackleford, Wood, & Worchel; Wagner, D. G., Ford, R. S., & Ford, T. W. (1986). Can gender inequalities be reduced? *American Sociological Review, 51,* 47–61; Davis, B. M. & Gilbert, L. A. (1989). Effects of dispositional and situational influences on women's dominance expression in mixed-sex dyads. *Journal of Personality and Social Psychology, 57,* 294–300; Dovidio, Ellyson, Keating, Heltman, & Brown; Brown, C. E., Dovidio, J. F., & Ellyson, S. L. (1990). Reducing sex differences in visual displays of dominance: Knowledge is power. *Personality and Social Psychology Bulletin, 16,* 358–368; Moskowitz, D. W., Suh, E. J., & Desaulniers, J. (1994). Situational influences on gender differences in agency and communion. *Journal of Personality and Social Psychology, 66,* 753–761; Hall, J. A., & Freidman, G. B. (1999). Status, gender, and nonverbal behavior: A study of structured interactions between employees of a company. *Personality and Social Psychology Bulletin, 25,* 1082–1091; Carli & Eagly.

21. Graham, K. (1997). *Personal history.* New York: Vintage, p. 419.

22. Elsass & Graves.

23. For reviews of theories supporting these views, see Tolbert, P.S., Graham, M. E., & Andrews, A. O. (1999). Group gender composition and work group relations: Theories, evidence, and issues. In G. N. Powell (Ed.), *Handbook of gender and work* (pp. 179–202). Thousand Oaks, CA: Sage; Riordan, C. M. (2000). Relational demography within groups: Past developments, contradictions, and new directions. In G. Ferris (Ed.), *Research in personnel and human resource management* (Vol. 19, pp. 131–173). New York: Elsevier; Konrad, A. M., Winter, S. & Gutek, B. A. (1992). Diversity in work group sex composition: Implications for majority and minority members. In P. S. Tolbert & S. B. Bacharach (Eds.), *Research in the sociology of organizations* (Vol. 10, pp. 115–140). Greenwich, CT: JAI.

24. Byrne, D. (1971). *The attraction paradigm.* New York: Academic Press; Tsui, A. S., & Gutek, B. A. (1999). *Demographic differences in organizations: Current research and future directions.* Lanham, MD: Lexington; Tolbert, Graham, & Andrews; Kanter, R. M. (1977a). *Men and women of the corporation.* New York: Basic; Ibarra, H. (1993). Personal networks of women and minorities in management: A conceptual framework. *Academy of Management Review, 18,* 56–87; Mehra, A., Kilduff, M., & Brass, D. J. (1998). At the margins: A distinctiveness approach to the social identity and social networks of underrepresented groups. *Academy of Management Journal, 41,* 441–452; Motowidlo, S. J. (1986). Information processing in personnel decisions. In K. M. Rowland & G. R. Ferris (Eds.), *Research in personnel and human resources management* (Vol. 4, pp. 1–44). Greenwich, CT: JAI.

25. Blau, P. M. (1974). Presidential address: Parameters of social structure. *American Sociological Review, 39,* 615–635; Kanter (1977a); Kanter, R. M. (1977b). Some effects of group proportions on group life: Skewed sex ratios and responses to token women. *American Journal of Sociology, 82,* 965–990; Brewer, M. B., & Miller, N. (1984). Beyond the contact hypothesis: Theoretical perspectives on desegregation. In N. Miller & M. B. Brewer (Eds.), *Groups in contact: The psychology of desegregation* (pp. 281–302). Orlando, FL: Academic Press; Tolbert, Graham, & Andrews; Tolbert, P. S., Andrews, A. O., & Simons, T. (1995). The effects of group proportions on group dynamics. In S. E. Jackson & M. N. Ruderman (Eds.), *Diversity in work teams: Research paradigms for a changing workplace* (pp. 131–159). Washington, DC: American Psychological Association.

26. Kanter (1977a, 1977b).

27. Elsass & Graves; Ashforth, B. E. & Mael, F. (1989). Social identity theory and the organization. *Academy of Management Review, 14,* 20–39; Turner, J. C. (1982). Social categorization and the self-concept: A social cognitive theory of group behavior. In E. J. Lawler, III (Ed.), *Advances in group process: A research annual* (Vol. 2, pp. 71–122). Greenwich, CT: JAI; Tajfel, H. (1981). *Human groups and social categories.* Cambridge, U.K.: Cambridge University Press; Deaux, K., & Major, B. (1987). Putting gender into context: An interactive model of gender-related behavior. *Psychological Review, 94,* 369–389; Brewer & Miller; Stangor, C., Lynch, L., Duan, C., & Glass, B. (1992). Categorization of individuals based on multiple social features. *Journal of Personality and Social Psychology, 62,* 207–218; Lau, D. C., & Murnighan, J. K. (1998). Demographic diversity and faultlines: The compositional dynamics of organizational groups. *Academy of Management Review, 23,* 325–340.

28. Turner, J. C. (1982). Towards a cognitive redefinition of the social group. In H. Tajfel (Ed.), *Social identity and intergroup relations* (pp. 15–40). Cambridge, U.K.: Cambridge University Press; Tsui & Gutek; Tolbert, Graham, & Andrews; Ely, R. J. (1994). The effects of organizational demographics and social identity on relationships among professional women. *Administrative Science Quarterly, 39,* 203–238; Swan, S., & Wyer, R. S., Jr. (1997). Gender stereotypes and social identity: How being in the minority affects judgments of self and others. *Personality and Social Psychology Bulletin, 23,* 1265–1267.

29. Tsui, A. S., Egan, T. D., & O'Reilly, C. A., III. (1992). Being different: Relational demography and organizational attachment. *Administrative Science Quarterly, 37,* 549–579; Chattopadhyay, P. (1999). Beyond direct and symmetrical effects: The influence of demographic dissimilarity on organizational citizenship behavior. *Academy of Management Journal, 42,* 273–287; Konrad, Winter, & Gutek.

30. Blalock, H. M., Jr. (1967). *Toward a theory of minority-group relations.* New York: John Wiley; Tolbert, Andrews, & Simons; Tolbert, Graham, & Andrews; Tolbert, P. S., Simons, T., Andrews, A., & Rhee, J. (1995). The effects of gender composition in academic departments on faculty turnover. *Industrial and Labor Relations Review, 48,* 562–579; Konrad, Winter, & Gutek; Allmendinger, J., & Hackman, J. R. (1995). Study of the inclusion of women in symphony orchestras. *Social Forces, 74,* 423–460.

31. Yoder, J. D. (1991). Rethinking tokenism: Looking beyond numbers. *Gender & Society, 5,* 178–192; Heikes, E. J. (1991). When men are in the minority: The case of men in nursing. *Sociological Quarterly, 32,* 389–401; Floge, L., & Merrill, D. M. (1986). Tokenism reconsidered: Male nurses and female physicians in a hospital setting. *Social Forces, 64,* 925–947; Fairhurst, G. T., & Snavely, B. K. (1983a). A test of the social isolation of male tokens. *Academy of Management Journal, 26,* 353–361; Israeli, D. N. (1984). The attitudinal effects of gender mix in union committees. *Industrial and Labor Relations Review, 37,* 211–221; Dworkin, A. G., Chafetz, J. S., & Dworkin, R. J. (1986). The effects of tokenism on work alienation among urban public school teachers. *Work and Occupations, 13,* 399–420; Ott, E. M. (1989). Effects of the male-female ratio at work: Policewomen and male nurses. *Psychology of Women Quarterly, 13,* 41–57; Zimmer, L. (1988). Tokenism and women in the workplace: The limits of gender-neutral theory. *Social Problems, 35,* 64–77; Fairhurst, G. T., & Snavely, B. K. (1983b). Majority and token minority group relationships: Power acquisition and communication. *Academy of Management Review, 8,* 292–300.

32. Kirchmeyer, C. (1995). Demographic similarity to the work group: A longitudinal study of managers at the early career stage. *Journal of Organizational Behavior, 16,* 67–83; Riordan, C. M., & Shore, L. M. (1997). Demographic diversity and employee attitudes: An empirical examination of relational demography within work units. *Journal of Applied Psychology, 82,* 342–358; Riordan, C. M., & Weatherly, E. W. (August, 1999). *Relational demography within groups: An empirical test of a theoretical model.* Paper presented at a meeting of the Academy of Management, Chicago, IL; Hinds, P. J., Carley, K. M., Krackhardt, D., & Wholey, D. (2000). Choosing work group members: Balancing similarity, competence, and familiarity. *Organizational Behavior and Human Decision Processes, 81,* 226–251; Chatman, J. A., & Flynn, F. J. (2001). The influence of demographic heterogeneity on the emergence and consequences of cooperative norms in work teams. *Academy of Management Journal, 44,* 956–974; Chatman, J. A., Polzer, J. T., Barsade, S. G., & Neale, M. A. (1998). Being different yet feeling similar: The influence of demographic composition and organizational culture on work processes and outcomes. *Administrative Science Quarterly, 43,* 749–780; Jehn, K. A., Chadwick, C., & Thatcher, S. M. B. (1997). To agree or not to agree: The effects of value congruence, individual demographic dissimilarity, and conflict on workgroup outcomes. *International Journal of Conflict Management, 8,* 287–305; Pelled, L. H. (1996). Relational demography and perceptions of group conflict and performance: A field investigation. *International Journal of Conflict Management, 7,* 230–246; Wharton, A., & Bird, S. (1996). Stand by your man: Homosociality, work groups, and men's perceptions of difference. In C. Cheng (Ed.), *Masculinities in organizations* (pp. 97–114). Thousand Oaks, CA: Sage; Baugher, D., Varanelli, A., Jr., & Weisbord, E. (2000). Gender and culture diversity occurring in self-formed work groups. *Journal of Managerial Issues, 12,* 391–407; Arrow, H. (1998). Standing out and fitting in: Composition effects on newcomer socialization. In D. H. Gruenfeld (Ed.), *Research on managing groups and teams* (Vol. 1, pp. 59–80). Stamford, CT: JAI; DiTomaso, N., Cordero, R., & Farris, G. F. (1995). Effects of group diversity on perceptions of group and self among scientists and engineers. In M. N. Ruderman, M. W. Hughes-James, & S. E. Jackson (Eds.), *Selected research on work team diversity* (pp. 99–119). Washington, DC and Greensboro, NC: American Psychological Association and Center for Creative Leadership; Cohen, L. L. & Swim, J. K. (1995). The differential impact of gender ratios on women and men: Tokenism, self-confidence, and expectations. *Personality and Social Psychology Bulletin, 21,* 876–884; Tolbert, Simons, Andrews, & Rhee; Yoder, J. D. (1994). Looking beyond numbers: The effects of gender status, job prestige, occupational gender-typing on tokenism processes. *Social Psychology Quarterly, 57,* 150–159; Tsui, Egan, & O'Reilly; Chattopadhyay; O'Reilly, C. A., III, Williams, K. Y., & Barsade, S. (August, 1999). *The impact of relational demography on teamwork:*

When differences make a difference. Paper presented at the meeting of the Academy of Management, Chicago, IL; Martin, P. Y., & Harkreader, S. (1993). Multiple gender contexts and employee rewards. *Work and Occupations, 20,* 296–336; Konrad, Winter, & Gutek; Allmendinger & Hackman.

33. Chatman & Flynn; Pazy, A., & Oron, I. (2001). Sex proportion and performance evaluation among high-ranking military officers. *Journal of Organizational Behavior, 22,* 689–702; Johnson, R. A., & Schulman, G. I. (1989). Gender-role composition and role entrapment in decision-making groups. *Gender & Society, 3,* 355–372; Kirchmeyer; Chattopadhyay; Gilson, L. L. (2001, August). *Diversity, dissimilarity, and creativity: Does group composition or being different enhance or hinder individual creative performance?* Paper presented at the meeting of the Academy of Management, Washington, DC.

34. Wood, W. (1987). Meta-analytic review of sex differences in group performance. *Psychological Bulletin, 102,* 53–71; Shaw, M. E. (1981). *Group dynamics: The psychology of small group behavior* (3rd ed.). New York: McGraw-Hill; Rogelberg, S. G., & Rumery, S. M. (1996). Gender diversity: Team decision quality, time on task, and interpersonal cohesion. *Small Group Research, 27,* 79–90.

35. Williams, K. Y., & O'Reilly, C. A., III. (1998). Demography and diversity in organizations: A review of 40 years of research. In B. M. Staw & L. L. Cummings (Eds.), *Research in organizational behavior: Vol. 20* (pp. 77–140). Stamford, CT: JAI; Pelled, L. H. (1996). Demographic diversity, conflict, and work-group outcomes: An intervening process theory. *Organizational Science, 7,* 615–631; Jehn, K. A., Northcraft, G. B., & Neale, M. A. (1999). Why differences make a difference: A field study of diversity, conflict, and performance in work groups. *Administrative Science Quarterly, 44,* 741–763; Owens, D. A., Mannix, E. A., & Neale, M. A. (1998). Strategic formation of groups: Issues in task performance and member selection. In D. H. Gruenfeld (Ed.), *Research on managing groups and teams* (Vol. 1, pp. 149–165). Stamford, CT: JAI.

36. Williams & O'Reilly; Tsui, Egan, & O'Reilly; Pfeffer, J. (1985). Organizational demography: Implications for management. *California Management Review, 18*(1), 67–81.

37. For an excellent summary of these two views, see Williams & O'Reilly; Jehn, Northcraft, & Neale; Pelled, L. H., Eisenhardt, K. M., & Xin, K. R. (1999). Exploring the black box: An analysis of work group diversity, conflict, and performance. *Administrative Science Quarterly, 44,*1–28; Jackson, S. E. (1992). Team composition in organizational settings: Issues in managing an increasingly diverse workforce. In S. Worchel, W. Wood, & J. A. Simpson (Eds.), *Group process and productivity* (pp. 138–173). Newbury Park, CA: Sage; Cox, T. H. (1993). *Cultural diversity in organizations: Theory, research, and practice.* San Francisco: Berrett-Koehler; Watson, W. E., Kumar, K., & Michaelsen, L. K. (1993). Cultural diversity's impact on interaction process and performance: Comparing homogeneous and diverse task groups. *Academy of Management Journal, 36,* 590–602; Elsass & Graves; Blau; Fields, D. L., & Blum, T. C. (1997). Employee satisfaction in work groups with different gender composition. *Journal of Organizational Behavior, 18,* 181–196.

38. Allmendinger & Hackman; Harrison, D. A., Price, K. H., & Bell, M. P. (1998). Beyond relational demography: Time and the effects of surface- and deep-level diversity on work group cohesion. *Academy of Management Journal, 41,* 96–107; Tolbert, Simons, Andrews, & Rhee; Mayo, M. C., Meindl, J. R., & Pastor, J. C. (1996). The cost of leading diversity: Effects of group diversity on leaders' perceptions. In M. N. Ruderman, M. W. Hughes-James, & S. E. Jackson (Eds.), *Selected research on work team diversity* (pp. 9–32). Washington, DC and Greensboro, NC: American Psychological Association and Center for Creative Leadership; Jehn, Northcraft, & Neale; Pelled, Eisenhardt, & Xin; Baugh, S. G., & Graen, G. B. (1997). Effect of team gender and racial composition on perceptions of team performance in cross-functional teams. *Group and Organization Management, 22,* 366–383; Chatman & Flynn; O'Reilly, C. A., III, Williams, K. Y., & Barsade, S. (1998). Group demography and innovation: Does diversity help? In M. A. Neale and N. A. Mannix (Eds.), *Research on groups and teams* (Vol. 1, pp. 183–207). Stamford, CT: JAI; Wheelan, S. A. (1996). Effects of gender composition and group status differences on member perceptions of group

development patterns, effectiveness, and productivity. *Sex Roles, 34,* 665–686; Lichtenstein, R., Alexander, J. A., Jinnett, K., & Ullman, E. (1997). Embedded intergroup relations in interdisciplinary teams: Effects on perceptions of level of team integration. *Journal of Applied Behavioral Science, 33,* 413–434; Williams & O'Reilly.

39. Williams & O'Reilly; Pelled, Eisenhardt, & Xin; Webber, S. S. & Donahue, L. M. (2001). Impact of highly and less job-related diversity on work group cohesion and performance: A meta-analysis. *Journal of Management, 27,* 141–162.

40. Lau & Murnighan; Brewer, M. B. (2000). Reducing prejudice through cross-categorization: Effects of multiple social identities. In S. Oskamp (Ed.), *Reducing prejudice and discrimination* (pp. 165–183). Mahwah, NJ: Lawrence Erlbaum.

41. Harrison, Price, & Bell; Pelled; Pelled, Eisenhardt, & Xin; Brewer & Miller; Watson, Kumar, & Michaelsen.

42. Lau & Murnighan; Jehn, Northcraft, & Neale; Pelled, Eisenhardt, & Xin; Fiske, S. T. (2000). Interdependence and the reduction of prejudice. In S. Oskamp (Ed.), *Reducing prejudice and discrimination* (pp. 115–135). Mahwah, NJ: Lawrence Erlbaum; Rudman; Brewer & Miller; Elsass & Graves; Larkey, L. K. (1996a). Toward a theory of communicative interactions in culturally diverse workgroups. *Academy of Management Review, 21,* 463–491.

43. Bhappu, Griffith, & Northcraft; Lind, M. (1999). The gender impact of temporary virtual work groups. *IEEE Transactions on Professional Communication, 42,* 276–285; Gopal, A., Miranda, S. M., Robichaux, B. P., Bostrom, R. P. (1997). Leveraging diversity with information technology: Gender, attitude, and intervening influences in the use of group support systems. *Small Group Research, 28,* 29–71; Savicki, V., Kelley, M., & Oesterreich, E. (1998). Effects of instructions on computer-mediated communication in single- or mixed-gender small task groups. *Computers in Human Behavior, 14,* 163–180; Savicki, V., Kelley, M., & Lingenfelter, D. (1996). Gender and group composition in small task groups using computer-mediated communication. *Computers in Human Behavior, 12,* 209–224; Savicki, V., Kelley, M., & Lingenfelter, D. (1996). Gender, group composition, and task-type in small task groups using computer-mediated communication. *Computers in Human Behavior, 12,* 549–565.

44. Milliken, F. J., & Martins, L. L. (1996). Searching for common threads: Understanding the multiple effects of diversity on occupational groups. *Academy of Management Review, 21,* 402–433; Larkey (1996a); Williams & O'Reilly; O'Reilly, Williams, & Barsade (1998); Riordan & Shore; Hinds, Carley, Krackhardt, & Wholey; Pelled, Eisenhardt, & Xin; Dworkin, Chafetz, & Dworkin.

45. Williams & O'Reilly; Baugh & Graen; Allmendinger & Hackman; Chatman & Flynn.

46. Mellor, S. (1995). Gender composition and gender representation in local unions: Relationships between women's participation in local office and women's participation in local activities. *Journal of Applied Psychology, 80,* 706–720; Ely (1994); Ely, R. J. (1995). The power in demography: Women's social constructions of gender identity at work. *Academy of Management Journal, 38,* 589–634; Elvira, M. M., & Cohen, L. E. (2001). Location matters: A cross-level analysis of the effects of organizational sex composition on turnover. *Academy of Management Journal, 44,* 591–605; Burke, R. J., & McKeen, C. A. (1996). Do women at the top make a difference? Gender proportions and the experiences of managerial and professional women. *Human Relations, 49,* 1093–1104.

47. Chatman; Chatman & Flynn.

48. Kossek, E. E., & Zonia, S. C. (1993). Assessing diversity climate: A field study of reactions to employer efforts to promote diversity. *Journal of Organizational Behavior, 14,* 61–81; Cox; Brewer & Miller; Larkey (1996a); Ely, R. J., & Thomas, D. A. (2001). Cultural diversity at work: The effects of diversity perspectives on work group processes and outcomes. *Administrative Science Quarterly, 46,* 229–273.

49. Milliken & Martins; Allmendinger & Hackman.

50. The trouble with teams. (1995, January 14). *The Economist,* p. 61; Thompson, L. L. (2000). *Making teams work: A guide for managers.* Upper Saddle River, NJ: Prentice Hall; Thompson, D. E., &

Gooler, L. E. (1996). Capitalizing on the benefits of diversity through work teams. In E. E. Kossek & S. A. Lobel (Eds.), *Managing diversity: Human resource strategies for transforming the workplace.* (pp. 392–437). Cambridge, MA: Blackwell.

51. Brewer; Heilman, M. E. (1994). Affirmative action: Some unintended consequences for working women. In B. M. Staw & L. L. Cummings (Eds.), *Research in organizational behavior* (Vol. 16, pp. 125–169). Greenwich, CT: JAI; Heilman, M. E., Block, C. J., & Stathatos, P. (1997). The affirmative action stigma of incompetence: Effects of performance information ambiguity. *Academy of Management Journal, 40,* 603–625.

52. Northcraft, G. B., Polzer, J. T., Neale, M. A., & Kramer, R. M. (1995). Diversity, social identity, and performance: Emergent social dynamics in cross-functional teams. In S. E. Jackson & M. N. Ruderman (Eds.), *Diversity in work teams: Research paradigms for a changing workplace* (pp. 69–96). Washington, DC: American Psychological Association; Owens, Mannix, & Neale; Tsui & Gutek.

53. Fiske; Brewer; Tsui & Gutek; Sessa, V. I., & Jackson, S. E. (1995). Diversity in decision-making teams: All differences are not created equal. In M. M. Chemers, S. Oskamp, & M. A. Costanzo (Eds.), *Diversity in organizations: New perspectives for a changing workplace* (pp. 133–156). Thousand Oaks, CA: Sage; Thompson & Gooler; Northcraft, Polzer, Neale, & Kramer; Donnellon, A. (1996). *Team talk: The power of language in team dynamics.* Boston, MA: Harvard Business School.

54. Tsui & Gutek; Thompson & Gooler.

55. Sessa & Jackson; Tsui & Gutek.

56. Larkey, L. K. (1996b). The development and validation of the workforce diversity questionnaire: An instrument to assess interactions in diverse workgroups. *Management Communication Quarterly, 9,* 296–337; Thompson & Gooler; Northcraft, Polzer, Neale, & Kramer.

57. Tsui & Gutek; Cox, T., Jr., & Beale, R. L. (1997). *Developing competency to manage diversity: Readings, cases, & activities.* San Francisco: Berrett-Koehler.

58. Tsui & Gutek; Adler, N. J. (2002). *International dimensions of organizational behavior* (4th ed.) Cincinnati, OH: South-Western; Shaw, J. B., & Barrett-Power, E. (1998). The effects of diversity on small work group processes and performance. *Human Relations, 51,* 1307-1325.

59. Tsui & Gutek.

60. Fairhurst & Snavely (1983b); Tsui & Gutek.

61. Northcraft, Polzer, Neale, & Kramer.

6

Leading People

TEACHING MEN THE RIGHT STUFF

Boys, it seems, can't afford to be boys anymore. At least not if they want to succeed as managers in the New Economy, where the old-school style of command-and-control is about as effective as getting blitzed in front of your boss at the company cocktail party.

With more and more studies showing that qualities typically associated with women are what New Economy businesses need to thrive, a new cottage industry is emerging that is taking the opposite view of Professor Henry Higgins in My Fair Lady: Why can't a man be more like a woman? "Men just don't have what it takes to be successful in the modern workplace," says London-based management guru James R. Traeger. "They are deskilled."

Sure, the baby-faced Traeger has an ax to grind—he runs a for-men-only training program that helps guys understand the value of emotion in work relationships. Through a three-month seminar that involves intense personal scrutiny, coaching, networking, and public speaking, Traeger tries to get men to recognize and improve their abilities to communicate, build teams, and develop flexibility. "If you were to ask which of these qualities men had an upper hand at, the answer would be none," he says.

Indeed, in this vise-tight labor market, execs who are prone to scoff at such "soft skills" have found they need to listen to Traeger and his cohorts. Managers everywhere are being forced to think more about creative leadership—the kind that can steer companies across the New Economy's bumpy terrain as well as hold on to valued workers who are constantly bombarded with new job offers. "The nature of modern business requires what's more typical to the female mold of building consensus as opposed to the top-down male military model," says Millington F. McCoy, managing director at New York–based executive search firm Gould, McCoy & Chadick Inc.

After Traeger helps participants identify the gender issues, they work on communication skills, feelings, and emotional expression. "The program is about breaking down the stereotype of an aggressive, controlling, and competitive man who always wants to be right, take charge, solve problems, and also has to have the last word," says David Bancroft-Turner, founder of 3D Training & Development, a U.K.–based consulting firm, who participated in the program. "It's about learning to listen and work in harmony."

—Pallavi Gogoi[1]

Management's face has changed dramatically over the last three decades. That face is now female almost half of the time. What are the implications of this change for the practice of management? How well do gender stereotypes, which represent general views of male-female differences, apply to the managerial ranks in particular? What kinds of prejudices are triggered by a manager's sex? Do female and male leaders[2] differ in their basic qualities and overall effectiveness? If there are sex differences in leadership qualities, which sex has more of the qualities that organizations need to thrive?

As a result of the increase in female managers, more employees than ever before have had a female boss at some time. Many employees have become accustomed to working for a woman, having had two or more female bosses in their careers. Despite the increase in women managers, people tend to prefer a male manager. The Gallup Organization asked people in 22 countries, "If you were taking a new job and had your choice of a boss, would you prefer to work for a man or a woman?" All over the globe, more respondents expressed a preference for a male boss.[3]

The preference for a male boss has decreased gradually over time. In the United States, 2000 poll results indicated that 45% of men and 50% of women preferred a male boss, whereas 19% of men and 26% of women preferred a female boss; other respondents did not express a preference. According to 1975 poll results, 63% of men and 60% of women preferred a male boss, whereas 4% of men and 10% of women preferred a female boss. At the end of the 20th century, a greater proportion of Americans preferred a female boss than at any previous time. However, about twice as many American men and women still preferred a male boss over a female boss.[4]

Why do people tend to prefer a male boss? There are several possible reasons. Stereotypes suggesting that leaders are more effective if they display personal characteristics associated with men rather than those associated with women may account for the preference for men as leaders. Prejudice directed toward female leaders may make it difficult for women to be as effective in the leader role as men and reduce their desirability as leaders. Women and men may differ in their actual behaviors in the leader role, with the behaviors exhibited by male leaders yielding better results for the organization and more satisfied subordinates, contributing to a preference for male leaders.

In this chapter, the stereotypes, prejudices, and behaviors associated with the managerial role today are examined. First, we compare stereotypes of leaders with gender stereotypes and examine whether leader stereotypes have changed over time. Second, the prejudices directed toward female leaders and the explanations that have been offered for such prejudices are considered. Third, we investigate whether (and if so, how) female and male managers differ in their behavior as managers and in their overall effectiveness as leaders. Traditionally, men have been regarded as having the "right stuff" to be leaders. More recently, it has been argued that women have the right stuff. We examine exactly what kind of "stuff" leaders need and whether men or women are more likely to have it.

Leader Stereotypes

Studies of the relationships among sex, gender stereotypes, and leader stereotypes were first conducted in the 1970s.[5] Virginia Schein compiled a list of 92 characteristics that people believe discriminate between men and women, the basis for gender stereotypes. She then asked a sample of U.S. middle managers to describe how well each of the characteristics fit women in general, men in general, or successful middle managers. Schein hypothesized that because the vast majority of managers were men, the managerial job would be regarded as requiring personal attributes thought to be more characteristic of men than women. In support of her hypothesis, she found that both male and female middle managers believed that a successful middle manager possessed personal characteristics that more closely matched beliefs about the characteristics of men in general than those of women in general.[6]

In more recent studies, U.S. women have not been inclined to view management as the domain of males. They now associate the managerial role equally with women and men, whereas U.S. men still associate the managerial role more with men than women. Male managers' tendency to link the managerial role with men is reduced when their descriptions of successful middle managers are compared with their descriptions of women and men managers or descriptions of *successful* women and men managers rather than with their descriptions of women and men in general. No matter what the comparison, male managers still associate men more than women with the managerial role. They also feel that women managers, when compared to men managers and successful middle managers, are more bitter, quarrelsome, jealous, and obsessed with the need for power and achievement. These terms conform to the notion of "bitch," which is often used to express reactions to high-powered career women.[7]

Men and women in Great Britain, Germany, Japan, and China hold views similar to those of U.S. men: They see men as more similar to successful managers than women are. Although these results are from a narrow range of countries, they suggest that international beliefs about managers may be expressed as "think manager—think male." U.S. women appear to stand alone in their dissension from that belief.[8]

Gary Powell and Tony Butterfield took a different approach to the analysis of leader stereotypes. As discussed in Chapter 3, the pioneering work of Sandra Bem brought considerable attention to the concept of androgyny, which represents a combination of high levels of masculine and feminine characteristics. Androgyny was offered as a unisex standard of psychological health that seemed more flexible than the dual standards of masculinity for men and femininity for women. Powell and Butterfield tested whether Bem's initial notions about the superiority of androgyny were consistent with individuals' beliefs about effective management. They asked part-time MBA students in the United States, nearly all of whom worked full-time, and undergraduate business students during 1976–7 to describe both themselves and a "good manager" using the Bem Sex-Role Inventory (BSRI).[9] They later rescored their results using only the items that belonged to the Short BSRI, the abbreviated version of Bem's original instrument.

In 1976, when Powell and Butterfield began their data collection, the proportion of women in management positions in the United States was 21%, an increase from 16% in 1970. Based on Bem's work and the recent increase in

Table 6.1   Descriptions of a Good Manager

Sample/Gender Identity	1976 to 1977	1984 to 1985	1999
Male undergraduates:			
Androgynous	26%	25%	29%
Masculine	54	62	44
Feminine	4	2	8
Undifferentiated	16	11	19
Female undergraduates:			
Androgynous	26%	24%	31%
Masculine	54	70	52
Feminine	5	3	4
Undifferentiated	15	3	13
Male part-time MBAs:			
Androgynous	30%	16%	16%
Masculine	62	63	57
Feminine	0	3	4
Undifferentiated	8	18	23
Female part-time MBAs:			
Androgynous	20%	25%	19%
Masculine	75	60	56
Feminine	0	0	0
Undifferentiated	5	15	25

SOURCE: Powell, G. N., Butterfield, D. A. & Parent, J.D. (2002). Gender and managerial stereotypes: Have the times changed? *Journal of Management, 28,* 177–193.
NOTE: All results are based on items included in the Short Bem Sex-Role Inventory.

the proportion of women in management, they hypothesized that a good manager would be seen as androgynous. Good-manager descriptions are summarized in the first column of Table 6.1. Contrary to their hypothesis, a good manager was seen as possessing predominantly masculine characteristics by a majority of respondents in all groups, including undergraduate and part-time graduate males and females. Powell obtained similar results in a separate study of actual managers' stereotypes of a good manager.[10] Thus, "think manager—think masculine" prevailed in these studies.

Powell and Butterfield conducted a replication of their original study during 1984–5. The proportion of women in management in the United States was 35% in 1984, a considerable increase from 21% in 1976. They hypothesized that this increase in the proportion of women in management since their earlier study would lead to a good manager's being viewed as androgynous. However, their new results (second column of Table 6.1) were consistent with their earlier results. A good manager was still seen as possessing predominantly masculine characteristics by the majority of respondents in all groups.[11]

By the end of the 20th century, the proportion of women managers in the United States was 45%, a further substantial increase from 35% in 1984. This proportion had more than doubled since 1976, when it was 21%, and now accounted for almost half of all managers. Management was no longer a male-intensive occupation, making it possible that the managerial role was no longer associated with predominantly masculine characteristics. Accordingly, Powell and Butterfield, now with Jane Parent, replicated their original study once again in 1999 with samples of undergraduate business students and part-time MBA students. The latest results appear in the third and last column of Table 6.1. The proportion of respondents from different groups that described a manager as possessing predominantly masculine characteristics was reduced. However, men and women still described a good manager in predominantly masculine terms.[12]

In summary, in studies conducted in three different decades, men and women at different career stages, including undergraduate business students preparing to enter the workplace, part-time MBA students preparing for managerial careers, and practicing managers, described a good manager as higher in stereotypically masculine traits than stereotypically feminine traits. Support for the masculine stereotype of the good manager has diminished somewhat over time but remains strong. Support for the stereotype of men as more suited for the leader role than women is also strong, except in the views of U.S. women. Overall, managerial stereotypes continue as "think manager— think masculine" and "think manager—think male."

Are stereotypes of managers as important as what actually makes a manager good or bad? Stereotypes as well as the realities of management are important. Leader stereotypes put aspiring women leaders at a distinct disadvantage, forcing them to deal with the perceived incongruity between the leader role and their gender role. If women conform to the female gender role by display-ing predominantly feminine characteristics, they fail to meet the requirements of the leader stereotype, which calls for stereotypically masculine characteris-tics. However, if women compete with men for leadership positions and con-form to the leader role by displaying predominantly masculine characteristics, they fail to meet the requirements of the female gender role, which calls for feminine niceness and deference to the authority of men.[13]

This incongruity between the leader role and the female gender role is demon-strated by further results from the studies by Gary Powell and his colleagues. In all of these studies, undergraduate business students exhibited stereotypical sex differences in their self-descriptions, with males seeing themselves as more masculine and less feminine than females. Female and male undergraduates agreed on a description of the good manager as highly masculine. As a result, undergraduate women tended to describe a good manager as less like themselves than undergraduate men did. Undergraduate women who do not see themselves as fitting the stereotype of a good manager may not develop management skills and may be diverted from pursuing managerial careers. Those who see themselves as fitting the stereotype may be the ones who go on to graduate business programs and eventually attain managerial positions.[14]

When women assume leader roles, leader stereotypes act as constraints on their behavior. Many organizations exert strong pressures on their members to conform to standards of behavior dictated by those in power. As long as men remain in the majority in the top ranks of management, the masculine leader stereotype is likely to prevail, and women throughout the organization will be expected to behave as men. Thus a masculine stereotype of the good manager is self-reinforcing and inhibits the expression of femininity by women in management positions.

In addition, the mismatch between the leader role and the female gender role may lead to discrimination against women managers. When performance evaluations are conducted, women may receive lower ratings than men for similar levels of performance. Women may also be subjected to discrimination when decisions are made about promotions into higher leadership positions, making it difficult for them to rise in managerial hierarchies. As a result, being competent does not assure a female manager the same amount of organizational success as her male equivalent.[15]

Female leaders encounter bias in a variety of organizational settings. For example, men and women in Texas A & M University's Corps of Cadets, a military training program, were asked to rate the typical male and female cadet and individual male and female classmates on psychological dimensions related to military performance. Each cadet's actual performance in the program was also assessed by objective measures. For both stereotypes and evaluations of individual cadets, men were believed to possess the motivation and leadership qualities necessary for effective military performance, whereas women were believed to possess more feminine attributes that impaired military performance. Male and female cadets, however, did not differ on any of the objective measures of military performance. Differences in the subjective evaluations of male and female cadets reflected the influence of gender stereotypes more than objective performance differences.[16]

Research results regarding leader stereotypes raise as many questions as they answer. The first question is: Do leader stereotypes depend on sex ratios in management ranks? If the proportion of women managers rises more, will there be some point at which stereotypes of managers no longer agree with the masculine gender stereotype? Probably not. As reported in Chapter 3, support for gender stereotypes has not diminished over time despite considerable changes in women's and men's roles in the workplace. Similarly, stereotypes of leaders have remained essentially the same despite the substantial increase in women managers in recent years. There is little reason to believe that these stereotypes will change if even more women become managers. The upper levels of management remain a male bastion despite the overall increase in the proportion of women managers. If stereotypes of leaders are influenced at all by sex ratios, they may be influenced most by the sex ratio of top executives.[17]

The second question is: Are stereotypes of leaders dependent on the racial and ethnic composition of the management ranks? Women currently hold slightly less than half (45%) of managerial positions in the United States. However, the vast majority of both female and male managers are non-Hispanic Whites. Of all the managerial positions held by women, non-Hispanic White women hold 81%, Black women hold 9%, Hispanic women hold 6%, and Asian women hold 4%. Similarly, of all the managerial positions held by men, non-Hispanic White men hold 84%, Black men hold 6%, Hispanic men hold 5%, and Asian men hold 4%. Thus, stereotypes of male and female leaders in general may largely reflect attitudes toward non-Hispanic White male and female leaders.[18]

The third and final question raised by leader stereotypes is: How well do they apply to the practice of management? Stereotypes are resistant to change and do not necessarily reflect current realities. Widely held stereotypes that men are better managers and that better managers are masculine may not reflect what makes good managers. Instead, these stereotypes may reflect only that most managers have been men and that most men have been expected to live up to the masculine stereotype. This question is addressed later in the chapter. The prejudices encountered by women seeking leader roles are considered next.

Attitudes Toward Women as Leaders

In 1965, *Harvard Business Review,* which then billed itself as "The Magazine of Thoughtful Businessmen" (you can see the bias), published results from a survey of male and female executives' attitudes toward women in managerial roles in an article entitled, "Are Women Executives People?" The article posed three general questions: whether women executives act as people, whether they think of themselves as people, and whether the business community treats them as people. These seem like strange questions from today's vantage point, but at that time women held a much smaller proportion of management positions.[19]

The survey results suggested that women were saying, "Treat us as people"; men were saying to women, "Act as people"; and successful women were saying to other women, "Think of yourselves as people." Most female executives (82%) had a basically positive attitude toward women in management; they believed that women should be treated as individuals rather than as a uniform group. In contrast, a large proportion of male executives (41%) had a basically negative attitude toward women in management. They believed not only that women were special but also that they had a special place, which was outside the ranks of management; this is what benevolent sexists would think. Older men tended to be more accepting of women in managerial roles than were younger men. Also, men who had been superiors or peers of women managers thought more favorably of them than men who had worked only for men. Overall, few men (27%) thought that they would feel comfortable working for a woman boss.

Respondents to the survey gave several reasons for their negative attitudes toward female executives. According to a large proportion of both male and female executives, women themselves were partially responsible for the negative attitudes because they had accepted their exclusion from managerial ranks without major protest. Societal prejudices against women working outside the home were also cited. Many men did not want to contend with women as well as with other men for the keenly competitive managerial jobs; younger men particularly may have felt in competition with women for managerial jobs.

In the next two decades, the composition of the managerial ranks changed considerably. According to a 1985 replication of the original *Harvard Business Review* survey, attitudes about whether women belong in leader roles also changed, especially among male executives. The proportion of male executives who expressed a basically negative attitude toward women in management dropped from 41% in 1965 to 5% in 1985, and the proportion who would feel comfortable working for a woman boss increased from 27% to 47%. In fact, male executives were more positive about how women executives were being accepted in business than the women themselves. The proportion of men who thought that a woman must be exceptional to succeed in business dropped from 90% in 1965 to 59% in 1985, whereas this proportion remained at about 85% for women. Similarly, the proportion of men who thought that the business community would never fully accept women executives fell from 61% in 1965 to 20% in 1985, whereas this proportion fell from 47% to only 40% for women. As in 1965, younger male executives expressed less favorable attitudes toward women managers than did older male executives.[20]

These two *Harvard Business Review* surveys present executives' attitudes toward women as leaders. Subordinates' attitudes are reflected in Gallup Poll results reported earlier in the chapter: people who have a preference want to work for a male boss more than a female boss. Another way of examining attitudes toward male versus female leaders is to conduct laboratory or field studies in which participants evaluate the behaviors of leaders. In laboratory studies, leader behavior is held constant; only the sex of the leader is varied. In field studies, real subordinates evaluate the behaviors of real managers.

A meta-analysis of laboratory studies of sex differences in evaluations of leaders found a tendency for female leaders to be evaluated less favorably than male leaders. This tendency, however, was more pronounced under certain circumstances. Female leaders were particularly devalued relative to male leaders when they (1) used a stereotypically masculine leadership style, (2) occupied a traditionally male-intensive leader role, and (3) were evaluated by males. These findings suggest that attitudes toward women as leaders are most negative when the leadership style or situation invokes traditional male norms. Women who exhibit the same leader behavior as men may be evaluated less favorably because of their sex.[21]

In studies of actual managers and their subordinates, subordinates typically express similar satisfaction with male and female managers. Subordinates do not appear to respond differently to male and female leaders for whom they have actually worked. The experience of having been supervised by a woman contributes to more positive attitudes toward women as leaders. Being in direct contact with or proximity to women as leaders may serve to dispel stereotypes about whether women belong in leader roles. However, individuals' attitudes toward women as leaders do not become more positive with experience unless that experience itself is positive. When individuals are more *satisfied* with their interactions with women leaders, they are more positive about women in leader roles.[22]

Overall, this review suggests that today's women managers are likely to encounter some prejudice, especially from subordinates. However, all individuals are not equally likely to hold prejudicial attitudes about female bosses. Men and hostile sexists of both sexes are most likely to endorse such attitudes. Although men's attitudes have become more favorable over time, men continue to hold more negative attitudes toward women as leaders than women do. This may be because men are more likely than women to possess traditional attitudes toward women's roles; men also score higher in hostile sexism toward women.[23]

The focus of this section has been on attitudes toward women, not men, as leaders. Male leaders essentially are taken for granted. Having a woman as a manager has only recently become a common experience for workers. As more people have more experience with women in leader roles, women leaders may elicit less negative reactions. However, ingrained prejudices against women as leaders resulting from sexist attitudes are unlikely to disappear completely.

Hostility toward women as leaders may be less openly expressed than in the past, but this does not mean that it does not exist. Women continue to face prejudices in the leader role that men do not face. These prejudices make it more difficult for women to be effective as leaders.

Leader Behavior and Effectiveness

We have examined stereotypes that favor male leaders and prejudices that target female leaders. When given the chance to be leaders, do women and men actually differ in their behavior on the job, as suggested by leader stereotypes?

This is a question of considerable public interest. As noted in Chapter 3, the study of sex differences is an international preoccupation. Corporate leaders also are given an enormous amount of attention, especially in societies that value individualism such as the United States, the United Kingdom, Australia, Canada, and the Netherlands.[24] In such societies, the success of large corporations is attributed to the wisdom, values, and practices of their founders or current leaders. When corporations fail to achieve expected results, their leaders are the first to be blamed. Consider the issues of sex differences and leadership together, and it is clear why so many people from all walks of life have strong opinions about whether there are sex differences in leader behavior.

Three distinct perspectives have emerged on whether there are basic behavioral differences between male and female leaders. First, men may be better prepared to be managers because of their unique socialization, including such factors as their greater participation in team sports during their formative years. In *The Managerial Woman,* one of the first books on the topic, Margaret Hennig and Anne Jardim concluded:

> We [see] that men bring to the management setting a clearer, stronger and more definite understanding of where they see themselves going, what they will have to do, how they will have to act and what they must take into account if they are to achieve the objectives they set for themselves. In contrast, we [see] that women are much less likely to bring to the same settings the insights, understanding and skills which from boyhood men have acquired and developed among themselves— a mind-set learned, acculturated and socialized which gives men an immediate advantage as they move into management positions.[25]

Although Hennig and Jardim saw women as lacking essential managerial skills coming out of childhood, they believed that women could be successful as managers and compete on an equal footing with men if they developed these skills later. However, even if women managers developed these skills, negative attitudes toward women as leaders could restrict the range of acceptable behavior for them and limit their approaches to managerial situations.

Second, as the opening passage to the chapter suggests, women may have the upper hand as leaders. Judy Rosener argued that the increased proportion of women managers has allowed them to behave in a manner more consistent with their socialization:

> The first female executives, because they were breaking new ground, adhered to many of the "rules of conduct" that spelled success for men. Now a second wave of women is making its way into top management, not by adopting the style and habits that have proved successful for men but by drawing on the skills and attitudes they developed from their shared experience as women. These second-generation managerial women are drawing on what is unique to their socialization as women and creating a different path to the top. They are seeking and finding opportunities in fast-changing and growing organizations to show that they can achieve results—in a different way. They are succeeding because of—not in spite of—certain characteristics generally considered to be "feminine" and inappropriate in leaders.[26]

In the same vein, Sally Helgesen, author of *The Female Advantage: Women's Ways of Leadership,* reported approvingly that Anita Roddick, founder and former CEO of The Body Shop, a London-based international chain of natural cosmetics stores, ran her company according to "feminine principles." Roddick defined feminine principles as

> principles of caring, making intuitive decisions, not getting hung up on hierarchy or all those dreadfully boring business-school management ideas; having a sense of work as being part of your life, not separate from it; putting your labor where your love is; being responsible to the world in how you use your profits; recognizing the bottom line should stay at the bottom.[27]

According to Helgesen, organizations need exactly what women, the carriers of feminine principles, are able to provide.

Similarly, Marilyn Loden, in a book entitled *Feminine Leadership, or How to Succeed in Business Without Being One of the Boys,* concluded that organizations need feminine leadership (i.e., female leaders) more than ever. Loden's view of male-female differences in the managerial ranks is captured in three words: "Vive la différence!" It seems the qualities associated with females increasingly are described in management texts as desirable for leaders.[28]

Third, the constraints of the leader role may minimize the effects of both men's and women's prior socialization on how they behave as leaders. Powerful forces influence the behavior of leaders of both sexes. These include

(1) self-selection, with men and women who decide on managerial careers sharing behavioral tendencies that are consistent with leader stereotypes; (2) organizational selection, with managers of both sexes being chosen according to similar behavioral criteria; (3) organizational socialization, with female and male managers being similarly socialized into proper role behavior early in their careers and rewarded for exhibiting the right kinds of behavior; and (4) organizational structure, with managers who hold positions with similar status, power, and compensation behaving similarly. Taking into account the sex differences in the jobs held and rewards received by female managers in comparison with male managers, men and women may act similarly in the leader role.[29]

This view was advocated by a team of researchers from The Center for Creative Leadership in a book titled *Breaking the Glass Ceiling: Can Women Reach the Top of America's Largest Corporations?* They concluded, "The basis for claiming differences between executive women and executive men—whether used to exclude or encourage women into these ranks—is suspect at best." Douglas Bray, who directed a major study of sex differences in leader behavior for AT&T, drew a more succinct conclusion: "Vive la no différence!"[30]

In summary, very different conclusions may be reached about whether and how sex differences in socialization experiences contribute to sex differences in leader behavior:

1. *Stereotypical differences favoring men.* Female and male managers differ in ways predicted by gender stereotypes due to early socialization experiences that make men better suited as managers.

2. *Stereotypical differences favoring women.* Female and male managers differ in accordance with gender stereotypes due to early socialization experiences, but femininity is particularly needed by managers to be effective in today's workplace.

3. *No differences.* Women who pursue the nontraditional career of manager do not adhere to the feminine stereotype and behave similarly to men who pursue managerial careers.

We now review the extent of the support for each of these perspectives. First, we consider how the major theories of leadership regard the merits of stereotypically feminine or masculine behaviors. Next, research evidence on sex differences in leader behavior and effectiveness is examined.

THEORIES

Early theories of what leaders do and what does and does not work well were based almost entirely on studies of male managers. A classic 1974 compendium of research results, *Handbook of Leadership,* discovered few studies that examined female leaders exclusively or even included female leaders in their samples.[31] When female managers were present in organizations being studied, they were usually excluded from the analysis because their inclusion might lead to distorted results. It was as if female managers were less legitimate or less worthy of observation than male managers. Although management researchers no longer exclude female managers from their samples, many of the existing theories of leadership were developed with male managers in mind. However, most theories refer to feminine as well as masculine characteristics. We briefly review some of the major behavioral theories of leadership.[32]

There are two distinct types of behavior that managers may use to influence the actions of their subordinates. The first type, *task style* or task accomplishment, refers to the extent to which the manager initiates and organizes work activity and defines the way work is to be done. For example, a manager who reorganizes a department, develops a description of the function of each department member, formulates department and individual goals, assigns projects, and gives details on how projects should be conducted may be considered high in task style. The second type, *interpersonal style* or maintenance of interpersonal relationships, refers to the extent to which the manager engages in activities that tend to the morale and welfare of people. For example, a manager who expresses appreciation to subordinates for work performed well, demonstrates concern about their job and work satisfaction, and tries to build their self-esteem may be considered high in interpersonal style. Task and interpersonal styles of leadership are typically regarded as independent dimensions. That is, a manager may be high in both task and interpersonal style, low in both, or high in one but not the other.[33]

Managers may also exhibit different decision-making styles. A leader who exhibits *democratic leadership* allows subordinates to participate in decision making, whereas a leader who exhibits *autocratic leadership* discourages such participation. These are generally considered to be opposite styles.[34]

Some theories regard one type or combination of behaviors as best in all situations. For example, Managerial Grid Theory proposes that the best manager is one who is high in both task style and interpersonal style in all situations. In addition, proponents of an ethical approach to management argue that a democratic decision-making style is superior to an autocratic style for the same reasons that democracy is superior to authoritarianism as a political system. In Western societies, management is seen as the last bastion of the autocratic style.[35]

Other theories regard different types of leader behavior as appropriate for different situations. For example, Situational Leadership Theory, offered by Paul Hersey and his colleagues, recommends that managers adopt high task/low interpersonal, high task/high interpersonal, low task/high interpersonal, and low task/low interpersonal styles in that order as their subordinates' maturity increases. More mature subordinates are more willing and able to take responsibility and have greater education and experience relevant to the task at hand. Also, Robert Tannenbaum and Warren Schmidt's leadership theory recommends that managers become more democratic and less autocratic in decision making as subordinates display a greater need for independence, readiness to assume responsibility, and ability to solve problems as a team.[36]

In recent years, leadership theories have become more dynamic and holistic by distinguishing between transformational, transactional, and laissez-faire leadership. *Transformational leaders* are regarded as superior. They motivate followers to transcend their own self-interests for the good of the group or organization by setting exceptionally high standards for performance and then developing subordinates to achieve these standards. In this way, they turn followers into leaders. Transformational leaders exhibit four types of behavior: (1) *charisma* by displaying attributes that induce followers to view them as role models and by communicating values, purpose, and the importance of the mission; (2) *inspirational motivation* by exuding optimism and excitement about the mission and its attainability; (3) *intellectual stimulation* by encouraging followers to question basic assumptions and consider problems and tasks from new perspectives; and (4) *individualized consideration* by focusing on the development and mentoring of followers and attending to their individual needs.[37]

In contrast, *transactional leaders* focus on clarifying the responsibilities of subordinates and then responding to how well subordinates execute their responsibilities. They exhibit two kinds of behavior: (1) *contingent reward* by promising and providing suitable rewards if followers achieve their assigned objectives and (2) *management by exception* by intervening to correct follower performance either in anticipation of a problem or after a problem has occurred. Transactional leaders who engage in *active* management by exception systematically monitor subordinate performance for mistakes, whereas those who engage in *passive* management by exception wait for subordinate difficulties to be brought to their attention before intervening. Transformational leaders may be transactional when it is necessary to achieve their goals. However, transactional leaders are seldom transformational. Distinct from both transformational and transactional leadership is *laissez-faire leadership*. Laissez-faire leaders avoid taking responsibility for leadership altogether. Such leaders refrain from giving direction or making decisions and do not involve themselves in the development of their followers.

The call for transformational leadership has been partly in recognition of the changing economic environment in which organizations operate. As global environments become more turbulent, highly competitive, and reliant on new technologies, they call for "high-involvement" organizations with decentralized authority, flexible structures, and few managerial levels. Individuals who are able to articulate and rally followers behind a unified vision, stimulate creativity in achieving the vision, and develop rewards, recognition, and career opportunities for high-performing specialists are best suited for leader roles in such organizations. In addition, participatory management approaches that emphasize open communications and delegation are most conducive to the rapid innovation and response to customers that organizations need to survive in such environments. As a result, organizations are shifting away from an authoritarian model of leadership and toward a more transformational and democratic model. If management is the last bastion of the autocratic style, fewer organizations are choosing this style.[38]

Several linkages may be made between gender stereotypes and behavioral theories of leadership. A high propensity to exhibit task-oriented behaviors such as setting goals and initiating work activity is associated with the masculine stereotype. The feminine stereotype is associated with a high propensity to exhibit interpersonally-oriented behaviors such as showing consideration toward subordinates and demonstrating concern for their satisfaction. When individuals are high in the propensity to exhibit both task-oriented and interpersonally-oriented behavior, they adopt the profile of an androgynous leader. However, when individuals are low in the propensity to exhibit either type of behavior, they may be regarded as undifferentiated. Thus, Managerial Grid Theory suggests that an androgynous leader will be effective in all situations. In contrast, Situational Leadership Theory suggests that leaders should be masculine, androgynous, feminine, and finally undifferentiated in turn as followers increase in maturity.[39]

The autocratic style of decision making is more associated with the masculine stereotype, reflecting a greater emphasis on dominance and control over others. In contrast, the democratic style of decision making is more associated with the feminine stereotype, reflecting a greater emphasis on the involvement of others. Tannenbaum and Schmidt's leadership theory suggests that leaders behave in an increasingly feminine manner as their followers gain independence, responsibility, and the ability to work well as a team.[40]

Although much of what makes a leader transformational does not pertain to either gender stereotype, the ability to offer individualized consideration to subordinates is more associated with the feminine stereotype because of its greater concern with relationships and the needs of others. In contrast, the primary activities of transactional leaders, including the granting of contingent rewards and active or passive management by exception, reflect a high task orientation that is more associated with the masculine stereotype. Thus, the argument that transformational leaders are superior to transactional leaders is more consistent with the notion that feminine characteristics are desirable in leaders than the notion that masculine characteristics are desirable.[41]

Recall that leader stereotypes place a high value on masculine characteristics. Even though early leadership theories were developed at a time when there were far fewer women in leader roles, the review of major theories does *not* support these stereotypes. Nor do leadership theories endorse feminine characteristics exclusively. The recent calls for transformational leadership over transactional leadership and democratic leadership over autocratic leadership place somewhat more emphasis on feminine characteristics than masculine characteristics. Other theories, however, recommend that leaders either act in an androgynous manner (Managerial Grid Theory) or vary the amount of masculine and feminine characteristics they display according to the situation (Situational Leadership Theory, Tannenbaum and Schmidt's leadership theory). Thus, leadership theories do not suggest that either stereotypically feminine or stereotypically masculine behaviors are the key to leader effectiveness.

EVIDENCE

Numerous studies have examined sex differences in the leader behaviors recommended by various leadership theories. Alice Eagly and Blair Johnson conducted a meta-analysis of studies that examined sex differences in task style, interpersonal style, and democratic versus autocratic decision-making style. Studies included in the meta-analysis were divided into three types: (1) laboratory experiments, which compare the behavior of male and female leaders in group simulations; (2) assessment studies, which compare the behavioral inclinations of men and women who do not currently hold leadership roles, such as business students; and (3) organizational studies, which compare the actual behavior of men and women in equivalent leadership roles.[42]

As gender stereotypes would predict, women tend to be higher in interpersonal style than men. This sex difference, however, appears only in laboratory experiments and assessment studies, not in organizational studies. That is, it is present only for individuals who participate in laboratory experiments and for nonleaders who are assessed on how they would behave if they actually were leaders. There is no sex difference in the interpersonal style of actual managers. Also, contrary to gender stereotypes, men and women do not differ in task style in any type of study.

There is a consistent sex difference in individuals' tendencies to adopt a democratic versus autocratic style of decision making. In support of gender stereotypes, women tend to be more democratic, less autocratic leaders than men. This sex difference is present for individuals in all settings and circumstances—actual leaders, nonleaders, and participants in laboratory experiments.

Several studies have examined sex differences in transformational and transactional leadership. Evidence suggests that female leaders are more transformational than their male counterparts. For example, in a sample of managers from nine nations, women rated higher than men on three dimensions of transformational leadership: charisma (especially attributes that motivate pride and respect), inspirational motivation, and individualized consideration. Women also rated higher than men on the contingent reward dimension of transactional leadership. In contrast, men rated higher than women on two dimensions of transactional leadership: active management by exception and passive management by exception. Men also rated higher than women in laissez-faire leadership.[43]

Other evidence suggests that all of the dimensions of transformational leadership and the contingent reward dimension of transactional leadership are positively associated with leader effectiveness as reflected in individual, group, and organizational performance. In contrast, passive management by exception and laissez-faire leadership are negatively associated with leader effectiveness.[44] Thus, the above results suggest that women rate higher than men in behavior that contributes to their effectiveness as leaders and lower than men in behavior that would detract from their effectiveness.

A separate meta-analysis by Eagly and her colleagues summarized the results of studies of sex differences in leader effectiveness. Most of the studies included in this meta-analysis were conducted in organizational settings. Women and men overall do not differ in their effectiveness as leaders. Men are more effective than women in military settings, which are extremely male-intensive, whereas women are more effective than men in education, government, and social service settings, which are less male-intensive. Neither men nor women are more effective in business settings. Men are more effective than women when the particular leader role examined is more congruent with the male gender role and there is a larger proportion of men as both leaders and subordinates. Further, men are more effective than women in lower-level management positions, whereas women are more effective than men in middle-level management positions. The position of middle manager is often regarded as requiring heavy use of interpersonal skills to wield influence, which would favor women according to gender stereotypes. There have not been enough studies of men and women in top management positions to allow a comparison using meta-analysis.[45]

In summary, the bulk of evidence regarding sex differences in leader behavior suggests the existence of stereotypical differences. As gender stereotypes predict, women are higher in interpersonal style than men in laboratory experiments and assessment studies and higher in democratic decision making style than men in all types of studies. Women are also higher than men in the individualized consideration dimension of transformational leadership, which is associated with the feminine stereotype, and lower than men in active and passive management by exception, which are associated with the masculine stereotype. However, offering some support for the "no differences" perspective, women and men do not differ in task style in any type of study. Contrary to gender stereotypes, women are higher than men in the contingent reward dimension of transactional leadership.

The evidence offers some support for the "stereotypical differences favoring women" perspective but not the "stereotypical differences favoring men" perspective. Women are higher than men in dimensions of transformational and transactional behavior that contribute to leader effectiveness and lower than men in dimensions of transactional behavior that detract from leader effectiveness. Women's greater use of a democratic decision-making style aligns them with what business ethicists regard as a superior approach to management. Moreover, trends in the economic environment seem to call for a transformational and democratic leadership style that is associated more with women than men.

Studies that directly measure leader effectiveness, however, rate women as no more or less effective than men. Additional evidence suggests that situational factors influence whether men or women are more effective as leaders. These factors include the nature of the organizational setting and leader role, the proportions of male leaders and followers, and the managerial level of the position. As a result, some leader roles are more congenial to male leaders, whereas other leader roles are more congenial to female leaders.

The evidence clearly refutes the stereotypes that men are better leaders and that better leaders are masculine. Effective leadership today requires a combination of traditionally feminine (individualized consideration), sex-neutral (inspirational motivation, charisma), and masculine (contingent rewards) behaviors. Women exhibit more of these behaviors than do men. However, situations differ in whether they favor women or men as leaders.

Promoting Effective Leadership

In Chapter 3, Sandra Bem was quoted as saying that "*behavior* should have no gender."[46] Ideally, to amend Bem's statement, *leader behavior* should have no gender. That is, the sex of individuals who hold leader roles should be of little concern. What should matter is how well individuals, male and female, respond to the demands of the particular leader role that they occupy. However, the sex of leaders does make an emphatic difference to others. Individuals describe leaders in stereotypical terms that favor males over females. They express personal preferences for male over female leaders. They also hold attitudes that make it more difficult for female leaders to be effective in their roles.

What is required to create a working environment in which members of both sexes with equal leadership abilities have an equal chance to be effective in the leader role? To achieve this objective, prejudices against women as leaders must be confronted. Such prejudices are most likely to be exhibited in masculinized work settings where the majority of both leaders and followers are male and the leader role is associated with the male gender role. In such settings, the playing field is tipped in favor of men.[47]

To give women a greater chance of being effective in highly masculinized settings, organizations need to consider the ways in which leaders are evaluated. When leaders in masculinized settings are evaluated on the basis of whether they promote group cohesiveness and develop subordinates for future roles as well as accomplish tasks, female leaders, who rank higher in individualized consideration than male leaders, have more of an opportunity to be seen as effective. To take advantage of this opportunity, they need to have resources to promote subordinate development.

Organizations also need to take steps to increase the legitimacy of female leaders. As for the selection of team members (see Chapter 5), the appointment of individuals to leadership roles should be accompanied by publicity about their special skills, expertise, and accomplishments. This information should be provided for *all* individuals who assume leader roles, not just women, to avoid drawing attention to female leaders as a group. Such an action will reduce the potential for stereotyping of leaders according to their sex because of insufficient or inaccurate information. In addition, management should monitor "the grapevine" for gossip about the reasons for leader appointments and try to quell untrue rumors.[48]

Female leaders in masculinized settings also may take actions to help themselves. For example, some situations truly call for the leader to direct and control others. When decisions need to be made on short notice, leaders may not be able to solicit and build on subordinates' ideas or involve them in decision making. Women should be as ready as men to respond to the demands and pressures of those situations.

Women who beat the odds and enter leadership levels previously controlled by men are often seen as powerful symbols of changing organizational realities. The appointment of women to top management positions may mean that the organization now values the attributes associated with women and may give newly appointed female executives a surprising degree of influence. They should be ready to take advantage of their status as symbols of change.[49]

Male leaders in settings that are more congenial to women face somewhat different issues. Because males have more status than females in patriarchal societies, they are likely to be granted higher status in a feminized work setting than female leaders are granted in a masculinized work setting. However, male leaders may still be subjected to negative attitudes. As discussed in Chapter 3, attitudes toward men range from hostility to benevolence, with women scoring higher in hostility toward men and lower in benevolence toward men.[50] Male leaders do not deserve to be the target of hostile sexist attitudes any more than female leaders do. When sexist attitudes are directed toward men, as well as women, in leader roles, they need to be addressed.

No matter what the setting, organizations need to be ready to act when their members embrace stereotypical views or display prejudices toward members of one sex as leaders. Although beliefs (e.g., leader stereotypes) and attitudes (e.g., prejudice against women as leaders) are difficult to change, organizations may take steps to counteract problematic beliefs and attitudes by sending employees to diversity training programs. Such programs should be designed to make individuals aware of the ways in which biases related to sex (as well as race, ethnicity, age, sexual orientation, etc.) can affect their decisions, and to teach them how to move beyond their own biases. For example, Levi Strauss put all of its executives, including the president, through an intense 3-day program designed to make them examine their attitudes toward women and people of color on the job.[51]

Organizations also need to encourage employees to engage in the right kinds of behavior, whatever their beliefs or attitudes may be. The performance measurement and reward system should be backed by top management and motivate managers to refrain from sex discrimination. Strategies for modifying employee beliefs and attitudes and for encouraging appropriate behaviors are discussed at greater length in Chapter 9.

In conclusion, evidence increasingly suggests that women are better suited than men to serve as leaders in the ways required in the global economy. This is not to say that organizations should choose women for leader roles on the basis of their sex. The challenge for organizations is to take advantage of and develop the capabilities of all individuals in leader roles and then create conditions that give leaders of both sexes an equal chance to succeed. The proper goal for leadership training programs is not to teach men how to behave more like women, as James Traeger is attempting in the program described in the opening passage. Nor is it to teach women how to behave more like men. Instead, the goal should be to enhance the likelihood that all people, women and men, will bring the right stuff to leader roles.

Notes

1. Gogoi, P. (2000, November 20). Teaching men the right stuff. *Business Week*, 84. Reprinted from the November 20, 2002 issue of *Business Week* by special permission. Copyright 2000 by the McGraw-Hill companies.

2. We use the terms "leader" and "manager" interchangeably throughout this chapter to refer to individuals who hold a *formal* leadership role in an organizational setting. We discuss how *informal* leaders emerge in work teams in Chapter 5.

3. Simmons, W. W. (2001, January 11). When it comes to choosing a boss, Americans still prefer men. *Gallup News Service.* Retrieved September 10, 2001, from http://www.gallup.com

4. Simmons.

5. Butterfield, D. A., & Grinnell, J. P. (1999). "Re-viewing" gender, leadership, and managerial behavior: Do three decades of research tell us anything? In G. N. Powell (Ed.), *Handbook of gender and work* (pp. 223–238). Thousand Oaks, CA: Sage.

6. Schein, V. E. (1973). The relationship between sex role stereotypes and requisite management characteristics. *Journal of Applied Psychology, 57,* 95-100; Schein, V. E. (1975). Relationships between sex role stereotypes and requisite management characteristics among female managers. *Journal of Applied Psychology, 60,* 340-344.

7. Heilman, M. E., Block, C. J., Martell, R. F., & Simon, M. C. (1989). Has anything changed? Current characterizations of men, women, and managers. *Journal of Applied Psychology, 74,* 935–942; Brenner, O. C., Tomkiewicz, J., & Schein, V. E. (1989). The relationship between sex role stereotypes and requisite management characteristics revisited. *Academy of Management Journal, 32,* 662–669; Schein, V. E., Mueller, R., & Jacobson, C. (1989). The relationship between sex role stereotypes and requisite management characteristics among college students. *Sex Roles, 20,* 103–110; Deal, J. J., & Stevenson, M. A. (1998). Perceptions of female and male managers in the 1990s: Plus ça change . . . *Sex Roles, 38,* 287–300.

8. Schein, V. E. (2001). A global look at psychological barriers to women's progress in management. *Journal of Social Issues, 57,* 675–688; Schein, V. E., Mueller, R., Lituchy, T., & Liu, J. (1996). Think manager—think male: A global phenomenon? *Journal of Organizational Behavior, 17,* 33–41; Schein, V. E., & Mueller, R. (1992). Sex role stereotyping and requisite management characteristics: A cross cultural look. *Journal of Organizational Behavior, 13,* 439–447.

9. Powell, G. N., & Butterfield, D. A. (1979). The "good manager": Masculine or androgynous? *Academy of Management Journal, 22,* 395-403.

10. Powell, G. N. (1978). Management styles. Address to Allstate Insurance Company, Farmington, CT.

11. Powell, G. N., & Butterfield, D. A. (1989). The "good manager": Did androgyny fare better in the 1980s? *Group & Organization Studies, 14,* 216–233.

12. Powell, G. N., Butterfield, D. A., & Parent, J. D. (2002). Gender and managerial stereotypes: Have the times changed? *Journal of Management, 28,* 177–193.

13. Eagly, A. H., & Karau, S. J. (2002). Role congruity theory of prejudice toward female leaders. *Psychological Review, 109,* 573–598; Rudman, L. A., & Glick, P. (2001). Prescriptive gender stereotypes and backlash toward agentic women. *Journal of Social Issues, 57,* 743–762; Rudman, L. A., & Glick, P. (1999). Feminized management and backlash toward agentic women: The hidden costs to women of a kinder, gentler image of middle managers. *Journal of Personality and Social Psychology, 77,* 1004–1010.

14. Powell, Butterfield, & Parent.

15. Eagly & Karau; Heilman, M. E. (2001). Description and prescription: How gender stereotypes prevent women's ascent up the organizational ladder. *Journal of Social Issues, 57,* 657–674.

16. Boldry, J., Wood, W., & Kashy, D. A. (2001). Gender stereotypes and the evaluation of men and women in military training. *Journal of Social Issues, 57,* 689–705.

17. Martell, R. F., Parker, C., Emrich, C. G., & Crawford, M. S. (1998). Sex stereotyping in the executive suite: "Much ado about something." *Journal of Social Behavior and Personality, 13,* 127–138.

18. U.S. Department of Commerce, Bureau of the Census. (2002). *Current Population Survey* (computed from data for January, 2002). Retrieved May 19, 2002, from http://ferret.census.gov; Parker, P. S., & Ogilvie, D. T. (1996). Gender, culture, and leadership: Toward a culturally distinct model of African-American women executives' leadership strategies. *Leadership Quarterly, 7,* 189–214.

19. Bowman, G. W., Worthy, N. B., & Greyser, S. A. (1965). Are women executives people? *Harvard Business Review, 4*(4), 14-28, 164-178.

20. Sutton, C. D., & Moore, K. K. (1985). Executive women—20 years later. *Harvard Business Review, 63*(5), 42-66.

21. Eagly, A. H., Makhijani, M. G., & Klonsky, B. G. (1992). Gender and the evaluation of leaders: A meta-analysis. *Psychological Bulletin, 111,* 3–22.

22. Eagly & Karau; Bass, B. M. (1990). Chapter 32, Women and leadership. In *Bass and Stogdill's handbook of leadership* (3rd ed., pp. 707–737). New York: Free Press; Bartol, K. M., & Martin, D. C. (1986). Women and men in task groups. In R. D. Ashmore & F. K. Del Boca (Eds.), *The social psychology of female-male relations: A critical analysis of central concepts* (pp. 259–310). Orlando, FL: Academic Press; Ezell, H. F., Odewahn, C. A., & Sherman, J. D. (1981). The effects of having been supervised by a woman on perceptions of female managerial competence. *Personnel Psychology, 34,* 291–299; Bhatnagar, D., & Swamy, R. (1995). Attitudes toward women as managers: Does interaction make a difference? *Human Relations, 48,* 1285–1307.

23. Dubno, P. (1985). Attitudes toward women executives: A longitudinal approach. *Academy of Management Journal, 28,* 235–239; Glick, P., Fiske, S. T., Mladinic, A., Saiz, J. L., Abrams, D., Masser, B., et al. (2000). Beyond prejudice as simple antipathy: Hostile and benevolent sexism across cultures. *Journal of Personality and Social Psychology, 79,* 763–775; Glick, P., Diebold, J., Bailey-Werner, B., & Zhu, L. (1997). The two faces of Adam: Ambivalent sexism and polarized attitudes toward women. *Personality and Social Psychology Bulletin, 23,* 1323–1334; Rudman, L. A., & Kilianski, S. E. (2000). Implicit and explicit attitudes toward female authority. *Personality and Social Psychology Bulletin, 26,* 1315–1328.

24. Hofstede, G. (2001). *Culture's consequences: Comparing values, behaviors, institutions, and organizations across nations* (2nd ed.). Thousand Oaks, CA: Sage, p. 215.

25. Hennig, M., & Jardim, A. (1977). *The managerial woman.* Garden City, NY: Anchor Press/Doubleday, p. 63.

26. Rosener, J. B. (1990). Ways women lead. *Harvard Business Review, 68* (6), pp. 119–120.

27. Helgesen, S. (1995). *The female advantage: Women's ways of leadership* (Paper ed.). New York: Currency Doubleday, p. 5.

28. Loden, M. (1985). *Feminine leadership, or how to succeed in business without being one of the boys.* New York: Times Books, p. 79; Fondas, N. (1997). Feminization unveiled: Management qualities in contemporary writing. *Academy of Management Review, 22,* 257–282.

29. Lefkowitz, J. (1994). Sex-related differences in job attitudes and dispositional variables: Now you see them, . . . *Academy of Management Journal, 37,* 323–349.

30. Morrison, A. M., White, R. P., Van Velsor, E., and The Center for Creative Leadership. (1992). *Breaking the glass ceiling: Can women reach the top of America's largest corporations?* (Updated ed.). Reading, MA: Addison-Wesley, p. 49; Bray, D. W. (September, 1988). *Ten important lessons about management success.* Presentation delivered at the Human Resources Meeting of the General Signal Company, Cambridge, MA.

31. Stogdill, R. M. (1974). *Handbook of leadership.* New York: Free Press.

32. For a more extensive discussion of theories of leadership, see Bass, Chapter 3, An introduction to theories and models of leadership (pp. 37–55).

33. Eagly, A. H., & Johnson, B. T. (1990). Gender and leadership style: A meta-analysis. *Psychological Bulletin, 108,* 233–256.

34. Eagly & Johnson.

35. Blake, R. R., & Mouton, J. S. (1964). *The managerial grid.* Houston: Gulf; Collins, D. (1997). The ethical superiority and inevitability of participatory management as an organizational system. *Organization Science, 8,* 489–507.

36. Hersey, P., Blanchard, K. H., & Johnson, D. E. (2000). *Management of organizational behavior: Utilizing human resources* (8th ed.). Englewood Cliffs, NJ: Prentice Hall; Tannenbaum, R., & Schmidt, W. H. (1958). How to choose a leadership pattern. *Harvard Business Review, 36*(2), 95–102.

37. Bass, B. M., Avolio, B. J., & Atwater, L. (1996). The transformational and transactional leadership of men and women. *Applied Psychology: An International Review, 45*(1), 5–34; Eagly, A. H., & Johannesen-Schmidt, M. C. (2001). The leadership styles of women and men. *Journal of Social Issues, 57,* 781–797.

38. Eagly & Karau; Drucker, P. F. (1988). The coming of the new organization. *Harvard Business Review, 88*(1), 45–53; Hitt, M. A., Keats, B. W., & DeMarie, S. M. (1998). Navigating in the new competitive landscape: Building strategic flexibility and competitive advantage in the 21st century. *Academy of Management Executive, 12*(4), 22–42; Useem, M. (1998). Corporate leadership in a globalizing equity market. *Academy of Management Executive, 12*(4), 43–59; Lawler, E. E., III, Mohrman, S. A., & Ledford, G. E., Jr. (1995). *Creating high performance organizations: Practices and results of employee involvement and total quality management in* Fortune *1000 companies.* San Francisco: Jossey-Bass.

39. Cann, A., & Siegfried, W. D. (1990). Gender stereotypes and dimensions of effective leader behavior. *Sex Roles, 23,* 413–419; Sargent, A. G. (1981). *The androgynous manager.* New York: AMACOM; Blake & Mouton; Hersey, Blanchard, & Johnson.

40. Tannenbaum & Schmidt.

41. Bass, Avolio, & Atwater; Eagly & Johannesen-Schmidt.

42. Eagly & Johnson; Eagly & Johannesen-Schmidt.

43. Eagly & Johannesen-Schmidt; Eagly, A. H. (August, 2002). *Leadership styles of women and men.* Paper presented at the meeting of the Academy of Management, Denver, CO; Bass, Avolio, & Atwater; Carless, S. A. (1998). Gender differences in transformational leadership: An examination of superior, leader, and subordinate perspectives. *Sex Roles, 39,* 887–902; Bass, B. M., & Avolio, B. J. (1994). Shatter the glass ceiling: Women may make better managers. *Human Resource Management, 33,* 549–560.

44. Eagly & Johannesen-Schmidt; Lowe, K. B., Kroeck, K. G., & Sivasubramaniam, N. (1996). Effectiveness correlates of transformational and transactional leadership: A meta-analytic review of the MLQ literature. *Leadership Quarterly, 7,* 385–425.

45. Eagly, A. H., Karau, S. J., & Makhijani, M. G. (1995). Gender and the effectiveness of leaders: A meta-analysis. *Psychological Bulletin, 117,* 125–145; Eagly & Karau.

46. Bem, S. L. (1978). Beyond androgyny: Some presumptuous prescriptions for a liberated sexual identity. In J. A. Sherman & F. L. Denmark (Ed.), *The psychology of women: Future direction in research* (pp. 1–23). New York: Psychological Dimensions, p. 19.

47. Yoder, J. D. (2001). Making leadership work more effectively for women. *Journal of Social Issues, 57,* 815–828.

48. Falkenberg, L. (1990). Improving the accuracy of stereotypes within the workplace. *Journal of Management, 16,* 107–118.

49. Adler, N. J. (1999). Global leaders: Women of influence. In G. N. Powell (Ed.), *Handbook of gender and work* (pp. 239–261). Thousand Oaks, CA: Sage.

50. Glick, P., & Fiske, S. T. (1999). The Ambivalence toward Men Inventory: Differentiating hostile and benevolent beliefs about men. *Psychology of Women Quarterly, 23,* 519–536.

51. Zeitz, B., & Dusky, L. (1988). *The best companies for women.* New York: Simon & Schuster.

7

Dealing With Sexuality in the Workplace

CRAMMING FOR THE EXOTIC U.S. WORKPLACE

The American workplace looks like a battlefield from over here [Tokyo], and Yukio Sadamori is mapping out the land mines for three U.S.–bound executives. . . .

"If female employees are put in a harsh environment where there are calendars with women in bikinis or porn magazines scattered around," he explains as the men take notes, "they will feel uncomfortable." One slip-up and you could face a sexual harassment case, warns Mr. Sadamori as a young woman serves tea. "The jury will see that you have black eyes and yellow skin," he says. "It's easy to see what side a juror would be on."

Mr. Sadamori, who runs Mitsui & Co.'s international personnel division, is teaching his charges the basics of managing in the U.S. He has given them a six-inch stack of homework: U.S. workplace regulations, Equal Employment Opportunity Commission guidelines, lists of forbidden job-interview questions, and manuals on how to get along with Americans and typical Japanese faux pas abroad.

Some of the practices alleged in the Mitsubishi case [a lawsuit filed by the U.S. government against Mitsubishi's U.S.

unit]—such as lewd pictures in the lavatories or teasing—would hardly raise an eyebrow in Japan. Businessmen openly thumb through porn at work, drink at hostess bars with clients and typically know few professional women. Tradition dictates that women belong at home. . . .

Western notions of equality do seem to be catching on with younger Japanese men. Though they have never worked with professional women, Mitsui's trainees seem convinced by Mr. Sadamori's presentation. "Respect for a woman as a person is very important," concurs Sadaharu Nomura, 34, who is bound for Mitsui's Sacramento, Calif., semiconductor-equipment office. "It's a very basic way of thinking. If we think this way, it's no problem."

—Valerie Reitman[1]

Issues pertaining to the expression of sexuality in the workplace arise in all cultures. In this chapter, we discuss *sexual harassment,* the directing of unwelcome sexual attention by one member of an organization toward another, and *workplace romance,* the sharing of welcome sexual attention by two members of an organization. Sexual harassment is a matter of public concern with potential legal ramifications. Workplace romances are a frequent subject of public debate: How should participants and their organizations handle them? Even when men and women in organizations do not participate in romances, they frequently have to deal with the intermingling of work roles and sexual roles by other employees.

Sexual harassment is a pervasive phenomenon. As discussed in Chapter 2, incidents such as those involving a U.S. Supreme Court nominee, senator, naval officers, and professional athletes have received considerable publicity. Such incidents represent only the tip of the iceberg. The proportion of women who report having experienced sexually harassing behavior at work has ranged from 40% to 68% in various studies, mostly conducted in the United States. The proportion of men who have been sexually harassed at work is not as high but worthy of note; 19% of male U.S. government employees reported having experienced sexually harassing behavior during the previous 2 years. In 2001, over 15,000 sexual harassment complaints were filed with the U.S. Equal Employment Opportunity Commission (EEOC), 14% of which were filed by men. Companies such as Mitsubishi, referred to in the opening passage, and Astra USA paid millions of dollars to settle sexual harassment charges filed by the EEOC on behalf of employees. The CEO of W. R. Grace was asked to resign by the board of directors because they believed that he sexually harassed female employees.[2]

Sexual harassment is a cross-cultural phenomenon. Studies have confirmed the prevalence of sexual harassment in these countries: Australia, Austria, Belgium, Canada, China, Denmark, Finland, France, Germany, India, Israel, Italy, Japan, the Netherlands, New Zealand, Norway, Portugal, Spain, Sweden, Turkey, and the United Kingdom. However, norms regarding the acceptability of sexually oriented behavior at work vary across national cultures. As the opening passage suggests, employees from a country with more relaxed norms who are assigned to work in a country with stricter norms (in this case, Japanese employees assigned to the United States) often need training on how to work within the norms of the unfamiliar country.[3]

Workplace romances receive extensive media coverage, especially when a public figure is involved as with President Bill Clinton and White House intern Monica Lewinsky. Sexual harassment is illegal but there are no laws against workplace romance. Also, sexual harassment typically victimizes and offends the target person. There is not necessarily a "victim" of a workplace romance, although one or both parties may pay a price in their emotional health, task assignments, or career advancement if others are offended by the romance. In such cases, the participants are seen as having brought on their own troubles rather than having been victimized by others.

In this chapter, we examine explanations for and experiences with both sexual harassment and workplace romances. In addition, we discuss what organizations and individuals can do in response to sexual harassment and workplace romances. As we will see, sexual behavior in the workplace poses a challenge for managers. Managers cannot ban sexuality at work, but they also cannot ignore it.

Sexual Harassment

In this section, we address the following questions: (1) How may sexual harassment be defined? (2) How may sexual harassment be explained? (3) What are peoples' experiences with sexual harassment?

DEFINITIONS

We need to consider how applicable laws define the types of sexually oriented behavior that constitute sexual harassment. Definitions of sexual harassment have been incorporated into law around the world. The European Union (EU) has established standards for what constitutes illegal sexual harassment.

A 1988 EU resolution stated that "conduct of a sexual nature, or other conduct based on sex affecting the dignity of women and men at work, constitutes an intolerable violation of the dignity of workers or trainees and is unacceptable." The resolution called for member states to inform employers that they have a responsibility to ensure that employees' work environments are free from sexual harassment and to develop campaigns to promote public awareness of the issue. The EU later issued a legally enforceable Code of Practice on sexual harassment. Most EU member countries have passed their own sexual harassment laws. For example, the United Kingdom passed the Sex Discrimination Act in 1975, and a landmark case in 1986 recognized sexual harassment as sex discrimination. However, in France, the definition of sexual harassment in a 1991 law was limited to supervisors' requests for sexual favors from subordinates in exchange for getting a job, promotion, or some other job benefit. Other countries with laws against sexual harassment include Australia, Canada, Israel, and New Zealand.[4]

The U.S. EEOC defines sexual harassment as an unlawful employment practice under Title VII of the 1964 Civil Rights Act. Its guidelines on sexual harassment state, "Unwelcome sexual advances, requests for sexual favors, and other verbal or physical conduct of a sexual nature constitute sexual harassment when (1) submission to such conduct is made either explicitly or implicitly a term or condition of an individual's employment, (2) submission to or rejection of such conduct by an individual is used as the basis for employment decisions affecting such individual, or (3) such conduct has the purpose or effect of unreasonably interfering with an individual's work performance or creating an intimidating, hostile, or offensive working environment." An employer is held responsible for acts of sexual harassment by its employees when it knew or should have known of the conduct, unless it can show that it took immediate and appropriate corrective action. According to the EEOC guidelines, an employer should take all steps necessary to prevent sexual harassment from occurring, including raising the subject, expressing strong disapproval, developing appropriate sanctions, informing employees of their right to raise the issue of sexual harassment and how to raise it, and developing methods to sensitize all concerned.[5]

The U.S. Supreme Court generally upheld the EEOC guidelines in *Meritor Savings Bank vs. Vinson,* the first case of sexual harassment it considered. It concluded that two types of harassment are actionable under Title VII, quid pro quo harassment and hostile environment harassment. In *quid pro quo* harassment, the harasser asks the victim to participate in sexual activity in return for gaining a job, promotion, raise, or other reward. In *hostile environment* harassment, one employee makes sexual requests, comments, looks, and so on toward another employee and thereby creates a hostile work environment. The

Supreme Court later affirmed in *Oncale vs. Sundowner Offshore Services* that the EEOC guidelines apply to same-sex as well as opposite-sex harassment. In federal court cases involving sexual harassment below the Supreme Court level, plaintiffs have been more likely to win their cases when (1) the harassment was more severe, (2) supporting witnesses were present, (3) supporting documents were available, (4) they had complained to superiors or management prior to filing charges, and (5) management took no action upon being notified of the alleged harassment. If plaintiffs have none of these factors in their favor, their odds of winning the case are less than 1%. If all five factors are in their favor, their odds of winning are almost 100%.[6]

Court decisions also may be influenced by the instructions that judges give to juries. Historically, judges have instructed juries, when making judgments about the guilt or innocence of a party accused of illegal behavior, to consider what a "reasonable person" would do in the same or similar circumstances. However, given that men have higher status in most societies than women, a juror, when asked to adopt the point of view of a "reasonable person," may adopt that of a "reasonable man." Such a tendency could affect the outcome of court decisions regarding sexual harassment because men are less likely than women to perceive behavior as sexual harassment. In some court cases, juries have been instructed to decide the case based on a "reasonable woman" rather than a "reasonable person" standard—would a reasonable woman consider the alleged conduct to be sufficiently severe or pervasive to alter conditions of employment and thus constitute sexual harassment? When a reasonable woman standard is used, jurors may be more likely to find alleged conduct as harassing than if a reasonable person standard is used.[7]

Although the legal definition of sexual harassment is complex and subject to interpretation by the courts, most people agree that some line needs to be drawn between acceptable and unacceptable sexually oriented behavior in the workplace. However, the question remains as to exactly what constitutes sexual harassment. Where should the line be drawn? To answer this question, we need to consider which types of sexually oriented behavior individuals find most offensive. Some types of sexually oriented behavior are universally regarded as more offensive than other types. However, judgments of which behaviors constitute sexual harassment may vary from person to person.[8]

Behaviors that may be considered sexual harassment include verbal requests, verbal comments, and nonverbal displays. Specific behaviors of each type may be classified from more severe (presented first) to less severe. *Verbal requests* include sexual bribery (pressure for sexual favors with threat or promise of reward), sexual advances (pressure for sexual favors with no threat or promise), relationship advances (repeated requests for date or relationship), and more subtle advances (questions about one's sex life). *Verbal comments* include personally-directed remarks (insulting jokes or remarks made directly to you), other-directed remarks (insulting jokes or remarks about you to others), and general sexual remarks (insulting sexual references about men or women in general). *Nonverbal displays* include sexual assault, sexual touching, sexual posturing (looks or gestures), and sexual materials (display of pornography or other materials). In addition, sexually oriented behavior is considered more severe when (1) the harasser is at a higher hierarchical level than the victim, (2) the harasser has behaved similarly toward the victim and others over time, and (3) there are job consequences for the victim.[9]

Individuals' definitions of sexual harassment differ according to their personal and job characteristics. The sex difference in definitions is strongest: Men perceive a narrower range of behaviors as constituting sexual harassment than women do. In addition, men are more likely than women to perceive victims as contributing to their own harassment, either by provoking it or by not properly handling "normal" sexual attention. There is also an age difference: Younger individuals have a broader, more lenient view of whether sexually oriented behavior constitutes sexual harassment than older individuals. Finally, perceptions of sexual harassment differ across managerial levels, with lower-level managers more likely to see sexual harassment as a problem than higher-level managers. Top executives are least likely to acknowledge the existence of sexual harassment.[10]

In conclusion, laws and court decisions define sexual harassment and dictate legally acceptable standards of behavior in the workplace. Individuals' own definitions of sexual harassment, however, influence the kinds of sexually oriented behaviors they feel entitled to initiate and their responses to behaviors initiated by others, whether they are jurors, victims, or simply bystanders. Individuals' definitions are in turn influenced by their personal and job characteristics, especially their sex. Thus, drawing a line between acceptable and unacceptable sexually oriented behavior in the workplace is not simple. Opinions differ over where the line should be drawn, making it difficult for organizations to fulfill their obligation to take corrective action against sexual harassment and to prevent it.

EXPLANATIONS

Several models have been offered as explanations for why sexual harassment occurs.[11] According to the *natural/biological model* of sexual harassment, sexual harassment represents a harmless behavior to be accepted rather than a problem to be solved. Individuals with strong sex drives are sexually aggressive toward others due to their biological needs. Therefore, it is not surprising or of particular concern that individuals exhibit sexual aggressiveness in work settings. Men and women are naturally attracted to each other and enjoy interacting sexually in the workplace. Targets of such attention should feel flattered, not offended.

According to the *sociocultural model,* sexual harassment has little to do with sexuality; it is an expression of power and dominance. In this view, individuals with the least amount of power in society are the most likely to be harassed. In a patriarchal society that rewards males for domineering behavior and females for compliant behavior, sexual harassment may be regarded almost as a male prerogative. Its purpose is to keep women economically dependent and generally subordinate.

The *organizational model* suggests that certain organizational characteristics set the stage for sexual harassment. For example, the hierarchical structure of organizations grants higher-level employees legitimate power over lower-level employees. Also, some employees, because they have gained critical expertise or information valued by other employees, may have personal power over others independent of their position in the organizational hierarchy. These power differentials allow some employees to use the promise of rewards or the threat of punishments to obtain sexual gratification from others. The reaction of the victim to the harasser varies according to the nature and strength of the harasser's power. However, individuals who have more access to formal grievance procedures or are more capable of obtaining other jobs may be less likely to tolerate sexual harassment derived from such abuses of power.[12]

In the *gender role spillover model,* the effects of gender role expectations are emphasized. The term *gender role spillover* refers to the carryover into the workplace of gender role expectations that are irrelevant to the conduct of work (e.g., expectations regarding sexual behaviors). Gender role spillover is most likely to occur when the sex ratio of a group is skewed, making members of the minority sex more noticeable and subject to special attention (see Chapter 5). Women in male-intensive groups and men in female-intensive groups experience gender role spillover because they are assumed to be basically different from members of the dominant sex and therefore are treated differently. They will experience more harassment than individuals who stand out less in their work environments.[13]

According to this model, incidents of sexual harassment vary according to the sex ratio of the pertinent group, which may consist of employees in the occupation, job, or immediate work group. The sex ratio of an occupation is determined by the proportions of men and women who hold jobs in it. The sex ratio of a job within a particular organization does not necessarily mirror the sex ratio of the occupation. Even if the sex ratio of an occupation is skewed in one direction, the sex ratio of the job may be skewed in the other direction. For example, more expensive restaurants tend to employ waiters rather than waitresses (see Chapter 4), even though waitresses comprise over two thirds of all food servers overall. Finally, the sex ratio of the individual's work group, consisting of the people with whom he or she interacts on a daily basis, may differ from the other two sex ratios.[14]

The three types of sex ratios vary in the immediacy of their impact on work experiences. The sex ratio of the occupation has the least impact on daily behavior at work, but it is part of the context in which this behavior occurs. The sex ratio of the job has some impact, but the sex ratio of the work group, those people with whom one most interacts, has the most immediate effect. In a work group with a skewed sex ratio, the greater visibility of members of the minority sex, especially if they are newcomers, may lead to their being scapegoats for the frustration of members of the majority sex. If they have peers who resent their presence, token members of work groups may be subjected to sexual harassment to make them feel so isolated and uncomfortable that they resign.

The *individual differences model* of sexual harassment recognizes that some people engage in sexual harassment and others do not, even when they live and work under the same conditions. Although most harassers are men, most men are not harassers, including those who live in a male-dominated society and hold positions of power in organizations. Most women are not harassers either. Individuals' tendencies to embrace benevolent sexism and/or hostile sexism may predict whether they will engage in sexual harassment. For example, male employees who are higher in benevolent sexism may direct milder forms of sexual attention toward female employees in the belief that they are flattering the targets. However, male employees who are higher in hostile sexism may direct more severe types of sexual attention toward female employees, thereby creating a hostile work environment for all employees.[15]

In summary, although the natural/biological model views sexual harassment as arising from individuals' basically sexual nature, other models suggest that power differences in society and organizations and the sex ratio of the occupation, job, and work group contribute to the occurrence of sexual harassment. However, individuals vary widely in their likelihood to harass others and their reactions to harassment by others. Each of these explanatory models may provide a partial explanation of why sexual harassment occurs. In addition, many of the factors described may operate simultaneously. To understand the relative merits of these models, we need to examine experiences with sexual harassment in a variety of work situations.

EXPERIENCES

An extensive survey of U.S. federal employees sheds light on the underlying causes and effects of sexual harassment.[16] In the survey, 44% of female and

19% of male federal employees said that they had been harassed at some time during the previous 2 years. Most male and female victims had experienced the milder forms of unwanted behaviors (e.g., sexual jokes, teasing, looks, gestures) rather than the more serious forms (e.g., pressure for dates or sexual favors, sexual assault).

The vast majority of female victims (93%) had been harassed by men, whereas most male victims (65%) had been harassed by women. About 1% of female victims had been harassed by women, and 21% of male victims had been harassed by men. The incidence of same-sex harassment among male federal employees suggests that the previously mentioned U.S. Supreme Court decision on same-sex harassment *(Oncale vs. Sundowner Offshore Services)* addressed a prevalent phenomenon. Other sources of harassment were mixed groups of men and women or unknown sources, as in the case of anonymous letters.

Female victims were harassed more by their immediate or higher-level supervisors (28%) than by their subordinates (3%). This difference supports the organizational model of sexual harassment. The power differential resulting from the relative positions in the organizational hierarchy of the harasser and victim appeared to contribute to the experiences of female victims. In contrast, male victims were harassed by their superiors (14%) and subordinates (11%) in similar proportions. However, coworkers and other employees without supervisory authority over victims were the most common harassers for both sexes (77% for female victims, 79% for male victims). (Percentages add to more than 100% because some victims had been harassed by more than one type of individual.)

In the federal survey, male and female victims of sexual harassment were more likely than nonvictims to work exclusively or mostly with members of the opposite sex, supporting the gender role spillover model. Victims of both sexes were more likely than nonvictims to be under the age of 35 and unmarried, which supports the natural/biological model, if younger and unmarried employees are assumed to be the more sexually attractive and available. Victims also were more likely than nonvictims to have gone to college.

In response to unwanted sexual attention, approximately equal proportions of female (45%) and male (44%) federal employees ignored the behavior or did nothing. Very few of the female (6%) and male (7%) victims went along with the sexual attention directed toward them, refuting the natural/biological model from the victim's perspective. Contrary to the sociocultural and organizational models, both of which assume a power differential favoring men, female victims (41%) were more likely to ask harassers to stop than male victims (23%). However, female victims (33%) were also more likely to avoid the harassers than male victims (20%). Few female (13%) or male (8%) victims reported the behavior to a supervisor or other official.

The costs of sexual harassment to individual federal employees and the federal government overall were high. Twenty-one percent of victims reported that they suffered a decline in productivity as a result of having been harassed, which would also affect the productivity of their work groups. About 8% used sick leave and 1% used leave without pay. Three percent received medical assistance and/or emotional counseling as a result of the unwanted attention, and 7% would have found such assistance or counseling helpful. Another 4% were transferred or fired, or quit without a new job. The cost of sexual harassment to the federal government over the 2-year period of the study was estimated to be $327 million.

Other studies have confirmed that the costs of sexual harassment are substantial. Across cultures, experiences with sexual harassment have negative effects on both physical health (e.g., headaches, sleep disturbance, fatigue) and mental health (e.g., loss of self-esteem and self-confidence, anxiety, depression). In addition, experiences with sexual harassment, even at low frequencies, exert a significant negative impact on individuals' job-related attitudes such as their sense of job satisfaction, organizational commitment, and feeling of involvement in their work and may negatively affect their careers.[17]

The general nature of the work environment influences employees' experiences with sexual harassment. Organizations and work groups vary in their tolerance for unprofessional behavior. When employees are treated in an unprofessional manner (e.g., expected to do tasks that are not formally part of their jobs or treated disrespectfully), they experience more sexual harassment and, as a result, more distress. In such an environment, victims' distress is likely to be exacerbated if they report their experiences to organizational authorities. Their complaints are unlikely to be taken seriously, especially if their harasser occupies a high-status position in the organizational hierarchy, and they may be subjected to retaliation.[18]

We have focused on the effects of sexual harassment on the immediate victim. However, sexual harassment may create a hostile work environment for employees not personally targeted by offensive behavior. The perspective of witnesses of sexual harassment is important. Witnesses' responses to unwanted sexual attention directed toward others range from ignoring the behavior, to intervening personally in an incident, to reporting it to authorities. Witnesses generally are more likely to take action when the behavior has more serious consequences for the victim, when they believe that most people would consider the behavior sexual harassment, and when they believe that the behavior poses a moral issue.[19]

In conclusion, women's and men's experiences with sexual harassment are considerably different. Although both sexes may be the targets of unwanted sexual attention, women are more likely to be harassed. It is not surprising that women see more sexual harassment in the workplace than men do: They are more conscious of sexual harassment than men because they experience it more. The personal costs of being harassed for both male and female victims are high. Their employers also face the prospect of diminished individual productivity, increased employee health care expenses, and costly litigation. Although sexual harassment may never be completely eliminated in the workplace, all parties benefit when its occurrence is minimized. In the last section of this chapter, we discuss steps that organizations and individuals can take to prevent sexual harassment and to deal with it when it occurs.

Workplace Romances

Sexual interest in a coworker is not always unwelcome.[20] In some cases, it is reciprocated and serves as the basis for a relationship between two employees that goes beyond their work roles. Workplace romances, or mutually desired relationships between two people at work in which some element of sexuality or physical intimacy exists, have become more prevalent in recent years due to fundamental changes in the workplace. Individuals have greater opportunity to become romantically involved with an organizational member of the opposite sex due to the increased proportion of women in the labor force in all regions of the world, especially in managerial and professional roles. Also, employees are expected to work longer hours, leading to their spending more time with coworkers and less time with family members. As a result, the work environment has become increasingly conducive to the formation of romantic relationships.[21] In this section, we examine the causes, dynamics, and consequences of workplace romances.

CAUSES

Robert Sternberg's triangular theory of love provides a perspective on loving relationships in general that may be applied to the formation of romantic relationships in the workplace. Love may be explained in terms of three components: *intimacy,* feelings of closeness and connectedness in a relationship; *passion,* feelings of romance and sexual attraction and the desire for sexual consummation; and *decision/commitment,* the decision that one loves someone else and the commitment to maintain that love. Intimacy is at the core of many kinds of loving relationships, such as love of parent, sibling, child, or close friend. Passion is linked to certain kinds of loving relationships, especially romantic ones involving sexual activity. Decision/commitment is highly variable over different kinds of loving relationships. The importance of these components depends in part on whether the relationship is short-term or long-term, with passion being prominent in short-term romances.[22]

Sternberg's theory may be used to distinguish between factors that contribute to interpersonal attraction (i.e., feelings of intimacy) and factors that contribute to romantic attraction (i.e., feelings of passion and, in some cases, decision/commitment as well as feelings of intimacy). Workplace romances take place in three stages. First, feelings of interpersonal attraction arise toward another organizational member. Second, feelings of romantic attraction toward the same person follow. Third, the decision is made to engage in a workplace romance.[23]

Interpersonal attraction is influenced by physical and functional proximity. *Physical* (or *geographical*) *proximity* refers to closeness that results from the location of employees' areas of work. *Functional proximity* refers to closeness that results from the actual conduct of work. Employees who are closer in rank and status are likely to be higher in functional proximity. Employees who interact with each other more frequently or more intensely because of ongoing work relationships are higher in both physical and functional proximity. Generally, employees with higher physical and functional proximity are more likely to be attracted to each other. Interpersonal attraction is also influenced by attitude similarity; individuals who are more similar in attitudes like each other more.[24]

Whether interpersonal attraction leads to romantic attraction is determined by the physical attractiveness of the other person and the amount of generalized physiological arousal. Whether romantic attraction leads to a workplace romance is influenced by several factors. Individuals' attitudes toward workplace romance in general influence whether they act on feelings of romantic attraction. There is a sex difference in attitudes toward workplace romances in general: Women have more negative reactions than men do. In addition, individuals may engage in workplace romances if they believe that doing so will fulfill job motives (e.g., desire for advancement, job security, financial rewards), ego motives (e.g., desire for excitement, adventure, ego satisfaction), or love motives (e.g., desire for intimacy, passion, and decision/commitment).[25]

The nature of individuals' jobs also influences whether they get involved in such relationships. Individuals whose jobs are more autonomous, allowing them to make more decisions about their own work and to move more freely inside and outside the organization, are less subject to the constraining presence of others and more likely to participate in workplace romances. Business trips, which entail high levels of both physical and functional proximity away from coworkers and supervisors, are particularly conducive to the formation of romantic relationships.

The prevailing culture in a work setting determines how much individuals risk violating workplace norms by pursuing a workplace romance. The distinction between conservative and liberal organizational cultures is useful. A *conservative culture* is characterized by an emphasis on traditional values and ways of doing things, whereas a *liberal culture* is characterized more by creativity and innovation. Conservative cultures are more steadfast in endorsing traditional gender roles and the separation of work and personal interests, and less flexible regarding appropriate employee behavior. Conservative cultures are less conducive to workplace romances. In contrast, liberal cultures are more supportive of the relaxed sexual mores that may be associated with workplace romances. Whether the cultures of work groups within organizations are conservative or liberal varies. In addition, professions as a whole differ in whether they emphasize the creativity and innovation associated with liberal cultures (e.g., advertising) or the adherence to formal work styles and practices associated with conservative cultures (e.g., accounting).[26]

The culture of the organization, work group, or profession regarding the acceptability of workplace romances may be influenced by the values of the organization's founders or top management. Younger and growing organizations are more likely to have a liberal culture regarding workplace romance. In addition, culture may be influenced by the sex ratio of an organization, department, or group. Recall that gender role spillover, or the carryover into the workplace of individuals' expectations based on gender roles, is more likely to occur when the sex ratio is skewed in favor of either sex. Employees may be more inclined to become romantically involved when the work setting is numerically dominated by one sex. In this kind of environment, employees may be more likely to see each other as sex objects and thereby search for romantic partners.[27]

In summary, interpersonal attraction created by high functional or physical proximity at work sets the stage for workplace romances. As employees interact, interpersonal attraction may evolve into romantic attraction, and, ultimately, a workplace romance. Romantic attraction is most likely to lead to an actual romance when employees have positive attitudes toward workplace romances and work autonomously in liberal organizational cultures.

DYNAMICS

Once two people enter into a workplace romance, what kinds of dynamics occur, and how do they evolve over time? Workplace romances differ according to the match between the motives (job, ego, love) of the two participants. Nine different combinations of these three motives are possible. However, four combinations of partners' motives tend to be present more than other combinations: (1) ego for both partners, a fling; (2) love for both partners, true love; (3) job for both partners, a mutual user relationship; and (4) ego for one partner and job for the other partner, a utilitarian relationship. Flings are characterized by high excitement for both participants and tend to be short-lived. True love relationships are characterized by the sincerity of both partici-pants and tend to result in marriage. Mutual user relationships are primarily job motivated. Utilitarian relationships involve a trade-off between different motives of the two participants, with the less powerful partner seeking to further job-related goals through involvement with a more powerful partner in pursuit of ego gratification.[28]

Power and dependency are key variables in understanding the dynamics of workplace romances. Lisa Mainiero depicted these dynamics as a function of the relative dependency of each participant on the other for resources being exchanged in the relationship. Three types of dependency may be present in a work relationship. *Task dependency* occurs when a worker depends on another in order to perform his or her function effectively. *Career dependency* occurs when individuals desire advancement that is dependent on the consent of others. In normal manager-subordinate relationships, managers depend on subordinates to perform tasks while subordinates rely on managers for career advancement. In a workplace romance, a *personal/sexual dependency* is intro-duced. The addition of this third dependency to the work relationship threat-ens the normal exchange of task and career dependencies.[29]

Whenever there is an imbalance of power in a romantic relationship, there is a high potential for exploitation of the participant with the higher level of depen-dency. The potential for exploitation is especially high in hierarchical romances (i.e., in which participants are at different organizational levels with high task and career dependency). For example, the higher-level participant in a hier-archical relationship can use the lower-level participant's personal/sexual depen-dency to force an increase in task performance. In addition, the lower-level participant can use the higher-level participant's personal/sexual dependency to argue for favorable task assignments or work conditions. When either of these instances occur, the relationship becomes utilitarian. Exploitation, however, is not limited to hierarchical romances, but also appears in lateral romances (i.e., in which participants are at the same organizational level with less task and career dependency). A power imbalance may occur in a lateral romance simply because one participant is more dependent on the personal/sexual exchange than the other.

Most couples try to keep their workplace romance hidden from coworkers but fail in the attempt. Conservative cultures, in particular, cause workplace romances to go underground with participants making a greater effort to keep the relationship secret because the consequences of exposure are more severe. The work roles of the two participants influence whether they attempt to keep the relationship secret. When teachers and students become romantically involved, for example, discretion is especially important because of the likelihood of negative reactions. Similarly, because coworkers disapprove of hierarchical romances more than lateral romances, participants in hierarchical romances are more likely to try to hide the relationship. Workplace romances in which one or both partners are married also create greater incentives for secrecy.[30]

The components of love, dependencies, and motives in workplace romances are seldom static and evolve over time. The levels of intimacy, passion, and decision/commitment felt by participants in a loving relationship seldom remain constant. Changes in task and career dependencies may alter the dynamics of their work relationship and romance. In addition, participants' motives for engaging in the romance may change. Growing satisfaction with the relationship may lead to increasing mutual commitment, or declining satisfaction may lead to terminating the relationship. Each participant has to deal with the others' changing feelings about the relationship, even if his or her own feelings remain the same.

There are great difficulties associated with the end of an affair and the return to being only coworkers, including the rejected lover's lower self-image and self-esteem. In addition, what was once workplace romance may become sexual harassment if only one participant desires to continue the relationship. Dissolved hierarchical romances between a supervisor and an immediate subordinate are the relationships most likely to become sexual harassment.[31]

We purposely have not distinguished between the dynamics of opposite-sex and same-sex workplace romances. We would expect the dynamics of both types of relationships to be similar. However, same-sex romances are particularly hazardous for participants due to general homophobia in the workplace. Because of this, individuals interested in same-sex romances face greater risks when they look for a partner at work than do straight individuals. Participants in a same-sex workplace romance, whether or not their sexual orientation is known to coworkers, have more reasons for secrecy: They face more serious repercussions.[32]

CONSEQUENCES

There are consequences of workplace romances for participants, coworkers, and the organization as a whole. Participants in workplace romances face a variety of outcomes. For example, their productivity, motivation, and involvement may decrease during the early stages of the romance (when they are more distracted) and increase in later stages of the romance (when it has become a normal part of their lives). Participants who are more satisfied with the romance tend to be more satisfied with other aspects of their jobs. In particular, workplace romance has a positive impact on the performance, motivation, and involvement of participants who enter the romance with a love motive. Love-motivated individuals may feel the need to impress their partners through higher productivity and to alleviate their supervisors' fears that the romance will negatively affect their work. On the other hand, love-motivated individuals may simply be happier because they have filled their need for companionship and now have more time and energy available for work.[33]

Romance within mentoring relationships, however, may lead to negative consequences for the protégé. Successful mentoring relationships, judged by the development of the protégé, are characterized by a productive level of intimacy between the mentor and protégé that does not result in workplace romance. Less successful mentoring relationships are characterized by either unproductive intimacy, leading to a romantic relationship and poor development of the protégé, or unproductive distance, which also leads to insufficient development of the protégé.[34]

Depending on the circumstances, coworkers' reactions to workplace romances range from approval to tolerance to outright objection. Workplace romance stimulates gossip among coworkers. Whether the gossip is positive or negative depends on the type of romance. True love relationships stimulate more positive gossip. Most people root for lovers in principle because they want to believe that romances can have happy endings. However, utilitarian relationships stimulate more negative gossip, especially if the romance is between a superior and subordinate. When coworkers strongly disapprove of a workplace romance, they may adopt extreme strategies such as blackmail (e.g., threatening to tell spouse), ostracism of participants through informal interactions, or quitting the organization to remove themselves from what they see as an intolerable situation.[35]

In general, people do not care what their fellow employees do as long as it does not affect the conduct of work. When coworkers perceive the lower-level participant in a hierarchical romance to be motivated by job concerns such as advancement or job security, however, they have strong negative reactions. These perceptions differ according to the sex of the lower-level participant. Women who are involved in hierarchical romances with senior-level executives are seen as more motivated by job concerns than men in similar relationships, leading coworkers to direct the most negative reactions to lower-level women.[36]

Why are lower-level women in hierarchical romances subjected to negative evaluations to a greater extent than are lower-level men? When a lower-level woman becomes involved with a higher-level man, coworkers tend to see the woman as motivated more by job concerns and the man by ego concerns. That is, coworkers perceive a utilitarian relationship, even if the relationship is better characterized as true love or a fling. In contrast, a workplace romance between a lower-level man and a higher-level woman is less likely to trouble coworkers. Although he may be seen as her "boy toy" if he is significantly younger than she, he is still seen as satisfying his ego needs. These perceptions work to the disadvantage of women.

Moreover, women are more likely than men to be the lower-level participant in hierarchical romances because the proportion of women decreases at progressively higher organizational levels. Due to their lesser power and status as well as negative perceptions of their motivation, female participants in workplace romances suffer more than their male counterparts when the relationship becomes public knowledge. One study found that women were twice as likely to be terminated by their companies as the men with whom they were involved.[37]

The managerial response to a workplace romance influences coworkers' reactions. Possible managerial actions, to be discussed at greater length in the last section of the chapter, range from ignoring the romance, to positive action (e.g., counseling), to punitive action (e.g., warning, reprimand, transfer, or termination). Coworkers prefer that punitive action be taken when the romance is hierarchical rather than lateral, one or both participants is motivated by job concerns, and there is a greater conflict of interest and disruption of the conduct of work. Contrary to past practice, when managerial action is to be taken, coworkers prefer that equivalent actions be directed toward both participants. Thus, coworkers' reactions are influenced by the ramifications of a workplace romance, not just the existence of the romance itself.[38]

In conclusion, as with sexual harassment, women's and men's experiences with workplace romance differ greatly. Women are more likely to be judged negatively, and suffer the consequences, if they engage in a hierarchical romance. Thus, it is not surprising that women have more negative attitudes toward workplace romance in general than men do. The overall effects of workplace romance on organizations vary widely. These effects may be positive (e.g., increased individual productivity, motivation, involvement; improved work climate), neutral (e.g., increased levels of gossip with no other impact), or negative (e.g., decreased productivity, work motivation, involvement; worsened work climate). When workplace romances have negative effects on the conduct of work, organizations need to be ready to act.

Addressing the Intersection of Sexuality and Work

SEXUAL HARASSMENT

Unless organizations address sexual harassment, they may be held in violation of the law and risk loss of productivity and alienation of a large portion of their work force. Many cases of sexual harassment, though not all, require managerial action. In addition, organizations and their employees benefit from managerial actions that discourage harassment from ever occurring.

Organizations must create cultures that reject sexual harassment by issuing strong written policies against it, educating employees about the issue, and establishing formal grievance procedures to deal with allegations of harassment. The organization's policy on sexual harassment should clearly specify the types of behaviors that are forbidden and their penalties. New employees should be informed of the policy on sexual harassment during their initial orientation. A training program for managers should detail the reasons for the policy, the variety of forms of sexual harassment, and proper responses to allegations of harassment. Managers should be made aware that sexual harassment could cost them their careers.[39]

Consider, for example, the training program described in the opening passage of the chapter. Employees of a Japanese firm about to begin jobs in the United States were counseled about inappropriate nonverbal displays in the U.S. workplace, such as leaving pornographic magazines lying around. They were also advised of relevant U.S. laws and regulations pertaining to sexual harassment and other matters. The program seems helpful because employees are coached on the differences in the norms and regulations in their new work environment from those in their own country. This is a good example of not only sexual harassment training, but also of cross-cultural training in general. The passage suggests that the employees who attended the training program were getting the point, even though it was difficult for them to absorb. By providing such training, organizations minimize the likelihood that their internal work environment is hostile for employees. In addition, they may reduce their legal liability if sexual harassment does occur within their boundaries.[40]

In dealing with cases of alleged harassment, organizations should follow this general principle: *The severity of the action taken should be based on the severity of the alleged offense and the certainty that an offense was committed.*

After a complaint of sexual harassment has been directed to a designated party, organizational policy can be effectively implemented by a formal grievance procedure such as the following:[41]

1. Interview the complainant, the accused, and possible witnesses.

2. Check personnel files for evidence that documents prior animosities between the parties, previous complaints against the accused or by the complainant, and recent discrepancies in the work record of the complainant or the accused.

3. Assess the severity of the alleged offense, considering the type of behavior, intent, power position of the accused relative to the complainant, and frequency of occurrence. Actions by complainants' supervisors should be considered more

serious offenses than the same actions by coworkers. Repeated incidents should be considered more serious offenses than isolated cases. The severity of both quid pro quo and hostile environment sexual harassment should be considered.

4. Assess the certainty that an offense was committed. Solid evidence, in the form of either witnesses or documents, to support the complaint provides assurance that there actually was an offense. Matters are less certain when there is less than overwhelming evidence to support the complaint. Whether an offense was committed is in greatest doubt when the only evidence to support the complaint is the complainant's word.

5. Determine appropriate actions to be taken. Severe actions (e.g., dismissal, demotion, suspension, transfer of accused) are to be taken when the alleged offense is severe and the certainty that it was committed is high. In such cases, the work record of the complainant should be restored if unjustly blemished. Mild actions (e.g., no record of complaint in file of accused, or record with annotation that accusation not proven; letter to the accused stressing organizational policy against sexual harassment; announcement reminding employees of organizational policy) are to be taken when the alleged offense is mild and the certainty that it was committed is low. Moderate actions (e.g., warning or disciplinary notice in file of accused with provision for removal of notice if no subsequent offense within a specified period of time; required counseling for accused) are to be considered in cases that fall between these two extremes. A combination of actions of different levels of severity may be appropriate.

Such a procedure demonstrates that an organization is willing to take action to minimize the incidence of sexual harassment. It also acknowledges individual differences in definitions of sexual harassment by matching the action taken with the severity of the offense and the certainty of its occurrence. Clear and objective administration of such procedures protects organizations from liability and increases the probability that their work environments are free of harassment.

Formal grievance procedures, however, have little effect if the organization exhibits "deaf ear syndrome" when it receives complaints of sexual harassment. Many organizations have poorly written policies and cumbersome reporting procedures. For example, one U.S. company stated its sexual harassment policy in a single paragraph in the middle of a 50-page handbook that no one was expected to read. Other organizations couch their policies in language that only a lawyer could understand. In another company, an employee reported a manager who would not stop making sexual comments to her after she repeatedly asked him to stop. She was told to keep notes on his actions. When the comments escalated to physical harassment, she left the company and reported the incident to headquarters. She finally filed a charge with the EEOC after headquarters failed to take any action. The company denied liability for its inaction, stating that the employee did not follow proper procedure and had reported the incidents to the wrong person. This is how *not* to administer a sexual harassment reporting procedure. Organizations also exhibit deaf ear syndrome by minimizing the seriousness of the offense, blaming the victim, protecting valued employees, ignoring habitual harassers, and retaliating against employees who "blow the whistle" on inappropriate behavior and on inadequate corporate responses to it.[42]

No matter how well intentioned a formal grievance procedure is, it will have little effect unless individuals who feel that they have been harassed are willing to make formal complaints against their harassers. Many victims are reluctant to use formal procedures. In the federal study described earlier, only 6% of victims used formal complaint channels. If they take any action at all, most victims choose to deal with the situation themselves. In fact, this may be their only recourse if they do not have solid evidence that harassment has taken place or if the organization turns a deaf ear to such complaints. Oral requests may alleviate harassment. In the federal study described earlier, this "knock-it-off" approach improved conditions for 60% of female victims and 61% of male victims. Telling colleagues, or threatening to tell, is also an effective response. On the other hand, going along with the offensive behavior, making a joke of it, or pretending to ignore it usually does not resolve the issue.[43]

If oral requests do not stop offensive behavior, victims may be more successful if they write a letter to the harasser. The letter should contain (1) a detailed description of the offending behavior, when it occurred, and the circumstances under which it occurred; (2) the feelings of the victim about the behavior and the damage that has been done (e.g., "Your behavior has made me feel uncomfortable about working in this unit"; "You have caused me to ask for a change in job"); and (3) what the victim wants in addition to an end to the harassment, such as the rewriting of an unjust evaluation that was prepared after the victim rejected sexual advances. The letter should be delivered in person with a witness present. The harasser will usually accept the letter and say nothing. There is rarely a response in writing, and, nearly always, the harassment stops.[44]

Victims' reluctance to make formal complaints does not relieve organizations of their obligations to create an environment free of sexual harassment and to provide support for employees who have been harassed. Even if no formal complaint has been filed, the organization should be prepared to initiate action if it uncovers significant evidence of wrongdoing. In investigating and redressing the wrongdoing, it should respect the wishes of those victims who wish to remain anonymous. The organization should also provide support for employees who have been harassed. Support should include off-the-record counseling to help victims identify and understand the available options for resolving the problem and to assist them in coping with the emotional consequences of harassment. They should be provided with the opportunity to discuss the harassment with a psychologist, personnel counselor, or some other person who is discreet and supportive of victims. For example, DuPont runs a 24-hour hotline that offers advice on personal security and sexual harassment. Callers may remain anonymous, and calling does not constitute bringing a charge. However, when a victim or a witness to harassment lodges a formal complaint, it is investigated immediately.[45]

In summary, we have detailed actions that organizations and individuals may take to deal with sexual harassment. Organizations should (1) establish a firm policy against sexual harassment; (2) provide training to employees about sexual harassment, including workplace norms and regulations in cultures with which they have contact; (3) set up and administer a formal grievance procedure; (4) ensure that employees are aware of both policies and procedures; and (5) provide counseling to help employees cope psychologically with harassment and decide what to do about it. Victims, however, should not bear the burden of solving the problems. Organizations have a responsibility to monitor the work environment and make it as harassment-free as possible.

WORKPLACE ROMANCES

There are sharp differences of opinion over whether workplace romance can and should be banned. Catharine MacKinnon, one of the first scholars of sexual harassment, argued that most of what passes for workplace romance is actually "coerced caring" or sexual harassment in disguise, resulting from a patriarchal system in which women are powerless to avoid being exploited sexually, and should be treated accordingly. Margaret Mead, a famed anthropologist, argued that, much like the taboos against sexual expression in the family that are necessary for children to grow up safely, taboos against sexual involvement at work are necessary for men and women to work together effectively. However, others claim that it is foolish to try to regulate welcome sexual attention. Lionel Tiger, another well-known anthropologist, argued that the U.S. Armed Forces' ban on sexual involvement among soldiers is preposterous because sexuality is an important, pervasive, and healthy life force that cannot be willingly and easily suppressed. As an IBM manager put it, "Trying to outlaw romance is like trying to outlaw the weather."[46]

In practice, most organizations choose to ignore workplace romance. Only one quarter of companies have written or unwritten policies about workplace romances, and most of these policies address only the most blatant instances when work is disrupted.[47] The two most frequent restrictions are bans on relationships between supervisors and subordinates (70%) and on public displays of affection (37%). Only 6% of corporate policies place restrictions on hierarchical, nondirect-report romances between employees who differ significantly in rank, even though those relationships may be as utilitarian in nature as romances between supervisors and subordinates. The reasons most frequently cited for restrictions on workplace romance include the fear of sexual harassment claims, concerns about the productivity of participants and the morale of coworkers, and the potential for retaliation if the romance ends.[48]

How should organizations respond when two employees become romantically involved? *The primary concern of management ought not to be who is involved with whom but whether the necessary work is getting done, and done well.* The general principle to follow in dealing with workplace romances is the same as that for dealing with sexual harassment: The severity of the action taken should be based on the severity of the alleged offense and the certainty that an offense was committed.

If there is no disruption to the accomplishment of work goals, then there is little need to take any action. However, a relationship in which there is the potential for task-related or career-related decisions to be influenced by romantic considerations presents some threat. Coworkers may fear that the relationship will influence the conduct of work or suspect that it is already having an effect, causing their morale and productivity to suffer. When the romantic partners have committed no actual offense but there is the potential for offense, management should step in. The couple should be told that if they continue the relationship, work assignments and/or reporting responsibilities will be changed to reduce the potential for disruption of the conduct of work. In this case, punitive action is not in order, but the situation does need to be addressed by management.

When it is certain that task-related or career-related decisions have been influenced by romantic considerations, there is greater cause for concern. This situation calls for punitive action against *both* participants. The hierarchical level of the participants should not be allowed to affect the actions taken. This recommendation runs counter to the common practice that the lower-status person bears the brunt of punitive action. However, when both individuals are punished, rather than only the person at the lower level, the appearance of an equitable decision will have the most positive effect on morale and productivity.

Management can also contribute to a satisfactory resolution of romance-related issues by offering counseling to all individuals involved—the couple, the managers of work areas that are disrupted by the relationship, and the coworkers in those areas. Coworkers need to have a designated neutral party with whom they can consult about a troublesome romantic relationship. As their manager may be one of the participants, they need freedom to report their concerns without fear of reprisal.

Individuals need to weigh the potential costs against the potential benefits when deciding whether to begin a workplace romance. The potential costs include negative effects of a workplace romance on their careers (e.g., loss of coworkers' respect, lack of advancement due to violations of workplace norms), self-esteem (e.g., questioning of basis for their work-related rewards), and family (e.g., marital strife, divorce). The potential benefits include meeting their personal needs at work and being happier as a result. When caught up in the passion of the moment, individuals may not be thinking clearly of the consequences of a workplace romance. Nonetheless, they may gain from considering these consequences before they act on their feelings.[49]

In conclusion, although they do not pose a legal threat, workplace romances pose potential problems for organizations. Two types of romances have the most damaging effects on individual, group, and organizational effectiveness: (1) hierarchical romances in which one participant directly reports to the other and (2) utilitarian romances in which one participant satisfies personal/sexual needs in exchange for satisfying the other participant's task-related or career-related needs. Negative effects of workplace romances on the conduct of work need to be addressed by organizations in some manner. Workplace romances often have only positive effects, such as when both participants are single and committed to each other. In such cases, coworkers may be happy for the couple, and organizations need not respond.

Although sexuality in the workplace cannot be fully "managed," we have outlined steps that organizations can take to respond to the negative effects of both sexual harassment and workplace romances. In taking such steps, organizations help create a more comfortable, if not asexual, work environment for their employees. We also have suggested actions that individuals may take to influence their own destinies. The workplace may be more exotic than ever before, but it need not be a battlefield over issues of sexuality and work. Borrowing from Sadaharu Nomura in the opening passage, respect for the feelings of other employees regarding expressions of sexuality is very important. It's a basic way of thinking. If everyone thinks this way, there's no problem.

Notes

1. Reitman, V. (1996, July 9). Cramming for the exotic U.S. workplace. *Wall Street Journal*, p. A15. WALL STREET JOURNAL CLASSROOM EDITION (STAFF PRODUCED COPY ONLY) by V. REITMAN. Copyright 1996 by DOW JONES & CO INC. Reproduced with permission of DOW JONES & CO INC. in the format Textbook via Copyright Clearance Center.

2. Glomb, T. M., Richman, W. L., Hulin, C. L., Drasgow, F., Schneider, K. T., & Fitzgerald, L. F. (1997). Ambient sexual harassment: An integrated model of antecedents and consequences. *Organizational Behavior and Human Decision Processes, 71,* 309–328; U.S. Merit Systems Protection Board. (1995). *Sexual harassment in the federal workplace: Trends, progress, and continuing*

challenges. Washington, DC: Government Printing Office; U.S. Equal Employment Opportunity Commission. (2002). *Sexual harassment charges, EEOC and FEPAs combined: FY 1992–FY 2001*. Retrieved May 20, 2002, from http://www.eeoc.gov; Miller, J. P. (1998, June 12). Mitsubishi will pay $34 million in sexual-harassment settlement. *Wall Street Journal*, p. B4; Maremont, M. (1998, February 6). Astra USA settles harassment suit; to pay $9.9 million. *Wall Street Journal*, p. B6; Lublin, J. S., & Simmons, J. (1995, April 5). A second CEO falls on charges of harassment. *Wall Street Journal*, p. B2.

3. Barak, A. (1997). Cross-cultural perspectives on sexual harassment. In W. O'Donohue (Ed.), *Sexual harassment: Theory, research, and treatment* (pp. 263–300). Boston: Allyn & Bacon; Webb, S. L. (1994). *Shockwaves: The global impact of sexual harassment*. New York: MasterMedia Limited; Shaffer, M. A., Joplin, J. R. W., Bell, M. P., Lau, T., & Oguz, C. (2000). Gender discrimination and job-related outcomes: A cross-cultural comparison of working women in the United States and China. *Journal of Vocational Behavior, 57,* 395–427; Wasti, S. A., Bergman, M. E., Glomb, T. M., & Drasgow, F. (2000). Test of the cross-cultural generalizability of a model of sexual harassment. *Journal of Applied Psychology, 85,* 766–778.

4. Collier, R. (1995). *Combating sexual harassment in the workplace*. Buckingham, UK: Open University Press; Webb; Bowes-Sperry, L., & Tata, J. (1999). A multiperspective framework of sexual harassment: Reviewing two decades of research. In G. N. Powell (Ed.), *Handbook of gender and work* (pp. 263–280). Thousand Oaks, CA: Sage.

5. U.S. Equal Employment Opportunity Commission. (2001). *Code of Federal Regulations, Title 29—Labor, Part 1604—Guidelines on discrimination because of sex, Section 1604.11—Sexual harassment*. Retrieved July 20, 2001, from http://www.eeoc.gov

6. Conte, A. (1997). Legal theories of sexual harassment. In W. O'Donohue (Ed.), *Sexual harassment: Theory, research, and treatment* (pp. 50–83). Boston: Allyn & Bacon; Meritor Savings Bank, FSB v. Vinson, 477 U.S. 57, 40 FEP Cases 1822 (1986); Oncale v. Sundowner Offshore Services, Inc., 118 S. Ct. 998 (1998); Terpstra, D. E., & Baker, D. D. (1992). Outcomes of federal court decisions on sexual harassment. *Academy of Management Journal, 35,* 181–190.

7. Wiener, R. L., & Hurt, L. E. (2000). How do people evaluate social sexual conduct at work? A psycholegal model. *Journal of Applied Psychology, 85,* 75–85; Gutek, B. A., & O'Connor, M. (1995). The empirical basis for the reasonable woman standard. *Journal of Social Issues, 5* (1), 151–166.

8. Bowes-Sperry & Tata.

9. Gruber, J. E., Smith, M., & Kauppinen-Toropainen, K. (1996). Sexual harassment types and severity: Linking research and policy. In M. S. Stockdale (Ed.), *Sexual harassment in the workplace: Perspectives, frontiers, and response strategies* (pp. 151–173). Thousand Oaks, CA: Sage.

10. Gutek, B. A., & Done, R. S. (2001). Sexual harassment. In R. K. Unger (Ed.), *Handbook of the psychology of women and gender* (pp. 367–387). New York: Wiley; Rotundo, M., Nguyen, D-H., & Sackett, P. R. (2001). A meta-analytic review of gender differences in perceptions of sexual harassment. *Journal of Applied Psychology, 86,* 914–922; Kenig, S., & Ryan, J. (1986). Sex differences in level of tolerance and attribution of blame for sexual harassment on a university campus. *Sex Roles, 15,* 535–549; Jensen, I. W., & Gutek, B. A. (1982). Attributions and assignment of responsibility in sexual harassment. *Journal of Social Issues, 38*(4), 121–136; Collins, E. G. C., & Blodgett, T. B. (1981). Sexual harassment: Some see it . . . some won't. *Harvard Business Review, 59*(2), 76-95.

11. Tangri, S. S., & Hayes, S. M. (1997). Theories of sexual harassment. In W. O'Donohue (Ed.), *Sexual harassment: Theory, research, and treatment* (pp. 112–128). Boston: Allyn & Bacon; Tangri, S. S., Burt, M. R., & Johnson, L. B. (1982). Sexual harassment at work: Three explanatory models. *Journal of Social Issues, 38*(4), 33-54.

12. Thacker, R. A., & Ferris, G. R. (1991). Understanding sexual harassment in the workplace: The influence of power and politics within the dyadic interaction of harasser and target. *Human Resource Management Review, 1,* 23–37; Cleveland, J. N., & Kerst, M. E. (1993). Sexual harassment and perceptions of power: An under-articulated relationship. *Journal of Vocational Behavior, 42,* 49–67.

13. Gutek & Done; Williams, C. L. (1989). *Gender differences at work: Women and men in nontraditional occupations.* Berkeley: University of California Press; DiTomaso, N. (1989). Sexuality in the workplace: Discrimination and harassment. In J. Hearn, D. L. Sheppard, P. Tancred-Sheriff, & G. Burrell (Eds.), *The sexuality of organization* (pp. 71–90). London: Sage.

14. Gutek, B. A. (1985). *Sex and the workplace: The impact of sexual behavior and harassment on women, men, and organizations.* San Francisco: Jossey-Bass; U.S. Department of Labor, Bureau of Labor Statistics. (2002). *Employment and Earnings* (computed from Table 39). Retrieved April 29, 2002, from http://www.bls.gov/cps

15. Gutek & Done; Pryor, J. B. (1987). Sexual harassment proclivities in men. *Sex Roles, 17,* 269–290; Perry, E. L., Schmidtke, J. M., & Kulik, C. T. (1998). Propensity to sexually harass: An exploration of gender differences. *Sex Roles, 38,* 443–460; Fiske, S. T., & Glick, P. (1995). Ambivalence and stereotypes cause sexual harassment: A theory with implications for organizational change. *Journal of Social Issues, 51*(1), 97–115.

16. U.S. Merit Systems Protection Board.

17. Dansky, B. S., & Kilpatrick, D. G. (1997). Effects of sexual harassment. In W. O'Donohue (Ed.), *Sexual harassment: Theory, research, and treatment* (pp. 152–174). Boston: Allyn & Bacon; Hanisch, K. A. (1996). An integrated framework for studying the outcomes of sexual harassment: Consequences for individuals and organizations. In M. S. Stockdale (Ed.), *Sexual harassment in the workplace: Perspectives, frontiers, and response strategies* (pp. 174–198). Thousand Oaks, CA: Sage. Fitzgerald, L. F., Drasgow, F., Hulin, C. L., Gelfand, M. J., & Magley, V. J. (1997). Antecedents and consequences of sexual harassment in organizations: A test of an integrated model. *Journal of Applied Psychology, 82,* 578–589; Wasti, Bergman, Glomb, & Drasgow; Schneider, K. T., Swan, S., & Fitzgerald, L. F. (1997). Job-related and psychological effects of sexual harassment in the workplace: Empirical evidence from two organizations. *Journal of Applied Psychology, 82,* 401–415.

18. Gutek (1985); Bergman, M. E., Langhout, R. D., Palmieri, P. A., Cortina, L. M., & Fitzgerald, L. F. (2002). The (un)reasonableness of reporting: Antecedents and consequences of reporting sexual harassment. *Journal of Applied Psychology, 87,* 230–242; Hulin, C. L., Fitzgerald, L. F., & Drasgow, F. (1996). Organizational influences on sexual harassment. In M. S. Stockdale (Ed.), *Sexual harassment in the workplace: Perspectives, frontiers, and response strategies* (pp. 127–150). Thousand Oaks, CA: Sage.

19. Bowes-Sperry, L., & Powell, G. N. (1999). Observers' reactions to social-sexual behavior at work: An ethical decision making perspective. *Journal of Management, 25,* 779–802; Bowes-Sperry, L., & Powell, G. N. (1996). Sexual harassment as a moral issue: An ethical decision-making perspective. In M. S. Stockdale (Ed.), *Sexual harassment in the workplace: Perspectives, frontiers, and response strategies* (pp. 105–124). Thousand Oaks, CA: Sage.

20. This section is primarily based on Powell, G. N., & Foley, S. (1999). Romantic relationships in organizational settings: Something to talk about. In G. N. Powell (Ed.), *Handbook of gender and work* (pp. 281–304). Thousand Oaks, CA: Sage; Powell, G. N., & Foley, S. (1998). Something to talk about: Romantic relationships in organizational settings. *Journal of Management, 24,* 421–448.

21. Powers, D. M. (1999). *The office romance: Playing with fire without getting burned.* New York: American Management Association.

22. Sternberg, R. J. (1998). *Cupid's arrow: The course of love through time.* Cambridge, UK: Cambridge University Press; Sternberg, R. J. (1986). A triangular theory of love. *Psychological Review, 93,* 119–135.

23. Pierce, C. A., Byrne, D., & Aguinis, H. (1996). Attraction in organizations: A model of workplace romance. *Journal of Organizational Behavior, 17,* 5–32.

24. Dillard, J. P., & Miller, K. I. (1988). Intimate relationships in task environments. In S. Duck (Ed.), *Handbook of personal relationships* (pp. 449–465). Chichester, UK: Wiley; Quinn, R. (1977). Coping with cupid: The formation, impact, and management of romantic relationships in organizations. *Administrative Science Quarterly, 22,* 30–45; Pierce, Byrne, & Aguinis.

25. Powell, G. N. (1986). What do tomorrow's managers think about sexual intimacy in the workplace? *Business Horizons, 29*(4), 30–35; Quinn; Pierce, Byrne, & Aguinis.

26. Mainiero, L. A. (1989). *Office romance: Love, power, and sex in the workplace.* New York: Rawson Associates.

27. Mainiero (1989); Gutek (1985).

28. Quinn; Dillard, J. P. (1987). Close relationships at work: Perceptions of the motives and performance of relational participants. *Journal of Social and Personal Relationships, 4,* 179–193.

29. Mainiero, L. A. (1986). A review and analysis of power dynamics in organizational romances. *Academy of Management Review, 11,* 750–762.

30. Mainiero (1989).

31. Pierce, C. A., & Aguinis, H. (1997). Bridging the gap between romantic relationships and sexual harassment in organizations. *Journal of Organizational Behavior, 18,* 197–200.

32. Mainiero (1989); Friskopp, A., & Silverstein, S. (1995). *Straight jobs, gay lives: Gay and lesbian professionals, the Harvard Business School, and the American workplace.* New York: Scribner.

33. Pierce, Byrne, & Aguinis; Dillard & Miller.

34. Clawson, J. G., & Kram, K. E. (1984). Managing cross-gender mentoring. *Business Horizons, 2* (3), 22–32

35. Dillard & Miller; Quinn; Pierce, Byrne, & Aguinis.

36. Powell, G. N. (2001). Workplace romances between senior-level executives and lower-level employees: An issue of work disruption and gender. *Human Relations, 54,* 1519–1544.

37. Quinn.

38. Foley, S., & Powell, G. N. (1999). Not all is fair in love and work: Coworkers' preferences for and responses to managerial interventions regarding workplace romances. *Journal of Organizational Behavior, 20,* 1043–1056; Powell (2001).

39. Gutek, B. A. (1997). Sexual harassment policy initiatives. In W. O'Donohue (Ed.), *Sexual harassment: Theory, research, and treatment* (pp. 185–198). Boston: Allyn & Bacon.

40. Reitman.

41. Powell, G. N. (1983). Sexual harassment: Confronting the issue of definition. *Business Horizons, 26*(4), 24–28.

42. Peirce, E., Smolinski, C. A., & Rosen, B. (1998). Why sexual harassment complaints fall on deaf ears. *Academy of Management Executive, 12*(3), 41–54.

43. U.S. Merit Systems Protection Board; Rowe, M. P. (1996). Dealing with harassment: A systems approach. In M. S. Stockdale (Ed.), *Sexual harassment in the workplace: Perspectives, frontiers, and coping strategies* (pp. 241–271). Thousand Oaks, CA: Sage; Knapp, D. E., Faley, R. H., Ekeberg, S. E., & Dubois, C. L. Z. (1997). Determinants of target responses to sexual harassment: A conceptual framework. *Academy of Management Review, 22,* 687–729; Malamut, A. B., & Offermann, L. R. (2001). Coping with sexual harassment: Personal, environmental, and cognitive determinants. *Journal of Applied Psychology, 86,* 1152–1166.

44. Rowe, M. P. (1981). Dealing with sexual harassment. *Harvard Business Review, 59* (3), 42–46.

45. Rowe (1981); Rowe (1996); Deutschman, A. (1991, November 4). Dealing with sexual harassment. *Fortune,* 145–148.

46. MacKinnon, C. A. (1979). *Sexual harassment of working women: A case of sex discrimination.* New Haven, CT: Yale University Press; Mead, M. (1980). A proposal: We need taboos on sex at work. In D. A. Neugarten and J. M. Shafritz (Eds.), *Sexuality in organizations: Romantic and coercive behaviors at work* (pp. 53–56). Oak Park, IL: Moore; Tiger, L. (1997, May 27). Sex in uniform. *Wall Street Journal,* p. A18; Hymowitz, C., & Pollock, E. J. (1998, February 4). Corporate affairs: The one clear line in interoffice romance has become blurred. *Wall Street Journal,* pp. A1, A8; Williams, C. L., Giuffre, P. A., & Dellinger, K. (1999). Sexuality in the workplace: Organizational control, sexual harassment, and the pursuit of pleasure. In K. S. Cook & J. Hagan (Eds.), *Annual review of sociology, 25* (pp. 73–93). Palo Alto, CA: Annual Reviews.

47. Society for Human Resource Management. (2002). *Workplace romance.* Retrieved February 5, 2002, from http://www.shrm.org

48. Society for Human Resource Management. (1998). *Workplace romance survey.* Alexandria, VA: Society for Human Resource Management.

49. Quinn; Mainiero (1986).

8

Pursuing Careers

THE BOARD DOESN'T WANT EXCUSES

[One] Saturday, Jennifer (not her real name) held a fiftieth birthday party for her mother. She worked for several months in arranging the party and in getting her family to agree to the arrangements. She lined up the restaurant at which the party would be held. She arranged the group gifts, prepared for the follow-up party to be held at her house afterwards, the whole works. It was going to be a special day for Jennifer, her mother, and everyone else involved. Early on that Saturday morning, Jennifer received a call from her boss and was told that she had to come to work that day. When she began to describe her plans for the day, she was cut off and told, "The board doesn't want excuses. The board wants work." The fiftieth birthday party was held, but without Jennifer present. She spent the whole Saturday at work. According to Jennifer, it wasn't even an emergency that led her to be called in.

—Gary N. Powell[1]

Ugly things are happening to employees in the business world. Horror stories like Jennifer's have become increasingly common. Many organizations expect employees to put work first at all times and to have an outside life only when granted permission to take time off from work. Such organizations, which we call *abusive organizations,* operate with callous disregard for their employees, not even displaying what might be considered a minimum amount of concern for employees' needs outside of work. Although abusive organizations have always been with us, their numbers seem to be multiplying.

In contrast, many other organizations have implemented work-family programs that help employees meet their family-related needs while maintaining high levels of performance. Such organizations, which we call *family-friendly organizations,* show greater concern for employees' lives outside of work and are less inclined to make unreasonable demands on a routine basis.[2] Thus, organizations vary widely in their attentiveness to employees' needs. The inconsistent nature of today's workplace is reflected in the large numbers of both abusive and family-friendly organizations.

Employees' needs vary widely as well. Many people are looking for flexible work schedules, child care and elder care assistance, telecommuting, part-time work, and other arrangements that family-friendly organizations offer to help employees meet their work and family needs. Not everyone, however, wants to work in a family-friendly organization. Work is the primary source of satisfaction in life for many people, including highly educated young professionals early in their careers, as well as senior executives further along in their careers.

This chapter is about pursuing a career—what people are looking for in a career, what opportunities are available to them, and how decisions made by individuals, organizations, and families influence careers. We define a *career* as the combination and sequence of roles played by a person during the course of his or her lifetime. These roles may include student, worker, spouse, parent, retiree, and so on. Not everyone plays all of these roles; some people never marry, have children, or reach retirement. According to this definition, you have a career even if you are not engaged in paid employment or preparing for such employment.[3]

At one time, describing the sequence of roles in individuals' careers seemed a straightforward task. Careers were viewed as a series of consecutive stages linked to an individual's age. For example, in one of the first formal theories of career development, Donald Super proposed that five career stages—growth, exploration, establishment, maintenance, and decline—captured an individual's work-related experiences from childhood to retirement. Individuals were assumed to go through each career stage only once in their lifetimes. In addition, work careers were assumed to be continuous within one occupation, perhaps with one or two employers, and devoid of major disruptions or redirections.[4]

Early theories of career development, however, were based primarily on observations of men's careers. Describing women's careers is a more challenging task. It may be easier to discuss what a woman's career *is not*—a lock-step progression of jobs at increasingly higher levels with a goal of upward mobility and objective career success regardless of the personal cost—than what it *is.* Former U.S. Secretary of State Madeleine Albright, the highest ranking woman in the history of the U.S. government, said, "Women's careers don't go in straight lines. They zigzag all over the place."[5]

In this chapter, we examine how individuals' work and nonwork lives evolve over their life spans and how organizational policies and practices influence the course of employees' lives. First, we consider exactly what constitutes career success for individuals. We then examine differences in the patterns of women's and men's careers, including experiences in advancing to top management positions. We consider the role played by organizations in employees' careers, including different kinds of work-family programs and the impact of the organizational culture on whether employees take advantage of such programs. We also consider the role played by family in careers, including the challenges of juggling work and family roles and the ways in which social support can help in meeting these challenges. Finally, we offer suggestions for enhancing men's and women's career success, including recommendations for both organizations and individuals.

What Makes a Career Successful?

Both objective and subjective measures may be used to assess career success.[6] In most research studies, career success has been measured by *objective* variables such as earnings, level of position in the organizational hierarchy, and rate of advancement or promotion. When such objective variables are used to measure career success, people's careers are deemed successful in relation to their receiving more pay, holding positions at higher levels, and advancing at a faster rate.

Career success also is measured by *subjective* variables that reflect individuals' satisfaction with various aspects of their work and nonwork lives, including their current job, potential for advancement, job security, relationships with family members, and opportunities to pursue hobbies and other personal interests. When such subjective variables are used to measure career success, people's careers may be considered successful at any level in the organizational hierarchy, no matter the amount of pay and how rapid their advancement. What counts is that they are satisfied with where they are and with their future.

Objective and subjective career success are positively related; people who achieve greater objective career success tend to be more satisfied with their careers. However, career success in objective terms does not necessarily lead to happiness. The factors that lead to objective career success may be very different from those that lead to subjective career success.[7]

Women and men tend to use different types of measures in assessing their own career success, with men focusing more on objective measures and women focusing more on subjective measures. Men's reliance on objective measures of success that emphasize "getting ahead" in organizations is consistent with the male gender role and corresponds with their interest in job attributes such as earnings, promotion opportunities, and authority (see Chapter 4). When men achieve greater objective success, they are better able to fulfill their traditional responsibilities as breadwinners for their families. In contrast, women's use of subjective measures of success is consistent with the female gender role. Women's focus on their feelings about their careers corresponds with the stereotype of women as expressive. In addition, the high value that women place on job attributes that promote positive interpersonal relationships, such as having good coworkers and opportunities to make friends and provide help to others, necessitates the use of subjective measures. The quality of relationships is best captured by subjective, not objective, measures.[8]

In summary, career success is not simply a function of concrete factors such as pay, organizational level, and rate of advancement. Individuals' feelings about their lives inside and outside of work also influence their assessments of their careers. People choose whether they rely more on subjective or objective measures of career success. Consistent with gender roles, women, in assessing their career success, generally place more emphasis than men on their own feelings and on their relationships with others and less emphasis on whether they are getting ahead.

Sex Differences in Careers

When we examine the levels of career success achieved by men and women, we find evidence of sex similarities and differences. Several studies have tracked the career success of male compared to female MBA graduates who earned their degrees from the same institutions during the same period of time. These studies have found no sex difference in the level of subjective career success achieved. Over time, as their common educational experience recedes, female MBA graduates are no more or less satisfied with their careers than their male counterparts. However, the same studies have found a sex difference in the level of objective career success achieved. Eventually, female MBA graduates lag behind their male counterparts in indicators of objective career success such as income and managerial level.[9]

A different picture emerges when examining sex differences in career success among Blacks, who generally experience less subjective and objective career success than Whites. Black male MBAs are less satisfied with their career advancement than Black female MBAs, even when they have achieved similar organizational levels.[10]

Next we review how the career patterns of women and men differ in ways that may contribute to the sex difference in objective career success.

EMPLOYMENT GAPS AND LEAVES OF ABSENCE

Women and men differ in the propensity to have gaps in their employment history. Employment gaps, periods of time without employment, may be either voluntary (e.g., for child rearing or due to personality mismatch on the job) or involuntary (e.g., due to downsizing and mergers). Women are more likely than men to have employment gaps early in their careers (first 12 years or so). Women's early-career gaps are longer than those of men and are more likely to be voluntary for child rearing.[11]

Women and men also differ in the propensity to take leaves of absence. A leave of absence is a paid or unpaid employer-approved period of time away from work. Due to both legislation and corporate policies, employees now have more opportunities to take leaves of absence. The Family and Medical Leave Act (FMLA) requires most U.S. employers to provide eligible employees up to 12 weeks of unpaid, job-protected leave each year to care for a newborn or newly adopted child, a seriously ill child, spouse, or parent, or to deal with their own illness. Many family-friendly organizations offer more extended leaves for similar purposes. Although the FMLA and most corporate programs offer the same leave opportunities to female and male employees, women are far more likely than men to take leaves.[12]

Sex differences in voluntary employment gaps and leaves of absence are due, in large part, to the differential impact of decisions about parenthood on the two sexes. Decisions about parenthood have a profound impact on the career patterns of women who want to have children. Because of the inescapable reality of their biological clocks, aspiring mothers feel compelled to incorporate motherhood into their career plans. In contrast, men are less likely to view fatherhood as a constraint on their work careers and feel less need to plan around it.

The way in which women incorporate motherhood into their careers affects whether they experience interruptions in employment. There are two patterns for the timing of motherhood, a sequential pattern of staggering or alternating a work career with the intensive years of motherhood (child bearing and early child rearing), and a simultaneous pattern of pursuing motherhood and a work career simultaneously, perhaps with a short maternity leave. There are three variations of the sequential pattern: (1) motherhood follows employment, when the mother embarks on her work career and then abandons it permanently upon birth of her first child; (2) employment brackets motherhood, when the mother takes time out from her work career to devote herself exclusively to raising her children and then resumes her work career when the children are older; and (3) employment follows motherhood, when the mother completes her parenting role before she begins her work career. Voluntary employment gaps occur when employment brackets motherhood.[13]

The stereotype of a successful career, largely based on the experiences of men, focuses on uninterrupted work. Such a career pattern is assumed to demonstrate stability and commitment to work. Time away from work, unless for the purpose of enhancing educational credentials, is often assumed to lead to deterioration of skills and knowledge and to reflect less commitment to work. As a result, when people choose to take time out from their work careers for any reason, their subsequent advancement and earnings are likely to suffer. Thus, women's greater tendency to have voluntary employment gaps and to take leaves of absence contributes to their achieving lower long-term objective career success.[14]

PART-TIME WORK

Women and men differ in the propensity to hold part-time rather than full-time jobs. Part-time jobs are in the minority in most countries, but their proportion is significant. To cite a few examples, the proportion of jobs that are part-time is 18% in the United States, 22% in the United Kingdom, 19% in Canada, 25% in Australia, 21% in Japan, and 24% in Sweden. Women hold two thirds or more of all part-time jobs in most countries. In the United States, women hold 67% of all part-time jobs; 25% of the U.S. female labor force and 11% of the U.S. male labor force are employed in part-time jobs. Women hold 86% of all part-time jobs in the United Kingdom, 69% in Canada, 73% in Australia, 68% in Japan, and 80% in Sweden.[15]

Part-time work offers many workers a better balance between work and family responsibilities, leisure, and civic activities. It also provides many workers a transition to or from full-time employment. For employers, part-time work permits greater flexibility in responding to changing market requirements. For governments, part-time work reduces the number of individuals who seek unemployment or welfare benefits. However, part-time work also has drawbacks for individuals. Part-time employees have lower status in organizations than full-time employees doing the same kind of work. Their hourly wages are lower, they are less likely to receive benefits such as health insurance, their jobs are less secure, and their career prospects are more limited. Although women's greater tendency than men to hold part-time jobs offers them advantages that may contribute to their subjective career success, it puts them at a disadvantage in achieving objective career success.[16]

DEVELOPMENTAL EXPERIENCES

Women and men in managerial positions differ in their access to key developmental experiences during their careers. Having a "stretch" assignment is an especially important developmental experience. In stretch assignments, managers learn to handle a variety of responsibilities in the spotlight and under fire. Male managers are more likely to receive these assignments. Men's jobs require them to handle high stakes (e.g., rigid deadlines, pressure from senior management, high visibility, responsibility for key decisions), manage business diversity (e.g., handle multiple functions, groups, products, customers, markets), and deal with external pressure (e.g., negotiate with unions or government agencies, cope with serious community problems). In contrast, women's jobs require them to function on their own with little support. Women are more likely to be excluded from key networks and receive little encouragement. The developmental challenges faced more by male managers contribute to career advancement, whereas those faced more by female managers hinder career advancement.[17]

Job opportunities that require relocation also enhance employees' development by providing them the chance to polish their skills, work on high-visibility projects, and gain exposure in a different geographic location. Employees who relocate gain valuable first-hand perspective on the problems and challenges faced in different corporate facilities. However, employees with equal qualifications do not have equal access to relocation opportunities. Married women are offered fewer job opportunities requiring relocation than married men. In addition, dual-career married employees receive fewer relocation opportunities than married breadwinners. Because the proportion of married women in dual-career relationships is larger than that of married men, the denial of women's access to relocation opportunities is reinforced.[18]

These differences in access to relocation opportunities reflect biased beliefs and assumptions about certain types of employees. Organizational decision makers may overlook employees in dual-career marriages when making relocation offers because they anticipate that such employees will be reluctant to relocate due to a working spouse's resistance. The same decision makers may believe that women will be less likely to accept relocation offers than men because they have less influence in their families regarding important decisions. In reality, women do not express less of a willingness to relocate than men. However, because they are perceived to be less willing to relocate, women experience lower geographic mobility than men, which restricts their objective career success.[19]

International assignments are particularly valuable relocation opportunities in multinational corporations. International business has become a major component of most corporations' operations, and not having an international assignment has increasingly become a liability for upwardly mobile managers. Female and male managers differ in access to international assignments. For example, only 13% of U.S. managers sent abroad are women, even though women represent 45% of U.S. managers overall. This is not because women express less interest in international assignments or careers than men. Instead, myths about the availability and suitability of women for international assignments prevail. Many executives and human resources professionals believe that women are just not interested in working abroad or that they do not want to move their families for this purpose, despite the fact that women are less likely to turn down an opportunity to work abroad than men. Another argument is that foreign clients are not as comfortable doing business with women as with men. However, most women who work abroad report that being a female has a positive or neutral impact on their effectiveness. Female managers' limited access to international assignments constrains their objective career success.[20]

Training programs, industry meetings, and professional conferences also enhance managers' development by building their skills, knowledge, and contacts off the job. Males are sent to a greater number of formal training programs and off-site development activities and receive greater financial support from their employers for outside educational programs (e.g., part-time MBA) than females. In addition, participation in such activities has a greater influence on male managers' than female managers' objective career success.[21]

Another important developmental experience is having a mentor. Mentors are senior individuals with advanced experience and knowledge who provide support and assistance to their protégés' careers. Although some organizations have formal programs that assign mentors to protégés, informal mentoring relationships are most common and tend to be most beneficial to protégés. Mentors help protégés in their career development by acting as coaches and sponsors, protecting them from hostile forces, and providing them challenging work assignments. Mentors also enhance protégés' satisfaction with their careers by offering personal support, friendship, counseling, and acceptance. Thus, mentors significantly contribute to their protégés' objective and subjective career success. Generally, the more well positioned the mentor is in the organization, the more positive the benefits for the protégé. Because White males hold the majority of top management positions, they are likely to be the most beneficial mentors for protégés.[22]

Mentors may be particularly helpful to female managers by buffering them from both overt and covert discrimination and helping them to overcome obstacles to attaining top management positions. Women, however, face greater barriers to developing informal mentoring relationships than men. Because the upper levels of management are male-intensive, men are in greater abundance than women as potential mentors. Male mentors may be reluctant to select female protégés because of concerns about possible sexual innuendoes or because they prefer to mentor people like themselves. In addition, women may hesitate to initiate mentoring relationships with men for fear that their actions will be misconstrued as sexual advances. Female managers are thereby less likely to be mentored than male managers. Even successful female executives are less likely than successful male executives to report that mentoring facilitated their advancement.[23]

TURNOVER

Women and men differ in the propensity to quit their jobs and leave their employers voluntarily. Women's turnover rates are higher than those of men in most occupations, including managerial and professional, in both the private and public sector. Some researchers have argued that a major cause of the sex difference in objective career success is that organizations associate "female" with "quitter." Women may be denied opportunities for development and advancement because it is thought to be inevitable that they will leave the organization to pursue motherhood. Women are, in fact, more likely to quit their jobs for family-related reasons than men, as seen in the sex difference in early-career voluntary employment gaps for child rearing.[24]

Female managers do not fulfill this expectation. Their decisions regarding whether to quit or to stay are influenced more by career-related concerns. Female managers who are frustrated at their lack of career opportunities are more likely to quit their jobs than male managers with a similar level of frustration. Female managers who receive a promotion during a given period of time, however, are less likely to quit their jobs than male managers who receive a promotion during the same period of time. Thus, female managers appear to have both a lower tolerance for career opportunities denied and a greater appreciation of career opportunities granted than male managers.[25]

ENTREPRENEURSHIP

When people are dissatisfied with the career opportunities available in organizations or want the challenge of making it on their own, they may start their own businesses. Women and men differ in the propensity to go into business for themselves. Privately held business firms are classified in U.S. government statistics as "men-owned" if the majority of owners are male, "women-owned" if the majority of owners are female, or "jointly-owned" if ownership is equally divided between males and females. Overall, 57% of firms are men-owned, 26% are women-owned, and 17% are jointly-owned. However, 91% of business revenues are generated by men-owned firms, 4% by women-owned firms, and 5% by jointly-owned firms. Women-owned firms tend to be younger and have fewer employees than men-owned firms.[26]

Women-owned business firms represent the fastest growth segment of privately held business firms. The proportions of women-owned firms, revenues generated by women-owned firms, and people employed by women-owned firms all have increased in recent years. These trends may be a consequence of other trends in women's employment and preparation for work in recent decades. First, women entered the labor force in greater numbers. Second, women earned more college degrees in all disciplines, including business, at both the bachelor's and master's levels. Third, women exercised increased decision making and authority in the business world by entering into managerial positions in greater numbers. Finally, women are starting businesses in greater numbers. The trend toward greater female involvement in entrepreneurial activity seems an inevitable consequence of greater female involvement in the labor force in other respects.

Consistent with the male gender role, male business owners tend to view their businesses as economic units independent from the rest of their lives. In contrast, consistent with the female gender role, female business owners tend to integrate their businesses into their lives, developing a network of business, family, societal, and personal relationships. Anita Roddick, founder and former CEO of The Body Shop, quoted in Chapter 6, expressed this perspective. Roddick described her work as a business owner as an integral part of her life and as a reflection of her societal concerns. Few business owners, female or male, are as explicitly socially conscious in their roles as Roddick. However, female entrepreneurs are more likely to adopt a holistic view of how their businesses fit into their lives rather than a compartmentalized view more characteristic of male entrepreneurs.[27]

Women who run their own businesses do not show up in published statistics about the proportion of women in top management because such statistics typically focus on large publicly held firms such as *Fortune* 500 corporations. Women business owners, however, are, in effect, the top management of their own firms.[28]

RETIREMENT

Near the end of their work careers, women and men differ in how they handle the issue of retirement. For married women, the odds of being retired at a given age are *higher* when they have a greater number of dependents in the household and when their husband's health is poor. However, for married men, the odds of being retired at a given age are *lower* when they have a greater number of dependents in the household and when their wife's health is poor.

Thus, women's retirement decisions are influenced by gender role expectations that they will be available to nurture others in need, the same expectations that led them to interrupt their work careers for child rearing. In contrast, men's retirement decisions are based more on their traditional gender role as providers of economic resources for their families.[29]

Women have more negative attitudes toward retirement and have a harder time adjusting to it than men. This may be because they are at an economic disadvantage when they retire. Retirement pensions are typically based on earnings at the time of retirement and years of continuous full-time employment with an organization, both of which tend to be smaller for women than men. As a result, men receive greater financial support after they retire. Retired men are more than twice as likely as retired women to receive a pension, and the size of men's pensions is more than 75% larger.[30]

In conclusion, there is considerable evidence of sex differences in career patterns throughout the life span, including differences in employment gaps, leaves of absence, part-time work, developmental experiences, turnover rates and causes, entrepreneurship, and retirement. These differences may account for why men on average achieve more objective career success than women. However, there is also evidence of sex similarity in subjective career success. Women and men who begin their work careers with similar backgrounds and credentials are similarly satisfied with their careers at later stages.

The Glass Ceiling

One of the most important signifiers of objective career success is advancement up the corporate ladder. Women and men differ in the attainment of top management positions. As reported in Chapter 1, although the proportion of women in the labor force and in management overall has increased in almost all countries, the proportion of women in *top* management positions remains small. Around the world, female managers are concentrated in the lower management levels and hold positions with less authority overall than men.

It does not seem to be only a matter of time until the gap between the proportions of women in top management and in management overall is closed. It also does not seem to be simply a matter of women's personal preference that there are fewer of them in top management. Although women tend to place less emphasis on objective career success, there would seem to be a sufficient number of highly qualified lower-level female managers interested in upward mobility to allow a substantial increase in the proportion of women in top management. Further, early sex differences in career patterns do not provide a sufficient explanation for why the top management ranks are so heavily male-intensive. Something more is going on when decisions are made about who will fill top management positions. The "glass ceiling" is restricting women's access to top management positions solely because they are women. Women are not allowed to advance in managerial hierarchies as far as men with equivalent credentials.[31]

Several factors contribute to the existence of the glass ceiling. The entry of women into top management is influenced by the structure of the decision-making process and the accountability of decision makers. Most organizations do not have a systematic procedure for making promotions to top management positions. Cases are handled on an ad hoc basis, and records of the promotional process are seldom kept. As a result, decisions about top management positions are relatively unstructured and unscrutinized, allowing decision makers to make biased decisions without fear of retribution. Decisions for lower-level management positions are typically more structured and based more on objective credentials that women can consciously acquire, such as education. These decisions may be scrutinized more readily, rendering decision makers more accountable.[32]

The glass ceiling also is perpetuated by decision makers' cognitive processes, including their stereotypes, prototypes, and preference for similar others. As discussed in Chapter 6, women who aspire to management positions in most societies contend with common stereotypes of their being unfit for those roles. These stereotypes disadvantage women at all levels of management. However, such stereotypes are most invoked when women are being considered for top-level management positions because women's presence at those levels violates the norm of male superiority. Having an abundance of masculine characteristics contributes to advancement in male-intensive management hierarchies, and such characteristics are associated with men more than women.[33]

As noted in Chapter 4, decision makers' prototypes or mental models of the attributes of the ideal jobholder influence their selection decisions. A prototype may be either sex-based, incorporating the sex of jobholders in some way, or sex-neutral, ignoring the sex of jobholders. The sex of the candidate is most likely to be incorporated into decision makers' prototypes when persons of one sex dominate both the pool of job incumbents and the pool of job candidates, typically the case for top management jobs.[34]

People also tend to make the most positive evaluations of and decisions about people whom they see as similar to themselves. Rosabeth Kanter characterized the results of such a preference in top management ranks as "homosocial reproduction." She argued that the primary motivation in bureaucracies in all decisions is to minimize uncertainty. Uncertainty is present whenever individuals are relied upon, and the effects of such uncertainty are greatest when these individuals hold significant responsibility for the direction of the organization. One way to minimize uncertainty in the executive suite is to close top management positions to people who are regarded as different. Thus, women have a difficult time entering top management positions because they are seen as different by male incumbents.[35]

Although the decision-making processes described above create the glass ceiling, women's reactions to these processes magnify its effects. When women believe that they are disadvantaged by the glass ceiling, they may be less likely to express an interest in open top management jobs than equally qualified men. This tendency contributes to maintaining the low proportion of women in top management, another self-fulfilling prophecy. However, the glass ceiling may be weakened if some women make it to the top of the organization. When women hold some of the top management jobs in an organization, cognitive biases favoring men are less likely to be used in the decision-making process because the prospect of adding women to top management is less uncertain. Further, women are more likely to express an interest in open management positions. The challenge then becomes getting women into top management jobs in the first place.[36]

The Intersection of Work and Family

Individuals' career patterns are influenced by the work environments that employers provide, as well as the nature of their family lives. To understand the dynamics of individuals' careers more fully, we examine the roles of both employers and employees in determining the intersection of work and family. First, we consider popular work-family initiatives and the influence of the organizational culture on whether employees participate in those initiatives. Next, we consider the differences in families and the consequences of these differences for the relationship between work and family in employees' lives.

WORK-FAMILY INITIATIVES

There are great differences in the extent to which organizations embrace work-family initiatives. Although many organizations take concrete steps to promote family-friendly environments, others treat employees in an abusive manner. Some organizations even offer work-family programs and then make it clear that employees will be sacrificing their future prospects for objective career success if they take advantage of the programs.

Employers may promote a family-friendly environment in many different ways. Work-family initiatives that have been adopted by organizations include dependent care; alternative work arrangements; employment assistance for spouses of relocated employees; partnerships with schools; gifts to community organizations; and workshops, support groups, and advisory task forces that address particular work-family issues. Firms with a higher proportion of professional employees and a higher proportion of female employees develop more extensive work-family initiatives and experience greater performance gains as a result of such initiatives.[37] Initiatives pertaining to dependent care and work arrangements are discussed in greater detail.

Organizations may offer employees valuable assistance with care of dependents, including preschool children, school-age children, and the elderly. Employees' needs for dependent care vary greatly, and organizations need to consider their financial resources and the diversity of their employees' family lives when deciding how best to address these needs. Even when resources are scarce, there are many kinds of actions that can be taken to assist employees with meeting these needs. These actions have a positive impact on recruitment, absenteeism, job satisfaction, and organizational commitment.[38]

For example, a corporate child care program may include any or all of the following actions: (1) Offer a caregiver fair. (2) Give employees information about existing caregivers and help them in making arrangements. (3) Grant employees financial assistance toward the costs of child care. (4) Work with school and community organizations to sponsor programs for school-age children of working parents. (5) Operate on-site or near-site centers that provide all-day and after-school care for employees' children. (6) Offer or sponsor child care programs for summer and school holidays.

Because of increased life spans, middle-aged adults often have to care for both their children and their elderly parents. Unlike child care, elder care may be complicated by distance if the adult dependent is not a member of the employee's household. A corporate elder care program may offer employees the following types of assistance: (1) Refer employees to existing elder care providers in various locations and assist them with making arrangements. (2) Grant employees financial assistance toward the costs of elder care. (3) Give employees information about government programs that address the needs of the aging. (4) Offer support to outside elder care centers. (5) Operate an on-site or near-site elder care center for employees' parents and elderly relatives.[39]

Flexibility in work arrangements makes it possible for many employees to combine work and dependent care. Organizations may offer employees a wide array of alternative work arrangements, including flextime, telecommuting, part-time work, paid leaves and sabbaticals, unpaid leaves beyond what is legally mandated, job sharing, phased-in work schedules following leaves, and phased-in retirement. In most cases, organizations do not need all of their employees to hold full-time jobs, adhere to rigidly defined work schedules, or work onsite all of the time. They can be more flexible in what they expect from employees regarding work arrangements, as long as employees are being productive.

Alternative work arrangements are highly popular with many employees because flexibility in their work schedules enables them to gain greater control over their work and family lives. For example, parents may find it easier to accommodate their children's regular schedules and predictable events such as teacher conferences. In addition, they may respond better to emergencies and unanticipated events such as sudden illnesses, weather-related school closings, and breakdowns in child care arrangements. Flexibility in work arrangements appeals to all employees, not just parents, because it symbolizes a focus on getting the work done rather than how, when, or where it is done. Alternative work arrangements yield benefits for employers such as decreased absenteeism and turnover and increased productivity.[40]

The most popular type of alternative work arrangement is flextime, which allows planned variations from normal work hours. Eleven percent of full-time U.S. workers participate in an employer-sponsored flextime program. Managerial and professional employees make the greatest use of flextime programs. Flextime may consist of changes to the starting and ending times of the workday, or compression of the workweek into fewer days (e.g., four 10-hour days instead of five 8-hour days). It may also allow variation in the work schedule from one workday to the next. Flextime has a positive impact on employees' productivity, absenteeism, job satisfaction, and satisfaction with their schedules, which benefits their employers as well.[41]

Telecommuting, being paid to do some or all of one's work away from the work site, is an increasingly popular type of work arrangement. About 3% of full-time U.S. workers have a formal arrangement with their employers to telecommute from home. As for flextime, telecommuting is most common for managerial and professional employees. It gives employees flexibility in the location and timing of work by allowing them to work with electronic tools out of a "virtual office." Telecommuters report that working at home increases their productivity by cutting down on interruptions and distractions and enhancing their concentration. It also helps employees to balance work and family; their increased presence at home enables them to better fulfill their childcare and household responsibilities and strengthens family relationships. However, telecommuting can blur the boundary between work and family roles in unproductive ways. Because electronic tools bring work-related messages into the home around the clock, telecommuters can feel pressures to always be working. Telecommuters, of course, also face interruptions and distractions from being at home. The challenge for telecommuters is to disengage from work or family when necessary. When this challenge is met, telecommuting benefits both employees and employers.[42]

ORGANIZATIONAL CULTURE

Promoting a family-friendly work environment involves more than offering a variety of work-family programs. It also means providing an organizational culture in which employees feel comfortable in taking advantage of programs that are intended to benefit them. Many organizations that consider themselves family friendly fail to provide such a culture. In an era of frequent downsizing, restructuring, and emphasis on short-term corporate performance, organizations are increasingly expecting their key male and female employees to act like traditional males. Employees are expected to complete their own jobs, as well as the jobs of coworkers who quit or were laid off, regardless of how many extra hours this work requires.

As a result, many employees are working long hours. In the United States, the average hours worked weekly by employed women has increased in recent years. In addition, the proportion of employed men working an extended workweek (more than 40 hours) has increased. Couples are spending more combined hours at work, and the proportion of couples in which both spouses work an extended workweek has increased. Moreover, employees are spending more unpaid hours using the Internet to work at home without cutting back on hours at the work site. These trends have resulted in a time bind for many workers. Although some employees welcome the opportunity to work long hours, organizations increasingly are pressuring employees to work long hours wherever they are and whether they want to or not.[43]

Other than the need to be competitive in the global economy, what leads organizations to adopt a culture in which employees' nonwork needs are ignored? Corporations tend to be run by workaholic male top executives, most of whom are married to women who are not employed full time. These executives strive for mastery and control in their lives and find that they are better able to exercise control at work than at home. They avoid intimacy in their relationships and are willing to sacrifice family and outside interests to fulfill business needs. They also set the standard by which lower-level managers are judged. Although the demands of most lower-level managerial jobs are less than those of most executive jobs, lower-level managers are expected to mimic top executives in their unwavering and absolute devotion to work, no matter how great the cost to their lives outside of work. A manager or professional in such an environment who does not adhere to this model and expresses an interest in a work-family program is committing career suicide, at least by objective measures of success.[44]

Thus, the message that many employers send to their employees is clear: Here is our wonderful array of work-family programs. Is this a great place to work or what? However, sign up for these programs at your own risk. Do not expect us to consider you for future career advancement unless you put us first.

WE ARE FAMILY

To understand the intersection of work and family, we also need to consider the nature of employees' family lives. If family life was fully determined by three variables—marital status (married or single), parental status (children or no children), and employment status of the spouse (employed or not employed)—six different combinations would result:[45]

1. Single, no children

2. Married, no children, spouse employed

3. Married, no children, spouse not employed

4. Single, children

5. Married, children, spouse employed

6. Married, children, spouse not employed

However, this categorization scheme for family life is much too simple. There are additional variations of marital status such as divorced, separated, widowed, or remarried. Single individuals may have a significant other who is as important as a legal spouse; unmarried same-sex and opposite-sex couples also have family lives. Couples, married or unmarried, may or may not live together. The numbers and ages of children vary, of course, as well as their places of residence. Younger children require different care than older children, and the rearing of multiple children is more demanding than that of a sole child. The employment status of the spouse or significant other also varies. Spouses and significant others differ in income contributed to the household and time and energy devoted to their work and family roles. Family members other than children and spouses may play important roles in people's lives.

Table 8.1 reports parental employment in U.S. families with children. The most prevalent combination of family and employment status is the dual-career couple, a married couple in which both parents are employed; 45.6% of families with children under age 18 and 41.9% with children under age 6 fall into this category.[46] The second most prevalent combination is the married couple in which only the father is employed; 21.3% of families with children under age 18 and 28.2% with children under age 6 fall into this category. This is the traditional family structure in which the male serves as breadwinner and the female as homemaker. The third most prevalent combination is the female-headed family in which the mother is employed; 16.6% of families with children under age 18 and 13.3% with children under age 6 fall into this category. The prevalence of single working mothers is a reminder that single as well as married people have family lives.

Table 8.1   Employment Status of Parents in U.S. Families With Children

Type of Family	Own Children Under Age 18 Percentage of Total	Own Children Under Age 6 Percentage of Total
Married-couple families:		
Both parents employed	45.6%	41.9%
Mother employed, not father	3.2	2.7
Father employed, not mother	21.3	28.2
Neither parent employed	2.1	2.1
Families maintained by women:		
Mother employed	16.6	13.3
Mother not employed	5.7	6.4
Families maintained by men:		
Father employed	4.7	4.5
Father not employed	.8	.7
TOTALS:	100.0%	100.0%

SOURCE: U.S. Department of Labor, Bureau of Labor Statistics. (2002). Employment characteristics of families (computed from 2001 data in Table 4). Retrieved May 25, 2002, from http://www.bls.gov
NOTE: No spouse was present in families maintained by women and families maintained by men. Own children include sons, daughters, stepchildren, and adopted children. Detailed percentages may not sum to totals due to rounding.

The family structures of women and men differ. Women are more likely to be single parents than are men. In married couples, women are less likely to be the sole breadwinner than are men. Even at top management levels, there is a sex difference in family structure. As women assume managerial positions at increasingly higher levels, they are less likely to be married or to have children than are men with equivalent responsibilities. In general, the more successful the man in objective terms, the more likely he is to have a spouse and children. The opposite holds true for women.[47]

Family structures are becoming increasingly differentiated around the world, as the traditional pattern of male breadwinner and female homemaker gives way to dual-career couples and other alternatives. Families with children exhibit several different structures, and of course, many families have no children or grown children who are no longer at home. As a result, there is considerable diversity in employees' family lives.[48]

A JUGGLING ACT

The roles of worker and family member are two of the most important roles that people play. Neither men nor women adopt a single approach to managing the interface between these two roles. Kathleen Gerson, in *No Man's Land: Men's Changing Commitments to Family and Work,* reported the results of interviews with men between the ages of 28 and 45 in both white-collar and blue-collar jobs. She concluded that the men she interviewed fell about equally into three categories: breadwinners, autonomous men, and involved fathers. Breadwinners seek to be the primary earner, whether or not their wives hold paying jobs, and resist involvement in care taking and domestic work; these men pursue the traditional male gender role in their work and family lives. Autonomous men seek to avoid parental responsibilities by not having children or by being estranged from their children; these men place a primary value on being in control of their lives inside and outside of work. Breadwinners and autonomous men segment their work and family lives by avoiding, or even shunning, domestic responsibilities. In contrast, involved fathers renounce workplace success as the sole measure of their manhood, and seek to participate significantly in the care taking aspects of parenthood, as well as provide economic support for their families. Rather than defining themselves rigidly as breadwinners or loners, involved fathers tend to be part of dual-career families and pursue a balance between their work and family lives.[49]

Women also differ in how they manage the interface between work and family roles over their careers. Women's careers are more complex than those of men and involve a wide panorama of choices, as well as constraints. Issues of balance, connectedness, and interdependence, in addition to issues of achievement and individuality permeate women's lives. At any point in her career, a woman may choose to place a greater emphasis on work or on family, or she may strive to achieve a balance between the two. If she emphasizes one role now, this emphasis may be part of a life plan that anticipates a future emphasis on the other role. As discussed earlier, what women emphasize at different points in time is influenced by their plans for motherhood. Women adopt different strategies for incorporating motherhood into their lives. However, not all women become mothers.[50]

For most individuals, participation in their work role influences and is influenced by participation in their family role. There are different schools of thought about the linkage between work and family roles. According to an optimistic view, people benefit from juggling their work and family roles. When people participate heavily in multiple life roles (e.g., engaged in employment outside the home while caring for those within), they are able to avoid the worst aspects of any one role. Their involvement in one role enhances their functioning in the other. As a result, they have a heightened sense of well-being and subjective career success. According to a pessimistic view, people suffer from trying to juggle their work and family roles. When people attempt to participate in both work and family roles to any significant extent, they face an inevitable time bind. Either they flee home in response to the pressures or appeals of work, or they sacrifice objective career success to devote themselves primarily to their families.[51]

The reality for many families lies somewhere between these optimistic and pessimistic views. A "tradeoffs" view suggests that there are benefits to juggling work and family roles as well as costs. The challenge for individuals is to maximize the benefits while minimizing the costs. Dual-career couples with children and working single parents face the biggest challenge in juggling work and family roles. A large proportion of families face such a challenge; in the United States, dual-career families and those headed by an employed single parent make up 66.9% of all families with children under age 18 and 59.7% of all families with children under age 6 (Table 8.1). Dual-career parents have to negotiate their responses to work and family demands and maintain some degree of objective and subjective career success. Single parents have to fill all the work and family roles in their households. Juggling is less of an issue in families with a male breadwinner and female homemaker because each parent is essentially in charge of one role, either work or family.

Individuals who attempt to juggle work and family roles, whether they are male or female, single parents or dual-career couples, are likely to experience some degree of work-family conflict. Such conflict may come about because work interferes with family, such as when long hours at work are required, or because family interferes with work, such as when a child is sick.

Three types of work-family conflict may occur for individuals: time-based, strain-based, and behavior-based.[52] *Time-based conflict* results from the finite amount of time that is available to handle both work and family roles. Time spent working generally cannot be devoted to family activities and vice versa. Parents experience more time-based conflict than nonparents, parents of younger children more than parents of older children, and parents of large families more than parents of small families.

In dual-career families, mothers are likely to experience more time-based conflict than fathers. This is because married mothers spend more time with their children and more time on household chores than married fathers do. This gap has narrowed as the proportion of women in the labor force, especially in managerial and professional jobs, has increased. Fathers have significantly increased the amount of time they spend with their children, and they have taken over more of the household chores as well. However, fathers who want to become more involved in family life tend to turn more to the nursery than to the kitchen or laundry room. As Kathleen Gerson put it, "Housework remains the last frontier that men want to settle."[53]

Strain-based conflict results when strain in one role spills over into the other role. Family strains may decrease performance at work and thereby negatively affect objective career success. On the other hand, strain at work may affect one's behavior as a parent or spouse. *Behavior-based conflict* occurs when incompatible behaviors are required for work and family roles, such as aggressiveness and objectivity at work and warmth and nurturance at home. Managers who are carrying out the masculine stereotype at work, whether female or male, may feel caught between the emotional detachment exhibited at work and the emotional expressiveness expected at home. "Shifting gears" between work and home is required to avoid this conflict.

Work-family conflict increases for individuals when the demands placed on them in either the work or family role increase. High levels of work-family conflict in turn produce feelings of dissatisfaction and distress within the work and family roles and detract from one's sense of well-being and life satisfaction. The greatest potential for conflict occurs when individuals face simultaneous demands to participate in both a work and a family activity and neither activity can be rescheduled. In the opening passage, Jennifer faced this kind of situation when she was forced to choose between an important work activity (emergency overtime work) and an important family activity (mother's birthday party). She made the difficult choice of going to work and missing the party. As a result, work heavily interfered with family for Jennifer that day, and she felt terrible about it. In general, when faced with such demands, individuals are likely to choose the activity about which others (e.g., boss, spouse) are pressuring them most. They are also likely to choose the activity in the role (work or family) that is most central to their identity.[54]

Work-family conflict may be alleviated by social support from the work and family spheres. Social support may include both tangible support (e.g., information, advice, assistance) and emotional support (e.g., affirmation, affection, trust). In the work environment, support generally comes from two major sources: family-supportive policies developed by organizations and a family-supportive manager who provides help and understanding to the employee in need. In the family, the most common source of support is the spouse or significant other, although other family members such as parents may provide support as well. Men and women who work for an organization that is family friendly and have a partner who provides great personal and career support tend to be more satisfied with their careers.[55]

Dual-career couples vary in how they support each other and deal with work-family conflict. Four types of dual-career couples may be identified:

superordinate partners, synchronized partners, synthetic partners, and severed partners.[56] *Superordinate partners* value both work and family activities and set the goal of achieving satisfaction in both domains for both partners. They may not achieve spectacular success in their work careers, because they do not devote their energies solely to objective career success, but they feel considerable satisfaction with their family lives and try to build a sense of interdependence among family members. They are people to whom work careers are important but not the only interest in life.

Synchronized partners help each other to achieve complementary individual goals. For example, one spouse may be interested primarily in career and less in family affairs while the other spouse is primarily interested in family and less in career pursuits. Couples possessing traditional gender identities, with the work-oriented man being more masculine and the family-oriented woman being more feminine, fit into this category. However, the combination of a family-oriented man and a career-oriented woman or combinations based on other factors (e.g., one partner's job requires extensive travel while the other's does not) are also possible.

Synthetic partners have relationships in which one or both members feel that they have compromised their aspirations. For example, the wife may feel that she has to subordinate her career to her husband's career to carry out family responsibilities, or the husband may feel that he has to suppress his involvement in his career to devote more of himself to the family. Such couples frequently experience frustrations and survive only through makeshift agreements or periodic resolution of tensions. However, the quality of family life is insecure at best.

Severed partners possess highly incompatible values, such as a nontraditional woman strongly committed to her career married to a traditional man who expects his wife to be more strongly committed to family. Such couples are the most contentious and require one member to make a considerable sacrifice in personal goals to preserve the relationship.

In dealing with work-family conflict, superordinate partners are likely to achieve the greatest amount of subjective career success across work and family roles. Synchronized partners are successful in a more limited way because each partner has chosen to specialize in a particular role. Synthetic and severed couples are less successful in agreeing on what their work and family roles will be. Single parents, of course, have to deal with work-family conflict alone. They are the individuals with the greatest need for social support in juggling their work and family lives.

Employees' experiences with work-family conflict and social support differ across national cultures. For example, Chinese employees are more likely to have their parents as live-ins or dependents than U.S. employees; two thirds of

Chinese parents who have adult children live with one of them. In addition, most adult children who do not reside with their parents live close to them. This high proximity facilitates the exchange of care between elderly parents and their married children. Elderly parents in China are more dependent economically and emotionally on their adult children than their U.S. counterparts, but also are more important providers of child care and household assistance to them. Although the net amounts of work-family conflict felt by Chinese compared to U.S. employees may be similar, dual-career couples in China experience both greater stress from having to provide for their parents and greater support from their parents than dual-career couples in the United States.[57]

In theory, corporate work-family programs represent an additional form of social support available to employees experiencing work-family conflict. However, employees may refrain from participating in such programs if the organizational culture tells them that their careers would suffer as a result. Men are especially likely to avoid work-family programs. When companies offer paid leaves for new parents, new fathers are much less likely to take advantage of the opportunity than new mothers. Also, when men participate in a work-family program, they are more inclined than women to try to disguise the reason for their participation. For example, although both men and women use flextime for family-related reasons, men are more likely to lead their coworkers and supervisors to believe that something else has motivated their change in schedule. In an unsupportive corporate culture, even involved fathers feel the need to be seen by their employers as putting work first in their lives.[58]

In conclusion, the challenge for all individuals, whatever their family status, is to manage the interface between their work and family lives. Meeting this challenge is no simple matter. The complexity of many employees' family situations can make the task of negotiating a balance between work and family interests seem like a full-time job in itself. Social support from family members and employers can make the task more manageable. However, many organizations send employees a mixed message: Corporate support is available to help you manage this interface, but at a cost to your advancement prospects.

Facilitating Employees' Career Success

Organizations cannot guarantee career success for their employees, but they can maximize employees' opportunities to have successful careers. Organizations should follow three general principles in their actions:

1. They should be bias-free in decisions made about employees except when consciously trying to offset the effects of past discrimination.

2. They should eliminate sex differences in access to important developmental experiences for employees with equivalent qualifications.

3. They should promote a family-friendly work environment, which may entail changing the organizational culture as well as adopting work-family initiatives.

BIAS-FREE DECISIONS

Organizations make numerous decisions about employees that ultimately determine what their career patterns will be, including decisions about task assignments, training and development, salary increases, and promotions. Once individuals join organizations, formal and informal evaluations of their past performance and potential for future performance influence virtually every major decision made about them. Biased performance evaluations can have a devastating effect on employees' career advancement. Management levels assume a pyramid shape in most organizations, with fewer positions at higher levels. As women attempt to climb the pyramid, only a small amount of sex bias in performance evaluations favoring men will effectively knock them "off course" and keep them from climbing any further. To give all employees a fair chance of objective career success, organizations need to eradicate the influence of biases of any type (gender, race, ethnicity, age, etc.) on performance evaluations and on decisions based on performance evaluations.[59]

Adoption of standardized promotion procedures similar to those used by the U.S. government to hire its top executives would be likely to reduce the influence of decision makers' personal biases on promotion decisions. The Senior Executive Service (SES) consists of the top 1% of government positions except those reserved for political appointees. Applicants for open SES positions are solicited through a public announcement. Then all promotion decisions are made using the same basic procedure. A review panel rates applicants based on their background, career history, and recent performance evaluations and chooses the applicants to refer to the selecting official, who makes the final decision. Finally, records are kept of the entire decision-making process for at least 2 years. These practices provide structure to the decision-making process and enable identification of decisions that are not properly made, thereby holding decision makers accountable. Although such practices are rare, especially in the private sector, greater use of such practices may result in more diverse top management teams.[60]

ACCESS TO DEVELOPMENTAL EXPERIENCES

Sex differences in access to developmental opportunities create barriers to women's advancement to top management. Organizations should ensure that members of both sexes have similar access to stretch assignments, as well as domestic and international relocation opportunities. Women also need access to advanced training and development activities, such as executive MBAs or executive leadership workshops.

Training and development programs targeted especially to women may offer them useful suggestions for dealing with prejudices in the work force, particularly in positions with top management responsibilities. For instance, The Women's Leadership Program is offered by the Center for Creative Leadership for women in middle- and senior-level management positions. Staffed only by women, its purpose is to provide female managers a safe setting in which to delve into "issues and perceptions surrounding women's leadership and work experiences. . . . [In the program] participants explore the choices and trade-offs they face as women juggling personal and professional objectives." However, women and men should be recommended for training and development programs according to their individual needs, not their sex. Many of the companies regarded as "the best companies for women" have no special programs for women; they simply assign the best and brightest people to developmental experiences regardless of sex.[61]

Being mentored is a job experience that can enhance objective and subjective career success. For reasons stated earlier, lower-level female managers have greater difficulty in establishing mentoring relationships than male managers at equivalent levels. Some companies try to overcome these difficulties by assigning highly placed mentors to promising lower-level managers, thereby ensuring that lower-level female managers will not be denied access to upper-level male mentors. Good mentoring relationships, however, cannot be engineered. They must emerge from the spontaneous and mutual involvement of two people who see value in relating to each other. If people feel coerced or mismatched in mentoring relationships, the relationships are likely to flounder. A better approach for organizations is to offer educational programs about mentoring and its role in career development and then identify good mentors and reward them.[62]

FAMILY-FRIENDLY ENVIRONMENT

Promoting a family-friendly environment involves more than offering well designed work-family programs. Supportive managers are a crucial link in creating a family-friendly environment. Employees are more likely to utilize work-family programs when they have supportive managers who empathize with their desires to balance their work and family lives. Moreover, having a family-supportive manager reduces employees' work-family conflict and gives them more incentive to stay with the organization.[63]

Despite the benefits of work-family programs for both employees and employers, managers may resist implementing them. Gary Powell and Lisa Mainiero conducted a study of the factors that affect managerial decisions about granting alternative work arrangements to employees. The most important factor affecting decisions was the criticality of the employee's job assignment. Employees whose work was more critical to the work unit were less likely to be granted alternative work arrangements than noncritical employees; employee sex had no effect on managers' decisions. These are curious results. Employees who are trusted with more critical job tasks would seem to deserve special treatment. According to this study, however, their managers view such employees as the *least* desirable candidates for alternative work arrangements. Critical employees should not have to transfer to less critical jobs to qualify for these arrangements. To reap the benefits of work-family programs, organizations need to educate their managers on the corporate benefits of these programs and provide incentives to managers to implement them.[64]

Promoting a family-friendly work environment also requires an organizational culture in which employees feel free to take advantage of work-family programs. Cultures that define a successful career as an uninterrupted sequence of promotions to higher levels, or assume that requests to take time out from career for family reasons reflect a lack of career commitment, discourage employees from taking advantage of work-family programs. Organizations that want to create family-friendly cultures need to expand their notions of what constitutes career success to include interruptions and lateral moves. They should encourage, rather than discourage, employees to take advantage of work-family programs, recognizing that employees who do so are likely to be more committed. In addition, family-friendly organizations set fair standards concerning the numbers of hours that employees will work; employees are not expected to work ridiculously long hours.

In conclusion, organizations may minimize artificial sex differences in career patterns by treating all employees fairly in decision making, ensuring that equally qualified employees have equal access to developmental experiences, and offering well designed work-family programs in supportive work environments. When organizations recognize that they are employing whole individuals, not just jobholders, they are more likely to be family friendly than abusive. They are also more likely to retain their most productive employees.

Succeeding on Your Own Terms

People are not lumps of clay, ready to be shaped by all those around them into any form, with no say in the nature of their work and family lives. As their careers unfold, women and men may set their own career goals and develop plans of action to achieve them, thereby shaping their own work and family experiences.[65]

Career success is enhanced by the use of career tactics that are carefully thought out, well timed, and appropriate for each career stage. A key step in the planning process is setting goals. Individuals need either social support or strong self-esteem to set goals that contribute to career success. Women traditionally have experienced less social support and lower self-esteem and thereby have been less competent in goal setting than men. Women, and men, who lack the necessary support may benefit from working with career counselors in the goal-setting process.[66]

Both men and women may further their success by obtaining mentors who provide social and instrumental support. Regardless of whether a mentor is available, however, members of both sexes will benefit from joining informal networks. Informal networks traditionally have been "old-boy" networks because, until recently, there have not been enough women managers to create "old-girl" networks. As more women enter management ranks, mixed-sex and old-girl networks are becoming more prevalent. Women who find it difficult to be accepted into predominantly male networks in their organizations might develop their networks by attending meetings of professional associations and trade groups.

Although techniques such as setting goals, establishing mentoring relationships, and networking are useful, there is no substitute for building competence and credibility. Careers are enhanced when people further their education, either prior to working or while working (e.g., part-time MBAs), thereby enhancing their skills and knowledge. Accepting difficult and highly visible stretch assignments and job transfers to domestic or international locations also benefits careers.[67]

Individuals also need to develop coping strategies to deal with stress from the demands of their work and family roles. Strategies that help individuals cope with stress in one role may not alleviate stress in the other role. For example, cognitive disengagement or detachment may be an effective strategy for coping with work-related stress, but not with family-based stress. Reassurances of emotional attachment and commitment may be effective when directed toward family members, but not when directed toward bosses, subordinates, and peers at work. Individuals need coping strategies for dealing effectively with stress in both spheres of their lives. In addition to unilateral coping strategies, couples may reduce their overall amount of stress by agreeing on what their work and family roles will be and providing mutual support.[68]

Couples who relocate as a result of international assignments need to devote particular attention to developing coping strategies. Although relocated employees often receive employer assistance in coping with their new environments, trailing spouses of relocated employees typically need to act on their own behalf. For example, a group of English-speaking men who trailed their executive spouses to Belgium formed their own support group, STUDS (Spouses Trailing Under Duress Successfully). The group provides the men a social network, which helps them settle in and adjust to their new location. STUDS brings these men together online and in person regularly for golf, fund raising, and social evenings. These men are not only helping themselves. They also better the lives of their executive partners. The failure of the trailing spouse to adjust is a frequent cause of early returns home or resignations of executives from international assignments.[69]

Entrepreneurial couples, couples who are married or unmarried and run a business together, face unique challenges. More than for dual-career couples or telecommuters, the boundary between work and family roles for entrepreneurial couples can become completely blurred. Each person in the couple may experience internal conflict in trying to handle both work and family roles. As a couple, together they may experience conflict in agreeing on the amount of time, energy, and attention that each will devote to work and family roles. Entrepreneurial couples who are better able to resolve such conflicts lead more satisfying work and family lives.[70]

In conclusion, when people are proactive and adopt suitable tactics for meeting their career goals, they are best able to succeed on their own terms. Developing skills for managing the stress created by the competing demands of work and family roles is also critical. Failure to develop and implement effective strategies for career advancement and stress management impairs career success and leads to anger, frustration, and disappointment.

The Rest of the Story

After beginning the chapter with Jennifer's story, we conclude by presenting the rest of the story. In the weeks that followed her decision to work overtime on the project that fateful Saturday and to miss the family birthday party for her mother, Jennifer felt considerable conflict and turmoil. Shortly thereafter, she found a new job in her field with an employer who treated her with much more respect. She was still in that job and enjoying it 2 years later.

Notes

1. Powell, G. N. (1998). The abusive organization. *Academy of Management Executive, 12*(2), p. 95. ACADEMY OF MANAGEMENT EXECUTIVE by G. N. POWELL. Copyright 1998 by ACAD OF MGMT. Reproduced with permission of ACAD OF MGMT in the format Textbook via Copyright Clearance Center.

2. Parasuraman, S., & Greenhaus, J. H. (Eds.). (1997). *Integrating work and family: Challenges and choices for a changing world.* Westport, CT: Quorum.

3. Super, D. E. (1980). A life-span, life-space approach to career development. *Journal of Vocational Behavior, 16,* 282–298.

4. Greenhaus, J. H. (2002). Career dynamics. In W. C. Borman, D. R. Ilgen, R. J. Klimoski, & I. B. Weiner (Eds.), *Handbook of psychology, industrial and organizational psychology* (pp. 519–540). New York: Wiley; Super, D. H. (1957). *The psychology of careers: An introduction to vocational development.* New York: Harper & Brothers; Schein, E. H. (1978). *Career dynamics: Matching individual and organizational needs.* Reading, MA: Addison-Wesley; Levinson, D. J., with Darrow, C. N., Klein, E. B., Levinson, M. H., & McKee, B. (1979). *The seasons of a man's life* (Paperback ed.). New York: Ballantine.

5. Gallos, J. V. (1989). Exploring women's development: Implications for career theory, practice, and research. In M. B. Arthur, D. T. Hall, & B. S. Lawrence (Eds.), *Handbook of career theory* (pp. 110–132). Cambridge, UK: Cambridge University Press; Campbell, S. (2002, May 20). An outspoken Secretary speaks. *Hartford Courant,* p. D2; U.S. State Department. (2001). *Biography: Madeleine Korbel Albright, U.S. Secretary of State.* Retrieved May 24, 2002, from http://secretary.state.gov

6. Powell, G. N., & Mainiero, L. A. (1992). Cross-currents in the river of time: Conceptualizing the complexities of women's careers. *Journal of Management, 18,* 215–237; Greenhaus.

7. Sturges, J. (1999). What it means to succeed: Personal conceptions of career success held by male and female managers at different ages. *British Journal of Management, 10,* 239–252; Bray, D. W., & Howard, A. (1980). Career success and life satisfactions of middle-aged managers. In L. A. Bond & J. C. Rosen (Eds.), *Competence and coping during adulthood* (pp. 258–287). Hanover, NH: University Press of New England; Judge, T. A., Cable, D. M., Boudreau, J. W., & Bretz, R. D., Jr. (1995). An empirical investigation of the predictors of executive career success. *Personnel Psychology, 48,* 485–519.

8. Konrad, A. M., Ritchie, J. E., Jr., Lieb, P., & Corrigall, E. (2000). Sex differences and similarities in job attribute preferences: A meta-analysis. *Psychological Bulletin, 126,* 593–641.

9. Kirchmeyer, C. (1998). Determinants of managerial career success: Evidence and explanation of male/female differences. *Journal of Management, 24,* 673–692; Schneer, J. A., & Reitman, F. (1995). The impact of gender as managerial careers unfold. *Journal of Vocational Behavior, 47,* 290–315; Cox, T. H., & Harquail, C. V. (1991). Career paths and career success in the early career stages of male and female MBAs. *Journal of Vocational Behavior, 39,* 54–75.

10. Cox, T. H., & Nkomo, S. M. (1991). A race and gender-group analysis of the early career experience of MBAs. *Work and Occupations, 18,* 431–446; Greenhaus, J. H., Parasuraman, S., & Wormley, W. M. (1990). Effects of race on organizational experiences, job performance evaluations, and career outcomes. *Academy of Management Journal, 33,* 64–86; Morrison, A. M., & Von Glinow, M. A. (1990). Women and minorities in management. *American Psychologist, 45,* 200–208; Davidson, M. J. (1997). *The black and ethnic minority woman manager.* London: Chapman.

11. Schneer, J. A., & Reitman, F. (1997). The interrupted managerial career path: A longitudinal study of MBAs. *Journal of Vocational Behavior, 51,* 411–434.

12. Judiesch, M. K., & Lyness, K. S. (1999). Left behind? The impact of leaves of absence on managers' career success. *Academy of Management Journal, 42,* 641–651; Sedmak, N. J., & Vidas, C.

(1994). Family and Medical Leave Act of 1993. In *Primer on equal employment opportunity* (6th ed., p. 27). Washington, DC: Bureau of National Affairs.

13.   Daniels, P., & Weingarten, K. (1982). *Sooner or later: The timing of parenthood in adult lives.* New York: Norton.

14.   Schneer & Reitman (1997); Judiesch & Lyness.

15.   Bollé, P. (2001). Part-time work: Solution or trap? In M. F. Loutfi (Ed.), *Women, gender and work: What is equality and how do we get there?* (pp. 215–238). Geneva: International Labour Office; U.S. Department of Commerce, Bureau of the Census. (2002). *Current Population Survey* (computed from data for January, 2002). Retrieved May 23, 2002, from http://ferret.bls.census.gov

16.   Bollé; Feldman, D. C. (1990). Reconceptualizing the nature and consequences of part-time work. *Academy of Management Review, 15,* 103–112; Higgins, C., Duxbury, L., & Johnson, K. L. (2000). Part-time work for women: Does it really help balance work and family? *Human Resource Management, 39,* 17–32; Catalyst. (2000). *Flexible work arrangements III: A ten-year retrospective of part-time arrangements for managers and professionals.* New York: Catalyst; Epstein, C. F., Seron, C., Oglensky, B., & Saute, R. (1999). *The part-time paradox: Time norms, professional life, family, and gender.* New York: Routledge.

17.   Ohlott, P. J., Ruderman, M. N., & McCauley, C. D. (1994). Gender differences in managers' developmental job experiences. *Academy of Management Journal, 37,* 46–67; Ragins, B. R., Townsend, B., & Mattis, M. (1998). Gender gap in the executive suite: CEOs and female executives report on breaking the glass ceiling. *Academy of Management Executive, 12*(1), 28–42; Mainiero, L. A. (1994). Getting anointed for advancement: The case of executive women. *Academy of Management Executive, 8*(2), 53–67.

18.   Eby, L. T., Allen, T. D., & Douthitt, S. S. (1999). The role of nonperformance factors on job-related relocation opportunities: A field study and laboratory experiment. *Organizational Behavior and Human Decision Processes, 79,* 29–55.

19.   Eby, Allen, & Douthitt; Brett, J. M., Stroh, L. K., & Reilly, A. H. (1993). Pulling up roots in the 1990s: Who's willing to relocate? *Journal of Organizational Behavior, 14,* 49–60; Stroh, L. K., Brett, J. M., & Reilly, A. H. (1992). All the right stuff: A comparison of female and male managers' career progression. *Journal of Applied Psychology, 77,* 251–260.

20.   Catalyst. (2000). *Passport to opportunity: U.S. women in global business.* New York: Catalyst; Linehan, M. (2000). *Senior female international managers: Why so few?* Aldershot, UK: Ashgate; Adler, N. J. (1984). Women do not want international careers: And other myths about international management. *Organizational Dynamics, 13*(2), 66–79; Antal, A. B., & Izraeli, D. N. (1993). A global comparison of women in management: Women managers in their homelands and as expatriates. In E. A. Fagenson (Ed.), *Women in management: Trends, issues, and challenges in managerial diversity* (pp. 52–96). Newbury Park, CA: Sage; Lyness, K. S., & Thompson, D. E. (1997). Above the glass ceiling? A comparison of matched samples of female and male executives. *Journal of Applied Psychology, 82,* 359–375; Lyness, K. S., & Thompson, D. E. (2000). Climbing the corporate ladder: Do female and male executives follow the same route? *Journal of Applied Psychology, 85,* 86–101.

21.   Tharenou, P., Latimer, S., & Conroy, D. (1994). How do you make it to the top? An examination of influences on women's and men's managerial advancement. *Academy of Management Journal, 37,* 899–931; Knoke, D., & Ishio, Y. (1998). The gender gap in company job training. *Work and Occupations, 25,* 141–167; Keaveny, T. J., & Inderrieden, E. J. (1999). Gender differences in employer-supported training and education. *Journal of Vocational Behavior, 54,* 71–81.

22.   Ragins, B. R. (1999). Gender and mentoring relationships: A review and research agenda for the next decade. In G. N. Powell (Ed.), *Handbook of gender and work* (pp. 347–370). Thousand Oaks, CA: Sage; Ragins, B. R., & Cotton, J. L. (1999). Mentor functions and outcomes: A comparison of men and women in formal and informal mentoring relationships. *Journal of Applied Psychology, 84,* 529–550; Dreher, G. F., & Cox, T. H., Jr. (1996). Race, gender, and opportunity: A study of compensation attainment and the establishment of mentoring relationships. *Journal of Applied Psychology, 81,* 297–308.

23. Ragins; Clawson, J. G., & Kram, K. E. (1984). Managing cross-gender mentoring. *Business Horizons 27*(3), 22-31; Ragins, B. R., & Cotton, J. L. (1991). Easier said than done: Gender differences in perceived barriers to gaining a mentor. *Academy of Management Journal, 34,* 939–951; Lyness & Thompson (2000).

24. Light, A., & Ureta, M. (1992). Panel estimates of male and female job turnover behavior: Can female nonquitters be identified? *Journal of Labor Economics, 10,* 156–181; Lewis, G. B., & Park, K. (1989). Turnover rates in federal white-collar employment: Are women more likely to quit than men? *American Review of Public Administration, 19,* 13–28; Keith, K., & McWilliams, A. (1999). The returns to mobility and job search by gender. *Industrial and Labor Relations Review, 52,* 460–477; Cotton, J. L., & Tuttle, J. M. (1986). Employee turnover: A meta-analysis and review with implications for research. *Academy of Management Review, 11,* 55–70.

25. Stroh, L. K., Brett, J. M., & Reilly, A. H. (1996). Family structure, glass ceiling, and traditional explanations for the differential rate of turnover of female and male managers. *Journal of Vocational Behavior, 49,* 99–118; Lyness, K. S., & Judiesch, M. K. (2001). Are female managers quitters? The relationships of gender, promotions, and family leaves of absence to voluntary turnover. *Journal of Applied Psychology, 86,* 1167–1178.

26. U.S. Small Business Administration, Office of Advocacy (2001). *Women in business, 2001.* Retrieved May 23, 2002, from http://www.sba.gov.

27. Brush, C. G. (1992). Research on women business owners: Past trends, a new perspective and future directions. *Entrepreneurship Theory and Practice, 16*(4), 5–30; Helgesen, S. (1995). *The female advantage: Women's ways of leadership* (Paperback ed.). New York: Currency Doubleday, p. 5.

28. Moore, D. P. (1999). Women entrepreneurs: Approaching a new millennium. In G. N. Powell (Ed.), *Handbook of gender and work* (pp. 371–389). Thousand Oaks, CA: Sage; Moore, D. P., & Buttner, E. H. (1997). *Women entrepreneurs: Moving beyond the glass ceiling.* Thousand Oaks, CA: Sage; Allen, S., & Truman, C. (Eds.) (1993). *Women in business: Perspectives on women entrepreneurs.* London: Routledge.

29. Talaga, J. A., & Beehr, T. A. (1995). Are there gender differences in predicting retirement decisions? *Journal of Applied Psychology, 80,* 16–28.

30. Kim, J. E., & Moen, P. (2001). Is retirement good or bad for subjective well-being? *Current Direction in Psychological Science, 10,* 83–86; Costello, C. B., & Stone, A. J. (2001). *The American woman 2001–2002: Getting to the top.* New York: Norton, pp. 294–295, Table 6–3.

31. Powell, G. N. (1999). Reflections on the glass ceiling: Recent trends and future prospects. In G. N. Powell (Ed.), *Handbook of gender and work* (pp. 325–345). Thousand Oaks, CA: Sage; Wirth, L. (2001). *Breaking through the glass ceiling: Women in management.* Geneva: International Labour Office; Catalyst. (2000). *Cracking the glass ceiling: Catalyst's research on women in corporate management 1995–2000.* New York: Catalyst; Davidson, M. J., & Cooper, C. L. (1992). *Shattering the glass ceiling: The woman manager.* London: Chapman; Morrison & Von Glinow; Morrison, A. M., White, R. P., Van Velsor, E., & the Center for Creative Leadership. (1992). *Breaking the glass ceiling: Can women reach the top of America's largest corporations?* (Updated ed.). Reading, MA: Addison-Wesley; Parkhouse, S. (2001). *Powerful women: Dancing on the glass ceiling.* Chichester, UK: Wiley; Marshall, J. (1984). *Women managers: Travellers in a male world.* Chichester, UK: Wiley.

32. Powell, G. N., & Butterfield, D. A. (1994). Investigating the "glass ceiling" phenomenon: An empirical study of actual promotions to top management. *Academy of Management Journal, 37,* 68–86; Antal, A. B., & Krebsbach-Gnath, C. (1988). Women in management: Unused resources in the Federal Republic of Germany. In N. J. Adler & D. N. Izraeli (Eds.), *Women in management worldwide* (pp. 141–156). Armonk, NY: Sharpe.

33. Tharenou, P. (2001). Going up? Do traits and informal social processes predict advancing in management? *Academy of Management Journal, 44,* 1005–1017.

34. Perry, E. L., Davis-Blake, A., & Kulik, C. T. (1994). Explaining gender-based selection decisions: A synthesis of contextual and cognitive approaches. *Academy of Management Review, 19,* 786–820.

35. Kanter, R. M. (1977). *Men and women of the corporation.* New York: Basic.

36. Cohen, L. E., Broschak, J. P., & Haveman, H. A. (1998). And then there were more? The effect of organizational sex composition on the hiring and promotion of managers. *American Sociological Review, 63,* 711–727; Kanter; Foley, S., Kidder, D. L., & Powell, G. N. (2002). The perceived glass ceiling and justice perceptions: An investigation of Hispanic law associates. *Journal of Management, 28,* 471–496.

37. Lobel, S. A. (1999). Impacts of diversity and work-life initiatives in organizations. In G. N. Powell (Ed.), *Handbook of gender and work* (pp. 453–474). Thousand Oaks, CA: Sage; Konrad, A. M., & Mangel, R. (2000). The impact of work-life programs on firm productivity. *Strategic Management Journal, 21,* 1225–1237; Perry-Smith, J. E., & Blum, T. C. (2000). Work-family human resource bundles and perceived organizational performance. *Academy of Management Journal, 43,* 1107–1117.

38. Rodgers, F. S., & Rodgers, C. (1989). Business and the facts of family life. *Harvard Business review, 67*(6), 121–129; Lobel.

39. Merrill, D. M. (1997). *Caring for elderly parents: Juggling work, family, and caregiving in middle and working class families.* Westport, CT: Auburn House.

40. Lobel; Rodgers & Rodgers; Thomas, L. T., & Ganster, D. C. (1995). Impact of family-supportive work variables on work-family conflict and strain: A control perspective. *Journal of Applied Psychology, 80,* 6–15; Grover, S. L., & Crooker, K. J. (1995). Who appreciates family-responsive human resource policies: The impact of family-friendly policies on the organizational attachment of parent and non-parents. *Personnel Psychology, 48,* 271–288; Pierce, J. L., Newstrom, J. W., Dunham, R. B., & Barber, A. E. (1989). *Alternative work schedules.* Boston: Allyn & Bacon.

41. U.S. Department of Labor, Bureau of Labor Statistics. (2002). *Workers on flexible and shift schedules in 2001.* Retrieved May 21, 2002, from http://www.bls.gov; Baltes, B. B., Briggs, T. E., Huff, J. W., Wright, J. A., & Neuman, G. A. (1999). Flexible and compressed workweek schedules: A meta-analysis of their effects on work-related criteria. *Journal of Applied Psychology, 84,* 496–513.

42. Mariani, M. (2000, Fall). Telecommuters. *Occupational Outlook Quarterly,* 10–17. Retrieved May 25, 2002, from http://www.bls.gov; Hill, E. J., Miller, B. C., Weiner, S. P., & Colihan, J. (1998). Influences of the virtual office on aspects of work and work/life balance. *Personnel Psychology, 51,* 667–683; Riley, F., & McCloskey, D. W. (1997). Telecommuting as a response to helping people balance work and family. In S. Parasuraman & J. H. Greenhaus (Eds.), *Integrating work and family: Challenges and choices for a changing world* (pp. 133–142). Westport, CT: Quorum.

43. U.S. Department of Labor (1999). Hours of work. In *Report on the American workforce 1999* (pp. 80–109). Washington, DC: U.S. Department of Labor; Nie, N. H., & Erbring, L. (2000). *Internet and society: A preliminary report.* Palo Alto, CA: Stanford Institute for the Quantitative Study of Society, Stanford University. Retrieved May 25, 2002, from http://www.stanford.edu

44. Kofodimos, J. R. (1990). Why executives lose their balance. *Organizational Dynamics,* 19(1), 58–73; Hewlett, S. A. (2002). Executive women and the myth of having it all. *Harvard Business Review, 80*(4), 66–73.

45. Schneer, J. A., & Reitman, F. (1993). Effects of alternative family structures on managerial career paths. *Academy of Management Journal, 36,* 830–843.

46. Although individuals have careers whether or not they are employed, we refer to couples in which both members are employed as "dual-career couples" for convenience.

47. Hewlett; Catalyst. (1996). *Women in corporate leadership: Progress and prospects.* New York: Catalyst; Korn/Ferry International and UCLA Anderson Graduate School of Management. (1993). *Decade of the executive woman.* New York: Korn/Ferry International.

48. Lewis, S., Izraeli, D. N., & Hootsman, H. (Eds.). (1992). *Dual-earner families: International perspectives.* London: Sage.

49. Gerson, K. (1993). *No man's land: Men's changing commitments to family and work.* New York: Basic Books; Kimmel, M. S. (1993). What do men want? *Harvard Business Review, 71*(6), 50–63.

50. Powell & Mainiero; Gallos; Gutek, B. A., & Larwood, L. (1987). Introduction: Women's careers are important and different. In B. A. Gutek & L. Larwood (Eds.), *Women's career development* (pp. 7–14). Newbury Park, CA: Sage; Abele, A. E. (2000). A dual-impact model of gender and career-related processes. In T. Eckes & H. M. Trautner (Eds.), *The developmental social psychology of gender* (pp. 361–388). Mahwah, NJ: Erlbaum; Astin, H. S. (1984). The meaning of work in women's lives: A sociopsychological model of career choice and work behavior. *The Counseling Psychologist, 12*(4), 117-126.

51. Greenhaus, J. H., & Parasuraman, S. (1999). Research on work, family, and gender: Current status and future directions. In G. N. Powell (Ed.), *Handbook of gender and work* (pp. 391–412). Thousand Oaks, CA: Sage; Edwards, J. R., & Rothbard, N. P. (2000). Mechanisms linking work and family: Clarifying the relationship between work and family constructs. *Academy of Management Review, 25,* 178–199; Ruderman, M. N., Ohlott, P. J., Panzer, K., & King, S. N. (2002). Benefits of multiple roles for professional women. *Academy of Management Journal, 45,* 369–386; Crosby, F. J. (1991). *Juggling: The unexpected advantages of balancing career and home for women and their families.* New York: Free Press; Miller, S. (1997). The role of a juggler. In S. Parasuraman & J. H. Greenhaus (Eds.), *Integrating work and family: Challenges and choices for a changing world* (pp. 48–56). Westport, CT: Quorum; Hochschild, A. R. (1997). *The time bind: When work becomes home and home becomes work.* New York: Metropolitan.

52. Greenhaus, J. H., & Beutell, N. J. (1985). Sources of conflict between work and family roles. *Academy of Management Review, 10,* 76-88.

53. Galinsky, E., & Swanberg, J. E. (2000). Employed mothers and fathers in the United States: Understanding how work and family life fit together. In L. L. Haas, P. Hwang, & G. Russell (Eds.), *Organizational change and gender equity: International perspectives on fathers and mothers at the workplace* (pp. 15–28). Thousand Oaks, CA: Sage; Gerson, p. 141; Kimmel; Pleck.

54. Greenhaus & Parasuraman (1999); Greenhaus, J. H., & Powell, G. N. (in press). When work and family collide: Deciding between competing role demands. *Organizational Behavior and Human Decision Processes*; Powell (1998).

55. Friedman, S. D., & Greenhaus, J. H. (2000). *Work and family—allies or enemies? What happens when business professionals confront life choices.* Oxford, UK: Oxford University Press; Greenhaus, J. H., & Parasuraman, S. (1994). Work-family conflict, social support and well-being. In M. J. Davidson & R. J. Burke (Eds.), *Women in management: Current research issues* (pp. 213–229). London: Chapman.

56. Sekaran, U. (1986). *Dual-career families.* San Francisco: Jossey-Bass.

57. Ling, Y., & Powell, G. N. (2001). Work-family conflict in contemporary China: Beyond an American-based model. *International Journal of Cross Cultural Management, 1,* 357–373; Bian, F., Logan, J. R., & Bian, Y. (1998). Intergenerational relations in urban China: Proximity, contact, and help to parents. *Demography, 35,* 115–124.

58. Powell, G. N. (1997). The sex difference in employee inclinations regarding work-family programs: Why does it exist, should we care, and what should be done about it (if anything)? In S. Parasuraman & J. H. Greenhaus (Eds.), *Integrating work and family: Challenges and choices for a changing world* (pp. 167–174). Westport, CT: Quorum; Pleck, J. H. (1993). Are "family-supportive" employer policies relevant to men? In J. C. Hood (Ed.), *Men, work, and family* (pp. 217–237). Newbury Park, CA: Sage; Judiesch & Lyness.

59. Bartol, K. M. (1999). Gender influences on performance evaluations. In G. N. Powell (Ed.), *Handbook of gender and work* (pp. 165–178). Thousand Oaks, CA: Sage; Martell, R. F., Lane, D. M., & Emrich, C. (1996). Male-female differences: A computer simulation. *American Psychologist, 51,* 157–158.

60. Powell & Butterfield.

61. Center for Creative Leadership. (2002). *The Women's Leadership Program.* Retrieved May 26, 2002, from http://www.ccl.org; Zeitz, B., & Dusky, L. (1988). *The best companies for women.* New York: Simon & Schuster.

62. Ragins; Ragins & Cotton (1999); Murray, M., with Owen, M. A. (1991). *Beyond the myths and magic of mentoring: How to facilitate an effective mentoring program.* San Francisco: Jossey-Bass.

63. Thompson, C. A., Beauvais, L. L., & Lyness, K. S. (1999). When work-family benefits are not enough: The influence of work-family culture on benefit utilization, organizational attachment, and work-family conflict. *Journal of Vocational Behavior, 54,* 392–415; Thomas & Ganster.

64. Powell, G. N., & Mainiero, L. A. (1999). Managerial decision making regarding alternative work arrangements. *Journal of Occupational and Organizational Psychology, 72,* 41–56.

65. Bell, N. E., & Staw, B. M. (1989). People as sculptors versus sculpture: The roles of personality and personal control in organizations. In M. B. Arthur, D. T. Hall, & B. S. Lawrence (Eds.), *Handbook of career theory* (pp. 232–251). Cambridge, UK: Cambridge University Press.

66. Inderlied, S. D. (1979). Goal setting and the career development of women. *New Directions for Education, Work, and Careers, 8,* 33-41.

67. Catalyst, Center for the Education of Women at the University of Michigan, & University of Michigan Business School. (2000). *Women and the MBA: Gateway to opportunity.* New York: Catalyst; Mainiero, L. A. (1994). On breaking the glass ceiling: The political seasoning of powerful women executives. *Organizational Dynamics, 22*(4), 5–20; Ragins et al.; Lyness & Thompson (1997, 2000).

68. Eckenrode, J., & Gore, S. (Eds.). (1990). *Stress between work and family.* New York: Plenum; Davidson, M. J., & Fielden, S. (1999). Stress and the working woman. In G. N. Powell (Ed.), *Handbook of gender and work* (pp. 413–426). Thousand Oaks, CA: Sage.

69. Jordan, M. (2001, February 13). Have husband, will travel. *Wall Street Journal,* pp. B1, B12; Linehan; Shaffer, M. A., & Harrison, D. A. (2001). Forgotten partners of international assignments: Development and test of a model of spouse adjustment. *Journal of Applied Psychology, 86,* 238–254; Shaffer, M. A., & Harrison, D. A. (1998). Expatriates' psychological withdrawal from international assignments: Work, nonwork, and family influences. *Personnel Psychology, 51,* 87–118.

70. Foley, S., & Powell, G. N. (1997). Reconceptualizing work-family conflict for business/marriage partners: A theoretical model. *Journal of Small Business Management, 35*(4), 36–47; Marshack, K. (1998). *Entrepreneurial couples: Making it work at work and at home.* Palo Alto, CA: Davies-Black.

9

Promoting Nondiscrimination, Diversity, and Inclusion

THEY GOT IT

The floor plan of the Chicago hotel conference room provided a compelling metaphor for the problem at hand. Seated in rows were 80 women, all partners at Coopers & Lybrand. Before them, atop a stage-like platform, presided eight senior members of the management committee. All eight were men. All eight were white.

Didn't these guys get it? Chairman and Chief Executive Nicholas G. Moore and his seven colleagues were there because Coopers' women wanted to know why, after a decade of gender-neutral hiring at the firm, females still made up just 8% of the 1,300-person partnership. Why weren't women responsible for more of the firm's key clients? Why did they head just 3 of 70 regional offices?

Answers came quickly in the ensuing exchange. Some men believed female partners didn't want to travel. Astounded, the women countered that in fact they were eager to get out and meet clients. Even though men said they were open to lunching with female counterparts, women said they felt excluded from such informal gatherings. Opinions also diverged over whether the road to partnership favored men. "If you're in an environment mostly dominated by a male culture, many of the things you must do to succeed are more comfortable for men than women," says Linda A. Hoffman, a 39-year-old partner who co-chaired the gathering. Recalls Moore: "That surprised me. But there were enough women who said it that I believe it's an issue."

The watershed confrontation . . . launched Coopers & Lybrand on a series of initiatives aimed at narrowing its gender gap. Two women now sit on the 14-person management committee, there's formal training and mentoring for up-and-comers, and a portion of partner bonuses is linked to performance on diversity issues.

—Linda Himelstein[1]

Throughout this book, we describe the effects of sex and gender in the workplace. We identify issues that arise as women and men seek employment, work together in teams, serve as leaders, exhibit sexual behavior at work, and pursue their careers. In general, organizations may take three types of actions to address these issues:

1. *Promote nondiscrimination* in treatment of people and decisions about people. This means promoting compliance by all employees with federal, state, and local equal employment opportunity (EEO) laws. Such laws ban discrimination on the basis of sex, race, ethnicity, national origin, age, religion, and other personal characteristics that are not relevant to the job at hand. It also means refraining from discrimination on the basis of job-irrelevant personal characteristics even if it is not illegal. For example, there is no U.S. federal law banning discrimination on the basis of sexual orientation, but such discrimination is just as unacceptable as sex or race discrimination.

2. *Promote diversity* among employees in all jobs and at all levels. The focus of promoting diversity is on the number or *quantity* of employees from various groups in different jobs and at different organizational levels. Affirmative action programs, which are legally mandated for most employers, represent attempts to ensure that organizational practices enhance the employment, development, and retention of members of protected groups such as women and people of color. Organizations also may attempt to increase the diversity of their labor force for business reasons.

3. *Promote inclusion* of employees from all groups in the organizational culture. The focus of promoting inclusion is on the nature or *quality* of work relationships between employees who belong to different groups. There are no laws that say that organizations ought to provide a work environment in which members of all groups feel comfortable and accepted. Organizations may engage in this kind of action if they see some advantage to doing so.

We suggest that organizations will benefit from pursuing all three types of actions: promoting nondiscrimination, promoting diversity, *and* promoting inclusion. An organization successful in these actions will be less likely to be the target of costly litigation. Its employees will bring a wider range of perspectives to work issues, which should result in more creative solutions to problems facing the organization. Such an organization will be most likely to attract and retain highly qualified employees from all groups and to take full advantage of their talents.

In this chapter, we consider what organizations need to do to achieve these benefits. First, we review the kinds of EEO laws with which organizations must comply. Second, we present the business case for going beyond minimal compliance with EEO laws. Third, we consider specific actions that organizations may take to promote a nondiscriminatory, diverse, and inclusive culture. Finally, we summarize the many positive actions identified in earlier chapters that are available to organizations and individuals.

Legal Requirements

Federal, state, and local laws govern the actions of employers, with federal laws having the broadest impact. Examples of federal EEO laws include Australia's Affirmative Action Act, Canada's Employment Equity Act, Japan's Equal Employment Opportunity Law, the United Kingdom's Sex Discrimination Act and Equal Pay Act, the Netherlands' Equal Pay Act and Equal Opportunities Act, Ireland's Anti-Discrimination (Pay) Act and Employment Equality Act, and Denmark's Equal Opportunities Act, Equal Treatment Act, and Equal Pay Act. Although the particulars of these laws vary, they share the general objective of banning sex discrimination in employment practices and promoting diversity on the basis of sex in organizations.[2]

We focus our attention in this section on federal EEO laws in the United States.[3] First, the legal requirements placed on employers to refrain from sex discrimination are described. Second, we consider the further requirements placed on many employers to take affirmative action to promote diversity on the basis of sex.

REFRAINING FROM DISCRIMINATION

Title VII of the Civil Rights Act of 1964 and the Equal Pay Act of 1963 are the most significant pieces of U.S. federal legislation that address sex discrimination. Title VII prohibits discrimination on the basis of sex, race, color, religion, or national origin in any employment condition, including hiring, firing, promotion, transfer, compensation, and admission to training programs. It has been extended to ban discrimination because of pregnancy, childbirth, or related conditions and to ban sexual harassment (see Chapter 7). The Equal Pay Act makes it illegal to pay members of one sex at a lower rate than the other if they hold jobs that require equal skill, effort, and responsibility under similar working conditions in the same firm.

Several agencies are involved in the administration and enforcement of federal EEO laws. The Equal Employment Opportunity Commission (EEOC) is charged with administering Title VII and the Equal Pay Act. It investigates and reconciles charges of discrimination against employers, unions, and employment agencies. The Department of Justice enforces Title VII in cases involving a state or local government agency or political subdivision. Individuals may also go to court in their own behalf or in behalf of a class of employees or potential employees to seek compliance with the laws.

Title VII. Two basic types of organizational practices are considered discriminatory under Title VII: those that involve disparate treatment and those that result in disparate impact.[4] *Disparate treatment discrimination* occurs when sex is intentionally used as a basis for treating people unequally. For example, one employer violated Title VII by asking a female applicant whether she planned to get pregnant and quit, and if her husband would mind when she had to "run around the country with men." Male applicants, obviously, were not asked such questions. Another employer violated Title VII by asking questions about child bearing and child rearing of only female applicants.[5]

Disparate impact discrimination occurs when an employment practice affects women and men unequally, unless it is job-related and justified by the needs of the business. For example, a company's minimum height requirement for a certain job was rejected as discriminatory when it was shown to rule out more women than men and was not essential to job performance. Under the disparate impact standard, whether the employer discriminates intentionally is irrelevant. All that matters is whether a practice has unequal results, and, if so, whether it serves a legitimate need (such as apprenticeship training for skilled craft positions and licensing requirements for nurses and teachers) that cannot be met by an alternative practice with less disparate impact.

The Uniform Guidelines on Employee Selection Procedures, used by government agencies to evaluate evidence in cases of alleged discrimination, suggest an 80% rule of thumb as a practical means of determining disparate impact. According to this rule, a rate of favorable decisions for one sex that is less than 80% of the rate of favorable decisions for the other sex may be regarded as evidence of disparate impact. For example, if a large marketing research firm hires 10% of all female applicants and 20% of all male applicants with similar qualifications for an entry-level analyst position, the hiring rate for women is 50% of that for similarly qualified men, suggesting disparate impact. This rule may be applied to all employment decisions. Employers are not required to meet hiring or promotion quotas for specific groups of workers (e.g., 45% of the area's labor force or population is female, thus 45% of new hires should be female). Hiring quotas may be allowed, however, to remedy an imbalance caused by past discrimination. If employers' past hiring practices promoted sex discrimination, they may be expected to take action to rectify these inequalities. In such cases, employers may give temporary preference to qualified applicants from underrepresented groups to achieve a long-term balance in the representation of those groups among their employees.

Although the vast majority of cases involving Title VII have dealt with discrimination against women, discrimination against men also is covered. For example, a court ruled against Pan American World Airways in the 1970s for limiting its flight attendants to women. Pan American cited survey results that passengers preferred female flight attendants, and a clinical psychologist testified that women are better at comforting and reassuring passengers simply because they are women. Nonetheless, Pan American lost the case. Male flight attendants are now common, and air travelers still manage to be served with some degree of comfort and reassurance.[6]

The Title VII ban on sex discrimination makes an exception when an individual's sex represents a legitimate condition of employment or "bona fide occupational qualification" (BFOQ). Employee sex may be specified as a BFOQ in situations involving hygiene (such as cleaning of washrooms during periods when they are in use), health care (such as counseling of rape victims), and safety. For example, women may be denied the opportunity to serve as guards in male prisons because of the possibility of assault by prisoners, but women cannot be denied the opportunity to be prison guards altogether. The sex of an employee also may be specified as a BFOQ for reasons of authenticity or genuineness; it is acceptable for theatres and movie producers to hire only women to act female parts and only men to act male parts. However, the refusal to hire an individual because of customer preferences or stereotypical characterizations of the sexes (as in the Pan American case) is illegal.

In a well-publicized case, the EEOC filed charges against Hooters, a restaurant chain that features voluptuous waitresses in short shorts and form-fitting tank tops or T-shirts, for requiring its wait staff ("Hooters Girls") to be female.

The issue was whether Hooters is in the restaurant business, as the EEOC saw it, or the sex business, as Hooters saw it. The EEOC claimed that "no physical trait unique to women is required to serve food and drink to customers in a restaurant." In response, Hooters argued that the primary job function of Hooters Girls is "providing vicarious sexual recreation" by wearing skimpy outfits that meet tight (pun intended) specifications. Hooters Girls also are expected to "enhance the titillation by their interaction with customers. They are to flirt, cajole, and tease the patrons." Ultimately, Hooters settled with the EEOC by paying $3.75 million to men who were denied the opportunity to serve as Hooters Girls and by creating support jobs such as bartender and host that would be filled without regard to applicant sex. However, Hooters was allowed to continue luring customers with an exclusively female wait staff of Hooters Girls.[7]

Another permissible exception to Title VII is discrimination based on a seniority system. For example, the U.S. Supreme Court ruled that an employer cannot be ordered to ignore a seniority system when making layoffs, even if the effect is to reduce the number of women hired under an affirmative action plan.

The Equal Pay Act. This law is based on the principle of equal pay for equal work. The equal work standard requires that jobs be only substantially equal, not identical. Equal work is defined by four factors: skill, effort, responsibility, and working conditions. *Skill* refers to the experience, training, education, and ability needed to perform the job. The skill level of the job, not the job holders, determines whether two jobs are equal. For example, female nursing aides and male orderlies in hospitals perform equal work because similar skills are required. *Effort* refers to the amount or degree of effort, mental or physical, required for a job. *Responsibility* refers to the degree of accountability required in the performance of a job. For example, a wage differential may be justified for employees who are required to become acting supervisor in the absence of a regular supervisor. *Working conditions* refers to the physical surroundings and safety concerns of a job, such as inside versus outside work and adequate heat and ventilation. The mere fact that jobs are in different departments is not sufficient to demonstrate a difference in working conditions.

Pay differences are permitted between men and women engaged in equal work if they result from a seniority system, a merit system, a system that measures earnings by quality or quantity of production (e.g., a piecework incentive system), or some job-related factor such as a shift differential or a difference in experience. For example, a court upheld higher pay for sales-people in the men's department of a clothing store over those in the women's department because the company demonstrated that the men's department was the more profitable. In another case, however, women received 10% less pay than their male counterparts who did the same basic job. The men occasionally did heavier work, but this was infrequent and not done by all men. The court, ruling that the employer's lower wage rate for women was based on an artificially created job classification and that the extra duties of some men did not justify paying all of them more, awarded back wages to the women.

Pay disparities are often linked to *job evaluation*, a measurement procedure that rates jobs on factors such as skill, effort, responsibility, and working conditions. Job evaluations typically focus on *key jobs*, characterized as having a standard and stable content across organizations and *job clusters*, which consist of groups of similar jobs. Job clusters may be determined on the basis of geographical location, stage of the production process, organizational level, or any other factor that makes the jobs comparable to one another and suggests that their wages be compared. Examples of job clusters include maintenance jobs, secretarial jobs, and an insurance claim processing team.[8]

The starting point for the setting of wages is what the marketplace currently pays for key jobs. Wages are assigned to key jobs according to the wages employers typically pay for that job. Wages for nonkey jobs are set according to how their job evaluation ratings compare with those for key jobs in the same job cluster. Ideally, the result is a pay structure that has both external equity— the pay for key jobs reflects the external marketplace—and internal equity— the relative pay for all jobs corresponds to their job evaluation ratings. Thus, wages for a software design job (typically a key job) should correspond to the wages for that job in the labor market. In addition, senior software design jobs that require familiarity with advanced design techniques or have more responsibilities should be rated higher, and thereby assigned higher wages, than lower-level jobs that require only familiarity with simple design techniques or have fewer responsibilities.

Employers need to make sure that sex discrimination does not enter into job evaluation or any other element of the compensation system. Sex discrimination does not legally exist if pay differences are due to differences in the value that the marketplace attaches to particular jobs or to differences in skill, effort, responsibility, or working conditions. However, if an organization has identified pay inequities that cannot be accounted for by job-related or market-related factors, then corrective action may be required. This does not necessarily mean immediately rectifying all differences or lowering anyone's pay, but it does mean fostering a commitment over the long run to eliminate unjustifiable disparities.[9]

In summary, EEO laws ban sex discrimination in several ways. Organizations may not discriminate in treatment of women and men in hiring, firing, promotion, layoff, compensation, and other types of employment decisions. They also may be held responsible for the unequal impact of their policies on men and women unless a legitimate business need is served by the policies in question.

TAKING AFFIRMATIVE ACTION

Affirmative action represents an extension of the notion of nondiscrimination. Its purpose is to overcome the effects of past discrimination by allowing members of a victimized group to compete on equal terms with members of the favored group. Legally mandated practices for this purpose have been called *affirmative action, employment equity, positive action,* and other terms in various countries. They were first introduced in the United States in the 1930s to compensate for past unfair labor practices against union organizers and members. They were later used to assist veterans' reentry to the workplace after World War II.[10]

Executive Order 11246, instituted in 1965, requires U.S. organizations with 50 or more employees and federal contracts exceeding $50,000 per year to prepare and implement written affirmative action plans. An acceptable affirmative action plan must contain an analysis of the sex composition of all major job classes and an explanation for the underrepresentation of women in any job class. It must also contain goals and commitments to relieve any deficiencies revealed by the analysis. Finally, the plan must describe detailed steps that the organization will take to make a good-faith effort to meet its goals and to remedy all other EEO deficiencies. These steps should include a program for outreach to and recruitment of women for the job classes in which they are underrepresented.

Thus, the goal of an affirmative action plan is to promote diversity on the basis of sex in job classes in which women are underrepresented. If the plan has its intended result, the outcome is that male-intensive job classes become more balanced in their sex composition. Organizations are not under a legal requirement to take affirmative action for the purpose of making female-intensive job classes more balanced.

The Office of Federal Contract Compliance Programs (OFCCP) is responsible for administering Executive Order 11246. Its guidelines specify that unless sex is a BFOQ for a job, employers must actively recruit members of both sexes for the job. Advertisements for jobs in newspapers and other media cannot express a sex preference for jobholders. Employers must take affirmative action to encourage women to apply for jobs from which they previously have been excluded. This can be accomplished by various means. For example, recruitment at women's colleges may be regarded as evidence of a good-faith effort to meet affirmative action goals. In addition, if women are underrepresented in managerial jobs and specific training programs have been demonstrated to enhance employees' chances of attaining management positions, a commitment to include women in such programs is an important element of an affirmative action plan. The OFCCP requires organizations to file periodic reports on their affirmative action initiatives and to make their records available to federal administrators.

In summary, U.S. organizations must comply with EEO laws banning sex discrimination in the workplace. In addition, most federal contractors are expected to take affirmative action to remedy the effects of past sex discrimination. Although we have focused on U.S. laws and regulations, the governments of other countries make similar demands on organizations.

Business Imperatives

Being charged with and convicted of illegal discrimination or failure to comply with affirmative action guidelines can be costly for a business firm. Convicted firms may incur direct costs from fines, punitive damages, and legal fees, and indirect costs from damage to their good will (i.e., image and reputation). Current and prospective employees may have less regard for the firm and act accordingly. Firms also suffer long-term financial consequences when convicted of discrimination. A study of *Fortune* 300 companies found that those convicted of discrimination involving either disparate treatment or disparate impact had lower returns on assets and sales in the 5 years following the conviction compared to companies that were not convicted. Some of these costs are incurred even if an accused firm is not convicted or admits no guilt. Defending a firm against charges of illegal discrimination consumes top management attention that is better directed elsewhere. The costs of violating EEO laws and regulations provide a persuasive business argument for refraining from discrimination and taking affirmative action.[11]

Business imperatives, however, encourage organizations to go beyond minimal compliance with governmental requirements and aggressively promote diversity and inclusion. In the remainder of this section, we summarize these imperatives.

WHY PROMOTE DIVERSITY?

Several economic trends suggest that it is advantageous for organizations to promote diversity. First, the U.S. labor force has become more diverse in recent years. Women now comprise 47% of all workers, up from 42% in 1980 and 45% in 1990. Minority group members, including Black, Asian, and Hispanic men and women, represented 17% of the labor force in 1980 and 21% in 1990;

they now represent 27% (men–14%, women–13%). Non-Hispanic White men, once the majority group in the labor force, now represent only 39%; non-Hispanic White women constitute 34%. As in many other countries, the U.S. labor force has become more heterogeneous on the basis of sex, race, and ethnicity. Organizations with management practices appropriate for a homogeneous group of employees need to rethink their human resource management strategies.[12]

Second, the relative skills that members of different groups bring to the workplace have changed. In particular, the educational attainment of female entrants relative to that of male entrants has risen dramatically. Within all racial/ethnic groups in the United States, women now constitute the majority of individuals who earn bachelor's and master's degrees across all disciplines (Table 2.2); the proportion of women earning these degrees has increased in many other countries as well. As a result, more women worldwide are prepared to enter the high-paying occupations that require advanced degrees. Organizations that promote diversity by attracting highly-educated women to historically male-intensive jobs and occupations are at an advantage in competing with organizations that do not.

Third, there has been a worldwide shift from a primarily manufacturing-based economy to an economy based more on the delivery of services. Service industries place greater importance on educational attainment and less on physical strength than do manufacturing industries. Because women and men compete for service jobs on more equal terms, service industries are more diverse on the basis of sex than are manufacturing industries. Companies in service industries have a greater proportion of women in jobs at all levels, including top management, than those in manufacturing industries. It is imperative that service firms implement human resource management programs and practices (e.g., work-family initiatives) that are appropriate for their diverse workforces.[13]

Service firms that aggressively promote diversity may be especially effective in the marketplace. Because services are both produced and consumed on the spot, employees have heightened contact with customers. Employees must be able to understand the customer's perspective, anticipate the customer's needs, and respond sensitively and appropriately. Employees whose demographic characteristics mirror the characteristics of their customers may be better able to do so. Also, customers may be more likely to purchase services from providers whose attributes match their own because they view such providers as more capable of understanding their needs. As the pool of potential customers becomes more diverse, the pool of employees with customer contact also needs to become more diverse for the organization to be successful.[14]

Fourth, the increasing globalization of business, including multinational business operations and worldwide marketing of products and services, calls for organizations to be responsive to customers who are increasingly diverse in national origin. Organizations that want to take advantage of global business opportunities face greater challenges than do those that confine their business activities to the home market. They must learn to attract, interact with, and satisfy customers from a variety of national cultures. Overall, a diverse workforce may be better able to design, market, and sell products and services that meet consumer needs in an increasingly diverse marketplace.[15]

All of these trends suggest that organizations benefit from promoting diversity. Recent evidence confirms the relationship between diversity and organizational performance. For example, a study of *Fortune* 500 companies found a strong correlation between a company's inclusion of women in its top management ranks over a 19-year period and its profitability at the end of the period. Companies with the highest proportion of women executives (i.e., greatest diversity in top management ranks on the basis of sex) earned much higher profits than other large companies in their industries.[16]

A separate study of the 200 U.S. firms with the largest market value found that those with a higher proportion of women managers at all levels scored higher on four measures of financial returns (return on sales, assets, income, equity). The researchers concluded that firms that employed more women managers had probably done a better job of recruiting capable managers from the available pool of talent. Their managerial contingents also better reflected the markets in which they competed. These two factors were likely to give them a competitive advantage over firms with fewer women managers.[17]

Finally, a study of private firms found that those with workforces that were about 50% female performed better in their industries than firms with lower or higher percentages of female employees. In this case, the performance measures included profitability, marketing, market share, and growth in sales compared to other firms in the same industry. Because firms with a 50–50 split between male and female employees are the most diverse on the basis of sex, greater diversity appears to be associated with stronger firm performance.[18]

Correlation, of course, does not prove causality. Although a company's long-term record of hiring and promoting women to all levels of managerial positions could lead to higher profitability, more profitable firms may feel freer to experiment with selecting women for previously male-intensive jobs. Profitable firms, however, typically attain their success by making smarter decisions than their competitors. One of these smart decisions may be promoting diversity in the executive suite, as well as the entire organization.[19]

In conclusion, evidence suggests that greater employee diversity on the basis of sex is associated with better organizational performance. The business case for promoting diversity is that it enhances the bottom line.

WHY PROMOTE INCLUSION?

Taking steps to promote diversity, but ignoring the need for inclusion, may limit an organization's ability to reap the full benefits of a diverse workforce. Although increased employee diversity may enhance organizational performance, it also poses potential problems. It is easier to maintain a sense of cohesiveness in homogeneous organizations than in diverse organizations. People tend to be more attracted to and feel more comfortable in social settings in which they interact primarily with people like themselves. Thus, diversity may be a double-edged sword, increasing decision-making creativity and the congruence of the organization with the marketplace but decreasing employees' satisfaction with being a member of the organization. Unless the potential problems associated with diversity are addressed, its potential benefits may not be fully realized. The organization's diversity culture, as demonstrated by how it deals with group differences, influences the extent to which these problems appear.[20]

Taylor Cox distinguished among three types of diversity cultures.[21] *Monolithic organizations* are characterized by a large majority of employees from one group (e.g., White men), especially in the managerial ranks. Differences between majority and minority group members are resolved by the process of assimilation, whereby minority group employees are expected to adopt the norms and values of the majority group to survive in the organization. Such organizations are characterized by low levels of intergroup conflict because there are few members of minority groups and these members have outwardly adopted, if not inwardly embraced, the majority's norms and values. Changes in workforce demographics have led to a reduction in the number of monolithic organizations with White male majorities. The diversity culture of monolithic organizations conveys a straightforward message to employees and potential job applicants: We do not particularly welcome diversity.

Plural organizations have a more heterogeneous workforce than do monolithic organizations, primarily because they have taken steps to promote diversity. These steps may include hiring and promotion policies that stress recruitment and advancement of members of minority groups and managerial training on equal opportunity issues. Plural organizations focus on the numbers of majority versus minority group members in different jobs and levels, not on the quality of work relationships between members of different groups. The primary approach to resolving cultural differences in plural organizations is assimilation, just as for monolithic organizations. Intergroup conflict is high in plural organizations if members of the majority group resent practices used to boost minority group membership. Even though overt discrimination may have been banished, prejudice is still likely in plural organizations. The diversity culture of plural organizations conveys a mixed message: We promote diversity, but we expect employees from minority groups to fit in with the majority group.

Multicultural organizations do more than promote diversity; they also promote a culture of inclusion. They respond to cultural differences by encouraging members of different groups to respect the norms and values of other groups, in contrast to the assimilation required by monolithic and plural organizations. Multicultural organizations attempt to bring about qualitative changes in their work environments through increased appreciation of the range of skills and values that dissimilar employees offer and increased use of teams that include members culturally distinct from the dominant group. The goal is to create a culture in which employees from all groups feel comfortable and appreciated and are given a chance to make meaningful contributions. In an inclusive culture, the knowledge, skills, insights, and experiences of employees from different groups are regarded as valuable resources that the organization may use to advance its mission. Intergroup conflict in multicultural organizations is low due to the absence of prejudice and discrimination accompanied by the appreciation of individuals from different groups. The diversity culture of multicultural organizations conveys a consistent message: We welcome members of all groups as full participants in our organizational culture, and we strive to take full advantage of what they have to offer.[22]

In the opening passage of the chapter, Coopers & Lybrand, a large global accounting firm that has since merged with Price Waterhouse to become PricewaterhouseCoopers, is addressing issues related to its diversity culture. Although the firm was not as monolithic as it once was, no women were on the management committee, which consists of the highest-status partners. The few women partners claimed that the firm's culture was more comfortable for men. Thus, Coopers & Lybrand had moved from being a monolithic organization toward being a plural organization, but it was not regarded as a multicultural organization by its women partners. The meeting in Chicago displays the intergroup conflict that is indicative of a plural organization. The fact that such a meeting was held at all, however, was a good sign. Actions taken after the meeting suggest that the firm was doing more to promote both diversity and inclusion.[23]

It is more difficult to assess the effects of promoting inclusion on organizational performance than the effects of promoting diversity. Researchers may obtain data on the sex composition and performance of corporations from publicly filed reports. Researchers, however, do not have the opportunity to assess the diversity cultures of organizations unless they are granted permission to do so. Organizations that do not want their business practices to be scrutinized, particularly those that are doing little to promote inclusion, are reluctant to grant researchers such permission. Organizations that are doing a better job of promoting inclusion may be more eager to showcase their progress.[24]

One study tried to get around these difficulties by examining the financial performance of 30 companies that received high ratings in *The 100 Best Companies to Work for in America* or *The Best Companies for Women*. The study compared the financial performance of these firms with their industry's average performance for a 10-year period. Overall, these companies outperformed their industry's average 60% of the time, a significant proportion. Although we cannot be certain that the companies included in this study did a better job of promoting inclusion than their competitors, their being cited in such books suggests that this may have been the case.[25]

As we note in Chapters 4 and 5, evidence suggests that inclusive cultures make it easier for organizations to attract employees and to facilitate the work of diverse teams. A study of college students' reactions to a fictitious recruitment brochure demonstrates the importance of an inclusive culture for applicant attraction. Students received either of two forms of the brochure. Both forms stated that the company is an affirmative action/equal opportunity employer, as many companies do in their recruitment literature. One of the forms also stated that the company values the contributions of a diverse workforce and has adopted programs to help teach all employees to recognize the strengths that individuals from diverse backgrounds can bring to the company. Students of both sexes and different races were more attracted to the company when they received a brochure with the additional statement about inclusion.[26]

In conclusion, promoting inclusion is likely to contribute to full utilization and retention of valued employees from all groups and enhance the bottom line. Employees from different groups, especially minority groups, can tell whether their organization is monolithic, plural, or multicultural. They are well aware of the message that the organization's diversity culture sends to people like themselves. They are most likely to be attracted to and commit themselves to an organization that promotes a culture in which members of all groups are valued and respected. Such organizations are likely to have a business advantage over competitors that are weaker in promoting inclusion or that fail to make the attempt.

Organizational Actions

We have presented the legal and business cases for promoting nondiscrimination, diversity, and inclusion. In this section, we consider these issues from a practical perspective—what organizations need to do. First, appropriate goals should be adopted and communicated. Second, the representation of women and men in different jobs and at different levels should be analyzed and a cultural audit performed to determine how well the company is achieving its diversity goals. Third, a management system should be adopted that sets concrete objectives for critical employees and provides incentives for them to meet these objectives. Fourth, employee network groups and advisory councils should be sponsored to stimulate employee involvement as well as to identify obstacles to the achievement of diversity goals. Fifth, employees should receive education and training that enhances their abilities and readiness to meet assigned objectives. Finally, changes in the organizational culture should be implemented as needed to ensure that goal achievement is sustained.[27]

SETTING AND COMMUNICATING GOALS

The first step to be taken is to set goals for the organization's diversity culture. We recommend that *all* organizations—large or small, public or private, profit or nonprofit—set the goals of being nondiscriminatory, diverse, and inclusive in their employment practices.

Assuming that an organization sets these goals, it then needs to communicate them to key employees. For example, United Technologies Corporation (UTC), one of the world's largest industrial companies, articulated its goals for a diversity culture in a brochure entitled *We Make United Technologies Strong* that was circulated at a corporate conference on managing diversity:

> What makes United Technologies strong? The diversity of its employees. People like these: a VP of helicopter manufacturing with more than 1,000 people reporting to her; a female Hispanic engineer in charge of developing jet-engine electronic controls; a blind engineer who uses customized computer equipment to perform his job. . . . That's diversity at work at United Technologies. UTC is a large, global company with many different businesses, and that compels us to develop a rich, diverse employee population where teamwork can thrive. . . . When diverse individuals bring their unique perspectives to the work place, the resulting environment generates excitement and evokes the best possible business decisions. So we encourage all of our associates to be innovative, to take risks and to tear down barriers that stand in the way of making a contribution. In this manner, UTC can become increasingly flexible and sustain its competitive advantage worldwide. Bottom line: Diversity makes good business sense.[28]

How an organization "sells" its diversity goals to employees plays a large role in determining whether those goals are achieved. They may be presented to employees as moral, legal, or business issues. Appeals to morality seldom work because few people do the "right thing" unless it is personally advantageous. The legal argument does not fully work either; it suggests that compliance with the law is most important, and thereby promotes only a minimal effort to achieve diversity goals. A pitch like UTC's is more effective in promoting nondiscrimination, diversity, and inclusion throughout the organization because it points to bottom-line profits, which most employees see as ultimately affecting their own livelihoods.[29]

Corporate communications should convey the message that promoting nondiscrimination, diversity, and inclusion are important organizational goals. These communications may include speeches by top executives, with transcripts or videos available to internal and external groups, newsletters, status reports, recognition events, special awards, and publicity for employees who have done good work toward these goals. The mission statement of the organization should state that the organization regards achievement of these goals as critical to its success.[30]

Top management commitment is critical to achieving diversity-related goals. The chief executive of an organization plays an important role in setting its primary values. In organizations such as Xerox and JCPenney with strong track records in managing diversity, the CEOs galvanized employees to take diversity seriously by making them aware of diversity issues facing the firm and by personally stimulating change. In addition, "champions of diversity" are needed—people who take strong public and personal stands on the need for cultural change in the organization and behave as role models in creating change. What better champion of diversity than the top executive?[31]

Assignment of responsibility and allocation of resources also demonstrate top management commitment. The person with primary responsibility for achievement of diversity goals should either report to or be a top line executive. This person should have immediate access to and control over the managers who determine program success or failure. For example, companies such as Corning and Allstate Insurance designate a manager to oversee diversity programs companywide. If this responsibility is buried in the professional ranks of the human resource management department, employees infer that promoting nondiscrimination, diversity, and inclusion are not top priorities, and there is less impact on the organization as a whole.[32]

IDENTIFYING AND REWARDING THE RIGHT BEHAVIOR

Making a good sales pitch for promoting nondiscrimination, diversity, and inclusion does not ensure that employees will act accordingly. An organization also needs a sound management system that encourages employees to engage in the right kinds of behavior on a regular basis. As one executive said in a Conference Board survey:

> How do you go about achieving [diversity] results in a company? The same way you achieve any other results. You analyze the problem carefully, determine what

you need to do, and then set up an overall management planning and control system to make very sure that it happens—and on schedule.[33]

First comes an analysis of what the organization needs to do to achieve its diversity goals. This analysis begins with an assessment of whether women are equitably represented throughout the organization. Required by Executive Order 11246 for U.S. government contractors, it should compare the number of women in each job category with the number of women in the relevant labor force who are qualified to fill jobs in that category. The relevant labor force may be defined as that located in the immediate city or town, the metropolitan area, or the nation, depending on the job category. Areas in which women are underemployed then become the appropriate targets of affirmative action programs. Although not required by law, this analysis could also identify areas in which men are underemployed.

The organizational analysis also includes a cultural audit, a snapshot of the current organizational culture. It assesses the nature of the organizational culture as experienced by employees, which is not necessarily what top management thinks the culture is or should be. It also assesses how the organizational culture influences the treatment of members of different groups. Surveys, interviews, focus groups, and meetings may be used to gather information for the audit. For example, meetings such as the one described in the opening passage may be a useful part of a cultural audit. A successful audit uncovers obstacles to the full attainment of diversity goals. Obstacles may include stereotypes and prejudices that affect employees' interactions with one another and managers' decisions regarding recruitment, performance appraisals, promotions, compensation, and other employment practices.[34]

Next comes the specification of objectives. Managers will put more effort into promoting nondiscrimination, diversity, and inclusion if they are expected to meet concrete objectives in pursuit of each of these goals. For example, the PQ Corporation, a specialty chemicals manufacturer, implemented a unique procedure to meet the objective of promoting nondiscrimination in employment decisions. The key to the procedure was the "selection checklist," a two-part document that a manager completed for each candidate interviewed for a position. The first part contained questions about each step in the selection process and the degree of possible discrimination (e.g., "Did you perform or do you have a current job analysis for this position?" "Was the position posted internally?" "Were reasons for rejection based on job-related deficiencies and not related to non-job related factors such as a handicap or religious beliefs?"). Each question had to be answered yes, no, or not applicable. The questions answered *no* reflected possible incidents of discrimination by the manager. The second part documented the correlation between the job criteria (i.e., skills and knowledge required to perform major job functions) and the attributes of the candidate.[35]

PQ's selection checklist was intended to make managers aware of the process they used to make their decisions. Objectives for managers were stated in terms of percentages of discriminatory incidents. Managers' checklists were passed on to their superiors, who could then assess how well the corporate goal of nondiscrimination was being achieved. If a manager fudged the checklist to cover up discrimination, he or she did so with the knowledge that this behavior could expose the company to an EEO lawsuit.

Managers should be expected to meet the objective of promoting diversity in their work units. In pursuing this objective, they may adopt either of two opposing affirmative action policies. According to one policy, competence is the first screening criterion for hiring or promoting individuals. Members of underrepresented groups such as women are then given preference if they pass the screen. According to the opposite policy, membership in an underrepresented group is the first screen, and competence is then used to choose among the candidates who remain. The first policy yields qualified and competent employees. The second policy yields the best of the available "affirmative action" candidates, whether qualified or not.

We recommend that organizations instruct their managers to follow the first policy in meeting their diversity objectives. The second policy tends to be detrimental to its intended beneficiaries and the organization in the long run. When employees believe that a woman has been hired under the second policy, they conclude that she must be incompetent. Such beliefs place women managers at a disadvantage. When women managers believe that they were hired primarily because of their sex, they tend to be less committed to the organization and less satisfied with their jobs than those who believe that sex was not an important factor in their selection. In contrast, when the organization makes it clear that merit considerations are central to the selection process, employees' reactions to the selection of a woman to be their boss are less pronounced. A woman who is selected for a leadership position under such conditions is more likely to see herself as competent and want to remain in the position. Other employees, even those who have been bypassed for the position, are less likely to stigmatize her as incompetent and grumble about her selection. Thus, organizations need to set objectives for promoting diversity that emphasize the role of merit in selection decisions.[36]

Managers also should be expected to meet the objective of providing their employees an inclusive work environment. Achievement of this objective may be measured by employee surveys. Monitoring of employee complaints will provide additional information about whether a manager has problems in this area that need to be addressed.

Once an organization develops and assigns specific objectives, they should become part of the manager's overall performance appraisal. Managers should be made aware that their success at promoting nondiscrimination, diversity, and inclusion will be evaluated by their supervisors. Good performance in these areas should be reinforced with tangible rewards such as promotions, salary increases, and favorable task assignments; failure to meet objectives should result in the withholding of such rewards. Actions speak much louder than words of approval or disapproval. By giving managers explicit knowledge of the organization's diversity goals and incentives to meet personal objectives consistent with these goals, an effective management system overcomes resistance from managers.

STIMULATING EMPLOYEE INVOLVEMENT

Organizations benefit when employees from all groups feel personally involved in the attainment of diversity goals. For example, Xerox stimulates employee involvement through its sponsorship of employee network groups: Hispanic Association for Professional Advancement, Black Women's Leadership Council, National Black Employee's Association (for all Black employees), Galaxe Pride at Work (for gay and lesbian employees), The Women's Alliance, and Asians Coming Together. Each group has a Corporate Champion assigned to it. Groups elect their own officers and run their own functions, including meetings, conferences, professional development activities, and outreach activities in the community. For instance, Black Women's Leadership Council takes an active role in encouraging and developing young Black women through a high school scholarship program. It also promotes mentoring and sponsorship of Black women at Xerox, celebrates their accomplishments, and surveys its members about corporate issues affecting them.[37]

Microsoft supports a wide variety of employee network groups initiated by its employees. Separate groups, some with overlapping interests, target women, fathers, parents, single parents, the hearing-impaired, employees affected by Attention Deficit Disorder, and gay, lesbian, bisexual, and transgendered employees. There are employee network groups for Black, Native American, Hispanic, Chinese, Taiwanese, Korean, Filipino, and Indian employees. These groups provide career development and networking opportunities and assist the company with college recruiting and cultural awareness activities.[38]

Organizations may form groups to involve employees in dealing with diversity issues. For example, one organization established an advisory council of a cross-section of employees. The council met monthly to discuss issues related to a diverse workforce. Corporate activities that resulted from the council included a diversity booth at the annual family picnic, articles on diversity in the company newsletter, training on refraining from discrimination, guidelines for first-line supervisors on appraising employees, and a suggestion box called "Dr. Equality." The council also assisted in the design of employee opinion surveys.[39]

Employee network groups and advisory councils serve several purposes that benefit both the organization and its members. Such groups help the organization to be aware of and address the concerns of employees. As a result, employees are more likely to feel that the organization cares about their concerns, which fosters their commitment to the attainment of corporate goals. The outreach activities of such groups also help the organization to be a good citizen in the community. Finally, they act as a vehicle for employee self-help by providing opportunities for networking, personal support, and career development.

EDUCATING EMPLOYEES

Educational initiatives serve to promote the organizational goals of nondiscrimination, diversity, and inclusion. Specific education and training programs may be designed to meet a range of objectives:[40]

1. Increase participants' knowledge about diversity issues, including EEO laws, changing societal demographics, and the business case for attention to these issues.

2. Increase participants' familiarity with organizational policies regarding inappropriate workplace behavior (e.g., sexual harassment) and what they should do if they experience or witness such behavior.

3. Increase participants' awareness of their own stereotypes and prejudices based on sex, race, ethnicity, age, national origin, sexual orientation, abilities/disabilities, and other primary and secondary dimensions of diversity.

4. Increase participants' skills in moving beyond their stereotypes and prejudices as they work with dissimilar customers and coworkers.

5. In multinational organizations, increase participants' fluency in other languages and knowledge of other national cultures.

6. Increase managers' skills in making bias-free decisions (e.g., decisions about selection, compensation, performance appraisal, promotion, and access to developmental experiences).

7. Increase managers' skills in dealing with diversity-related incidents.

8. By addressing the above objectives, change the organization's diversity culture itself.

Diversity training programs should have an expected outcome: As a result of the program, something should change. To determine whether the desired change has occurred, program outcomes should be measured on a long-term basis, not just at the end of the last session. For example, participants' assessment of what was most useful about a program and how it helped them may be solicited 3, 6, or 12 months afterwards. If the program's objective is to modify the organization's diversity culture, periodic employee surveys of employees' attitudes toward diversity may provide information on whether this objective is being met.[41]

One issue that arises is whether participation in a diversity training program should be voluntary or mandatory for employees. Allowing voluntary participation may suggest that top management does not regard the program as particularly important and that employees themselves are free to determine its importance. Making participation mandatory sends the message that top management regards the program as critical to achievement of corporate goals. If participation is mandatory, however, the program facilitator faces the challenge of dealing with reluctant participants. Under these circumstances, the facilitator must get *all* participants to believe that they have something to gain from the program, or its objectives may be thwarted. Programs that are designed to get everyone working toward the same corporate goals, not to embarrass or blame anyone, are most likely to encourage involvement.[42]

According to a survey of human resource professionals, a diversity training program is more likely to be effective when (1) top management support for achievement of diversity goals is strong and visible; (2) participation is mandatory for managers; (3) program success is evaluated over the long term; (4) managers are rewarded for promoting diversity in their work units; and (5) a broad definition of "diversity" is used that acknowledges the needs and concerns of all employees, including White males.[43] Organizations should use education and training initiatives at all levels to promote achievement of diversity goals. Achievement of diversity goals is enhanced if employees know why they are being asked to work toward these goals and are taught the necessary skills.

IMPLEMENTING CULTURAL CHANGE

An organization's diversity culture influences how group differences are taken into account. It consists of a general perception of the value the organization places on being nondiscriminatory, diverse, and inclusive. Organizational culture is an elusive concept. It lies beneath the surface of organizational life, yet it influences every aspect of how employees are treated and work is conducted. Because organizational culture is deep-seated, often going back to the values of the founder, it cannot be changed overnight. If an organization sets goals of promoting nondiscrimination, diversity, and inclusion and its culture does not fully support achievement of these goals, some form of cultural change is needed.[44]

The first step in implementing cultural change is to decide, based on a cultural audit and corporate goals, how the culture needs to be improved.[45] Cultural change will be especially critical for monolithic organizations. Plural organizations, which are promoting nondiscrimination and diversity but not inclusion, will also need to make some changes to their cultures. Even organizations that are already multicultural may benefit from some modifications to their diversity cultures.

The second step is to develop a plan that charts the course for cultural change. The plan may include revisions to existing policies and practices, including the management system, and new programs such as education and training initiatives. Top management support of the plan for cultural change is crucial, but not sufficient, to bringing about cultural change. The participation of first-line supervisors in development of the plan also is critical to its success. First-line supervisors are those most responsible for getting work done in organizations. If they are told by top management to implement a plan for cultural change but do not participate in its development, they will not be committed to the plan. Long-lasting cultural change can be brought about only when the change is accepted and owned by all of the employees who will be involved in making the change effective.[46]

The third step is to launch the change effort itself. For the launch to be effective, leaders of the change effort need to specify objectives, achieve early results to demonstrate the value of the effort, and assess progress along the way. The management system should reward behavior that contributes to achievement of needed cultural change.

The final step, once the initial change effort is complete, is to ensure that cultural changes take hold and are not temporary. Long-term maintenance of the organizational culture is necessary. Maintenance involves monitoring the results of the change effort to guard against backsliding and motivating employees to confront and overcome obstacles to sustained cultural change. Cultural audits should be repeated on a regular basis to determine whether intended changes are in place and to identify further needs for change.

Multinational corporations face additional challenges in changing their diversity cultures. Change efforts are especially likely to fail if managers in the home office impose their notions of diversity on operations in other areas of the world. Such efforts may be viewed as cultural imperialism and resented by managers outside the home office. The challenge for a multinational organization is to engage in efforts to influence the *organizational* culture while taking internal differences in *national* culture into account.[47]

All organizations benefit from promoting nondiscrimination, diversity, and inclusion. Even organizations with a history of such actions need to continue to make special efforts to attract qualified applicants from all groups, offering satisfying jobs and a welcoming culture. When organizations take such actions and achieve the goal of being multicultural in their management practices, they are likely to attract the best talent available, stimulate employee involvement and commitment, and enhance the bottom line.

Conclusions for the Book

In Chapter 1, we posed the question: Is it only a matter of time until the proportions of women and men in all managerial levels and all occupations become essentially equal, until women and men are paid equal wages for equal work, and until individuals' work experiences are unaffected by their biological sex? Our answer is that it depends on the actions that organizations and individuals take.

In the ensuing chapters, we elaborated on this answer. We offered numerous recommendations for improving interactions between, and encouraging the full utilization of, women and men in the workplace. Boxes 9.1 and 9.2 list specific actions that we recommend for organizations and individuals respectively. In these tables, we identify more actions for organizations than for individuals. However, organizations consist of people who work together to provide products or services. Thus, *all* of our recommendations are for actions that people may take. Although this book's title stresses the managerial role, *all* of us—current and future members of the labor force, managers and non-managers—may contribute toward making a better workplace.

In all likelihood, some sex differences in preferences for job attributes, styles of interacting with others at work, and career patterns will remain. Our intent is to report the facts about sex differences, not to suggest what they should be. Our overriding concern is with gender differences, beliefs about how males and females differ. When gender differences are guided more by stereotypes than by facts about actual sex differences, they have a corrosive impact on interactions between the sexes at work. The goal is the creation of a nondiscriminatory, diverse, and inclusive workplace—a world in which members of both sexes are valued for what they bring to the workplace and are granted the opportunity to make full use of their talents. By taking actions such as the ones we have recommended, all of us will contribute to establishment of such a world. What a wonderful world this would be.

Box 9.1   Recommended Actions for Organizations

---

1. Distribute promotional materials to school systems that send a message that both sexes belong in available occupations.

2. Publicize employees who hold jobs that are atypical for their sex.

3. Develop job descriptions that include the full range of activities associated with the job.

4. Seek applicants from multiple sources rather than rely only on referrals.

5. Screen recruiters to determine whether they endorse traditional gender stereotypes.

6. Train recruiters to avoid biased decisions and discriminatory behavior in interviews.

7. Formalize and standardize practices used in selection and promotion decisions.

8. Assess the effectiveness of all selection practices.

9. Reward recruiter effectiveness based on long-term results.

10. Strive to have diverse work teams and management teams, but do not select team members or managers solely on the basis of sex or other visible characteristics.

11. Select team members with values and skills conducive to teamwork.

12. Publicize qualifications of all individuals assigned to teams and leadership positions.

13. Address sexist attitudes displayed toward team members and leaders.

14. Reward team performance in addition to individual performance.

15. Encourage rotation of roles and tasks to develop team members to play future roles.

16. Structure work assignments to require some level of cooperation among team members.

17. Train team members on how to manage team processes and how to deal with the difficulties created by stereotyping and dissimilarity.

18. Coach leaders to encourage expression of diverse points of view.

19. Evaluate leaders on the basis of task accomplishment, group cohesiveness, and development of subordinates for future roles.

20. Develop the capabilities of all individuals to play leader roles.

21. Create conditions that give leaders of both sexes equal chances to succeed.

22. Issue a strong written policy against sexual harassment.

23. Train managers to recognize and deal with sexual harassment.

24. Designate a party to whom employees may bring complaints of sexual harassment and other offensive behavior without fear of reprisal.

25. Investigate employee complaints and take appropriate action.

26. Offer counseling to employees who need help in handling sexual, or other types of harassment, and workplace romances.

27. Take action when workplace romances affect the conduct of work, but ignore them otherwise.

28. Train employees to minimize biases in performance evaluations.

29. Adopt a flexible model of the successful career that does not penalize employment gaps, leaves of absence, and lateral moves.

30. Ensure that all qualified employees have access to developmental opportunities.

31. Educate employees about the value of mentoring and being mentored.

32. Reward employees who are good mentors.

33. Offer assistance to employees in meeting child and elder care needs.

34. Offer flexible work arrangements to employees when possible.

35. Provide incentives for managers to permit subordinates to take advantage of flexible work arrangements.

36. Set reasonable standards for the number of hours employees are required to work.

37. Do not act as if all employees have stay-at-home spouses.

38. Remove all constraints on career success that are not based on an individual's past accomplishments or future potential.

39. Offer counseling to employees and their family members when organizational decisions will affect the family (e.g., relocation).

40. Set and communicate the goals of promoting nondiscrimination, diversity, and inclusion.

41. Comply with all EEO laws.

42. Make sure that employees understand how affirmative action works in the organization.

43. Work with employee network groups formed out of employees' common interests in planning and implementing cultural change.

44. Provide diversity training that educates employees about the organization's diversity goals and gives them the knowledge and skills they need to work toward these goals.

45. Analyze the organization's composition and culture to determine what specific improvements are needed and then set objectives for attaining them.

46. Ensure that the achievement of diversity goals and objectives is rewarded by the management system and supported by the organizational culture.

47. Continually monitor the organization's progress relative to its diversity goals and take appropriate actions to ensure that improvements are permanent.

Box 9.2   Recommended Actions for Individuals

1. In interactions with young people, understand the powerful effect of your own gender role expectations on their behavior.

2. Encourage young people to pursue activities and interests that they enjoy, regardless of whether those activities and interests are consistent with traditional gender roles.

3. Engage in self-exploration activities to identify your preferred occupations and job attributes.

4. Use a broad range of job search methods.

5. Practice how you will conduct yourself before a job interview.

6. Do research on potential employers before you contact them.

7. Select the job that best matches your preferred job attributes.

8. Be ready to negotiate your starting salary when you take a job.

9. Understand how your sense of self-identity influences your interactions with others.

10. Guard against your own stereotypes and prejudices as you evaluate others' behavior.

11. Build good relationships with other members of your team.

12. If people like you are in the majority on a team, do not subject minority team members to performance pressures or exaggerate differences between you and them simply because they are in the minority.

13. If people like you are in the minority on a team, take actions to enhance your own power and guard against stereotypes that limit your behavior.

14. If you are the first woman to hold a particular leadership position, take advantage of being seen as a symbol of change.

15. Do not ignore sexual harassment or other offensive behavior directed toward you or others thinking that it will eventually cease; either confront the offending party directly or use your organization's procedure to file a complaint.

16. Weigh the potential costs of a workplace romance against the potential benefits before getting involved.

17. Adopt career tactics that are well thought out.

18. Establish a network of business contacts and get a mentor if possible.

19. Build your competence by furthering your education and being receptive to stretch assignments that come your way.

20. Deal with stresses in your career, both inside and outside work, by adopting appropriate coping strategies.

21. Reach accommodations with partners about the role that work and family concerns will play in each other's lives.

22. If you are a trailing partner, join a support group or form one with others in similar positions.

23. Be a champion of diversity; take strong public and private stands on diversity issues in the workplace and behave as a role model for others.

Notes

1. Himelstein, L. (1997, February 17). Breaking through. *Business Week,* p. 64. Reprinted from the February 17, 1997 issue of *Business Week* by special permission. Copyright 1997 by the McGraw-Hill companies.

2. Davidson, M. J., & Cooper, C. L. (Eds.). (1993). *European women in business and management.* London: Chapman; Konrad, A. M., & Linnehan, F. (1999). Affirmative action: History, effects, and attitudes. In G. N. Powell (Ed.), *Handbook of gender and work* (pp. 429–452). Thousand Oaks, CA: Sage; Wirth, L. (2001). *Breaking through the glass ceiling: Women in management.* Geneva: International Labour Office, pp. 139–151; Leck, J. D., & Saunders, D. M. (1992). Hiring women: The effects of Canada's Employment Equity Act. *Canadian Public Policy–Analyse de Politiques, 18*(2), 203–220; Cannings, K., & Lazonick, W. (1994). Equal employment opportunity and the "managerial woman" in Japan. *Industrial Relations, 33,* 44–69.

3. The description of legal requirements placed on U.S. employers is based primarily on the following two sources: Sedmak, N. J., & Vidas, C. (1994*). Primer of equal employment opportunity* (6th ed.). Washington, DC: Bureau of National Affairs; Gamble, B. S. (Ed.). (1992). *Sex discrimination handbook.* Washington, DC: Bureau of National Affairs.

4. Gold, M. E. (1993). *An introduction to the law of employment discrimination.* Ithaca, NY: ILR Press.

5. Sedmak & Vidas, p. 39.

6. Ledvinka, J., & Scarpello, V. G. (1991). *Federal regulation of personnel and human resource management* (2nd ed.). Boston: PWS-Kent, p. 60; Sedmak & Vidas, p. 44.

7.   Bovard, J. (1995, November 17). The EEOC's war on Hooters. *Wall Street Journal*, p. A18; Hooters of America, Inc. (2002). *Media statement*. Retrieved May 20, 2002, from http://www.hootersofamerica.com; Reiland, R. (1998). Selecting targets. *The Free Market, 16*(1). Retrieved February 19, 2002, from http://www.mises.org

8.   Schwab, D. P. (1984). Job evaluation and pay setting: Concepts and practices. In E. R. Livernash (Ed.), *Comparable worth: Issues and alternatives* (2nd ed., pp. 49–77). Washington, DC: Equal Employment Advisory Council; Mahoney, T. A. (1990). Compensation functions. In G. R. Ferris, K. M. Rowland, & M. R. Buckley (Eds.), *Human resource management: Perspectives and issues* (2nd ed., pp. 226–236). Boston: Allyn & Bacon.

9.   Sape, G. P. (1985). Coping with comparable worth. *Harvard Business Review, 63*(3), 145-152.

10.   Aeberhard, J. H. (2001). Affirmative action in employment: Recent court approaches to a difficult concept. In M. F. Loutfi (Ed.), *Women, gender and work: What is equality and how do we get there?* (pp. 441–468). Geneva: International Labour Office.

11.   Baucus, M. S., & Baucus, D. A. (1997). Paying the piper: An empirical examination of longer-term financial consequences of illegal corporate behavior. *Academy of Management Journal, 40*, 129–151.

12.   U.S. Department of Commerce, Bureau of the Census. (2002). *Current Population Survey* (computed from January, 2002 data). Retrieved March 1, 2002, from http://ferret.bls.census.gov; U.S. General Accounting Office. (1992). *The changing workforce: Demographic issues facing the federal government*. Washington, DC: U.S. General Accounting Office, p. 27.

13.   Gutek, B. A., Cherry, B., & Groth, M. (1999). Gender and service delivery. In G. N. Powell (Ed.), *Handbook of gender and work* (pp. 47–68). Thousand Oaks, CA: Sage; Jackson, S. E., & Alvarez, E. B. (1992). Working through diversity as a strategic imperative. In S. E. Jackson & Associates (Ed.), *Diversity in the workplace: Human resources initiatives* (pp. 13–29). New York: Guilford; Blum, T. C., Fields, D. L., & Goodman, J. S. (1994). Organization-level determinants of women in management. *Academy of Management Journal, 37*, 241–268; Goodman, J. S., Fields, D. L., & Blum, T. C. (in press). Cracks in the glass ceiling: In what kinds of organizations do women make it to the top? *Group & Organization Management*.

14.   Gutek, Cherry, & Groth; Jackson & Alvarez; Loden, M., & Rosener, J. B. (1991). *Workforce America: Managing employee diversity as a vital resource*. Homewood, IL: Business One Irwin.

15.   Jackson & Alvarez; Cox, T., Jr. (1993). *Cultural diversity in organizations: Theory, research and practice*. San Francisco: Berrett-Koehler.

16.   Women and profits. (2001). *Harvard Business Review, 79*(10), 30; Adler, R. D. (2001). *Women in the executive suite correlate to higher profits*. Malibu, CA: Glass Ceiling Research Center. Retrieved January 18, 2002, from http://glass-ceiling.com

17.   Shrader, C. B., Blackburn, V. B., & Iles, P. (1997). Women in management and firm financial performance: An exploratory study. *Journal of Managerial Issues, 9*(3), 355–372.

18.   Frink, D. D., Robinson, R. K., Reithel, B., Arthur, M. M., Ammeter, A. P., Ferris, G., et al. (in press). Gender demography and organization performance: A two-study investigation with convergence. *Group & Organization Management*.

19.   Adler.

20.   Cox (1993); Milliken, F. J., & Martins, L. L. (1996). Searching for common threads: Understanding the multiple effects of diversity in organizational groups. *Academy of Management Review, 21*, 402–433.

21.   Cox (1993); Cox, T., Jr. (1991). The multicultural organization. *Academy of Management Executive, 5*(2), 34–47.

22.   Ely, R. J., & Thomas, D. A. (2001). Cultural diversity at work: The effects of diversity perspectives on work group processes and outcomes. *Administrative Science Quarterly, 46*, 229–273.

23.   Himelstein; PricewaterhouseCoopers. (2002). *Our history*. Retrieved February 12, 2002, from http://.pwcglobal.com

24.   Gilbert, J. A., & Ivancevich, J. M. (2000). Valuing diversity: A tale of two organizations. *Academy of Management Executive, 14*(1), 93–105.

25. Simmons, B. L., & Nelson, D. L. (August, 1997). *The diversity advantage?* Paper presented at the meeting of the Academy of Management, Boston; Levering, R., & Moskowitz, M. (1993). *The 100 best companies to work for in America* (Revised ed.). New York: Doubleday; Zeitz, B., & Dusky, L. (1988). *The best companies for women.* New York: Simon & Schuster.

26. Williams, M. L., & Bauer, T. N. (1994). The effect of a managing diversity policy on organizational attractiveness. *Group & Organization Management, 19,* 295–308.

27. Lobel, S. A. (1999). Impacts of diversity and work-life initiatives in organizations. In G. N. Powell (Ed.), *Handbook of gender and work* (pp. 453–474). Thousand Oaks, CA: Sage; Arredondo, P. (1996). *Successful diversity management initiatives: A blueprint for planning and implementation.* Thousand Oaks, CA: Sage; Gardenswartz, L., & Rowe, A. (1993). *Managing diversity: A complete desk reference and planning guide.* Burr Ridge, IL and San Diego, CA: Business One Irwin and Pfeiffer.

28. United Technologies Corporation. (1995). *We make United Technologies strong.* Hartford, CT: United Technologies Corporation.

29. Cox (1993).

30. Lobel.

31. Gilbert & Ivancevich; Cox, T. H., & Blake, S. (1991). Managing cultural diversity: Implications for organizational competitiveness. *Academy of Management Executive, 5*(3), 45–56; Morrison, A. M. (1992). Step two: Strengthen top-management commitment. In *The new leaders: Guidelines on leadership diversity in America* (pp. 183–200). San Francisco: Jossey-Bass.

32. Cox & Blake.

33. Schaeffer, R. G., & Lynton, E. F. (1979). *Corporate experiences in improving women's job opportunities.* New York: Conference Board, p. 21.

34. Gardenswartz & Rowe. Conducting a diversity audit: Taking an organizational snapshot, pp. 263–312; Cox & Blake; Himelstein.

35. Poole, J. C., & Kautz, E. T. (1987). An EEO/AA program that exceeds quotas—It targets biases. *Personnel Journal, 66*(1), 103-105.

36. Crosby, F. J., & VanDeVeer, C. (Eds.). (2000). *Sex, race, and merit: Debating affirmative action in education and employment.* Ann Arbor: University of Michigan Press; Konrad & Linnehan; Aeberhard; Kravitz, D. A., Harrison, D. A., Turner, M. E., Levine, E. L., Chaves, W., Brannick, M. T., et al. (1997). *Affirmative action: A review of psychological and behavioral research.* Bowling Green, OH: Society for Industrial and Organizational Psychology; Chacko, T. I. (1982). Women and equal employment opportunity: Some unintended effects. *Journal of Applied Psychology, 67,* 119-123; Heilman, M. E., Battle, W. S., Keller, C. E., & Lee, R. A. (1998). Type of affirmative action policy: A determinant of reactions to sex-based preferential selection? *Journal of Applied Psychology, 83,* 190–205.

37. Xerox Corporation. (2002). *Diversity at Xerox.* Rochester, NY: Xerox Corporation. Retrieved March 22, 2002, from http://www.xerox.com; Xerox Corporation, Black Women's Leadership Council. (2002). *Mission.* Rochester, NY: Xerox Corporation. Retrieved March 22, 2002, from http://www.bwlc.com; Sessa, V. I. (1992). Managing diversity at the Xerox Corporation: Balanced workforce goals and caucus groups. In S. E. Jackson & Associates (Ed.), *Diversity in the workplace: Human resources initiatives* (pp. 37–64). New York: Guilford.

38. Microsoft Corporation. (2002). *Employee resource groups.* Seattle, WA: Microsoft Corporation. Retrieved March 22, 2002, from http://www.microsoft.com

39. Gilbert & Ivancevich.

40. Ferdman, B. M., & Brody, S. E. (1996). Models of diversity training. In D. Landis & R. S. Bhagat (Eds.), *Handbook of intercultural training* (2nd ed., pp. 282–303). Thousand Oaks, CA: Sage; Arredondo, The role of education and training, pp. 125–145. Although some writers distinguish between "education" and "training," we use the terms interchangeably.

41. Arredondo.

42. Arredondo.

43. Rynes, S., & Rosen, B. (1995). A field survey of factors affecting the adoption and perceived success of diversity training. *Personnel Psychology, 48,* 247–270.

44. Kossek, E. E., & Zonia, S. C. (1993). Assessing diversity climate: A field study of reactions to employer efforts to promote diversity. *Journal of Organizational Behavior, 14,* 61–81; Beyer, J., & Trice, H. M. (1987). How an organization's rites reveal its culture. *Organizational Dynamics, 15*(4), 4–24.

45. Numerous models of how to implement organizational change have been offered. The model we describe is based on Reardon, K. K., & Reardon, K. J. (1999). "All that we can be": Leading the U.S. Army's gender integration effort. *Management Communication Quarterly, 12,* 600–617.

46. Scheflen, K. C., Lawler, E. E., III, & Hackman, J. R. (1971). Long-term impact of employee participation in the development of pay incentive plans: A field experiment revisited. *Journal of Applied Psychology, 55,* 182–186.

47. Bloom, H. (2002). Can the United States export diversity? *Across the Board, 39*(2), 47–52; Fulkerson, J. R., & Schuler, R. S. (1992). Managing worldwide diversity at Pepsi-Cola International. In S. E. Jackson & Associates (Ed.), *Diversity in the workplace: Human resources initiatives* (pp. 248–276). New York: Guilford.

INDEX

About the Authors

Gary N. Powell, Ph.D., is Professor of Management and Ackerman Scholar at the University of Connecticut. He is a recognized scholar on gender and diversity issues in the workplace. He is editor of *Handbook of Gender and Work*, author of two earlier editions of *Women and Men in Management*, and author of *Gender and Diversity in the Workplace: Learning Activities and Exercises*. His graduate course on women and men in management won the American Assembly of Collegiate Schools of Business Committee on Equal Opportunity for Women Innovation Award and first led to the writing of this book. He has received the University of Connecticut President's Award for Promoting Multiculturalism.

He is a former Chair, Program Chair, and Executive Committee member of the Women in Management (now Gender and Diversity in Organizations) Division of the Academy of Management, and received both the Janet Chusmir Service Award for his contributions to the division and the Sage Scholarship Award for his contributions to research on gender in organizations. He has published numerous articles in journals such as *Academy of Management Journal, Academy of Management Review, Journal of Applied Psychology,* and *Organizational Behavior and Human Decision Processes,* and presented numerous papers at academic meetings. He has served on the Board of Governors of the Academy of Management and is a Past President, Program Chair, and Fellow of the Eastern Academy of Management. He also is a former Co-Chair of the Status of Minorities Task Force of the Academy of Management and has served on the Editorial Board of *Academy of Management Review, Academy of Management Executive,* and *Journal of Management.*

Prior to joining the faculty at the University of Connecticut, he worked at General Electric, graduating from its Manufacturing Management Program. At GE, he designed and implemented automated project scheduling systems as well as systems for inventory control, materials procurement, and so on. He has provided management training and development for many companies, including The Hartford Financial Services Group, The Implementation Partners (TIP), GE-Capital, General Signal, Apple Computer, Monroe Auto Equipment, Allstate, and CIGNA, and has conducted numerous other workshops. He holds a doctorate in organizational behavior and a master's degree in management science from the University of Massachusetts, and a bachelor's degree in management from MIT.

Laura M. Graves, Ph.D., is Associate Professor of Management at the Graduate School of Management at Clark University. She is a recognized scholar on diversity issues in the workplace. Her work has examined gender and race effects in the workplace, particularly gender bias in employment interviewers' decision processes and the effects of demographic diversity on work teams. She received the Sage Scholarship Award from the Gender and Diversity in Organizations Division of the Academy of Management for her contributions to the management literature. Her research has appeared in leading academic journals including *Academy of Management Review, Journal of Applied Psychology,* and *Personnel Psychology.* In addition, she has contributed chapters to several books and presented numerous papers at academic meetings. She has served on the Editorial Board of *Academy of Management Journal* and as a Guest Editor for an *Academy of Management Journal* special research forum.

She is a former Chair, Chair-Elect, Program Chair, and Executive Committee member of the Gender and Diversity in Organizations Division of the Academy of Management. She also has held several positions in the Eastern Academy of Management, serving on its Board and chairing both the Organizational Behavior and Human Resources Management programs for its annual meeting.

Prior to joining the faculty at Clark, Graves worked in Corporate Human Resources at Aetna, where she was engaged in internal management consulting. She was also a member of the management faculty at the University of Connecticut. She holds a doctorate and a master's degree in social psychology from the University of Connecticut and a bachelor's degree in psychology from the College of William and Mary.